394.26

15.00

6-99

Festivals
and Holidays

MACMILLAN
PROFILES

Festivals and Holidays

MACMILLAN LIBRARY REFERENCE USA
New York

Macmillan Library Reference USA
1633 Broadway
New York, New York 10019

Manufactured in the United States of America

Printing number
1 2 3 4 5 6 7 8 9 10

Cover design by Berrian Design

Library of Congress Cataloging-in-Publication Data

Festivals and holidays.
        p.   cm. — (Macmillan profiles)
        Includes bibliographical references (p.   ) and index.
        ISBN 0-02-865378-5 (hardcover : alk. paper)
        1. Festivals Encyclopedias   2. Holidays Encyclopedias.   3. Fairs
Encyclopedias.   I. Series.
GT3925.F47   1999
394.26′03—dc21   99-26394
                                                               CIP

Cover design: © 1998 PhotoDisc, Inc.

This paper meets the requirements of ANSI/NISO A39.48-1992
(Permanence of Paper)

Contents

Macmillan Profiles: *Festivals and Holidays* is a unique reference featuring over one hundred articles describing celebrations, rituals, feast days, observances, festivals, fairs, and holidays from around the world. Macmillan Library Reference recognizes the need for reliable, accurate, and accessible reference works covering important aspects of the social studies and history curriculum. The Macmillan Profiles series can help meet that need by providing new collections of articles that were carefully selected from distinguished Macmillan sources. Macmillan Library Reference has published a wide array of award-winning reference materials for libraries across the world. It is likely that several of the encyclopedias on the shelves in this library were published by Macmillan Reference or Charles Scribner's Sons. Approximately one-third of the articles in *Festivals and Holidays* were drawn from Macmillan's 16-volume *Encyclopedia of Religion*, published in 1983. Individual articles were also drawn from the *Encyclopedia of Africa South of the Sahara*, the *Encyclopedia of Latin American History and Culture*, and the *Dictionary of the Middle Ages*. All extracted articles were recast and tailored for a younger audience by a team of experienced writers and editors. Seventy-four articles were newly written for this title.

Every culture sets aside special days for people to pray and give thanks, to honor individuals and events from the past, to solidify family and community relationships, to draw attention to important social issues, or simply to stop working and have fun. Some holidays are somber and serious, others are lighthearted and merry, but all holidays reveal something about the people and societies that celebrate them. The articles in *Festivals and Holidays* provide the history and significance of special days of all sorts, including all major Buddhist, Christian, Hindu, Islamic, and Jewish holidays; national holidays from around the world; ancient festivals that form the foundation of many modern celebrations; and newly established holidays like Earth Day and United Nations Day. The article list was based on the following criteria: relevance to the social studies and history curriculum of American high schools and middle schools and representation of as broad a cultural range as possible. The article list was refined and expanded in response to advice from a lively and generous team of librarians from school and public libraries across the United States.

FEATURES

Festivals and Holidays is part of Macmillan's **Profiles Series.** To add visual appeal and enhance the usefulness of the volume, the page format was designed to include the following helpful features:

- ■ Time Lines: Found throughout the text in the margins, time lines provide a quick reference source for dates and important events in the history of these festivals and holidays.

- ■ Definitions and Glossary: Brief definitions of important terms in the main text can be found in the margin. A glossary at the end of the book provides students with an even broader list of definitions.

- ■ Sidebars: Appearing in shaded boxes throughout the volume, these provocative asides relate to and amplify topics.

- ■ Pull Quotes: Found throughout the text in the margin, pull quotes highlight essential facts.

- ■ Suggested Reading: An extensive list of books and articles about the festivals and holidays covered in the volume will help students who want to do further research.

- ■ Index: A thorough index provides thousands of additional points of entry into the work.

ACKNOWLEDGMENTS

We thank our colleagues who publish the Merriam Webster's Collegiate Dictionary. Definitions used in the margins and many of the glossary terms come from the distinguished Webster's Collegiate Dictionary, Tenth Edition, 1996.

The biographies herein were written by leading authorities at work in the field of world history. *Festivals and Holidays* contains 85 photographs. Acknowledgments of sources for the illustrations can be found on page 429.

This work would not have been possible without the hard work and creativity of our staff. We offer our sincere thanks to all who helped create this marvelous work.

Macmillan Library Reference

Abu Simbel Festival

The Abu Simbel Festival celebrates the illumination of the inner sanctum of the Abu Simbel temple with the sun's rays. The festival is held twice a year—on February 22, the anniversary of the coronation of Egyptian pharoah Ramses II, and October 22, the anniversary of his birth.

The Abu Simbel temple, actually two temples, was built by Ramses II and is located on the banks of the Nile in the Aswan region of southern Egypt. The larger of the two temples is the tomb of Ramses II and the smaller, the tomb of his queen, Nefertary. Ramses II lived at least three thousand years ago and construction of the temples began around 1270 B.C.E. Abu Simbel is built into the face of the 300-foot sandstone cliffs that form the banks of the Nile. The front of the temple is adorned with massive statues of Ramses II and is situated so that as the sun rises above the opposite shore the first rays of light shine through the entrance. The temple is designed in such a way that on February 22 and October 22, and only on these days, the sun's rays reach all the way into the inner sanctum, which is carved 180 feet into the living rock directly following the line of the sun on those dates. The inner sanctum contains statues of four gods, Ptah, Amen-Re, Ramses, and Re-Horakhty seated side by side on a giant throne. At the center of the sanctuary there is a stone that once held the wooden boat that the pharoah would use to travel to the next world.

Abu Simbel is located far from the main population centers of Egypt and lay covered in sand until it was rediscovered in 1812 by the Swiss explorer Johann Burckhardt. In 1964 the

> The Abu Simbel temple is designed in such a way that on February 22 and October 22, and only on these dates, the sun's rays reach all the way into the temple's inner sanctum.

1

Ancient Egyptian architects designed the Abu Simbel temple in such a way that twice each year the sun's rays reach the inner sanctum.

temple was threatned by the building of the Aswan dam. The dam flooded the Nile and would have submerged the temples had they not been taken apart into two thousand pieces and reassembled 180 feet higher up the cliff. At this new location the inner sanctum is still illuminated on the twenty-second of February and October, although not as perfectly as in the original location.

Scholars of Egyptian history believe that ancient Egyptians probably held ritual celebrations at the temple on days when the sun reached the inner sanctum. Today, the Abu Simbel festival draws thousands of tourists from Egypt and other countries. The festival occurs outside the temple and is marked by performances of authentic Nubian dances and other celebrations of ancient Egyptian culture and folklore. ◆

All Saints' Day

All Saints' Day, on November 1, the day after Halloween, is dedicated to honoring all saints, particularly those whose feast days tend to pass unnoticed. The holy day was proclaimed by Pope Gregory IV in the year 837 to replace, or overlay, an ancient pagan festival of the dead on this day. All Hallow's Eve, known today as Halloween, was the medieval English name for the night before All Saints' Day. (*Hallow* comes from an Old English word that means "holy" or "saint.")

The feast of Samhain was an ancient Celtic festival marking the waning of the sun, after the autumn harvest: a two-day celebration that began at sundown on Halloween. Samhain, or the feast of Saman, lord of death, was a time of remembering and honoring one's ancestors through ceremonies intended to give honor and thanks to those who came before. The late Canadian novelist Robertson Davies has written that Halloween was the night when certain souls, displeased by the neglect of the living, sought vengeance on their thankless descendants: "To be out on Halloween was to run great risk of physical or psychological harm, for it was then that the underworld of chaos and death settled old scores."

There is no knowing how European (and, by extension, world) history and culture might have developed had the early Christian church allowed "heathen, pagan" practices to coexist alongside the new religion that was spreading over the continent. In any case, such "inclusiveness" would have been unthinkable in a **monotheistic** religion. In their efforts to spread the gospel of

monotheistic: belief on only one god.

4

Jesus Christ, believed to be essential for the salvation of souls, early Christian evangelists asserted that prior beliefs had to give way to the new religion (there is but one true God). Churchmen found "good fits" between certain new holy days (a saint's feast day, for example) and ancient festivals; the Christian practice was superimposed on the pagan rites (just as some European churches are said to have been built on ground formerly used in **Druid** rituals); and by a process of blending and gradual submersion of the old, the new Christian holy day took root and the old rituals withered, though they never disappeared entirely. (In a similar way, the celebration of the birth of Christ was moved from springtime to December 25 to coincide with and eventually replace the Roman Saturnalia; likewise, the Romans' all-out-wild Lupercalia in late February was replaced by Carnevale, Shrove Tuesday, or Mardi Gras, as it has been variously known.)

Druid: a member of an ancient Celtic priesthood.

In the fourth century, the Eastern church (Greek) observed a feast of all martyrs on May 13. The martyrs, such as saints Stephen, Bartholomew, Perpetua, and Felicity, attracted a strong following in the fourth century and later. The martyrs, who in constancy to their faith had often died gruesome deaths, were regarded as having already attained the heavenly inheritance to which all believers looked forward. They were not dead, but transformed: they were saints living in the presence of their Lord. So strong were the pious devotions to the martyrs that their feast days became a permanent part of the Church's calendar of public worship.

In 609 Pope Boniface IV dedicated the Pantheon in Rome—originally a temple for the worship of "all gods"—to the Blessed Virgin Mary and all the martyrs. The earliest sign of November 1 as the date for venerating the martyrs, and of opening the holy day to include the saints as well, was during the reign of Pope Gregory III (731–741); Gregory chose November 1 to dedicate a chapel in honor of all saints in St. Peter's in Rome. All Saints' Day was observed by the early Christian scholar Alcuin (735?–804) on November 1 in the year 800, and the holy day also appeared on the first of November in a ninth-century English calendar. Pope Gregory IV made it official in 837 when he ordered that all churches set aside November 1 as the day to honor all the saints.

In European countries like France, Spain, Italy, Germany, and Portugal, All Saints' Day is a public holiday, whereas its observance is limited in the English-speaking (and generally more Protestant) countries. The holiday tends to be observed primarily in countries with a large Catholic population, thus it is an important event in Latin America and places in the United States with a predominantly Catholic population.

Perhaps nowhere in the United States is All Saints' Day observed with greater "mass reverence" or with such a long tradition as in Louisiana, where old French and Spanish customs influence life even to this day. As Henri Schindler explains in *Mardi Gras: New Orleans*, "The dead were not only remembered by the Creoles, they were venerated. They were buried with funeral processions, and the cemeteries were the scenes of one vast family reunion on All Saints' Day." All Saints' Day was more than a religious holiday; it was a social occasion. In New Orleans, whose cemeteries of aboveground tombs and mausoleums are commonly known as "cities of the dead," it was the custom in bygone days to spend the entire day at the cemetery, visiting, paying respects, and, if you were a child, playing hide-and-seek among the avenues and allées between the tombs. From mid-October, the cemeteries were busy with people whitewashing tombs, cleaning the grave sites, and placing flowers and candles by the tombs of their loved ones. In the weeks before the holy day, vendors would sell flowers and fruits and cakes, and boys would stand outside the gates of the cemetery, offering to clean and whitewash the tombs (for a price, naturally). Families would bring flowers (usually chrysanthemums), candles, and a picnic basket, and everyone wore their best winter clothes for the first time. Creole women would wear their *robe de la toussaint* (All Saints' dress), and many of the wealthier families built wrought iron or stone benches beside their family tomb, where they would sit all day and receive visitors, speak fondly of the dead, and gossip.

In some parts of Latin America, a particularly beautiful All Saints' tradition is the flying of giant kites. In the village of Santiago Sacatepéquez, fifteen miles from Antigua, Guatemala, villagers gather and move in a procession through the streets to the cemeteries. Once there, they fly giant kites to communicate with loved ones who have passed away. The kites have messages tied to the tails for the deceased and special petitions to God. The celebration ends with a traditional meal called Fiambre. ◆

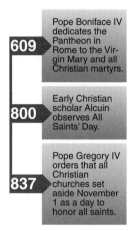

609 Pope Boniface IV dedicates the Pantheon in Rome to the Virgin Mary and all Christian martyrs.

800 Early Christian scholar Alcuin observes All Saints' Day.

837 Pope Gregory IV orders that all Christian churches set aside November 1 as a day to honor all saints.

All Souls' Day

All Souls' Day, November 2, is the third in a sequence of special days traditionally set aside to honor the dead. Halloween (October 31), All Saints' Day (November 1), and All Souls' Day have different origins, however—some pagan and some Christian—and have come to be grouped together by the gravitational forces of religion, natural affinity, and culture and history rather than by design.

All Souls' Day, primarily a Catholic, Anglican, and Orthodox holy day, appears to have developed from a custom originated by the **abbot** Odilo of Cluny, in France, in the tenth century. St. Odilo (d. 1049) proposed that his parish observe the day after All Saints' Day (by then a regular part of the church calendar) in honor of all the departed, particularly those whose souls were still in purgatory (the temporary state after death in which a soul destined for heaven is purified). Traditionally, November 2 is a day to visit family graves and pray for the souls of one's ancestors. The evening of November 1 (All Saints' Day) is often called All Souls' Eve, and is a time to tidy and decorate graveyards and light candles in memory of the dead. On All Souls' Day, the Catholic church gives a **requiem** Mass (from the opening words, *Requiem aeternam dona eis, Domine,* "*Eternal* rest grant unto them, O Lord [and let perpetual light shine upon them]") to honor and assist the souls of the departed. Priests celebrating the mass traditionally wear vestments of black (for mourning), violet (penance), or white (the hope of resurrection).

abbot: the head of a monastery.

requiem: a service for the dead.

Aymara Indians in Peru celebrate All Souls' Day in the cemetery near the graves of their dead ancestors.

In France, *Le Jour des Morts* (the Day of the Dead) is widely celebrated, as is the day before, *La Toussaint* (All Saints). Church services are held in memory of all the saints on November 1, but by the evening, attention turns toward the less exalted. People go to the cemeteries to tend the graves and decorate them with flowers and candles in homage to deceased family members.

Italy's Il Giorno dei Morti begins at dawn with a solemn requiem Mass. Church bells toll, and, as in France, people clean and decorate their family's graves. Although the day is serious and respectful, it is not all somber: in Sicily, children who have prayed for the *morti*, or souls of the departed, leave their shoes outside, where they are filled with gifts or candy. And in Rome, it is customary for young people to choose *Il Giorno dei Morti* as the day to announce their engagement (perhaps to please their ancestors?).

November 2 in Germany is *Allerseelen*, a day for tending graves, lighting candles in memory of the departed, and care-taking of souls. At noon, church bells begin ringing and may toll for an hour, freeing the souls until noon the next day. It is a tradition that no knife should be left with its blade upturned, lest passing souls hurt themselves. Stoves are kept lit to warm the souls, bowls of butter and fat may be left out to soothe their wounds, and cold milk to cool them.

In Mexico, *el Día de los Muertos* (the Day of the Dead) is a national holiday. Many believe that on this day the spirits of the dead return to visit their friends and relatives. Before sunrise, people gather in cemeteries with candles, flowers, and food in the shape of, or decorated with, symbols of death: children eat sugar funeral wreaths, candy skulls and coffins, and little chocolate hearses. The occasion is festive, though, because the departed loved ones and the living are reunited.

Although it has a large Catholic population, the United States has historically not made much of All Souls' Day (or All Saints', for that matter), except in southern Louisiana. There the population is heavily Catholic, and to this day the culture remains much influenced by the old customs of the French and Spanish settlers who developed and governed "la Louisiane" for nearly a hundred years before the Louisiana Purchase in 1803 brought the vast territory into the possession of the United States. All Souls' Day was essentially a continuation of All Saints'. On the evening of All Saints' (also known as All Souls' Eve), people light candles on the tombs, often replacing them throughout the night, until the morning of All Souls' Day. A New Orleans *Picayune* from 1859 reports that "with unusual pomp and much of the display introduced by old Spanish colonists, the clergy surrounded a tall black cross in the cemetery centres and chaunted the imposing anthem for repose of departed souls."

A more recent and more widespread cultural phenomenon expanding American awareness of All Souls' Day has been the settlement of Mexican and Central American immigrants throughout the United States, especially since the 1980s. In Texas, Mexican Americans tend to call November 2 *el Día de los Difuntos* (the Day of the Deceased), or *de los Finados* (the Finished, or Departed). The day is an occasion for cleaning and decorating the family graves, and for graveside social gatherings, where people tell stories about the deceased and recall old times. As a woman in San Antonio said, "On this day we remember those who are there in the earth. They expect us to come to remember them." ◆

All Souls' Day is an occasion for cleaning and decorating the family graves and for graveside social gatherings, where people tell stories about the deceased and recall old times.

Anthesteria

ANCIENT GREECE ● SPRING

Attic: of ancient Athens.

The Anthesteria was the main spring festival in the Greek **Attic** calendar, celebrated in the middle of the month Anthesterion (mid-February to mid-March). Dedicated to Dionysos, the ceremonies lasted for three days, from the eleventh to the thirteenth of the month. The days were respectively known as Pithoigia, Choes, and Chutroi, meaning "opening of the barrels," "cups," and "pots." Starting at sunset before the festive days began, people brought their agricultural tools and vessels in from the fields and vineyards.

On the first day the ceremonies started with a tasting of wine cellared the previous autumn at a small sanctuary of the god of the wine Dionysos en Limnais (Dionysos of the marshes) that was open only during this time, all other sanctuaries being closed. Everybody, including children over the age of three, began drinking at the same time on the order of the king and at the sounding of trumpets, but each individual sat alone and in silence. The celebrants thus renounced the **conviviality** that normally accompanies food, drink, and table talk. The drinking culminated in a contest, the winner being the first to empty a two-liter jug. During the festival, distinctions of rank and status were abolished. The solemnity of the occasion may derive not only from the **etiological** myth about the reception of Orestes, who had been polluted by slaying his mother, but also from the belief that the spirits of the dead rose on this "day of pollution," as Choes was also called. People chewed **buckthorn** and painted their doors with pitch to ward off these evil spirits.

conviviality: a festive, social atmosphere.

etiological: relating to cause or origin.

buckthorn: a small, thorny tree containing clusters of berries.

The second day ended where the first had started: the drunken revelers carried their ivy-decorated drinking cups back to the sanctuary of Dionysos, handing them over to the women's collegiate of the fourteen Geraiai (the venerable ones), led by the queen. The queen, consort of the *archon basileus* (king of ruling houses), then performed the central rite of the festival through her communion with Dionysos in the *hieros gamos* (sacred marriage), a nocturnal rite attended only by the women's priestly college. Though the concrete consummation of this divine marriage is shrouded in mystery, the mythical origin of the ritual dramatization clearly refers to the Greek myth of the marriage between the ill-fated Ariadne and Dionysos, another somber connection between Dionysos and the world of the dead.

The third day was completely given over to Hermes Chthonios, ruler of the underworld of the dead. Various cereals were cooked in honey and the meal was offered to the *keres*, spirits that might otherwise become noxious. The day ended with the invocation, "Out of the doors, ye *keres!* The Anthesteria is over." Before that, however, a number of contests were held, the most enigmatic being one where unmarried girls swing on chairs hung from trees. This is said to have been the reenactment of the unhappy death of Erigone, daughter of Ikarios, the bringer of wine (Ikarios was a double of Dionysos): when her father was slain by drunken herders, Erigone hanged herself on the branches of a tree that grew out of his body. This points to the double aspect of the festival: the darker side of the realm of the dead, and of sacrifices by hanging, and the brighter side of the promise of resurrection, marriage, and fertility in spring. ◆

Anzac Day

AUSTRALIA AND NEW ZEALAND ● APRIL 25

1914 Anzac soldiers are sent to Egypt to train for battle during World War I.

1915 Anzac forces fight a bloody eight-month battle against Turkish forces on the Gallipoli Peninsula in Turkey.

1916 Anzac soldiers in London and Egypt observe the first anniversary of the April 25 Gallipoli landing.

1920 The Australian government declares April 25 a national holiday.

1929 The Australian War Memorial in Canberra is dedicated.

Anzac Day, a national holiday in both Australia and New Zealand, commemorates a painful time in their history. When World War I began in 1914, both countries were young and had only recently organized their own military forces, under the training of British instructors. Their combined forces became known as "Anzac" (Australia and New Zealand Army Corps).

In late 1914 the Anzac soldiers eagerly sailed off to war, expecting to fight in western Europe. But they were sent for months of training in Egypt instead, and their final destination turned out to be the Gallipoli Peninsula in Turkey. The goal of the campaign was to seize the peninsula and allow the Allied forces to sail into the Black Sea. The Anzac landed on April 25, 1915, at a place that later came to be known as Anzac Cove. The Allied leaders had expected a quick victory over the Turkish forces, but their mistake was soon obvious; the battle was bloody and lasted for eight months. Conditions were dreadful, with intense heat and little drinking water.

The Allied forces finally were evacuated in December, 1915, after both sides had suffered terrible losses; an estimated 33,000 Allied soldiers and 86,000 Turkish soldiers died. Among the Anzac forces that suffered the highest casualties was the Maori Pioneer Battalion, a 476-man unit of New Zealand natives who many people had predicted would not fight well. The Maoris proved the skeptics wrong, and fought so fiercely that only sixty of them survived the battle. Numerous military experts and historians now agree that the Allied campaign was

---

Anzac Biscuits

When people from the British Isles migrated to Australia and New Zealand during the eighteenth and nineteenth centuries, they carried with them a custom of baking simple, hearty biscuits from oats. Before long they modified the traditional recipe by adding coconut, which is plentiful in countries of the South Pacific. During World War I, the biscuits became associated with the Australia New Zealand Army Corp (Anzac) when charity organizations began selling them to raise funds for the war effort. After the war, the biscuits (now dubbed Anzac biscuits) were sold to raise money for needy veterans. Today, people in Australia and New Zealand serve Anzac biscuits on Anzac Day in remembrance of their countrymen who have fallen in battle. There are many different ways to make Anzac biscuits. All recipes include oatmeal and some type of sweet syrup; most also include shredded coconut. The following recipe is typical.

1 cup of rolled oats	3/4 cup shredded coconut
1 cup sugar	1/2 cup butter
1 tablespoon light corn syrup	1 teaspoon baking soda
2 tablespoons boiling water	1 cup flour

Mix oats, flour, sugar, and coconut together in a large bowl. Set aside. Melt the corn syrup and butter together in a saucepan. Dissolve the baking soda into the boiling water and add to melted butter and syrup. Slowly pour the liquid into the flour mixture and stir until evenly moistened. Place tablespoonfuls of the dough about three inches apart on a well-greased baking tray. Bake at 350° for 15 to 20 minutes.

---

badly planned and doomed from the beginning. Despite the slaughter, the campaign achieved no military goals. C. E. W. Bean, who became the official historian of the battle, said that it represented "reckless valour in a good cause, . . . enterprise, resourcefulness, fidelity, comradeship and endurance." The 1981 Australian motion picture *Gallipoli*, directed by Peter Weir and starring Mel Gibson, presents the history and a very graphic depiction of the battle.

On April 25, 1916, the first anniversary of the landing on Gallipoli, soldiers from Australia and New Zealand who were stationed in London commemorated the occasion with a march. Troops stationed in Egypt, some of whom were survivors of the battle, did the same. In Sydney, Australia, wounded soldiers were driven through the streets with their nurses. When the war ended in 1918, many soldiers remained on duty. In 1920, with the forces finally home, April 25 was declared a national holiday, a day to express both pride and mourning. In later years the day also became a commemoration of the dead from other wars involving Australia and New Zealand, much like Memorial Day and Veterans Day in the United States. Australian and New Zealand dead from World War II, the Korean War, the Vietnam War, the Persian Gulf War, and other military actions are all honored on Anzac Day.

Anzac Day is an extremely important national holiday throughout Australia and New Zealand. It is marked by religious services held at dawn, plus ceremonies at cemeteries and war memorials. A period of silence at 9 A.M. recalls the time when the landing began. Wreaths are laid that contain both laurel, a symbol of honor dating back to ancient Rome, and rosemary, signifying remembrance. Poppies are associated in these countries with Remembrance Day (November 11, the anniversary of the armistice that ended World War I), but poppies are now used on Anzac Day as well. They are placed in cemetery wreaths and are sold individually to raise funds for veterans. People also eat little oatcakes called "Anzac biscuits," which are similar to biscuits sold during and after World War I to raise money for soldiers and veterans.

Members of Australia's armed forces march in an Anzac Day parade in Sydney.

During the ceremonies, poems honoring soldiers who died in battle are read. One frequent choice is "For the Fallen" by British poet and scholar Laurence Binyon, which reads in part:

> They went with songs to the battle, they were young,
> Straight of limb, true of eye, steady and aglow.
> They were staunch to the end against odds uncounted;
> They fell with their faces to the foe.
> They shall not grow old, as we that are left grow old;
> Age shall not weary them, nor the years condemn.
> At the going down of the sun and in the morning
> We will remember them.

This poem, written in 1914, became associated with Anzac Day when it was placed on the cover of a collection of sermons and speeches at a ceremony in Queensland in 1921; Binyon's poem was also read when the Australian War Memorial in Canberra was dedicated in 1929. Another traditional Anzac Day reading is "In Flanders Fields" by J. M. McCrae, a Canadian medical officer who served during World War I. The "Last Post," a military trumpet or bugle call, is usually sounded at the end of Anzac Day ceremonies.

In Turkey, visitors from Australia, New Zealand, and other nations that fought in World War I gather at dawn on the beach at Anzac Cove to remember the soldiers who perished there. On the war memorial at Anzac Cove, there is an inscription written by Mustafa Kamal (also known as Ataturk), who led the Turkish forces and later became a noted statesman. It concludes: "After having lost their lives on this land they have become our sons as well." ◆

April Fools' Day

April Fools' Day has been seen as commemorating the wandering from place to place of the raven and dove Noah sent from the ark to search for dry land after the flood.

The first day of April, known as April Fools' Day or All Fools' Day, is traditionally marked by the custom of playing jokes (usually on friends) and engaging in frivolous activities. It stands as one of the few spring festivals in Christian Europe unaffected by the date of the celebration of Easter. April Fools' Day should not be confused with the Feast of Fools, the medieval mock-religious festival involving status reversals and parodies of the official church by low-level cathedral functionaries and others (held on or about January 1). April Fools' Day activities, however, are related in spirit to this once-licensed kind of revelry.

The actual origins of April Fools' practices and their connection to the first of April are unknown. The day and its traditions appear to reflect some of the festive characteristics of such non-Christian religious celebrations as the Hilaria of ancient Rome and the Holi festival of India (both held in spring). Traditional celebrations related to the vernal equinox and to the arrival of spring in the Northern Hemisphere, as well as that season's playful and often fickle weather, may also have contributed to the timing and persistence of April Fools' customs.

The development of April Fools' Day has been the subject of much popular speculation. The day has been seen as commemorating the wanderings from place to place of the raven and dove Noah sent from the ark to search for dry land after the biblical flood. It has also been thought to memorialize in an irreverent way the transfer of Jesus from the jurisdiction of one governmental or religious figure to another in the last hours before his crucifixion. In either case, the events in question were believed to have occurred on or near the first of April.

An intriguing explanation for April Fools' Day customs in France, on the other hand, concerns confusion over the change in the date for the observance of the New Year. Those who recognized March 25 as the beginning of their year (a number of different dates were used to mark this occasion in medieval Europe) culminated their eight-day celebration of this event on April 1. When in 1564 Charles IX changed the official date to January 1, some people either resisted the change or failed to remember when the year was to begin. This confusion led to the practice of exchanging false greetings for the first of the year on the old day of its observance (April 1) and of sending false gifts, as a joke, to those who expected the customary holiday presents on that day. Thus some scholars believe that jests of all sorts soon came to be associated with this date. The French term *poisson d'avril*, literally translated as "an April fish," is still used to describe the foolish victim of an April Fools' Day prank.

The custom of "April fooling," known and practiced in many European countries, was brought by English settlers to the United States. Here, any person of any age or rank is susceptible to being made a fool on April first; tradition demands, however, that these jokes take place only within the twelve-hour period from midnight to noon (with the rest of the day reserved, no doubt, for apologies). Today, the practice is usually observed by children, although some adults continue to perpetrate both simple and complex jests and hoaxes on unsuspecting individuals on this day. ◆

Any person of any age or rank is susceptible to being made a fool of on April first.

Arbor Day

UNITED STATES AND CANADA ● VARIOUS DATES

Arbor Day is a holiday devoted to the planting and care of trees, and to public education about conservation and recycling. Every American state and most of the provinces of Canada celebrate Arbor Day. In most states, Arbor Day is observed during the last week in April, but the exact date varies from state to state to coincide with the best tree-planting weather. Warm southern states observe Arbor Day early in January, February, or March. People in Alaska, Maine, North Dakota, and other northern states with long winters observe Arbor Day in May. Hawaiians celebrate Arbor Day in November. In California, Arbor Day comes on March 7, the birthday of naturalist Luther Burbank.

The first Arbor Day was celebrated in Nebraska in 1872. Julius Sterling Morton, who had migrated from Detroit, Michigan, to the treeless plains of the Nebraska Territory in 1854, came up with the idea. Morton, who was the editor of the *Nebraska City News*, was interested in conservation and used his newspaper as a forum to encourage people to plant trees, thereby making the prairie a good place for people to live. Morton believed that the prairie needed more trees to serve as windbreaks and shade, to hold moisture in the soil, and to provide lumber for housing and fuel, fruit for food, and habitat for birds, squirrels, and other wildlife. Morton first proposed a tree-planting holiday in January 1872 at a meeting of the Nebraska State Board of Agriculture. He suggested naming the holiday "Arbor Day" after the Latin word for "tree." In response, the Board passed the following resolution, which included an offer

1854 Arbor Day founder Julius Sterling Morton immigrates from Detroit to treeless plains of the Nebraska territory.

1872 Nebraska celebrates America's first Arbor Day.

1875 Arbor Day is designated a legal annual holiday in Nebraska; other states soon follow Nebraska's lead.

Johnny Appleseed

Although Julius Sterling Morton deserves credit as the founder of Arbor Day, the holiday's spiritual forefather was a man named John Chapman, better known as Johnny Appleseed. Chapman was born in Leominster, Massachusetts, on September 26, 1774. As a young adult, Chapman became a professional nurseryman, raising and selling young trees and planting numerous orchards in New York and Pennsylvania. During this time, the American frontier began to move west into what is now Ohio, Indiana, and Illinois. Chapman was aware that few fruit trees grew in these territories and he realized that settlers would be deprived of fruit until orchards could be planted and grown. He therefore resolved to carry flower and fruit tree seeds, especially apple seeds, to the west from Pennsylvania. Beginning in 1797, he wandered alone through Ohio and Indiana ahead of the settlers, searching for good land to plant trees. When he found a spot he established an orchard to be ready for the use of the settlers when they arrived. Chapman owned many orchards and made a living selling trees to settlers. He died in 1845 near Fort Wayne, Indiana.

After his death Chapman became an American folk hero. Dubbed Johnny Appleseed, he is usually pictured barefoot, wearing ragged clothing, with a tin cup around his neck and a bag of seeds slung across his shoulder. According to legend, he wandered the American frontier scattering appleseeds and giving away apples to everyone he encountered. His fame was greatly enhanced in 1871 when an article entitled "Johnny Appleseed, a Pioneer Hero," written by W. D. Haley, appeared in *Harper's New Monthly Magazine.* Although many of the stories about Johnny Appleseed are probably not true, there is no doubt that he loved and cared for trees and that he planted large numbers of them, especially in Ohio and Indiana. His name and spirit are often invoked during Arbor Day festivities.

of prizes for the individual and county that planted the most trees.

> *Resolved,* That Wednesday, the 10th day of April, 1872, be, and the same is hereby especially set apart and consecrated for tree planting in the State of Nebraska, and the State Board of Agriculture hereby name it "ARBOR DAY," and urge upon the people of the State the vital importance of tree planting, hereby offer a *"Special Premium"* of *one hundred dollars* to the County Agricultural Society of that county in Nebraska which shall *upon that day* plant, properly, the largest number of trees, and a *Farm Library of Twenty-five Dollars* worth of books to that person who on that day shall plant, properly, in Nebraska, the greatest number of trees.

More than one million trees were planted in Nebraska on the first Arbor Day. Two years later, Robert W. Furnas, the governor of Nebraska, proclaimed Arbor Day a state day of observance. The following year, Arbor Day became a legal holiday in

Many schoolchildren, like this boy in Long Beach, California, learn how to plant and care for trees on Arbor Day.

Nebraska, and April 22, Morton's birthday, was selected as the permanent date for its observance. In the decades that followed conservationists like B. G. Northrup, George P. Marsh, and A. S. Draper, as well as President Theodore Roosevelt, promoted the establishment of Arbor Day observances in other states and the holiday was eventually observed throughout the United States and Canada.

Many other countries also have holidays devoted to tree planting and public education about conservation. In Israel, for example, people plant trees during the Bi-Shevat festival in late January or early February. People in Japan plant trees on Greenery Day, which falls on April 29, the birthday of their late emperor Showa.

Most Arbor Day observances take place in schools, where children learn about the role of trees in the ecosystem and their value to human beings and animals. Many teachers ask their students to write reports, prepare exhibits, and design posters about trees, conservation, and paper recycling. In some schools, each student plants tree seeds or a seedling in a pot on Arbor

Neighborhood tree-planting ceremonies, like this one in Seattle in 1995, take place in many American towns and cities on Arbor Day.

Day; the student cares for the young tree while it grows, then plants it outdoors when it is large enough. Students may also plant larger trees outdoors, then learn how to care for them. They eat apples, pears, and other fruits that grow on trees; they sometimes have picnics under older, full-grown trees after they have planted new ones. Tree giveaways are held around the country during which thousands of trees are offered at no cost to residents who promise to plant them. People in some neighborhoods organize block parties where they plant new trees and help one another water, prune, and care for older trees. Every year, the United States president and his family observe Arbor Day by planting a young tree on White House grounds in Washington, D.C.

The Nebraska estate of Arbor Day founder Julius Sterling Morton is now an educational institution open to the public. Along with many of its original buildings, gardens, and orchards, the grounds now include nature trails lined with many species of trees. The Morton estate also encompasses facilities for testing and demonstrating the use of trees for erosion control, a wind-break arboretum to show how trees can protect buildings and fields from harsh weather, and a fuel-wood plantation where fast-growing trees are planted and harvested in planned cycles. ◆

Armed Forces Day

UNITED STATES ● THIRD SATURDAY IN MAY

On September, 18, 1947, some two years after World War II ended, the United States government decided to combine the nation's armed forces into a single entity, the Department of Defense, with four branches: the Army, the Navy, the Air Force, and the Marines. Before then, the separate branches had set aside special days on which they honored their members. After the new department was created, they were asked to display their unity by participating in Armed Forces Day, a single day to honor all of the members of the armed forces.

Armed Forces Day was first proclaimed on August 31, 1949, by Secretary of Defense Louis Johnson. The third Saturday in May was selected as the permanent date for the celebration. The "Cold War" between the United States and the Soviet Union had just begun, and it was probably by design that Armed Forces Day closely followed the May Day celebrations in which communist countries traditionally displayed their military might.

President Harry Truman issued a presidential proclamation on February 27, 1950, proclaiming May 20, 1950, to be "the first parade of preparedness by the unified forces of our land, sea, and air defense." The theme of the first Armed Forces Day was "Teamed for Defense." Activities included parades, air shows, and public tours of military facilities and battleships used in World War II. Both veterans and active-duty military personnel marched in Washington, D.C., and in New York City, where 250 military planes also flew overhead. Themes of later years

1947 The Department of Defense is created, combining the nation's separate armed forces into one entity.

1949 Secretary of Defense Louis Johnson proclaims the first Armed Forces Day, to be observed the following May.

1950 President Harry Truman issues a proclamation directing Americans to set aside May 20 as Armed Forces Day.

Holiday Proclamations

In 1950 President Harry Truman issued a proclamation directing American citizens to set aside May 20 of that year to honor "the unified forces of our land, sea, and air defense." Proclamations are issued by American political executives to notify the public about some governmental action or, more often, to designate a legal holiday or special observance. Proclamations related to governmental action include those issued by the president or a governor when an emergency situation requires the establishment of martial law, as in the case of Abraham Lincoln's Proclamation of 1861 at the beginning of the Civil War. Governmental proclamations may also be issued when it is necessary to order troops into a troubled or afflicted area to protect life and property and maintain order, without martial law, as in some strike situations; or when a sudden turn of events requires executive action, as in the case of Lincoln's Emancipation Proclamation of 1863, President Andrew Johnson's Proclamation of Amnesty of 1865, President Woodrow Wilson's Armistice Proclamation of 1918, or President Franklin D. Roosevelt's Bank Holiday Proclamation of 1933.

Most proclamations, however, are simple ceremonial notices issued in connection with the observance of legal holidays. For example, on Thanksgiving it has become customary for the president and governors, as the heads of state, to issue annual proclamations calling upon the people to cooperate in the appropriate observance of the day. Similar proclamations are issued to commemorate significant events in national or local history, like the anniversary of a state's admission to the union. Proclamations are also issued for publicity purposes, as when a day, week, or month is designated to call the public's attention to the contributions of a designated minority group or the importance of an industrial or agricultural product.

have included "Deter If Possible, Fight If Necessary," "Power for Peace," and "Arsenal of Freedom and Democracy."

A parade is still held in New York City every year, although most Armed Forces Day ceremonies occur on military bases. One of the key activities occurs at Andrews Air Force Base in Maryland, where there is a joint services open house. Air shows featuring parachute jumps and precision flying teams take place on at different locations across the country. Tours of military bases serve as public relations vehicles to display facilities and equipment, as well as opportunities for visitors who are considering military careers to meet with recruiters.

Today Armed Forces Day has been expanded to Armed Forces Week, which begins on the second Saturday of May and honors the members of the Army, Navy, Air Force, Marines, and Coast Guard. The separate branches of the armed forces have also continued to honor their members on separate dates: April 6 (Army); second Saturday in September (Air Force); October 27 (Navy); and November 10 (Marines, officially part of the Navy).

Other countries celebrate similar holidays. For example, Egypt celebrates Armed Forces Day on October 6. This date is the anniversary of the beginning of the October War (Yom Kippur War) of 1973, in which Egypt attacked Israel to regain territory it had lost during the Six Day War in 1967. Egyptian president Anwar Sadat was assassinated during a 1981 Armed Forces Day parade in Cairo. ◆

Ash Wednesday

CHRISTIAN ● SPRING

Ash Wednesday is the first day of Lent, a season preceding Easter that is observed by western Christian churches, especially Roman Catholic, Anglican, and Lutheran. In Eastern Catholic and Eastern Orthodox churches, Lent begins on a Monday, which is sometimes called Pure Monday or Clean Monday. For Roman Catholics and Protestants, Lent starts on Ash Wednesday and ends with the Mass of the Lord's Supper, celebrated on Holy Thursday, two days before Easter Sunday. Ash Wednesday is a day of fasting and abstinence.

Although Lent is traditionally a time of self-discipline and penance, the modern church teaches the faithful to appreciate the symbolism and spirit of the season rather than applying rigid practices. Catholics learn that the season is a time to emulate the journey of Jesus; to experience the descent into death (the self-denial of Lent) and rebirth into life (Easter).

The main ritual of Ash Wednesday takes place within a church service, such as mass. The priest or minister blesses the ashes of incinerated palm branches from the previous year's Palm Sunday. The clergyperson then makes a cross on the foreheads of each worshiper with the ashes while saying, "Remember that you are dust, and unto dust you shall return." This custom symbolizes an Old Testament practice of public penance in which people cover themselves with ashes and clothe their bodies with **sackcloth**. Christians repent of their sins during Lent. Lent lasts 40 days, symbolizing the 40 days Jesus spent in the wilderness fasting and praying, which in turn signified the

sackcloth: a coarse cloth worn as a sign of penitence.

25

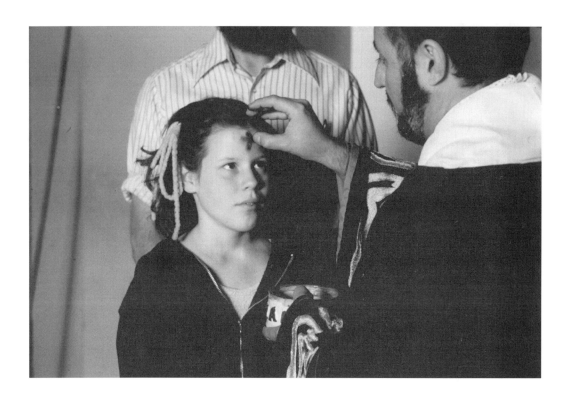

A priest makes a cross on the forehead of a girl during Ash Wednesday services.

40 years Moses wandered the desert with the Israelites. Lent ends in Holy Week, which begins with Palm Sunday, celebrating Jesus' arrival in Jerusalem, and ends with Easter, celebrating the resurrection of Jesus after being crucified.

Many practices of Lent can be traced to early Christian customs. The eve of Easter became a time to baptize Christian converts and to accept repentant Christians back into the faith. In the weeks before Easter, converts fasted and received religious instruction. By the 900s, Lent had become a time of penance and preparation for all Christians. The placing of ashes on the forehead is thought to have been introduced by Pope Gregory I and became universal after a special church council in 1091.

Early practices of Lent involved rigid fasting requirements, which changed throughout Christian history. For some periods, Christians abstained from any food of live creatures for the 40 days of Lent. Others ate fish only. Some ate birds and fish; others abstained from fruit and eggs. Some ate dry bread only. In the 900s, abstinence from eggs, cheese, and fish was a mark of exceptional virtue. But abstaining from flesh meat, and from all things that come from flesh, such as milk, cheese, and eggs, became the common law of the Church. The prohibition of eggs during Lent led to the popular custom of making gifts of eggs at Easter.

Practices in the length of the fast also evolved through the years. In the early Middle Ages only a single meal was permitted in the evening. Soon it became acceptable to break the fast at three o'clock. That changed to midday through the years. Eventually, people were allowed a cup of liquid with a fragment of bread or toast in the early morning. By the early 1990s Catholics could eat meat once a day in Lent except on Fridays, Ash Wednesday, and Holy Saturday. In 1966 Pope Paul VI declared fasting and abstinence during Lent obligatory only on Ash Wednesday and Good Friday.

Some unusual Ash Wednesday practices include burial of a strip of meat as thin as a sardine in Spain. It is thought to have originated with a fertility custom symbolizing the burial of winter. The ceremony also symbolizes the burial of worldly pleasures and acts as a reminder to abstain from meat. In England, people used to make a straw figure dressed in old clothes called Jack-o-Lent. The figure represented Judas Iscariot, who betrayed Jesus, and the people burned it. The self-denial expected during Lent gave rise to elaborate celebrations before Lent. On Shrove Tuesday, the day before Ash Wednesday, many people celebrate Mardi Gras (Fat Tuesday), a lively, colorful occasion of celebratory excess. ◆

The placing of ashes on the forehead is thought to have been introduced by Pope Gregory I and became universal after a special church council in 1091.

Ashura

MUSLIM ● FIRST DAY OF MUHARRAM

Ashura, sometimes called "Husayn Day," is a Muslim holiday commemorating the death of Husayn ibn Ali, the grandson of the prophet Mohammed. Ashura falls on the tenth day of Muharram, the first month of the Muslim calendar. Its general significance as a fast day for Muslims derives from the rites of the Jewish Yom Kippur (Day of Atonement). The Arabic term *ashura* is based on the Hebrew word *asor* with the Aramaic **determinative** ending.

Scholars are not agreed as to the exact day on which Ashura was observed in early Islam. Early **hadith** tradition seems to indicate that the day possessed special sanctity in Arab society even before Islam. Thus the Jewish rite, which the Prophet observed in Medina in 622 C.E., only helped an already established Arab tradition to acquire religious content and hence greater prestige. The Jewish character was soon obscured, however, through its incorporation into the Muslim calendar and its observance as a Muslim fast day. With the institution of the fast of Ramadan in the second year of the **Hijrah**, Ashura became a voluntary fast.

For over thirteen centuries the Muslim Shiah community has observed the day of Ashura as a day of mourning. On October 10, 680 Husayn ibn Ali, the grandson of the Prophet and third **imam** of the Shiah Muslims, fell in battle on the plain of Karbala, a small town on the banks of the Euphrates in Iraq. Muawiyah, the first Ummayad **caliph**, had died in the spring of the same year and was succeeded by his son Yazid. This heredi-

determinative: concerning a part of a word that determines the class to which it belongs.

hadith: the collected body of traditions relating to Mohammed and his companions.

Hijrah: the term for Mohammad's flight from Mecca to Medina in 622, which marks the first year of the Muslim calendar.

imam: a Muslim leader.

caliph: a successor of Mohammed as political and religious leader.

tary appointment met with strong opposition in many quarters of the Muslim community, which was already torn by conflict and dissension. Among the dissenting groups was the party of Ali.

The events leading to Husayn's death, which were subsequently elaborated and greatly embellished, helped to heighten the drama of suffering and martyrdom. With his family and a small following, Husayn encamped in Karbala on the second day of Muharram. During the week of his fruitless negotiations with Umar ibn Saud, the Iraqi governor's representative, Husayn and his family were denied access to the Euphrates, a river in southwestern Asia. The thirst of the women and children and their pathetic entreaties for water provided one of the major themes of suffering and heroism for the drama of Karbala. In the fateful battle between Husayn's small band of less than one hundred and the four-thousand-strong army of Ubayd Allah ibn Ziyad, governor of Iraq, Husayn and nearly all his followers fell. The women and children were carried captive first to Ubayd Allah ibn Ziyad in Kufa, and from there to Damascus, where Yazid received them kindly and at their own request sent them back to Medina.

The death of Husayn produced an immediate reaction in the Muslim community, especially in Iraq. It is reported in al-Majlisi's *Bihar alanwar* that when the people of Kufa saw the head of the martyred imam and the pitiful state of the captives they began to beat their breasts in remorse for their betrayal of the grandson of the Prophet and son and heir of Ali. This reaction produced an important movement known as al-Tawwabin (the Repenters), which nurtured a spirit of revenge for the blood of Husayn and provided fertile soil for the new Ashura cult.

Ali Zayn al-Abidin, the only surviving son of Husayn, was proclaimed fourth imam by a large segment of the Shiah community. His house in Medina and those of subsequent imams became important centers for the growth of the Ashura celebration, where commemorative services (*majalis al-aza*) were held. At first, these consisted of recounting the tragedy of Karbala and reflecting on its meaning and reciting **elegies** (*marathi*) in memory of the martyred imam. Soon, the shrines of the imams became important places of pilgrimage (*ziyarah*), where the pious continue to this day to hold their memorial services.

During Ummayad rule (680–750) the Ashura cult grew in secret. But under the Abbasids (750–1258), who came to

elegy: a song or poem expressing sorrow.

dirge: a slow, solemn
song of grief.

power on the wave of pro-Alid revolts, it was encouraged, and
by the beginning of the tenth century public commemorations
were marked by a professional mourner *(naih)*, who chanted
elegies and led the faithful in the **dirge** for the martyred imam
and his followers.

In 962, under the patronage of the Buyids (an Iranian
dynasty with deep Shii sympathies that held power in Iraq and
Iran from 932 to 1055), Ashura was declared a day of public
mourning in Baghdad. Processions filled the streets, markets
were closed, and shops were draped in black. Special edifices
called *husayniyat* were built to house the Ashura celebrations.
Such buildings eventually became common in Cairo, Aleppo,
and many Iranian cities.

The greatest impetus for the development of the Ashura
celebration as a popular religious and artistic phenomenon
came with the rise of the Safavid dynasty in Iran in 1501. The
Safavids adopted Shiism as Iran's state religion and worked tire-
lessly to consolidate and propagate it. It was during their rule
that the literary genre known as *taziyah* (passion play) was
highly developed and popularized. From Iran the Ashura celebration spread first to the Indian subcontinent and from there
to other areas influenced by Iranian language and culture.

Some scholars have postulated a direct relation between
the Ashura celebration and ancient rites dedicated to the Sym-
marian god Tammuz and the mythical Greek youth Adonis, but
the extent of such influence can never be determined. The fact
that Husayn died on the very spot where they were observed
may simply be a historical coincidence, and it is perhaps more
plausible that parallels between these two phenomena are due
to human psychology and the need to express strong emotions
through a common form of myth and ritual. ◆

Bastille Day

FRANCE ● JULY 14

Bastille Day is the French national holiday, comparable to the American Fourth of July, that commemorates the day in 1789 when citizens of Paris overthrew the Bastille, a medieval fortress (and later a prison) in the early days of the French Revolution. *Le 14 juillet* ("the Fourteenth of July" in French) is a grand national festival of speeches, military parades, dances, and cookouts in the town square. Bastille Day is marked by extravagant fireworks displays—particularly fireworks of blue, white, and red, the colors of the French flag. From military processions on the great Champs-Elysées in Paris to the plazas of provincial villages, Bastille Day is an occasion of strong national pride and a reinforcement of the Revolution's principles of liberty, equality, and brotherhood.

The Fortress. The Bastille (from Old French *bastide*: fortress) was originally built on orders from King Charles V as a stronghold on the east side of Paris along a wall around the city, a forbidding defense in case of attack by the English. The first stone was laid on April 22, 1370. With eight towers, an imposing height of 100 feet, and surrounded by a moat more than eighty feet wide, the medieval superstructure dominated the Paris skyline. The fortress went through many structural modifications over the next four centuries, but one thing that remained unchanged was the Bastille's imposing presence over the city, both a stalwart defense and, increasingly during the reign of the Bourbon kings, an offensive sight.

During the 1600s the Bastille began to be used as a state prison, usually holding no more than forty prisoners at a time.

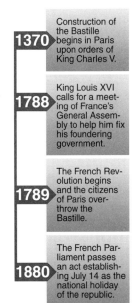

1370 Construction of the Bastille begins in Paris upon orders of King Charles V.

1788 King Louis XVI calls for a meeting of France's General Assembly to help him fix his foundering government.

1789 The French Revolution begins and the citizens of Paris overthrow the Bastille.

1880 The French Parliament passes an act establishing July 14 as the national holiday of the republic.

Bastille Day, the national holiday of France, is marked by a huge parade through Paris's Arc de Triomphe and along the Champs-Elysées.

Most of the prisoners were taken captive by direct orders from the king—as written in the dreaded *lettres de cachet*—from which there was no recourse, no appeal. Many prisoners were taken arbitrarily and secretly; it is probably this aspect of the imprisonment that gave rise to legends of horror and oppression, for most of the inmates were political prisoners of rank and influence, and they were generally treated mildly.

Under Louis XIV (1638–1715)—also known as the Sun King—the Bastille became a place of judicial detention, where prisoners could be held by the lieutenant of police. Suspects being tried by the Parlement were held there during the regency of Philippe II, duc d'Orléans, as were prohibited books that had been confiscated from booksellers.

The French Revolution. In 1788, after decades of foreign wars, court extravagance, and mounting debt (all compounded by a tax-gathering bureaucracy that was as chaotic as it was unfair), the treasury of France was empty, and the government on the brink of bankruptcy. In the fiscal crisis the king, Louis XVI, called for a meeting of the Estates-General, an assembly of representatives of the three estates—nobles, clergy, and commoners—that had not been called together in 175 years. The

A couple in Paris celebrate Bastille Day in costumes of 18th-century French nobility.

Estates-General, an advisory, not legislative, body, was expected to supply funds and to advise the king on ways to reform the government. The flood of opinions and demands pouring in from around the country showed an impressive consistency in ideas and (high) expectations. Many wanted a constitutional monarchy, like that of Britain, to replace the absolute monarchy France had endured since the days of Louis

The storming of the Bastille during the early days of the French Revolution quickly came to symbolize the end of the old order.

XIV. In general, the people did not want to abolish the monarchy as an institution, but only to rein in the abuses of despotism—the maddening, arbitrary control of the national bureaucracy.

In the national emergency, Louis XVI had granted freedom of the press in an effort to stimulate reforms and win public acceptance of them. The abbé Sieyès jolted the French people when he wrote in a brief manifesto, "The Third Estate [the commoners] is the whole country—a complete nation." (Sieyès would later contribute to the contents of the famous Declaration of the Rights of Man and the Citizen.) In the spring of 1789 the Third Estate declared itself the National Assembly (the commoners are the nation), and forced the king to legalize the National Assembly. In July Louis surrounded his palace at Versailles with troops, and dismissed Jacques Necker, his popular minister of finances.

Amid unbearable political and social tensions, on the morning of July 14, 1789, a crowd of Parisians seized weapons from the armory at the Invalides and then marched toward the Bastille. They demanded the release of the arms and munitions stored there. At the time, the prison part of the Bastille held only seven captives. Infuriated by the prison governor's lack of cooperation, the mob stormed and captured the Bastille. The taking of the Bastille quickly came to symbolize the end of the ancien régime, or old order.

La Fête Nationale. The very next year, the Fête de la Fédération held on July 14 celebrated the insurrection, and in ensuing years the Parisian Revolutionary Directory promoted the anniversary as a great national holiday, one of several created to replace the old festivals associated with the "enemies of the people," the monarchy and the Catholic church. July 14 became an anniversary to celebrate the people's freedom from the oppressions of despotic kings and the triumph of "Liberté, Égalité, Fraternité."

Celebrations diminished through the years, however, until 1880, when leaders of the Third Republic chose July 14 as a day for celebrating the foundation of that relatively new government. On July 6, 1880, the French Parlement passed an act establishing the Fourteenth as the national holiday of the Republic.

Among the most exuberant celebrations of Bastille Day were in 1919, after France's unspeakable sufferings through

World War I, and the three days of jubilation in July 1945 after the Allied victory over Nazi Germany in World War II.

The festivities of July 14 are as popular today as ever. Amid shouts of "Vive la France!" and "A bas la Bastille" (down with the Bastille!), armed forces parade down the wide boulevard of the Champs-Elysées, air force fighters with blue, white, and red jet plumes roar over the Arc de Triomphe, and civic officials give speeches extolling the ideals of liberty and equality. Families gather for huge feasts, townspeople come together in the square for a traditional méchoui (lamb roast on a spit) amid blue, white, and red lanterns, and bands play pop music and popular accordion tunes. The beloved national anthem, "La Marseillaise," is sung over and over ("*Allons enfants de la patrie . . .*"). As with the American Fourth of July, the crowning delight is a spectacular fireworks display, emphasizing the national tricolors. But even after the fireworks, the people press the band to play on, "just one more—the last," and the dancing continues long into the night. ◆

Boxing Day

GREAT BRITAIN ● DECEMBER 26

Boxing Day is celebrated as a national holiday in Great Britain on the day after Christmas. Boxing Day began in England, probably during the Middle Ages. According to the generally accepted version of the holiday's origins, the lords and ladies of English feudal manors gave their servants and other dependents modest gifts in Christmas boxes on December 26. A variation on this account says that in the great houses of medieval England, a ceramic box was placed in the entrance hall and that visitors dropped coins into the box as a thank you to the manor staff. The box was opened on December 26 and the contents were disbursed among the staff. A minority view is that Boxing Day's roots go back to the churches' practice of distributing the contents of their charity boxes on the day after Christmas, which was also St. Stephen's Day.

In more recent history Boxing Day has lost its original meaning, especially since the early nineteenth century, when the Industrial Revolution began to depersonalize economic relationships and when the manors began their decline. Now it is, as one observer has said, "a sort of **anachronistic** gift," a day to recover from the heavy eating and drinking and general hubbub of Christmas Day. While Christmas means spending time with family and exchanging presents, Boxing Day is for relaxing. The day has no religious significance and imposes no social or family obligations, an ironic shift from its charitable origins.

Leftover food from Christmas, such as turkey and ham, is consumed on the holiday. When the Christmas meal is so

anachronistic: existing in a time where it does not belong.

Boxing Day Bubble-and-Squeak

Bubble-and-squeak is a classic British dish that is prepared on Boxing Day using foods left over from the Christmas feast of the day before. Every cook makes bubble-and-squeak differently, without a recipe, tossing into the pan whatever leftover foods are available. The dish usually includes boiled potatoes, onions, and often cabbage, all fried together in butter or meat drippings. Some people add cheese, meat, or leftover vegetables, such as turnips, carrots, and Brussels sprouts. The name comes from the bubbling and squeaking sounds the food makes as it fries. Below is a simple, traditional version of bubble-and-squeak.

1/4 cup butter
1 medium onion, chopped
3 or 4 large potatoes, boiled and mashed
1 cup shredded, boiled cabbage
salt and pepper

Melt the butter in a large frying pan. Add the onion and fry, stirring constantly, until softened. Add the potatoes and cabbage (and any vegetables or meat). Add salt and pepper to taste. Fry over medium heat for 10 to 15 minutes until browned.

bountiful that people cannot make it to the traditional plum pudding, it is consumed on the following day. A common Boxing Day dish is called bubble and squeak, consisting of mashed potatoes and other vegetables that are fried in a pan. Another is tatie pot, a combination of beef, black sausage, and potatoes.

For many, heavy television viewing is the day's major activity. Programming includes a healthy dose of holiday fare, including Frank Capra's film *It's a Wonderful Life* (1946). In contrast to the family gatherings of Christmas, Boxing Day is a time for visiting friends. It is also the biggest sports day of the year in Britain, with fans turning out for soccer, rugby, and horse racing. For England's elite, December 26 is a day for fox hunting.

In almost every English village, Boxing Day is a time for performances of "pantomimes," which are bawdy farces based on old stories such as "Cinderella." The actors commonly cross-dress: attractive young women play male heroes, while men play dowdy women. Actors often make names for themselves as pantomime players before moving on to radio and television.

Boxing Day is also a national holiday in Ireland (as it is in Canada and New Zealand) but there, not surprisingly, it is celebrated with an anti-English twist. On December 26, 1601, at the Battle of Kinsdale, the call of a wren supposedly awoke English troops in time for them to thwart an attack by Irish fighters. Since then, Hunting the Wren has been a popular pastime on Boxing Day. Groups of people traditionally captured wrens, killed them, and impaled each on a hot stick; today, paper wrens are usually substituted. In either case the "wren boys" then bring their prey from door to door, perform traditional mime and song, and receive food and drink in return. ◆

Buddha's Day

Buddha's Day, also called Vesak or Visakha Puja, is a holiday commemorating the birth, enlightenment, and death of Siddhartha Gautama, the founder of Buddhism. Siddhartha Gautama is usually called simply "Buddha," which means "enlightened one." This day is considered by many to be the most holy day in the Buddhist year. Although all Buddhist countries observe the birth, enlightenment, and death of Buddha, these three events are not always celebrated on the same day. Japanese Buddhists, for example, celebrate Buddha's birth on April 8, the enlightenment on December 8, and the death on February 15. Buddhists who follow the Theravada school, however, believe that Buddha was born, enlightened, and died miraculously on the same day of the week. Therefore, Theravadan countries, which include Burma, Cambodia, Laos, Sri Lanka, and Thailand, celebrate the three events on a single day during the full moon of the sixth month, called Vaisakha, which occurs in April or May.

Siddhartha Gautama was born during the 400s or 500s B.C.E in southwest Nepal, near the border with India, where he led a life of ease and luxury. When Gautama was twenty-nine years old, he experienced a series of visions that convinced him that life was filled with suffering and unhappiness. Gautama then left his wife and child and became a wanderer in search of truth. After six years, Gautama gained enlightenment, which taught him how people can overcome suffering and achieve nirvana, a state of complete happiness and peace, by freeing themselves of the desire for worldly things. For the rest of his life, Buddha

"Not to do evil, to cultivate good, to purify one's mind—this is the teaching of the Buddhas."
Dhammapada,
183

This boy in Singapore symbolically cleanses himself by pouring water over an image of Buddha on Buddha's Day.

relic: an object that is venerated because of its association with a holy person.

Bodhi: a type of fig tree under which Buddha is said to have obtained enlightenment.

reliquary: a container for sacred relics.

preached the message of his enlightenment and gained many followers. He died when he was about eighty years old.

Vesak celebrations in Southeast Asia focus on the Buddhist monastery. Devotees observe the precepts and listen to sermons on the life of the Buddha. In Thailand, the traditional Vesak sermon, the *pathama-sambodhi*, continues throughout the entire night. It begins with the description of the wedding of Suddhodana and Mahamaya, the Buddha's parents, and concludes with the distribution of the Buddha's **relics** and an accounting of the reasons for the decline of Buddhism in India. The text is a composite of scripture and popular commentary in which the Buddha is depicted as a teacher and miracle worker. In addition to attendance at monastery services, other common Vesak practices include watering **Bodhi** trees within monastery compounds, circumambulation of a special **reliquary** at night with incense and candles, acts of social service such as feeding the poor and treating the sick in hospitals, pilgrimage to sacred sites, and the bathing of Buddha images.

The celebration of Buddha's Day is both ancient and widespread. The seminal events of the Buddha's career coalesced into Vesak by the Theravādins are acknowledged independently in other Buddhist cultures. In Tibet, for example, the traditional religious year included celebration of the Buddha's conception or **incarnation** on the fifteenth day of the first lunar month, the attainment of enlightenment on the eighth day of the fourth month, the Buddha's death on the fifteenth day of the fourth month, and the Buddha's birth on the fourth day of the sixth month of the Tibetan year. The first of these events, the Buddha's incarnation, occupied a preeminent place in the Tibetan religious year, in part because of its assimilation into the New Year carnival. It was a day when special respects were paid to the Dalai Lama, and the Buddha's mother, Mahadevi, was solicited for special **boons**. In China, Korea, and Japan, the Buddha's birthday has been marked, in particular, by a procession of Buddha images and the bathing of these images. These traditions associated with Buddha's Day or Buddha's Birthday appear to be of early origin.

> **incarnation**: the embodiment of a deity in earthly form.

> **boon**: a favor or blessing.

Sacred Buddhist writings mention a procession of Buddha images during the reign of Indian Prince Duṭṭhagamaṇi (101–77 B.C.E), for which the **prototype** may well have been a ceremony described in ancient Indian emperor Asoka's Fourth Rock Edict. The tradition of bathing Buddha images appears to be symbolized by the legend that two serpents, Nanda and Upananda, bathed the Siddhartha Gautama after his birth. Another sacred Buddhist writing describes a similar event where the Buddha is bathed by the Hindu god Indra and four *deva* kings. It designates the eighth day of the fourth lunar month as the time when all devotees should wash his images in respect of the Buddha's power to grant boons.

> **prototype**: the original model.

> **deva**: a benign Hindu deity.

Although relatively free of non-Buddhist elements, the focus on the Buddha image has primarily a mythic and/or magical significance. The Buddha is honored as a being greater than any other deity, and as a granter of boons. On the popular level, this aspect of Buddha's Day has assumed a greater importance than remembrance of the Buddha as the Enlightened One and great teacher. ◆

Butter Sculpture Festival

Butter Sculpture Festival is part of a Tibetan celebration of the Buddhist New Year. It is celebrated on the fifteenth day of the first lunar month of the year, which usually falls in February. The event is part of the annual Great Prayer Festival, which started in the fourteenth century.

The festival occurs after a two-week period of prayer following Losar, the Tibetan New Year. As with other Asian cultures, the Tibetans view Losar as a time of transition and efforts are made to set a proper tone for the coming year. Homes are cleaned and refurbished, debts are paid, and everyone tries to avoid negative states of mind. The monks perform ceremonies to drive out the negative forces of the old year. Many offerings are made to the gods in appreciation for what the gods have done for people. Juniper and other purifying herbs are also burned, a ritual through which the blessings of the Buddhas descend from the heavens and provide guidance and protection to all beings.

yak: a long-haired ox native to central Asia.

On the day of the festival, monasteries display elaborate sculptures made of colored **yak** butter. Yak butter is one of the most ubiquitous substances in Tibet. It is used in candles, on women's hair, as a flavoring and source of nourishment in tea and *tsampa*, the traditional Tibetan food made with roasted barley flour, and in other ways. Tibetans believe that yak butter has healing qualities.

The most famous sculptures are on view at the Jokhang monastery in Lhasa, the capital of Tibet. Each year, monks base their works of art on a different theme, such as a depiction of a

certain legend that describes a traditional Buddhist teaching. The images show a variety of characters and scenes and include ornamental representations of famous men, dragons, flowers, animals, and gods. Sculptors work with cold, hardened yak butter and use dyes to color their creations.

Buddhist monks from a lamasary in Tibet carry a sculpture made from yak butter.

Months of work go into the creation of each sculpture. Their materials include different shades of colored butter set up on long palettes and a supply of warm water for cleaning their fingers and cold water for chilling their fingers before handling the butter. Each sculpture is painstakingly created, layer by layer. The works of art are fastened to tall wooden frames for display purposes. On the fifteenth day of the New Year, they are unveiled after dusk and illuminated by yak butter candles. People come from miles around to view the displays and give their opinion of the skill of the depiction. The government offers a prize every year to the best sculpture.

Monks consecrate the sculptures, inviting the Buddhas to come into the display. The sculptures are left on view until dawn. Then, based on how brightly the candles are shining and what the weather is like, predictions about the success of the next harvest are made because the New Year is also associated with the coming of spring and the planting season. At the end of the festival, a ceremony is performed to invite the Buddhas to leave the sculptures. The sculptures are pulled down and the color scraped off and mixed with ash, the mixture of which will serve as the first coat of the next year's sculptures. ◆

Canada Day

CANADA ● JULY 1

Canada Day, celebrated annually on July 1, is Canada's major national holiday. The holiday commemorates the British North America Act (also called the Constitution Act) of 1867, which united the British colonies of New Brunswick, Nova Scotia, Upper Canada (now Ontario), and Lower Canada (now Quebec) into one country called the Dominion of Canada. The holiday was called Dominion Day until 1982, when Canada's constitution was revised. Canadians celebrate the holiday with patriotic events and celebrations that include parades, fireworks, and the display of flags.

Like independence celebrations of many countries, Canada Day marks a major turning point in the nation's history. Prior to 1867, French and English colonists fought each other in four wars and by the mid-1800s, ethnic tensions remained. Political instability prevailed between the colonies of Upper Canada, populated mainly by Protestant British business owners, and Lower Canada, populated mainly by Roman Catholic French farmers. In late 1837 a revolt broke out in Lower Canada, setting off rebellion in Upper Canada. The British Parliament tried to contain the turmoil by uniting the two Canadas into one colony, the Province of Canada, in 1841.

Gradually, Britain granted all the Canadian colonies self-government in local affairs. Soon, colonial leaders moved for a confederation of the colonies and gathered in Quebec City to work out final details. The results of their meeting became the British North America Act, which the British Parliament

> *"It shall be lawful for the Queen, by and with the Advice of Her Majesty's Most Honourable Privy Council, to declare by Proclamation that, on and after the passing of this Act, the Provinces of Canada, Nova Scotia, and New Brunswick shall form and be One Dominion under the Name of Canada."*
>
> The British North America Act, 1867

A young girl expresses her patriotism by wearing flags in her hair on Canada Day.

passed and proclaimed in Canada on July 1, 1867. The new nation was called the Dominion of Canada and was a federation of the provinces of Nova Scotia, New Brunswick, Québec, and Ontario. The Dominion remained under the authority of the British Crown, but had its own parliamentary government. The Act allowed for other provinces to join the Dominion, and by the early 1900s, nine provinces spanned the continent.

Canada Day is always observed on July 1, unless that date falls on a Sunday, in which case it is observed the following day. Banks, government offices, and most businesses close for the holiday. In the nation's capital, Ottawa, a day of ceremonies includes raising the Canadian flag, singing the national anthem, "O Canada," and a large parade. In Montreal, Catholics celebrate mass, and flag-raising ceremonies are held with singing of the national anthem and cutting the Canada Day cake.

Throughout the country, cities and towns of all sizes celebrate with speeches, parades, and flag displays. Many people

Canada's National Aboriginal Day

In 1996 the people of Canada began celebrating a new annual holiday on June 21—National Aboriginal Day. The holiday was established to celebrate the distinct culture of Canada's first inhabitants and to educate people about their contributions to the country. A movement to establish a holiday celebrating aboriginal Canadians began in 1982 when Canada's Assembly of First Nations passed a resolution to recognize June 21, the summer solstice, as National Solidarity Day for Indian Peoples. The summer solstice was chosen because it had been observed as a festival day by Canada's native peoples for many years. In 1990 the legislature of Quebec proclaimed June 21 a provincial holiday to celebrate Aboriginal culture. In 1995, Elijah Harper, member of Parliament from Manitoba, proposed that the holiday be established as a national observance and the idea was widely supported. The late June date was retained because it allowed the holiday to coincide with celebrations for the Feast of Saint John the Baptist on June 24 and Canada Day on July 1.

National Aboriginal Day is observed in every Canadian province and festivities focus on the culture of the aboriginal groups that live in that region. Activities include banquets featuring the traditional foods of Canadian aboriginal people; demonstrations and exhibitions of native arts and crafts such wood and antler carving, beadwork, and basket weaving; and performances of aboriginal music and dances. In many provinces National Aboriginal Day is also marked by serious educational activities such as lectures about the history, lifestyle, and philosophy of native Canadians and lessons in their traditional languages. Some provinces invite aboriginal groups from other parts of the world, such as Australia and South America, to come to Canada and join the festivities.

have the day off and take advantage of the summer weather to relax at picnics and barbecues. Civic organizations host such events as dances, baseball games, musical performances, concession booths, storytelling, crafts displays, carnivals, fishing derbies, sports tournaments, and cultural entertainment. Many towns and cities host fireworks in the evening. Detroit, Michigan, and Windsor, Ontario, which share a common border, celebrate Canada Day with an International Freedom Festival. The two cities mark their international friendship with a day of exhibitions, competitions, and parties.

Two national holidays leading up to Canada Day create a festive summer season. Some festivities start with National Aboriginal Day, a June 21 holiday declared by the Canadian government in 1996 to honor the country's large Native American population. Events such as special museum exhibits and Native American dances, crafts demonstrations, and food

Detroit, Michigan, and Windsor, Ontario, celebrate Canada Day with the International Freedom Festival, featuring a parade along their shared national border.

tastings take place. On June 24, many Canadians celebrate the feast day of St-Jean-Baptiste (Saint John the Baptist), an official holiday in the largely French province of Quebec. Both Quebec City and Montreal are the sites of boisterous celebration in what has become a rallying occasion for Quebec nationalists, though some leaders try to promote it as a more reflective holiday. ◆

Carnival

CHRISTIAN ● SPRING

Carnival is a Christian festival that takes place in the spring on Shrove Tuesday, the eve of Ash Wednesday. In its widest sense, however, the Carnival period is of much longer duration, beginning right after Christmas, the New Year, or the Feast of Epiphany, depending on the region.

The **etymological** roots of the name Carnival may be the Latin *caro* (meat) and *levara* (to remove, to take away), which in vulgar Latin became *carne levamen*, and afterward *carne vale*. Some etymologists also link it to *carnis levamen*, "the pleasure of meat," the farewell to which is celebrated in the festivities that come immediately before the **prohibitions** of Lent. Another hypothesis links it etymologically to the *carrus navalis*, the horse-drawn, boat-shaped carriage that was paraded in Roman festivals in honor of the god Saturn, carrying men and women who, in fancy dress and wearing masks, sang obscene songs.

If it is problematic to identify the etymological roots of Carnival, it becomes even more difficult to determine the historical origins of the celebration itself. However, the Roman feasts of Saturn, the Saturnalias, are generally recognized as the ancient forerunner of Carnival festivities. They embodied the essential carnival spirit, strongly characterized by the transgression of daily conventions and excesses of behavior. In these feasts, which took place in the midst of great **licentiousness**, slaves banqueted together with their masters, whom they insulted and admonished. From among them was elected a King of Chaos who, for the period of Saturnalia only, gave ridiculous orders that had to be obeyed by everyone. At the end of the fes-

etymological: relating to the origin and history of words.

prohibition: an act that is forbidden.

licentiousness: disregard for traditional moral and legal restraints.

49

tivities, however, he was unthroned and, in the earliest form of the rite, sacrificed to signal a return to order.

Although far in meaning from the Christian Carnival, these Roman rituals contained some elements that would come to define the later and more universal concept of the feast. The inversion of prevailing norms—as when servants rule masters—is of particular importance; the **burlesque parodies** of power and order, as seen in the dramatization of the Jester King, and the element of exaggeration, both in terms of libidinous excesses and in the inordinate consumption of food and drink, have also become prominent characteristics of Carnival. This unruliness that temporarily suspends the recognized world order has the corollary of introducing a contrast to the parameters of daily life. In other words, these cyclical rituals of disorder and rebellion show themselves incapable of administering real life because they foster the confusion of roles, licentiousness, and the mockery of power; they thus serve as a reminder of the necessity for order, which is reestablished at their conclusion.

In *Rabelais and His World* the Russian essayist Mikhail Bakhtin presents an interesting interpretation of the meaning of Carnival in the context of the Middle Ages and the Renaissance. He treats Carnival as the most evident expression of a joking popular culture with its roots in the Roman Saturnalias, which reflected the playful, irreverent side of human nature and the indestructible festive element in all human civilizations. During the whole of the Middle Ages and the Renaissance, this culture of laughter resisted the official, serious culture. In opposition to the mysticism and dogmatism of the ecclesiastical culture and rigidity of the prevailing political structures, the joking popular culture revealed a world in which a playful **mutability** was possible and provided an experience, at once symbolic and concrete, of the suspension of social barriers. By dramatizing the comic and relative side of absolute truths and supreme authorities, it highlighted the ambivalence of reality, coming to represent the power of both absolute liberty and farce.

Using these distinctions, Bakhtin contrasts the official and ecclesiastical ceremonies of ordered society with the festivities of carnivalesque culture. He characterizes the former as rituals of inequality because they reinforce the dominant order and seek justification of the present in the past. The latter he regards as rituals of equality because they parody the stratification of power and the cult of religion, as well as provide a symbolic suspension

burlesque: broadly humorous mockery.

parody: a comic imitation.

mutability: tendency to change.

A Brazilian samba dancer performs during Carnival in Rio de Janeiro, Brazil.

of norms and privileges, harboring a seed of social reaction in satire.

Thus, inversion is universally at the root of Carnival symbolism, and explains the presence of such customs as cross-dressing, or clothes worn inside out, the poor playing the role of the rich, and the weak that of the powerful. This interpretive perspective also makes sense of the symbolism of death, common in Carnival celebrations; here it implies revitalization. Similarly, the dethroning and burning in effigy of the Jester King marks the end of a cycle and suggests the commencement of another. From this point of view, one can also amplify the concept of "carnivalization" to include all the symbolic processes that bring about transformations in the representation of social reality.

The most notable carnivalization of late medieval European society was to be found in the Feast of Fools, also called the Feast of Innocents. Although it took place in churches between Christmas and Epiphany, this festival was both an extreme satire of the mannerisms and mores of the court and the high church and a radical mockery of ecclesiastical structure and religious doctrine. The low church and the lower orders played an important part in it, while the high church and the nobility were its principle targets.

For the festival, a King of the Fools or a Boy Bishop, chosen from among the local choir boys, was elected to act out a parody of **episcopal** functions, including the distribution of blessings to the crowd from a balcony. A comic version of the holy mass was enacted, in which obscene parodies such as "The Liturgy of the Drunkards," "The Liturgy of the Gamblers," and "The Will of the Ass" were substituted for the **canticles** and prayers. Masked and painted, wearing the garb of the high church or dressed up as women, the revelers danced freely in the cathedrals and banqueted on the altars. The burning of old shoes replaced incense. Meanwhile, riotous processions of other revelers, wearing goat and horse masks, paraded dancing and singing through the streets.

Dances in churches are not totally unheard of in the history of Christianity; so-called shrine dances, for example, were frequent in the first centuries of its development. However, with the consolidation and institutionalization of the church, these dances were gradually abolished. In any case, the Feast of Fools had an entirely different sense. Its most striking characteristic was that of grotesque buffoonery, and in it the carnivalesque inversion was carried to its ultimate extreme. Focusing on the ecclesiastical hierarchy and religious ethics, the Feast of Fools pointed out the critical relations of medieval society and demonstrated that such a society was capable of self-criticism.

The Feast of the Ass, which took place principally in France, was a variation within the same category of rituals of carnivalesque inversion. Also part of the Christmas cycle, it theoretically commemorated Mary's flight to Egypt. The central character was, however, the ass, or rather the Ass Prince, who was richly adorned and brought in procession under a luxurious canopy to the church, where a mass was celebrated in its honor, punctuated with braying noises to which the celebrants responded by also braying.

By the end of the Middle Ages, the trend everywhere was to discipline Carnival, restricting the extremes of its licentiousness and violence, while encouraging its artistic aspects. To control carnivalesque rebelliousness was, however, the work of centuries. The introduction of masked balls in the sixteenth century in Italy was the first step on the festival's path to a predominantly poetic character. Parades of floats began to compete

episcopal: relating to a bishop.

canticles: short hymns.

for a place in the disorderly street processions. From the combination of these two new currents flowered the fusion of carnival with art.

In Renaissance Florence, Italy, Carnival songs made fun of the private lives of certain social groups, with themes like "the goldsmith's song," "the song of the poor who accept charity," and "the song of the young wives and the old husbands"; by means of their festive **ambivalence**, they revealed the ridiculous—and usually censored—side of social conventions. Under the patronage of the Medici family, who ruled Florence from the early 1400s to 1737, the Florentine Carnival was typified by the singing of these songs on flower-covered, ornamented triumphal carts, which were the models for the later Carnival floats of the later Baroque and Romantic periods in Italy. In Turin, too, there were parades of flower-covered carts and floats as well as tournaments and **cavalcades**. In Venice, as throughout the Italian Peninsula, masks were the distinguishing feature of Carnival. Celebrated with the great solemnity afforded by the presence of the city's mayor and his wife and accompanied by a fireworks display, it contrasted with what happened in the streets, where there were battles between rival groups and a bull was sacrificed. Another element of Venetian Carnival was the flight of a man on ropes to the top of the bell tower of Saint Mark's, since Carnival was also a time to challenge and exorcise the forces of nature.

ambivalence: contradictory attitude, uncertainty.

cavalcade: a procession of riders and carriages.

Carnival in Rome was typified by a complex symbolism of violence, death, and resurrection. In Pope Paul II's time, in the fifteenth century, it was transferred to the Via Latta, which became the traditional setting for the carnivalesque parades called Corso. The Roman Carnival was essentially a series of masquerades and horse parades—these abolished only in 1833—culminating on Shrove Tuesday with an impressive candlelight procession, in which the participants, shouting "Death to him who has no candle," tried in whatever ways they could to put out one another's candles. In the carnivalesque revelry, the literal meaning of the threat of death was tempered, blending into the essential ambivalence of Carnival imagery. The procession ended with a feast in the early morning of Ash Wednesday, during which immense quantities of meat were consumed in anticipation of the Lenten fast to follow.

As a result of the Romantic movement in the late 1700s and mid 1800s, the following centuries saw a growing beautification

Carnival in Rio de Janeiro, Brazil, is a world-famous four-day celebration marked by numerous parades featuring huge, elaborate floats, brightly costumed samba dancers, and thousands of lively musicians and singers.

of Carnival. Flowered carriages, parades, floats that grew ever more majestic and complex, and fancy-dress balls became permanent features of the celebration, wherever it still existed. The elements of violence lessened: fighting, verbal abuse, and the various forms of mock aggression—water jets, the hurling of oranges, plaster confetti—gradually gave way to battles of flowers and colored paper confetti that were the new and prominent aspect of nineteenth-century street Carnival. In this way, the masses of revelers were gradually transformed from participants to spectators and the crowds grew more controlled. In Nice, for example, where Carnival still preserved its rich tradition, a festival committee was set up in 1873. The functions of this committee were to organize the festivities, parades, and flower battles and to award prizes for the allegorical floats, functions that still exist today.

These artistic and commercial innovations passed by the Carnival in Portugal. The typical form of Portuguese Carnival, like that of the whole Iberian Peninsula, was the *Entrudo*, a rowdy celebration in which flour, eggs, **lupines**, mud, oranges, and lemons were thrown on passersby. Dirty water, glue, and various other liquids were also poured onto the crowd, and gloves heavy with sand were dropped from windows. Repeating a common New Year's custom, pots and pans and all sorts of useless kitchen utensils were also thrown out of the windows, perhaps symbolizing the discarding of the old, or perhaps heralding the Lenten fast. Fierce battles were waged with plaster eggs, wax lemons, corncobs, and beans blown fiercely through glass or cardboard straws. Blows with brooms and wooden spoons were dealt out liberally. Apart from the violence and filth, the Entrudo was also a Carnival of **gluttony**: in the better stocked houses—from whose windows cakes and pastries were pitched—guests feasted sumptuously. Even in the convents cakes were widely distributed.

lupine: a plant in the pea family.

gluttony: greedy or excessive eating and drinking.

In Galicia, Spain, the Carnival of flour, eggs, and water was similar. It began with a chariot attack by one neighboring village on another and ended with the mock burial of a character called Señhor Antroido, for whom a **eulogy** was written, satirizing the most notable local people and the most notorious events of the previous year.

eulogy: a formal statement of high praise.

In nineteenth-century Portugal, there were flower battles in Oporto and Lisbon. Nevertheless, the form of Carnival introduced into the American colonies by Portugal and Spain was, in substance, the Entrudo.

In Europe, it was a weakened Carnival that greeted the contemporary age. In the scientific **dogmatists** of the end of the nineteenth century, Carnival inspired suspicion and contempt and was viewed as an irrational, primitive, and inexplicable rite. Lacking spontaneous popular support in Europe, Carnival has, with rare exceptions, gradually lost its force in the twentieth century, until it has become a subject of interest chiefly for academics and those who have a strong affection for the past.

dogmatist: a person who asserts opinions in an authoritative, but often arrogant, manner.

In Brazil, meanwhile, Carnival assumed the proportions of a national festival. Because of Brazil's multiethnic population and nearly continental proportions, its Carnival drew on many different cultural and folkloric sources, becoming the melting pot of indigenous, African, and European influences. Instead of surviving merely as a curious **anachronism**, it is today a living, dynamic phenomenon, modifying itself even in conjunction with the modern resources of mass communications. The Brazilian Carnival, like those of all Hispanic America, stems from the Entrudo. Begun with the Portuguese colonization in the sixteenth century, the Entrudo lasted more than three centuries before collapsing in the first years of the Brazilian republic. Prohibitions against it, however, date from its very introduction. The first recorded one is a decree of 1604, the first of many that produced no result, despite the stipulated punishments. A decree of 1853 imposed fines and detention for free men and caning and prison sentences for slaves participating in the Entrudo; nevertheless, another with identical content had to be issued in 1857.

anachronism: something that is placed in a time to which it does not belong.

The Brazilian Entrudo was very close to its Portuguese source: it involved the throwing of a lot of water and various small projectiles, later substituted by wax lemons. During the Entrudo, so much water was used in Rio de Janeiro that the newspapers invariably warned about risks to the city's water supply. The Entrudo was played even in the imperial palace, and whole families with their slaves dedicated weeks on end to the fabrication of wax lemons. Daniel Kidder, an American missionary who visited Brazil in the nineteenth century, advised in his *Sketches of Residence and Travel in Brazil* (1845) that people leaving their houses on these days should take their umbrellas with them to protect themselves against missiles and water.

With the abolition of slavery at the end of the nineteenth century, massive rural contingents migrated to the larger urban centers, bringing with them a great variety of regional folkloric contributions. In the first decades of the twentieth century, the activities involved in Carnival expanded, and a multiplicity of organizations, structured to a greater or lesser extent, began to make their presence felt in the street Carnival.

The Congo, a popular festivity with African roots alluding to the coronation of the "Congolese kings," began to make its contribution at this time. It was made up of several elements, among which were processions and warlike dances. From these came the majestic Maracatus, making their appearance in the

Carnival of northeastern Brazil; these are choreographed processions derived from the Congo, with king, queen, and a court of princes, ladies, ambassadors, and standard- and sunshade-bearers, along with a percussion section of rhythmic drums and triangles. There was also an increase in the number of *cordões*—loose groupings of people with masks depicting old people, the Devil, kings, queens, clowns, Indians, bats, Death, and so forth, who sang and danced frenetically to the accompaniment of percussion instruments.

An innovation in the Carnival of the south of Brazil were groups of local dancers and musicians called *ranchos de reis* (ranch of kings), which were taken from devotional Christmas dramatizations performed in procession, reproducing the journey of the Three Kings to Bethlehem to visit the infant Jesus. They were, however, stripped of their religious allusions, carnivalized, and took the form of *rancho carnavalesco*—a slow-march procession accompanied by brass and string instruments, during which costumed male and female choruses, carrying small allegorical images, narrate lyrical stories while singing and dancing.

The most complete expression of the contemporary Brazilian Carnival is the samba school. These schools, which are actually associations, present a kind of mobile popular opera, each year worked around a different theme. This theme is narrated through the music and words of the Carnival samba song (*samba-enredo*), and the characters are represented collectively by groups of dancers and singers in costume, with the scenery mounted on allegorical floats. A samba school is divided into three basic sections: first comes the drum section (*bateria*), which has between two hundred and four hundred instrumentalists, who play big bass drums (*surdos*), side drums, tambourines, triangles, and bells, among other percussive instruments; second is the group (*ala*) of composers; and last is the main body of dancer-singers and other performers of the school. Schools compete with one another during the festival. The increasing complexity of the parade, and its internal regulation, have brought about the creation of a great number of both financial-administrative and technical-artistic posts, organizing the samba schools to meet certain commercial norms. There are more than a hundred samba schools, concentrated principally in Rio de Janeiro, where they originated, each one with between two thousand and four thousand members.

The samba schools have now developed into extraordinarily complex institutions, in both their actual parades and their daily organization. They continue to function throughout the year as modest community clubs, always, however, with an eye to raising money for their Carnival expenses. As Carnival draws closer, they open up to allow the participation of the upper classes, until the parade at the climax festival, which is itself a rite of total social integration. Afterward, they retract again to their more modest dimensions. The themes of the parade refer to folkloric tales and events from Brazil's history, which, in the language of Carnival, are translated into an idealized vision of Brazil, depicted as a rich and generous mother country in which the contributions of the three races—white, black, and **indigenous**— join them in harmony, and where there is always room for hope and optimism. In reality, Brazil is a country marked by deep inequalities, still struggling in its uphill battle for development.

indigenous: native to a region.

In its historical and contemporary manifestations, the common denominator of Carnival is still the process of the inversion of reality. This inversion is of a symbolic and temporary nature, which classifies as a process of ritual transformation. As a ritual, Carnival allows a glimpse of the **axiomatic** values of a given culture, as well as its underlying contradictions. The language that relates these contradictions to one another is principally that of satire. But the carnivalesque inversion can equally be expressed through violence and exaggeration. In the Carnival context, violence symbolizes an attack on order, classifying the festival, in this case, as a ritual of rebellion, of which the Entrudo is the clearest example. Carnival retains a close correlation with daily life, though during its celebration the normal and **quotidian** are inverted and lived as a festival. In this way, carnivalesque rebellion and provocation become a parody of true rebellion and provocation. In any case, ambivalence is inherent in Carnival symbolism, since Carnival itself is on the threshold between order and disorder, hierarchy and equality, real and ideal, sacred and profane. Essentially, Carnival represents confrontation of the antistructure with the structure of society, constituting a channel through which utopian ideals of social organization find expression and suppressed forms of human behavior are released from the restrictions of daily life.

axiomatic: taken for granted.

quotidian: occurring every day; ordinary.

The inversion of the social order inherent in Carnival, when applied to a larger scale, represents the inverted, profane extreme of the sacred religious festival that Carnival immediately precedes. The two are inextricably interwoven and find their opposites in each other. ◆

Chinese New Year

The Chinese New Year is the longest, the busiest, and the most important annual festival in China and Taiwan. The festival is observed by Chinese communities throughout the world. Chinatowns in New York City, San Francisco, and other American cities boast colorful and noisy New Year's celebrations.

For the Chinese the New Year begins in the middle of the twelfth month with the Wei-ya (tail end of the year) observance and continues through to the full moon of the first month (usually late January to early February). In former times all business came to a virtual standstill during most of this period; nowadays the length of the holiday has been considerably curtailed, but many traditional practices are continued. On "tail end of the year," the twelfth day of the twelfth month, sacrifices are made to T'u-ti-kung (the local earth god), the all-important **tutelary** deity of household and community. On this evening the proprietors of businesses hold feasts for their employees to thank them for their hard work and to wish for a successful new year.

tutelary: having guardianship.

According to Chinese tradition on the twenty-fourth day of this month, the deity Tsao-chun (lord of the cooking stove) leads the various deities assigned to **terrestrial** duties to the court of Yu-huang Shang-ti (supreme emperor of jadelike augustness), ruler of the bureaucratic pantheon in Heaven; there he makes the required annual report. Tsao-chun is in effect the spirit overseer of the household. Presumably because his report will influence the life span of humans as recorded in

terrestrial: earthly.

longevity: long life.

the heavenly registers, he also is considered one of the *ssu-ming fu-chun* (arbiters of **longevity**). On this day, Chinese families place a paper image of Tsao-chun above the stove. They smear the deity's mouth with something sweet so that he will have only sweet things to report. The paper icon of Tsao-chun is then burnt, the smoke conveying the report directly to Heaven. Once the deities have left for the court of Heaven, the house undergoes a thorough cleaning, which also gets rid of any *hui-*

inauspicious: unlucky.

ch'i (**inauspicious** breaths). The next day, celestial deities, deputed by the Supreme Emperor of Jadelike Augustness, arrive to make their inspection during the absence of the terrestrial deities. Everyone is on good behavior during this inspection period.

New Year's Eve is called Kuo-nien (the passing of the old year) or Ch'u-hsi (the eve of the passing year). It is observed by seven traditional practices.

1. *Tz'u nien* (bidding farewell to the old year). Sacrifices are offered to gods and ancestors, to Tsao-chun, and to Ch'uang-mu, the tutelary "mother of the bed." **Propitiary** sacrifices are

propitiary: intending to pacify or reduce anger.

also placed at the gate for *hao-hsiung* (good elder brothers), that is, bereaved spirits, souls denied their rightful sacrifices, whose resentment constitutes a menace to the living. On the family altar in the main hall are set offerings of cooked rice, other foods, and strings of money. After the sacrifices have been made, firecrackers are set off to scare off demons.

2. *T'uan-yüan-fan yu wei-lu* (family reunion meal and surrounding the stove). The gathering of the family from far and near for the communal meal is also called *shou-sui-chiu* (wine that safeguards the New Year). A **brazier** placed under the

brazier: a large metal pan for burning coal.

round table is festooned with coins and described as "warm as spring, the prospering breath of wealth." The family gathering is thus called "surrounding the stove"; should there be a family member who cannot attend the feast, some of his clothing is draped over an empty chair to indicate his symbolic presence and that the family is thinking of him. At this meal the last course is a fish, which must not be eaten, however, for the Chinese word for "fish" is pronounced the same as the word for "having abundance" (*yu*).

3. *Ya-sui-ch'ien* (money of the year that is given away). After the communal feast the elders hand out money to the youngsters. This is also called *fen kuo-nien-ch'ien* (dividing the money of the passing year). In the past, one hundred coins were

strung together (the old copper coins had a square hole in the center), and even though these have now been replaced by paper money, the meaning is still "may you live one hundred years."

4. *Shou-sui* (safeguarding the year). After the elders give money to the children, the family sits around the stove, chatting, joking, and playing games to see the old year out. "Safeguarding the year" is said to contribute to the longevity of the parents.

5. *T'iao huo-p'en* (jumping over the fire pan). After the feast, all male members of the family take turns jumping over a pan filled with burning rice straw in front of the family gate. They call out certain auspicious phrases as they do so. The passing over fire signifies purification or making a new beginning.

6. *T'ieh ch'un-lien* (pasting up spring scrolls). To welcome the new year, "spring scrolls" bearing auspicious words are pasted on the gateposts. Pieces of lucky red paper with the graph for "spring" written on them are pasted on such places as the leaves of the gate and the rice barrels. Other **felicitous** phrases are pasted elsewhere. The pasting up of spring scrolls

Chinese communities across the United States and Canada celebrate the Chinese New Year with parades, like this one in Honolulu, Hawaii, featuring colorful dragons carried on the backs of dozens of people.

felicitous: pleasant.

derives from the ancient practice of hanging peachwood amulets at the gate to guard against evil. There are colored paper scrolls hung over the lintel on blue paper if a male infant has died during the year or on yellow paper if a female infant has died.

7. By ancient custom, on New Year's Eve people attended plays held in front of a temple. If a debtor stayed until dawn of New Year's Day, his creditor would not dare to disturb the gathering by trying to collect the debt. The debt, collectible before the new year, could then be postponed because the new year had arrived. These events were thus called *p'i-tse-hsi* (fleeing-from-debt plays).

The first five days of the new year are called Hsin-cheng (correct, or fixed, beginning) or Hsin-ch'un (beginning of the new spring). They are greeted with the spring scrolls, firecrackers, and music, while people crowd the streets in a happy bustle. On the first day people eat long noodles symbolic of their hope for a long life. Dressed in new clothes and bearing fruits and other offerings, they go to the temples to burn incense and worship the deities. Then they pay a New Year's call on friends and relatives. On this day everyone takes care to avoid saying or doing things of bad omen. No work is done, and everyone enjoys himself. On the second day newly married girls pay a visit to their **natal** homes. On the fourth day the deities who had been away at their annual audience at the court of Heaven return to this world and are received with offerings and prayers for good fortune during the new year. With day five life returns temporarily to normal, but the season is not yet over. On the evening of the eighth day everyone takes a bath and observes a fast called Shou-shou (safeguarding longevity) until midnight. Then, led by the head of the family, all members of the household perform Ta-li, the "great ritual," consisting of "three kneelings and nine knockings" (*k'e-t'ou,* or "kowtow" as it is known in the West) and the presentation of incense. Thus is marked the beginning of the ninth day, the birthday of the Supreme Emperor of Jadelike Augustness, by whose indulgence all beings are born and nurtured.

The fifteenth day marks the close of the New Year festivities. It is called Shang-yuan Chieh (festival of the First **Primordial**). The triad Shang-ÿuan, Chung-yüan, and Hsia-yüan, of whom the first is recognized here, are otherwise known in Taoism as the San Kuan (three controllers), supervisors of the

natal: relating to one's place of birth.

primordial: earliest or original being.

realms of Heaven, earth, and the waters. In popular religion they are also identified with the three sage-kings of legendary antiquity: Yao, who attained perfect goodness, is the Celestial Controller; Shun, who reclaimed the land, is the Terrestrial Controller; and Yü, who tamed the floods, is the Controller of the Waters. The birthday of each controller is widely celebrated. Sacrifices to the Celestial Controller are presented at dawn on the fifteenth.

The major event of the day, however, takes place in the evening and is called Yuan-hsiao Chieh (festival of the First Primordial night) or Teng-chieh (lantern festival). The family again gathers at a communal feast, and special round dumplings of the First Primordial night *(yuan-hsiao yuan-tzu)* are eaten. The roundness of the dumplings is like this first full moon of the year and symbolizes the complete family circle as well as completeness or perfection in general. After dark everyone takes to the streets and temples to show and view ingeniously designed lanterns and to enjoy the boisterous dragon and lion dances accompanied by the din of gongs and drums, and the acrobatics of martial arts troupes. With this festival the season comes to an end. ◆

Christmas

CHRISTIAN ● DECEMBER 25

Romance languages: French, Italian, Spanish, and other languages developed from Latin.

Christmas is the Christian celebration of the birth of Jesus Christ. The name, English in origin, means "Christ's Mass," that is, the mass celebrating the feast of Christ's nativity. Names for Christmas in **Romance languages** are derived from the Latin *nativitas*. The French *Noël* comes from either *nativitas* or *nowell*, meaning "news." German employs the term *Weihnachten*, meaning "holy (or blessed) night." Another name for the whole season is *Yule*. Originally this name did not have Christian connotations but derived either from the Germanic *jol* (turning wheel), with reference to the gain of sunlight after the winter solstice, or from the Anglo-Saxon *geol* (feast). The name of this pre-Christian winter feast of the solstice was eventually applied to the whole of the Christmas season.

There is no certain knowledge of the origin of the Christmas feast. It may have been celebrated as early as the beginning of the fourth century in North Africa, but certainly it was observed at Rome by the middle of the same century. Two theories have been advanced for the occurrence of the feast on December 25. One theory argues that Christmas originated in Christian opposition to or competition with the pagan Roman Feast of the Invincible Sun (Sol Invictus) that had been celebrated on the old date of the winter solstice. The computation theory, on the other hand, argues that the birth of Christ was calculated on the basis of the idea that the conception of Christ coincided with his death, which supposedly occurred on March 25.

Christmas and the First Amendment

During the last decade, fierce public debates have erupted in the United States over the place of Christmas in a secular and pluralistic society dedicated to the separation of church and state. That government offices and many schools and businesses are closed for two Christian holidays, Christmas and Good Friday, seems to be generally tolerable to Christians and non-Christians alike; but battle lines have been drawn over the issue of placing Christian holidays symbols, such as Christmas trees and nativity scenes, in government spaces like post office lobbies, public schools, or the corridors of city hall. Indeed, the appearance of civil liberties lawyers in court to argue against such displays has become almost as regular a feature of the American Christmas season as the descent of Santa Claus into shopping malls.

Some people argue that the Christmas tree is a folkloric symbol, drained of specific religious content, that has become the common property of all Americans. Others attempt to balance Christian imagery in government spaces with holiday icons of other faiths, a gambit known as the "menorah defense." A minority of Americans defend the display of Christian symbols on the grounds that the United States is in ideals and history a Christian nation, however religiously diverse it has become, but the nation's courts have found this argument unpersuasive. The debate over the appropriate place of religious imagery in a secular society continues, however, and has transformed Christmas into an ongoing examination of the First Amendment, which guarantees both religious freedom and the freedom of speech.

By the end of the fourth century the observance on December 25 of the feast of Christ's nativity has spread throughout most of the Christian world. In the mid-fifth century the Christian church in Jerusalem accepted the December 25 date, which then replaced the older celebration of the nativity there on January 6. The Armenians, however, have never accepted December 25 as the Feast of the Nativity.

The Western Christian observance of Christmas was strongly influenced by the celebration of this feast in the city of Rome. Three masses came to be celebrated by the pope on Christmas Day. The original mass was held at Saint Peter's Basilica on Christmas morning. But in the course of the fifth century a second mass was added "in the middle of the night" (first at cockcrow and later at midnight) at the shrine of Christ's crib, which had been erected at the Church of Santa Maria Maggiore as a replica of the crib at Bethlehem. Finally, during the Byzantine period of the sixth century a third mass was added in Rome, this one at dawn at the Church of Sant' Anastasia, a martyr whose feast was celebrated in Constantinople on December 25. Probably for the sake of convenience, in the course of the eleventh century the original mass celebrated at Saint Peter's was transferred to Santa Maria Maggiore, already the site of the second mass. Since the eighth century the Western Christian celebration of Christmas has been provided with an octave, or eight days of liturgical observance, in imitation of the feasts of Easter and Epiphany.

In the weeks before Christmas, children can visit Santa at shopping malls and department stores.

In the early sixth century the Byzantine emperor Justinian made Christmas a public holiday. The feast was extremely popular in all European countries during the Middle Ages, inspiring the composition of music and liturgical drama. The observance of Christmas received added impetus in the early thirteenth century when Francis of Assisi originated the devotion of the Christmas crib.

After the sixteenth century most of the Reformation churches retained the Christmas feast. Martin Luther, for example, showed great devotion to Christmas in his preaching. However, the English Puritans tried to do away with the celebration of Christmas altogether in the course of the seventeenth century. The feast was revived with the restoration of the English monarchy in 1660, but on a somewhat more **secular** basis. Under the Puritan influence in early America, especially in New England, Christmas was a regular workday until the middle of the nineteenth century.

The customs of Christmas in the Northern Hemisphere include, in addition to Christian religious practices and midwinter feasting, various celebrations of the returning light of the sun. In northern European folklore, the twelve days

During the Christmas season, many Christian churches present living nativity scenes with real people and animals.

secular: not religious.

between Christmas and Epiphany are a time when the evil spirits are considered to be especially active, combating the coming of spring and the gradual victory of sunlight over darkness that follows the winter solstice; thus Christmas Eve is called there "the devil's funeral." To celebrate the victory of life over winter's death and to combat evil spirits, homes are decorated in this darkest period of the year with lights and evergreens of all kinds. Similarly, the Yule log was kindled on Christmas Eve in northern countries and kept burning until Epiphany, and remains of the log were kept to kindle the next year's Yule fire. The Christmas tree itself seems to be of rather recent origin: it may be as late as the sixteenth century that Germans first decorated a fir tree with lights, fruits, and tinsel. From Germany the custom spread quickly and became universally popular, even in the Southern Hemisphere.

The custom of sending special greeting cards at Christmas originated in nineteenth-century England. Giving gifts at Christmas probably originated with the pagan Roman custom of exchanging gifts *(strenae)* at the New Year. The popular gift bringer, Santa Claus, is a nineteenth-century American invention; he combines features of the traditional children's saint, Nicholas of Myra, with some elements of the Germanic fire god, Thor, who fought the giants of ice and snow from his home in the polar regions.

Other customs of the Christmas season include the baking of special foods, the cooking of poultry dinners on Christmas Day, and the singing of special songs, notably carols, a species of simple song that originally had wider application than as Christmas music. The celebration of Christmas thus includes both Christian observances and wider folkloric customs, the latter relating to general festivity at the time of the winter solstice. ◆

Cinco de Mayo

Cinco de Mayo (Fifth of May) is a Mexican national holiday commemorating the triumph of the Mexican army over the French on May 5, 1862, in the battle of Puebla. In the United States, Cinco de Mayo has become the largest ethnic celebration of many Mexican Americans, even though it is not the top holiday in their native land. As with many Americans, celebrations related to their homeland become a major occasion for ethnic sentiment and cultural pride.

Prior to 1862, Mexico struggled to reach independence after breaking away from Spain in the early 1820s. Turbulent years followed the split with Spain, and several leaders gained and lost power. In 1862 Emperor Napoleon III of France took advantage of the political chaos and sent troops to conquer Mexico. The troops landed at the port city of Veracruz on the Gulf of Mexico and began their march to the center of Mexico. When the troops reached the city of Puebla, in east-central Mexico, General Ignacio Zaragoza faced them in battle on May 5, 1862. He led a Mexican army of about 2,000 soldiers along with armed citizens. The Mexicans bravely fought the French army, which was a force three times larger than them, some 6,000 well-equipped professional soldiers. By sunset, the Mexican army had amazingly defeated the French and forced them to withdraw.

In spite of the Mexican victory at Puebla, French troops battled their way into the heart of Mexico for a year, finally entering Mexico City in June 1863. In 1864, the Austrian archduke Maximilian became emperor of Mexico and established a

1862 Mexican troops defeat invading French forces in the Battle of Puebla.

1863 French troops enter Mexico City.

1864 Archduke Maximilian becomes emperor of Mexico.

1867 Maxmilian is deposed and executed; Benito Juarez reestablishes the Mexican republic.

Costumed musicians perform traditional Mexican music for the 1998 Cinco de Mayo celebration on Olvera Street in Los Angeles.

French-supported government. However, the victory at Puebla had inspired the Mexican people to fight with new determination. Mexican resistance helped force France to withdraw its troops from Mexico in 1866 and 1867. The French-backed government soon fell. In 1867, President Benito Juarez was able to reestablish the Mexican republic.

In honor of the victory, Mexico established the fifth of May as a holiday, and it became an important national symbol of courage and solidarity. Mexicans celebrate Cinco de Mayo

throughout the nation with parades, festivals, music, and dancing. The city of Puebla celebrates their heroic victory with special vigor. Puebla hosts parades and battle reenactments that use fruit as ammunition. The citizens revel with dances, parties, fireworks, and favorite national foods, such as *mole*, a sauce made of crushed chile, nuts or seeds, and chocolate served over meat or poultry. Many visitors come to celebrate in Puebla, a town famous for the beauty of its classic Spanish colonial architecture.

In the United States, patriotic celebrations by Mexican Americans began in the 1870s. These celebrations helped strengthen community ties and increase cultural awareness. Cinco de Mayo became much celebrated in the United States, especially in the Southwestern states and cities with large communities of Mexican origin, such as Los Angeles, Chicago, Denver, Dallas, and Houston. Celebrations often include parades, folk dancing, speeches, carnival rides, battle reenactments, and Mexican music. The victory of a small disorganized army against a powerful enemy at Puebla strikes a sympathetic chord for many Americans, who share a similar pride in their nation's struggle for independence from a colonial power. Many

Many Cinco de Mayo celebrations include historical reenactments of the May 5, 1862, Battle of Puebla.

Americans join with their Mexican-American neighbors to celebrate the holiday that is a source of such pride for the Mexican people. This identification with the struggle for independence often leads Americans to confuse Cinco de Mayo with the Mexican independence day, which is celebrated on September 15. ◆

Columbus Day

AMERICAS ● SECOND MONDAY IN OCTOBER

Columbus Day commemorates the day Christopher Columbus landed in the Bahamas in 1492. Born in 1451 in the republic of Genoa, later part of Italy, Columbus was a leading navigator of his day. Underestimating distances, he believed that by sailing westward from Europe he could establish a shorter route to the Asian spice trade. Backed by King Ferdinand and Queen Isabella of Spain, he left the port of Palos, Spain, with three ships on August 3, 1492, and landed on the small island of San Salvador in the Bahamas on October 12, 1492. He is generally regarded as the first European to land in the Americas, although claims have been made for others.

The first formal celebration in the United States of Columbus's landing was a dinner in his honor on October 12, 1792. Organized by the Society of St. Tammany, also known as the Columbian Order, it marked the 300th anniversary of his landing. During the early decades of the nineteenth century, celebrations of Columbus Day were in the hands of Protestants, who then made up the overwhelming majority of Americans. Commemorations took the form of dinners and speeches, at which Columbus's Catholic religion along with his sponsor, Spain, were often denigrated while he was hailed as a man of daring and genius who, as an unwitting tool of Divine Providence, made possible the establishment of a great Protestant democracy in the Americas.

As immigration changed the population mix during the latter half of the century, Columbus Day observances came more and more under the purview of Catholic and Italian-American

"At two o'clock in the morning the land was discovered, at two leagues' distance; they took in sail and remained under the square-sail lying to till day, which was Friday, when they found themselves near a small island, one of the Lucayos, called in the Indian language Guanahani."

Journal of Christopher Columbus, October 11, 1492

73

Columbus Quincentenary

The year 1992 marked the quincentenary, or 500th anniversary, of the landing of Christopher Columbus on the shores of what came to be called the Americas. Major events marking the anniversary took place in Spain and in many countries in North and Latin America, including a $5 billion world's fair in Seville, Spain, with exhibits from 110 nations; the opening of the world's largest monument to Columbus, a 390-foot lighthouse in Santo Domingo in the Dominican Republic; and the largest flower show ever held in the Western Hemisphere, the AmeriFlora exposition in Columbus, Ohio. Nevertheless, the numbers of visitors to these events were fewer than expected, media attention was scanty, and financial goals were not met. A quincentenary encyclopedia was published in the United States, but several planned public events and scholarly meetings were either curtailed or canceled.

Several factors explain the failure of the quincentenary to evoke enthusiasm. One frequently cited reason was lack of money, public and private, because of a worldwide recession. Another was a sense that Columbus should not be honored for having "discovered" a world where 200 million people already lived. The central reason was probably opposition raised by indigenous peoples in both North and South America to the idea of celebrating a man they believe brought conquest, colonization, and environmental exploitation to the Americas, accompanied by the transmission of diseases that killed 90 percent of the original inhabitants. Most of the quincentenary festivities and exhibits combined celebration and protest, and coverage of the occasion, popular and scholarly, was similarly mixed. One benefit of the 1992 observances was that previously uncritical treatments of Columbus and his achievement—such as at the World's Columbian Exposition of 1893 in Chicago—gave way to a more profound understanding of the explorer's purposes and goals.

sponsorship. The first Italian-American celebration took place in New York City on October 12, 1866, organized by the Compagnia del Tiro al Bersaglio di New York (the [Italian] Sharpshooters' Association of New York). By 1869 Italian-American organizations were commemorating Columbus Day in St. Louis, Philadelphia, Boston, Cincinnati, New Orleans, and San Francisco. In the last city, the parade was followed with a dinner sponsored by the Garibaldi Guard.

In the late nineteenth and early twentieth centuries, parades became the most common way of celebrating of Columbus Day. They were showcases of religious and ethnic pride, used by Italian Americans and Catholics in their efforts to win acceptance as full Americans. Hailing Columbus's arrival in the Americas, the parades typically included floats carrying impersonators of Columbus and Queen Isabella and replicas of Columbus's flagship, the *Santa María*, and sometimes the *Niña* and the *Pinta* as well.

The Knights of Columbus, a Catholic fraternal lay organization founded in 1882, soon began pressing for recognition of Columbus Day as a legal national holiday. President Benjamin Harrison declared such a holiday in 1892, but only for that year, the 400th anniversary of Columbus's voyage. In 1937 President Franklin D. Roosevelt proclaimed every October 12 as Columbus Day, but it did not become a federal holiday until 1972, to be celebrated by act of Congress on the second Monday of October rather than on October 12. At the state level, in 1907 Colorado became the first state to make Columbus Day a legal holiday, persuaded by prominent local Italians with help from the Italian consul in Denver. By the mid-1990s, thirty-nine states had a legal Columbus Day holiday.

Celebrations grew during the course of the twentieth century. In San Francisco a Grand Ball was held on the evening before Columbus Day to select the young woman who would impersonate Queen Isabella. Columbus Day itself began with a Solemn High Mass at a church in North Beach, the district

A replica of the *Santa María* appears in a Columbus Day parade in San Francisco, California.

where most of the city's Italian Americans lived. Several thousand marchers then paraded through town. Marchers and spectators then gathered at Aquatic Park. There, three boats rigged up by local Italian fishermen to resemble Columbus's vessels entered the adjacent cove and cast anchor near the shore. A Columbus impersonator then came ashore in a rowboat.

In New York City the 1972 parade up Fifth Avenue drew more than 100,000 marchers and over one million spectators. The participants included bands from Columbus societies made up of Italian Americans from city departments and other public agencies, and marching groups from the Knights of Columbus and the Order of the Sons of Italy. Terence Cardinal Cooke, the archbishop of New York, and other Catholic leaders stood on the steps of St. Patrick's Cathedral to greet the marchers.

Beginning in the 1970s, the shape of Columbus Day celebrations changed sharply as the indigenous peoples of the United States and the rest of the Americas began organizing politically to assert their rights. To many of these Native American activists, Columbus was a villain who brought in his wake conquest, disease, slavery, and centuries of oppression for indigenous peoples. This point of view won wide support among non-Indians, including educators, and it began to influence the way the historical significance of Columbus was taught to schoolchildren. Even the traditional view that Columbus "discovered" America became taboo for many, who asked how Columbus could have discovered a world that was already well known to American Indians.

This new perspective made itself decisively felt in 1992, on the 500th anniversary Columbus's landfall. In San Francisco demonstrators disrupted the coronation of a Queen Isabella impersonator and prevented the landing of a modern-day Columbus. The Denver parade was canceled after a group of American Indians and their supporters vowed to stop it. Columbus Day protests were held in New York City; Columbus, Ohio; Las Vegas, Nevada; and elsewhere. The Berkeley, California, city council responded to the controversy by voting to proclaim October 12 "**Indigenous** People Day."

Many mainstream organizations paid respect to the Native American perspective on Columbus Day in 1992. The National Italian-American Foundation announced a scholarship enabling an Italian American to study American Indian history, and another for an American Indian to study the Italian

> *"In the morning, I ordered the boats to be got ready, and coasted along the island toward the north-north-east to examine that part of it, we having landed first at the eastern part. Presently we discovered two or three villages, and the people all came down to the shore, calling out to us, and giving thanks to God."*
>
> Journal of Christopher Columbus, October 14, 1492

indigenous: native to a region.

Renaissance. The National Council of Bishops condemned the violence used against American Indians, and the archbishop of Seattle had a Native American dinner and then listened to the grievances of indigenous groups. Some schools invited Native American speakers to present their views as Columbus Day approached.

Columbus Day was traditionally celebrated in the Caribbean, Central America, and South America, and there, too, the voices of Native Americans and their sympathizers were heard in 1992. Several thousand demonstrators from Alaska to Chile marched on Mexico City, where some of the protestors defaced a Columbus statue.

In the years just after 1992, protestors continued to make themselves heard in the Americas. Indians in Honduras, for example, marked Columbus Day in 1997 by pulling down a Columbus statue in the capital of Tegucigalpa and painting it red, the symbol of blood. Yet many Columbus Day celebrations proceeded in the old-fashioned way. New York City's 1997 parade, attended as usual by office seekers in the upcoming November elections, proceeded without disruption. The following year, the celebration in Albany, New York, was described by a reporter as a tribute to "Italian-American values and traditions." ◆

Confederate Memorial Day

Confederate Memorial Day is a holiday to honor Confederate soldiers who died during the Civil War in America (1861–65). The custom of honoring the Confederate war dead arose spontaneously in various towns across the South almost as soon as the Civil War ended. In 1865 a group of women in Vicksburg, Mississippi, gathered to decorate the graves of more than 18,000 men who had been killed during the siege of Vicksburg (May–July 1863). In 1866 the women of Columbus, Mississippi, laid magnolia blossoms on the graves of Confederate and Union soldiers alike. In addition to Vicksburg and Columbus, Mississippi, the towns of Columbus, Georgia, Petersburg, Virginia, and Charleston, South Carolina, have all claimed to have been the first to honor the fallen.

The first observances were simple and loose-knit, as families would walk to the cemetery or local battlefield and place flowers or wreaths on the graves of the soldiers. Usually the early remembrances were led by women—often the widows. During the next fifty years, the custom spread, and more southern towns began holding organized and formal programs to honor the memory of the dead. The services were usually organized by a women's memorial association, and later by the United Daughters of the Confederacy, whose members' relatives had served in the war.

Because many of a town's men had been killed and buried far away, citizens erected statues and monuments to honor the soldiers' sacrifice. To these statues and monuments the townspeople brought flowers and wreaths, and here they gathered on a chosen day, usually in the spring, to hear music by military

> In 1866 the women of Columbus, Mississippi, laid magnolia blossoms on the graves of Confederate and Union soldiers alike.

Confederate Memorial Day observances often include reenactments of Civil War battles. These men in Georgia play the role of Confederate soldiers.

bands, sermons, prayers for the dead, and speeches by veterans and civic leaders. Speakers often praised the courage and sacrifice of the fallen and extolled the nobility of the southern cause. Occasionally, former slaves viewed as loyal would be invited to speak; their presence lent a sort of moral authority to the proceedings, and likely served to reinforce the white citizens' conviction that indeed the war had been fought for a cause that was just in every respect.

Eventually, as the grief of loss and defeat was eased by the passage of time, the ceremonies grew less mournful and became more spirited. Bands played lively versions of "Dixie," and the speakers' emphasis shifted to reconciliation—sometimes former Union soldiers were invited to participate onstage with former Confederates—and to looking forward together to a future of peace and prosperity in a nation reunited.

The dates of observance have varied. Sometimes the date of celebration would be determined by an event of local importance, such as a battle, or the death of a local hero. Most commemorations were held in the spring—April and May particularly. By 1916 ten states had designated June 3, the birthdate of Confederate president Jefferson Davis. Other dates for Confederate Memorial Day have included the fourth Monday in April (Alabama and Mississippi); April 26, the anniversary of the surrender of General Joseph E. Johnston (Florida and Georgia); and May 10, the date of Stonewall Jackson's death in 1863 and Jefferson Davis's capture in 1865 by Federal troops (the Carolinas). Texas celebrates Confederate Heroes' Day on January 19, the birthday of Robert E. Lee. The various dates of celebration reflect, although in a milder form, the "decentralized" and independent nature of the Confederate government itself, as was seen in the states' rights arguments that made **con-scription** of troops and efforts toward centralized government an endless struggle for President Jefferson Davis.

conscription: compulsory military service, draft.

Confederate Memorial Day is not what it used to be. In the decades since the Civil Rights movement of the 1950s and 1960s, heightened sensitivity to the long history of injustices suffered by African Americans has made it difficult—some say indefensible—to celebrate soldiers whose victory would have preserved slavery. At the same time, to the dismay of many descendants of southern soldiers, the Confederate battle flag has been appropriated by white supremacist groups to a degree that makes white friends of civil rights ashamed to be associated with a symbol that once made them proud.

Although as time passes the commemorations are less attended by newer generations—true also of the national Memorial Day and of Armistice Day—Confederate Memorial Day is still observed in towns and cities with a local chapter of the United Daughters of the Confederacy, a group based in Richmond, Virginia, that has kept lit the flame of memory for their ancestors who gave their lives in what some still regard as the War for Southern Independence. ◆

Confucius's Birthday

Confucius's Birthday commemorates the birth of Confucius, one of the most influential and respected teachers in Chinese history. It is celebrated on September 28 in parts of China and Taiwan. The Chinese also celebrate Teacher's Day on September 28, by honoring all teachers for all their hard work during the year.

Confucius was born in Tzouyi (present-day Qufu in Shandong Province) in 551 B.C.E. His real name was Kong Qiu. The name *Confucius* comes from the Latin form of the title *Kongfuzi*, which means *Great Master Kong*. The ideas and philosophy of Confucius are called Confucianism.

Confucianism greatly influenced education, government, and social behavior in China for hundreds of years. It taught that people should respect their ancestors and government authority, and it stressed the importance of good moral character. The philosophy also emphasized the need for a well-ordered society in which parents rule their children, men rule women, and the educated rule the uneducated.

Confucius developed his philosophy at a time of much warfare and turbulence among the states of China. He thought that if all people, rulers included, adhered to a system of high moral standards and lived more disciplined lives, the chaos of the times would end and society would improve. Confucius was not widely known at the time of his death in about 479 B.C.E., but his teachings were spread by his disciples, who recorded his sayings and short dialogues in a collection called *The Analects*. Emperor Wudi, who ruled from 140 to 87 B.C.E., made Confu-

> *"When you know a thing, to hold that you know it; and when you do not know a thing, to allow that you do not know it—this is knowledge."*
>
> Confucuis, *Analects*

Taiwanese students dressed in traditional Chinese costumes perform the ancient eight-row dance on Confucius's Birthday.

cianism the state religion or philosophy. From the 100s B.C. to the C.E. 1900s, Confucianism served as the state religion of China. For a time, all candidates for government positions had to pass tests on Confucian doctrine before taking their positions.

When China became a Communist state in 1949, the Chinese government condemned Confucianism because of its emphasis on the past rather than the future. Opposition to Confucianism ended in Communist China in 1977. Today, Confucius's birthday is celebrated at the largest and oldest Confucius Temple in China, which is located in Qufu. There, a two-week-long festival is held that includes performances of ancient music and dance as well as exhibitions and lectures on the life and teachings of Confucius. Out of respect for all teachers on this day, students often give their teachers cards.

In Taiwan all the Confucius temples hold ceremonies in honor of the sage. The ceremony in Taipei, the capital of Taiwan, begins with a dawn ritual. It opens with drumming and a welcoming of the spirit of Confucius by officials. Buddhist scriptures are read, and dancers perform the ritualistic eight-row dance, in which eight dancers in eight rows perform an ancient dance dressed in clothing styles from the Ming and Qing dynasties. Musicians play ceremonial music and eulogies are chanted. The spirit is then sent off with the conclusion of the ceremony. Students in Taiwan also show respect for their teachers on this day, with cards or small gifts. ◆

Corpus Christi

Roman Catholics celebrate Corpus Christi on a Thursday in late May or early June. On the church calendar, Corpus Christi falls on the Thursday after Holy Trinity Sunday, which depends on what date Easter falls on. In the United States and some other countries, the solemnity is held on the Sunday after Trinity Sunday. Corpus Christi is Latin for "body of Christ," and the feast is celebrated to commemorate the institution of the Holy Eucharist.

The Eucharist is a central rite of many Christian religions. In the Eucharist, bread and wine are **consecrated** by a minister or priest and consumed by members of the congregation. The ceremony repeats the Last Supper of Jesus and his apostles and symbolizes the union of Jesus and His followers. Among Catholics, the Eucharistic bread is believed to be wholly transformed into the body of Christ. This belief is called the doctrine of transubstantiation, an official teaching of the Roman Catholic church since the Middle Ages.

Sources trace the feast of Corpus Christi to St. Juliana of Mont Cornillon, Belgium, who was born in 1193. She became a nun who greatly **venerated** the Eucharist and worked for a special feast in its honor. She is said to have had a vision of the church under a full moon having one dark spot, which signified the absence of such a feast. She made her ideas known to church leaders, and in 1264 Pope Urban IV published a decree extolling the love of Jesus as expressed in the Holy Eucharist and ordering the annual celebration of Corpus Christi.

consecrated: made sacred.

venerate: esteem highly, worship.

Europeans celebrated the feast of Corpus Christi with grand outdoor processions of merchants, members of the nobility and clergy, and guild members. Guilds were organizations of tradesmen and craftsmen. Guild members produced and performed mystery plays in town squares for Corpus Christi. Mystery plays were a type of Biblical drama that came to be called Corpus Christi plays because most were presented during Corpus Christi.

In the early 1500s, the Reformation resulted in the establishment of Protestant churches. Protestants rejected a number of Catholic teachings, including transubstantiation, and the custom of Corpus Christi processions gradually stopped everywhere except in Roman Catholic countries. Today, celebrations of Corpus Christi are found in predominantly Catholic countries. Throughout rural Austria, colorful processions and religious rituals celebrate Corpus Christi. On Traun and Hallstatter lakes, people decorate boats and barges for water processions. In several towns of Italy, cobblestone streets are carpeted with carefully arranged flowers on the morning of Corpus Christi. Solemn processions then walk over the flowers.

Peruvian villagers carry a block of ice to Cuzco to make a sacrifice to their patron saint on Corpus Christi.

People in Peru celebrate Corpus Christi with brass brands, masked dancers, feasts, and drinking. Peruvian villagers bring statues of their patron saints to the city of Cuzco in colorful processions. The statues stay in the cathedral alone and are said to dance together during the night. In many Venezuelan towns during Corpus Christi, dancers move through the streets dressed as devils, banging on drums and shaking **maracas**. In some areas, they dance to fulfill a holy vow and in other places dancers portray the devil's submission to the Eucharist. The celebration of Corpus Christi is one Panama's greatest festivals, going back to the early years of Spanish colonial rule. It is held in the central cities of Chitre and Los Santos, and features dances of good devils (angels) and bad devils.

The town of Papantla de Olarte in the state of Veracruz, Mexico, is famous for the parades, dances, and unusual rituals of its Corpus Christi festival. The Totonac Indians perform a "flying dance" called the *voladores,* in which men leap from a high pole with ropes tied to their ankles. In the Southwestern United States, some areas that were settled by Spain celebrate Corpus Christi, especially some small villages of Colorado and New Mexico. ◆

maracas: rattles made from gourds.

Day of the Dead

MEXICO AND CENTRAL AMERICA ● NOVEMBER 1

The Day of the Dead has grown into one of Mexico's most popular holidays, and is based on two Roman Catholic holy days. All Saints' Day, November 1, celebrates all saints, whether known or unknown. It was established by the church in the 800s to Christianize the **Celtic** festival of the dead, Samhain. All Souls' Day, November 2, is based on the doctrine that some departed souls, unprepared for heaven, can receive help from the prayers of the living. Ironically, All Souls' Day took on many Samhain rituals. When Spaniards conquered Mexico in the early 1500s, they brought these Catholic practices, which then mingled with ancient Indian practices. The Aztec Indians had a month dedicated to the dead in which the goddess Mictecacihuatl presided over festivities. Indians viewed death as a natural stage of life, which carried over to the unique Day of the Dead celebration in Mexico and Central America. Unlike the American celebration of Halloween, El Dia de los Muertos is not frightening. It is a time of happiness in which the souls of loved ones return to visit and celebrate with the living.

Los Dias de los Meurtos, as the holiday is called in Spanish, begins on the evening of October 31 as women prepare by cleaning house, making candles, and cooking large quantities of food, including tortillas, chicken, *atole* (a thick drink made of corn meal), hot chocolate, and special bread called *pan de meuerto* (bread of the dead).

Indians believed that dead people need some of the same things that living people do, so families construct elaborate, colorful altars to make offerings to the dead. The souls of dead

Celtic: relating to a group of ancient European peoples called Celts.

The Aztec Indians' belief that death was a natural stage of life carried over to the unique Dias de los Meurtos celebration in Mexico and Central America.

87

Pan de Muerto (Bread of the Dead)

On the Day of the Dead, Mexican bakers make their famous *pan de muerto* (bread of the dead)—delicious, sweet loaves, usually seasoned with anise and cinnamon. Some bakers shape the dough into a skull or skeleton. Others braid the dough, then decorate it with crossbones, sometimes covering the crossbones with white icing. Some bakers even hide a tiny toy skull or skeleton inside the bread.

1/4 cup milk	2 eggs
1/4 cup butter	3 cups flour, unsifted
1/4 cup sugar	1/2 teaspoon aniseed
1/2 teaspoon salt	1/2 teaspoon cinnamon
1 package active dry yeast	2 teaspoons sugar
1/4 cup very warm water	

Pour milk into a saucepan and bring to a boil; immediately remove from heat. Stir butter, 1/4 cup sugar, and salt into the milk. In a large bowl, mix yeast with warm water until yeast is dissolved. Let stand five minutes. Add the milk mixture. Separate the yolk and white of one egg. Add the yolk to the yeast mixture, but save the white for later. Now add another whole egg to the yeast mixture. Measure the flour and add to the yeast and eggs. Stir well until dough is formed.

Flour a pastry board and place the dough in the center. Knead until smooth (5 to 8 minutes). Return the dough to the large bowl and cover with a damp cloth. Let rise in a warm place for 90 minutes. After 90 minutes, knead the dough again. Divide the dough into four pieces and set one aside. Roll the remaining three pieces into ropes. On a greased baking sheet, pinch three rope ends together and braid. Finish by pinching the ends together on opposite side. Divide the remaining dough in half and shape into two "bones." Lay them in a cross atop the braided loaf. Cover the bread with a dish towel and let rise for 30 minutes. Meanwhile, grease a baking sheet and preheat the oven 350°. Mix aniseed, cinnamon, and sugar together. Beat egg white lightly. After 30 minutes, brush top of bread with egg white and sprinkle with sugar mixture (except on crossbones). Bake at 350° for 35 minutes.

infants and children, called Angelitos (Little Angels), begin to return on October 30 and 31, sometimes following a path of marigold flowers families set out to show the way home. On All Saints' Day, the Angelitos partake in the altars set for them with toys, non-spicy foods, and candy. Candy skulls (*calaveras*) and skeletons are made of *alfenique*, a confection similar to marzipan. Some families place miniature cups, saucers, and even miniature *pan de muerto* on the altars. The living children of the family can eat the special treats later.

Adults are honored on All Souls' Day with elaborate three-level altars. Prominently displayed on the altar is a picture of the beloved, and the tiers are covered in brightly colored paper with cut-out designs. Important colors are purple for pain, white for hope, and pink for celebration. Candles cover the altar to light the way for the dead to return. Bad spirits must be swept away to leave a clear path for the soul, which can be done by burning *copal*, an incense made from tree resin. Other objects on the altar include saint statues and symbolic items from the family.

The family places favorite dishes of their loved ones on the altar as well as other foods the women have prepared. *Pan de muerto*, a sweet, egg-rich bread, varies regionally, with bakeries competing to create interesting shapes. The most common is round or oval, to resemble the soul, while others are created in the shapes of people or animals. Some are sprinkled with white sugar with a crisscrossed bone shape on top. Main holiday dishes are *mole* (a thick sauce made from chilis, ground seeds or nuts, and chocolate) with meat or poultry. Tamales are popular, with special sweet ones for children. Water is placed on the

On the Day of the Dead a Mexican family sits in the cemetery in Tzintzuntzan, Mexico, after spending the night there to honor relatives who have died.

On the Day of the Dead bakeshops and markets across Mexico are filled with pastries and candies formed in the shape of little skulls.

altar to quench the spirits' thirst. Often a bottle of tequila (a liquor) or *pulque* (a homemade fermented liquor) and even cigarettes are laid out for adult spirits. After the spirits consume the aromas and essence of the foods, the family eats the food or gives it away.

Day of the Dead celebrations proceed to the cemetery where families gather to clean and repaint graves of loved ones. They often place on the grave huge flower arches with pictures of the deceased set into them. Several hundred candles may be placed around the grave, and a picnic is set up. As families keep a nightlong vigil, the scene becomes festive and lovely. Musicians stroll from one gravesite to another, singing favorite songs for a fee. The mood of the evening is respectful yet social. Catholic priests often visit gravesides to pray with families.

Dia de los Muertos traditions vary from town to town throughout Mexico. In a famous Janitzio Island celebration, beautifully dressed Tarascan Indian women file to the cemetery carrying huge baskets of food and gifts, while the men sing solemnly through the night. In Yalalag, Zapotec Indians wear white shrouds, carry torches, and wail in a procession to the cemetery. Villagers in the state of Oaxaca make altars as large as rooms. Many areas feature skeletal puppets and masked figures, called *calacas*, that appear at festivals and invite children to dance with them.

Many Mexicans and Central Americans dropped the holiday when they came to the United States. However, in the early 1970s, many immigrants revived Day of the Dead celebrations. In cities with large Latin American neighborhoods many people come together for public celebrations of the Day of the Dead. Museums and art galleries in such places as New York City, Chicago, Phoenix, and Houston feature special exhibits and other events to celebrate the holiday. Many Hispanics in the border states of California, Arizona, New Mexico, and Texas celebrate Dia de los Muertos. ◆

Dionysia

Only traces of Dionysia remain today; one modern Dionysian celebration is a twelve-day festival of food and wine in the town of Limassol on the island of Cyprus.

nymphs: minor nature deities.

Dionysia was a series of festivals in ancient Greece to honor Dionysus, the Greek god of wine and agricultural fertility. Bacchus, the god of wine in Roman mythology, was nearly identical to Dionysus. The Romans began to worship Bacchus after coming into contact with Greek culture in the 700s B.C.E., and the Bacchanalia became their version of the Dionysia. The time of year for celebrating Dionysia varied.

Dionysus was not a major god of Olympus, but he was an important deity. Greek legend tells of Dionysus's conception by Zeus, king of the gods, and Semele, a mortal princess of the city of Thebes. Dionysus, the only god with a human parent, was not yet born when his mother died. Zeus saved him and kept the fetus in his side until it matured. When the baby reached full term, Zeus sent the infant to be raised by the **nymphs** at Nysa, a valley where the finest grapes grew. Dionysus grew up to wander the world teaching humans how to turn the juice of grapes into wine.

As a god of vegetation, Dionysus is often pictured with a drinking horn and vine branches. He is also associated with the fir tree and with ivy. His symbol, the *thrysus*, which his worshippers carry, is a branch or stalk of fennel twined with ivy leaves and tipped with a pine cone. Dionysus was often paired with Demeter, goddess of grain. Dionysus was usually represented wearing a bull's hide, complete with head, horns, and hoofs draped about him. He is sometimes shown as a calf-headed child with horns on his head and grapes about his brow.

Another animal associated with Dionysus is the goat. At one point, Zeus changed the young Dionysus into a goat to save him from the jealous Hera, the wife of Zeus. Followers of Dionysus were said to tear goats into pieces and eat the flesh to take into themselves the revered qualities of their god. The mythical *maenads*, or *bacchantes*, were female devotees who left their homes to roam the wilderness and dance madly on mountainsides in ecstatic devotion to Dionysus. They wore fawn skins and were believed to possess mystical powers.

The Greeks honored Dionysus in festivities that featured new wines, feasts, processions, dancing, and singing. These celebrations became known as Dionysias and, though sometimes celebrated at the end of harvest, probably originated in spring nature festivals. They also featured great dramatic competitions of comical and **satirical** plays, or Dionysiac **mysteries**. These plays gradually evolved into the structured form of Greek drama. The most important festival, the Greater Dionysia, was held in Athens for five days each spring. In time, the mysteries associated with Dionysus became occasions for drunkenness and flagrant sensual behavior. Eventually, they were forbidden at Thebes and later elsewhere in Greece. Greeks were aware of the dual nature of wine its positive and negative qualities and this was mirrored by the dual nature of Dionysus. The god of wine could be either kind or cruel. Worshiping him could bring either ecstasy or chaos. According to tradition, Dionysus died each winter and was reborn in the spring. To his followers, this cyclical revival, accompanied by the seasonal renewal of the fruits of the earth, embodied the promise of the resurrection of the dead.

Dionysus became known to the Romans as Bacchus. The Romans held an annual festival honoring Bacchus called the Bacchanalia, which featured drinking and wild behavior. These frenzied celebrations became popular by the second century B.C.E. in Roman Italy. The excesses of the Bacchanalia became increasingly extreme. At first the mysteries were celebrated only by women, but when they were opened to men, the gatherings became more lewd and depraved. The celebrations were prohibited by the Roman senate in 186 B.C.E.

Only traces of Dionysia remain today. One modern celebration of Dionysia is a festival of food and wine in the town of Limassol on the island of Cyprus near Greece. The festival began in 1960 as an effort of local wineries. Local musicians, dancing groups and actors perform for the event. Many people

satirical: relating to literary works that use wit and irony to ridicule or attack.

mysteries: religious dramas.

travel to Limassol from all over the island to attend the festivities and are joined by tourists from all over the world. The festivities last for twelve days and twelve nights. Local wine pours freely and local dishes are served.

As the Roman empire spread into northern Europe, some Roman practices merged with existing religious practices in those regions. The major Celtic feast of Beltane, or May Day, shared characteristics of Dionysia. Beltane, a celebration of spring, includes dancing around maypoles to celebrate the fertility of the earth and is still observed in parts of Ireland, Scotland, and Wales. In addition, a modern religious movement known as neopaganism has revived some of these ancient rituals. Neopagans draw from ancient religions that showed an awareness of nature with seasonal cycles as well as the cycles of human life. The neopagans reinvent some of those religious practices to fit their contemporary lives. ◆

Divali

Divali, also known as Dewali, Dipavali, or the Festival of Lights, is an important renewal festival celebrated all over India in the autumn at the time of the equinox. Divali marks the end of the rainy season and the harvest of the summer crops. The Hindi word *Divali* can be translated as "row of lights," in reference to lights lit on the nights of the transition from the waning to the waxing moon. These lights stand for the hope kindled by the new season that comes at the end of the dangerous **monsoon**. In many ways the festival is a celebration of a new year. Accordingly, debts are paid off, and merchants close their accounts in anticipation of new wealth.

monsoon: a season of wind and heavy rain.

Divali is a three-night festival, the last night of which is the first night of the waxing moon. The celebrations incorporate a number of mythic elements, many of which find colorful regional variations. As in any renewal rite, care is taken to clean and purify homes and shops, and people make certain to perform special **ablutions** in a ritual bath. The festival is most obviously characterized by the seemingly infinite number of oil lamps that are lit everywhere, as well as by the noise of exploding firecrackers that are said to frighten away evil spirits and to welcome the arrival of Laksmi, the Hindu goddess of prosperity. In some parts of India people welcome Laksmi by painting elaborate designs called *alpanas* on the walls and floors of their home. In some regional practices the lamps are said to light the darkness for departed ancestors or to welcome the demon king Bali.

ablutions: washing the body as a religious rite.

Young women in
Saputara, India, paint
designs on the wall of
their house as part of
the Divali celebration.

Puranic: relating to
sacred Hindu writings
called the Purana.

It is to Laksmi, however, that the people offer jewels and
money, delicate foods, and special new clothes made for the
occasion. Much importance is placed on the giving of gifts to all
members of the family and to the neighborhood servants who
help people throughout the year. Men gamble at various games
in a ritual reenactment of the dice tournaments played by the
gods to determine the fate of human beings.

The festival is associated with several **Puranic** myths. Their
underlying idea calls forth what was at issue during the rainy
season and centers on the notion, which holds true for ancestors as well, that underworld creatures play a crucial role in the
acquisition of wealth. A well-known myth relates how the
dwarf Vamana (an incarnation of the Hindu god Visnu) asked
Bali to grant him as much land as he could cover in three steps.
The generous demon king agreed. To his amazement, two of the
dwarf's steps covered the earth and the sky; the third, planted
on Bali's head, sent the demon to the underworld, a region that
became his domain. For his generosity, Bali was then allowed to
come to the surface of the earth during Divali in order to bestow
wealth on human beings.

Another myth, one in which the god Krishna is said to slay Naraka (or Narakasura, the "demon of hell"), similarly marks the momentary halt of evil underworld powers. Naraka is the son of Bhudevi, the earth goddess, and Varaha, the incarnation of Visnu as a boar, who had rescued the goddess when she lay buried under the waters of the sea. Although he was ultimately killed by Krishna —as all demons must eventually be killed by a god—Naraka, like Bali, is nevertheless paid homage when the question of wealth is at stake.

In North India the second day of Divali is reserved for the worship of the hill Govardhana, near the town of Mathura, a site of deep religious significance for devotees of Krishna. Once Indra had captured all of the world's cattle, Krishna freed the cows, but the enraged Indra flooded the earth with a downpour of rain to drown the valuable animals. Krishna then raised Govardhana so that the cows would be saved. The importance of the myth is clear in the context of Divali, for in Hindu thought the cow is a powerful and evocative symbol of prosperity. The ritual here primarily involves worship of cattle, but—in a play on the word *govardhana* (lit., "cow-increasing")—offerings are made to mounds of cow dung (*govar*) to ensure continued prosperity and wealth (*dhana*).

One final ritual marks the celebration of Divali. Girls and women, who at the onset of the rainy season had tied protective threads around their brothers' wrists, now invite the boys and men for delicacies in exchange for gifts. This rite is accompanied by the worship of Yama, lord of the dead, and his twin sister, Yami. Yama is also known as Dharmaraja (king of the social and cosmic order), for that very order is then restored with the return of prosperity, which is dependent upon women and on controlled underworld powers. ◆

On Divali, girls and women, who at the onset of the rainy season had tied protective thread around their brothers' wrists, now invite the boys and men for delicacies in exchange for gifts.

Dragon Boat Festival

<small>CHINA AND TAIWAN ● EARLY SUMMER</small>

Dragon Boat Festival is a lively celebration that began as an occasion for driving off evil spirits and later incorporated activities honoring the Chinese classical poet Qu Yuan. Chinese people in China, Taiwan, Canada, the United States, Malaysia, and other places celebrate the Dragon Boat Festival on the fifth day of the fifth month of the Chinese lunar calendar, which falls between May 28 and June 28.

Long ago, the "Double Fifth"—fifth day of the fifth month—was a time when people were reminded to take care of their health. The day falls in the summer, when the climate is hot and sticky, and infectious diseases and harmful insects thrive. On this day, people engaged in various activities to drive off evil spirits and pests that cause disease. Some people hung up pictures of Zhong Kui, an ancient scholar who was considered the **nemesis** of evil spirits. Many burned the foul-smelling mineral realgar, or arsenic disulfide, using it as a pesticide. People also drank realgar wine and smeared it on the ears, nose, and forehead of children because it was believed to cure illness and **exorcise** evil spirits.

Some Chinese hung bunches of moxa above their doors to prevent pestilence. Moxa is a substance made from the leaves of certain Chinese or Japanese wormwood plants. Others hung branches of mugwort plants on the doorjamb of their houses. The evil spirits were said to be terrified of these branches. Many girls wore colored silk pouches filled with aromatic flowers and herbs believed to bring luck and ward off evil. Some Chinese ate cakes shaped like the "five poisonous creatures"—which in

nemesis: rival or opponent.

exorcise: to get rid of evil spirits with prayers or rituals.

98

The team of rowers aboard this dragon boat won its race during the Dragon Boat Festival in Hong Kong.

some areas were the centipede, house lizard, scorpion, snake, and spider. People believed that the image of the evil creatures could combat the real pests, and eating the image was considered preventative medicine. An image of a tiger was also believed to be a potent force against evil. A number of these traditions continue today, including displaying the image of Zhong Kui, hanging bunches of moxa and mugwort, and wearing sachets.

About 2,000 years ago, the "double fifth" became associated with Qu Yuan, a famous court poet and government official. Qu lived in the state of Chu (present-day Hubei and Hunan province) during the period of warring states, when feudal lords waged brutal battles over control of land. Qu tried repeatedly to advise his king during the turbulent times, but his advice went unheeded. Consequently, the despondent Qu threw himself into the Yangtze River on the fifth day of the fifth month. The poem he supposedly wrote before his suicide, "**Elegies** of Chu," is one of the most important classical poems in Chinese literature.

elegy: a song or poem expressing sorrow.

When people heard of Qu's suicide, they searched the river in boats for his body, but he was never found. Some say that people cast bamboo sections stuffed with rice into the river to honor Qu and give his spirit sustenance. Other stories say that rice balls were flung into the river to feed the fish and keep them from eating Qu's body. According to yet another story, people threw the rice-stuffed bamboo into the river for Qu, but the river dragon ate it all and Qu's soul was starving. A spirit told the people that they must wrap the bamboo sections in chinaberry leaves and sew the bundles with silk thread in five different colors. The dragon would not eat such bundles, so that Qu could get them.

Today, colorful dragon boat races held in many large Chinese communities around the world combine the customs of the Double Fifth with the legend of Qu. Traditionally, dragons were believed to help prevent disease. So, the dragon boats served as a potent force in protecting the people, especially the rowers, against the pests and diseases of the season. Today, the boat races also represent a reenactment of the search for Qu's body. The long boats with elaborately decorated dragon heads and tails hold dozens of crew members, who row in unison to the rhythm of pounding drums. Spectators line the river banks, cheering on the rowers.

> When people heard of Qu Yuan's suicide, they searched the Yangtze River for his body, but he was never found.

A traditional holiday food eaten in memory of Qu during the festival is *zong zi*, a steamed rice dumpling mixed with dates, peanuts, pork, salted eggs, or other fillings and wrapped in banana, palm, or bamboo leaves to form pyramid-shaped dumplings. The dumpling recalls the bundled rice cast into the river in honor of Qu. ◆

Earth Day

APRIL 22

The first Earth Day took place on April 22, 1970, and has become the largest environmental event in the world. Earth Day events range from tree plantings and community cleanups to waste reduction programs to ecology fairs, workshops, and parades. Earth Day focuses attention on environmental problems of the planet. People use the day to apply solutions for pollution, habitat destruction, extinction of plant and animal species, and the depletion of nonrenewable resources.

In September 1969, Senator Gaylord Nelson of Wisconsin announced a national environmental teach-in for the spring of 1970. He wanted to place environmental concerns in the center of the national dialogue and decided to follow the model of antiwar teach-ins he saw on college campuses. Nelson raised funds and sent letters to civic leaders requesting that they issue Earth Day proclamations. He sent an Earth Day article to college newspapers and published one that reached most elementary and high schools. News sources soon picked up the story, and letters and phone calls poured in. Nelson opened an office to serve as a national clearinghouse for Earth Day activities.

An estimated twenty million people nationwide participated in peaceful demonstrations on April 22, 1970. Events included speeches, seminars, and practical actions. In New York City, over 100,000 people attended an ecology fair in Central Park. The United States Congress adjourned for the day and many of its members attended "teach-ins" at universities or made speeches about the environment. New York's governor

"Earth Day achieved what I had hoped for. The objective was to get a nation-wide demonstration of concern for the environment so large that it would shake the political establishment out of its lethargy and, finally, force this issue permanently onto the national political agenda. It was a gamble, but it worked."

Earth Day founder Gaylord Nelson, 1990

101

The Environmental Movement

The publication in 1962 of Rachel Carson's *Silent Spring* is one of the markers of the beginning of the environmental movement. Carson's book argued that chemicals in the air and water, especially DDT, were killing "birds, mammals, fishes, and indeed practically every form of wildlife." Out of the shock engendered by Carson's book grew a new sensibility about and a dedication to saving and protecting the natural environment. An older form on environmentalism, usually called conservationism, had existed for decades and was associated with John Muir, Aldo Leopold, William O. Douglas, and David Brower, among others, but the effort that emerged in the 1960s was the first concerted, vocal, active, and influential movement. The decade ended in 1970 with the first Earth Day, an outpouring of environmental sentiment involving an estimated 20 million people that, according to its chief organizer, Senator Gaylord Nelson of Wisconsin, sent "a big message to the politicians—a message to tell them to wake up and do something." In response Congress established the Environmental Protection Agency in 1970, and passed the Clean Air Act of 1970, the Pesticide Control Act and the Clean Water Act of 1972, the Endangered Species Act of 1973, the Ocean Dumping Act of 1977, and numerous other laws designed to protect the environment.

After the first Earth Day, the growing acceptance of the nation's environmental crisis became evident as membership in older environmental groups, such as the Sierra Club and the National Audubon Society, rose dramatically, and new organizations such as Greenpeace and the Cousteau Society were established. These national groups began to exercise their political influence in Washington, where many of them maintained headquarters, moving with increasingly sophisticated tactics to get Congress to pass far-reaching environmental legislation during the 1980s and 1990s. By the late 1990s, the effect and importance of environmentalism had become a fact of life in the United States and many other countries, and Earth Day had grown into a widely observed international holiday.

signed a measure coordinating pollution abatement and conservation activities.

For the next twenty years, interest in Earth Day wavered, as there was no central organization. However, a temporary organizing body helped to vigorously resurrect Earth Day for its twentieth anniversary in 1990. Over 200 million people in 140 countries celebrated the occasion. Around the world, people held marches, rallies, concerts, festivals, street fairs, cleanups, plantings, and other environmental events.

In Chicago, 10,000 bicyclists rode in a twenty-five-mile "Ride for Clean Air," and more than 150,000 people attended a one-day celebration and concert at Chicago's Lincoln Park. In New York City, celebrations began in Times Square where a

On Earth Day, young people across the United States pitch in to pick up trash along roads and highways.

crowd gathered for an "Earth Rising" ceremony, and close to a million people attended an Earth Concert in Central Park. About fifty Cree Indians kayaked down the Hudson River from Canada to call attention to the role of native peoples in environmental preservation. In France, people formed a 500-mile human chain. In Italy, 5,000 people created a "lie-down" to protest car exhaust fumes. Japanese divers pulled garbage out of

A group of Earth Day celebrants in Washington, D.C., spells out "Love Your Mother" before a huge balloon of the earth.

the sea, and 35,000 people gathered on an island in Tokyo Bay built from the city's garbage.

The organizing body closed its doors following Earth Day 1990, but soon a group of people formed Earth Day USA in order to keep the momentum going. Earth Day USA began providing services such as organizer manuals, activity ideas, newsletters, posters, fund-raising ideas, conferences, and official T-shirts. Earth Day USA continued to gather information about thousands of events and activities and hosted an Internet site with an events calendar.

By 1998 Earth Day had taken root in many parts of the world, especially Europe, Asia, and Latin America. In Israel, groups of musicians, jugglers, and environmental activists traveled widely, conducting mini-festivals. In Malaysia, the Future in Our Hands Society hosted a tree planting. Filipinos hosted a free Earth Day concert and fair, featuring artists, musicians, environmental groups, contests, games, and activities for kids. In the Sultanate of Oman, students collected used newspapers for recycling.

South American Earth Day activities in 1998 included a Biosferic Awareness Day in Chile that featured art, dance, native Indian ceremonies, and vegetarian food. In Peru, a student's group presented a weeklong celebration that included photographs of Peru's ecological sanctuaries and videos about endangered Peruvian ecosystems. The city of Paramaribo, Suriname, featured neighborhood tree plantings and cycling tours for youngsters. Around London, England, boys and girls performed musical presentations and students cleaned out a school pond and planted plants. In Belfast, Ireland, volunteers sponsored construction of a new path in the Green Park Woodlands. The Czech Republic celebrated enthusiastically with concerts, plantings, exhibitions, fairs, seminars, lectures, excursions, and demonstrations.

Throughout the United States, small towns hosted such events as cleanups of communities, beaches, public parks, and wetlands areas. Many groups hosted tree plantings, especially of endangered species. The University of Chicago hosted an Earth Day Fair that filled the campus with environmental exhibits, food, music, and entertainment. In Montana, an American Indian group featured a cleanup week of their reservation followed by a community picnic. In Bakersfield, California, the American Wind Energy Association hosted a wind-power conference to show wind energy as a clean power source. In San Francisco, an architectural group presented environmentally friendly architectural products.

The first Earth Day gave the modern environmental movement a major push. By the late 1900s, most Americans considered themselves environmentally conscious. Even traditionally conservative lawmakers supported such efforts as saving tropical rain forests and protecting the marine environment. Businesses also participated in environmental concerns. Some companies perform environmental audits into their own policies and practices. American automakers created cars that were, on average, 60 percent more fuel efficient in the 1990s than they were in 1970 and some invested in the development of electric-powered vehicles. Other manufacturers engaged in recycling and more efficient manufacturing processes to conserve resources. Many corporate leaders had once been college students who participated in the first Earth Day. ◆

"We joined together to save the natural beauty and all the resources that God has given us, and to pass it on to our children and grandchildren. For a quarter of a century now, Americans have stood as one, to say no to dirty air, toxic food, poison water, and yes, to leaving a land to our children as unspoiled as their hopes."

President Bill Clinton, on the 25th anniversary of Earth Day, 1995

Easter

CHRISTIAN ● SPRING

Romance language: French, Italian, Spanish, and other languages developed from Latin.

E aster, the most important of all Christian feasts, celebrates the passion, the death, and especially the resurrection of Jesus Christ. The English name *Easter* probably derives from *Eostur,* the Norse word for the spring season. In **Romance languages** the name for Easter is taken from the Greek *Pascha,* which in turn is derived from the Hebrew *Pesaḥ* (Passover). Thus Easter is the Christian equivalent of the Jewish Passover, a spring feast of both harvest and deliverance from bondage. The Eastern Slavs call Easter "the great day" and greet one another, as do the Greeks, with the words "Christ is risen," receiving the response "He is risen indeed."

Easter is the earliest of all annual Christian feasts. It may originally have been observed in conjunction with the Jewish Passover on the fourteenth day of the month Nisan. Gradually, however, it was observed everywhere on Sunday, the day of Christ's resurrection. The Council of Nicaea (325) prescribed that Easter should always be celebrated on the first Sunday after the first full moon following the spring equinox.

Easter was fundamentally a nocturnal feast preceded by a fast of at least one day. The celebration took place from Saturday evening until the early morning hours of Sunday. In the fifth century Augustine of Hippo called this "the mother of all **vigils**." From at least the time of the early Christian scholar Tertullian (third century) the Easter Vigil (also called the Paschal Vigil) was the favored time for baptism, since the candidates for initiation mirrored the new life won by Christ from the darkness of death.

vigil: the day before a religious feast observed as a day of spiritual devotion.

106

The symbolism of light became an important feature of this nocturnal festival. It was customary on the Saturday evening of the Easter Vigil to illuminate not only churches but entire towns and villages with lamps and torches; thus the night was called "the night of illumination." From at least the end of the fourth century in Jerusalem the lighting of lamps at **vespers** took on a special character at this feast. In northern European countries the use of special lights at Easter coincided with the custom of lighting bonfires on hilltops to celebrate the coming of spring; this is the origin of the Easter fire later kindled in Western Christian Easter vigils. Large Easter candles also became the rule, and poems were composed in honor of them and thus of Christ the light, whom they symbolized. Such poems stem from as early as the fourth century; the most famous, still employed in various versions, is the *Exultet*, which originated in the seventh or eighth century. In the East, among the Orthodox, Holy Saturday night is celebrated with a candle-light procession outside the church building. After a solemn entrance into the church, bells peal and the Great Matins or Morning Prayer of Easter begins. It is followed by a solemn celebration of the Eucharist according to the liturgy of Saint Basil.

vespers: late afternoon or evening services.

The Easter vigil also contains a number of biblical readings. In the East the baptisms took place during the long readings of the vigil, whereas in the West a procession to the baptistery took place after the readings had been completed. In both cases the celebration of the Eucharist followed the baptisms. With the decline in adult conversions and, hence, in Easter baptisms during the Middle Ages, the time for the vigil service (and thus the end to fasting) was moved up to Saturday morning; however, the Roman Catholic church restored the nocturnal character of the service in 1952 and other rites relating to Holy Week in 1956. In the current Roman Catholic, Lutheran, and Episcopalian rites the Paschal Vigil is the high point of a *triduum*, or three days of services, celebrating the death and resurrection of Christ.

From at least the end of the fourth century, Easter was provided in Jerusalem with an octave, eight days of celebration. With the medieval decline in the octave celebration, Monday and Tuesday of Easter week nevertheless retained the character of holidays. In a larger context the whole of the fifty days from Easter Sunday to Pentecost was properly called Easter, and so constituted a feast in its own right; the eight-day octave, however, was a time of special recognition of the newly baptized.

"And entering into the sepulchre, they saw a young man sitting on the right side, clothed in a long white garment; and they were affrighted. And he saith unto them, Be not affrighted: Ye seek Jesus of Nazareth, which was crucified: he is risen; he is not here: behold the place where they laid him."

King James Bible, Mark 16:5–6

The Sunday after Easter was called the "Sunday in white" because the newly baptized wore their baptismal garments for the last time on that day, and among the Orthodox the octave of Easter is still called "the week of new garments."

Devotions tied to the liturgy of Easter are the origins of liturgical drama. In the Middle Ages it was customary to bury the consecrated host and a cross, or simply a cross, in an Easter **sepulcher** on Holy Thursday or Good Friday. The host or cross was retrieved on Easter Sunday morning and brought to the altar in procession. From this practice developed a brief Easter play called the *Visitatio sepulchri* (Visit to the Tomb), which enacted the visit of the two women to Christ's empty tomb. The same dramatic dialogue can be seen in the eleventh-century poetic sequence *Victimae paschali laudes* (Praise to the Paschal Victim), which became part of the Western liturgy.

> **sepulcher**: a receptacle for religious relics.

A number of popular customs mark Easter Sunday and the rest of Easter week. One such custom, allied to the coming of spring with its earlier sunrise, is an outdoor sunrise service celebrating the resurrection. Such celebrations are especially popular among American Protestants. Since Easter was a time in which the newly baptized wore shining white garments, it became customary to wear new clothes on Easter Sunday and to show them off by walking around town and countryside; thus originated the Easter promenade or Easter parade, popular in many places.

Among the most familiar Easter symbols are the egg and rabbit. The egg symbolizes new life breaking through the apparent death (hardness) of the eggshell. Probably a pre-Christian symbol, it was adapted by Christians to denote Christ's coming forth from the tomb. In many countries the exchange of colored or decorated eggs at Easter has become customary. The Easter bunny or rabbit is also most likely of pre-Christian origin. The rabbit was known as an extraordinarily fertile creature, and hence it symbolized the coming of spring. Although adopted in a number of Christian cultures, the Easter bunny has never received any specific Christian interpretation.

> **The Easter bunny is most likely of pre-Christian origin; the rabbit was known as an extraordinarily fertile creature, and hence it symbolized the coming of spring.**

Among Easter foods the most significant is the Easter lamb, which is in many places the main dish of the Easter Sunday meal. Corresponding to the Passover lamb and to Christ, the Lamb of God, this dish has become a central symbol of Easter. Also popular among Europeans and Americans on Easter is ham, because the pig was considered a symbol of luck in pre-Christian European culture.

Every year on the day after Easter, children are invited to roll Easter eggs down the south lawn of the White House in Washington, D.C.

Every year in Washington, D.C., the president and his wife invite children to roll Easter eggs down the sloping lawn behind the White House on the first Monday following Easter. The tradition began in the mid-1900s, when local children would roll Easter eggs down the lawn of the Capitol building. Congress prohibited the practice in the 1870s because the eggs damaged the grass. However, Rutherford B. Hayes, who was president at the time, invited the children to roll their eggs on the White House grounds. Today, in addition to rolling eggs, children hunt for special wooden Easter eggs, some of them signed by the president, that are hidden in the grass. ◆

Emancipation Day

Emancipation Day is the blanket name for the various days of the year on which African Americans celebrate their liberation from slavery. Some of the days reflect local or regional history, while others have spread across the United States.

Early celebrations of victories over slavery began well before the Civil War. African Americans commemorated January 1, 1808, the day on which Congress's ban on the importation of slaves took effect. African Americans in New York observed July 4, 1827, the day on which state legislation providing for the complete abolition of slavery took effect. Beginning August 1, 1834, African Americans annually marked Britain's abolition of slavery in its West Indian possessions. On October 1, 1851, white abolitionists in Syracuse, New York, sent a fugitive slave named Jerry off to freedom in Canada, and the date was subsequently observed as Jerry Rescue Day.

Since 1863 most emancipation celebrations have commemorated the complete abolition of slavery in the United States as a consequence of the Civil War. President Abraham Lincoln's Emancipation Proclamation, freeing slaves then in Confederate-controlled territory, took effect on January 1, 1863, and set off a wave of enthusiastic celebrations by African Americans. In the years soon following, January 1 became Emancipation Day primarily in New York City, Boston, and the Deep South states. Later, the holiday spread to the Upper South and then to the North.

> *"That on the 1st day of January, A.D. 1863, all persons held as slaves within any State, or designated part of a State, the people whereof shall then be in rebellion against the United States, shall be then, thenceforward, and forever free."*
>
> Emancipation Proclamation, September 22, 1862

President Lincoln's Emancipation Proclamation

President Lincoln's Emancipation Proclamation was issued on September 22, 1862, to take effect on January 1, 1863. The Proclamation stated that "all persons held as slaves within any State, or designated part of a State, the people whereof shall then be in rebellion against the United States, shall be then, thenceforward, and forever free." With these words, Lincoln freed all persons held as slaves in those parts of the country that were in a state of rebellion against the United States. The proclamation also stated that freed slaves "of suitable condition will be received into the armed service of the United States," encouraging many black men to enlist in the Union army and navy.

The Emancipation Proclamation was an exercise of presidential power, issued by the president who had previously refused to permit his generals to free slaves in the slave-holding areas that they conquered. Lincoln based his Proclamation on his powers as commander-in-chief. It was a war measure, designed to strengthen northern military forces and destroy the war-making power of the South. The Emancipation Proclamation was issued the day after the Union military victory at Antietam. It became an important element in the Union war strategy, as a morale builder for the North, and an additional burden for southerners fighting for the Confederacy. Eventually, a very large number of slaves were set free by the Emancipation Proclamation, although its effect was not felt immediately on January 1, 1863. Confederates who held slaves did not obey it, of course. Final emancipation of all slaves did not come about until the passage in December 1865 of the Thirteenth Amendment to the Constitution, which freed slaves in loyal states as well as those held in Confederate states.

The most widely celebrated Emancipation Day at the end of the twentieth century is June 19, or Juneteenth. Originally a Texas holiday, it dates back to June 19, 1865, when Union major general Gordon Granger arrived in Galveston and announced that Texas's slaves were free under the provisions of the Emancipation Proclamation. Annual celebrations soon followed in East Texas, western Louisiana, southwestern Arkansas, and southern Oklahoma. Juneteenth was carried to the North during the black migration of the years before and during World War I. After World War II, black migrants carried the holiday to California. By the end of the twentieth century, Juneteenth was observed in some thirty states, making it the most widely celebrated Emancipation Day. It is also the only Emancipation Day that has become an official holiday, recognized as such by the state of Texas in 1979.

There are many other dates for Emancipation Day on the calendar. Particular ones are favored by various regions; often, the reason why a date was chosen is lost to history. May 8 is marked in eastern Mississippi. August 4 and 8 are days of celebration in north-central Tennessee, southwestern Kentucky, northeastern Arkansas, and central Oklahoma. May 20 is celebrated throughout Florida, while May 28 and 29 are commemorated in many Alabama and Georgia towns along the Chattahoochee River.

In some cases the reason for the choice of day is known. May 9 became a regional day of commemoration in the southeast because on May 9, 1862, Union general David Hunter issued an order freeing all slaves in South Carolina, Georgia, and Florida. The commemoration stuck even though President Lincoln revoked the order. September 22 became a date of celebration in some localities because on that day in 1862 Lincoln issued his preliminary proclamation, which announced his intention of issuing the Emancipation Proclamation on the following January 1.

The most recently created Emancipation Day was initiated in 1940, when February 1 was set aside to mark the adoption of the Thirteenth Amendment, which freed all slaves in the United States. It is celebrated in Philadelphia.

Emancipation Day has been celebrated in a variety of ways. January 1 celebrations of the Emancipation Proclamation have been marked in a serious fashion. They are usually conducted in a church, with the observances including prayers, sermons, readings of the Emancipation Proclamation, and the singing of "Lift Every Voice and Sing," known as the Negro National Anthem. Other celebrations have had pleasure as their sole purpose. August 8 observances, for example, are held in community parks and on church lawns and include baseball games, barbecues, dancing, and the drinking of alcohol (sometimes excessively). Still other celebrations, including many held on Juneteenth, have mixed serious purpose with pleasure, featuring speeches and readings from historical documents along with picnics, parades, dances, and so on.

Just as blacks have debated since the early nineteenth century whether they should try to assimilate into American society or retain their separate identity, so they have long debated whether to celebrate their own Emancipation Day or observe July 4 along with the rest of the country. During the second half of the twentieth century, some members of the growing black middle class began to feel more comfortable with the mainstream July 4 observance than did earlier generations of African Americans. But in the 1980s and 1990s there was a

"Neither slavery nor involuntary servitude, except as a punishment for crime whereof the party shall have been duly convicted, shall exist within the United States, or any place subject to their jurisdiction."

13th Amendment to the U.S. Constitution, section 1

countertrend, with many African Americans placing greater stress on the importance of black identity and self-awareness. This inclination made itself felt in the celebration of Emancipation Day. African fairs, African storytelling, and reenactments of episodes of African-American history became part of the observance in many instances.

Some other countries where people once lived as slaves also celebrate an Emancipation Day. People in the Bahamas celebrate Emancipation Day on August 5. In 1985 Trinidad and Tobago eliminated its Columbus' Discovery Day and replaced it with Emancipation Day, celebrated on August 1 in commemoration of the abolition of slavery there in the 1830s. ◆

Epiphany

Epiphany is the Christian feast of the **manifestation** of Jesus Christ. Traditionally celebrated on January 6, it is also celebrated by the Roman rite in some places on the Sunday following the octave of Christmas. The feast is called Epiphania (manifestation) among Western Christians and Theophaneia (manifestation of God) among Eastern Christians. That the feast is of Eastern origin is indicated by the Greek origin of both names. Epiphany is one of the twelve major feasts of the Orthodox church year.

The origins of Epiphany are obscure and much debated. It was originally either a feast of Christ's baptism in the Jordan or of his birth at Bethlehem. The theory that the date of January 6 corresponded to an old date for the Egyptian winter solstice has been largely discredited. The date may have at first been observed as a feast of the baptism of Christ among second-century **gnostics**. In the fourth century it was certainly a feast of the nativity of Christ, celebrated with an octave, or eight days of celebration, at Bethlehem and all the holy places of Jerusalem.

At the end of the fourth century, when the Western feast of the nativity of Christ came to be observed in the East on December 25, January 6 came to be widely celebrated as the feast of Christ's baptism, although among the Armenians of western Asia Epiphany is the only nativity feast celebrated to this day. As the feast of Christ's baptism, Epiphany became for Eastern Christians a major baptismal day, and hence it was given the Greek name Ta Phota (the lights); baptism itself was called *phōtismos* (enlightenment).

manifestation: the act of showing or displaying.

gnostics: adherents of an early Christian doctrine that believed that spiritual knowledge was essential to salvation.

115

Men dressed as the three kings parade on horseback during an Epiphany procession in Colombia.

At the same time as the East was accepting the Western Christmas, the Feast of Epiphany was being adopted in the West. Outside of Rome it was celebrated as the Feast of the Three Miracles, comprising the visit of the Magi (the three kings), the baptism of Christ, and the miracle of changing water into wine at the wedding feast of Cana. In Rome, however, the feast concentrated solely on the visit of the Magi, connoting Christ's manifestation to the gentiles. With their adoption of the Roman liturgy all other Western Christians eventually came to observe Epiphany as the Feast of the Magi.

Among Eastern Christians the celebration of Epiphany is notable for several reasons. At Alexandria the patriarch would solemnly announce the date of Easter for the current year on January 6. Throughout the East, Epiphany, together with Easter, was a special day for performing baptisms. The most enduring custom, however, has been the blessing of the waters on Epiphany. There are two blessings. The first takes place during the vigil of Epiphany in the evening and is followed by the priest's sprinkling of the town or village with the blessed water. The second blessing takes place on the day of Epiphany itself, when the local waters of stream, lake, or sea are blessed by having a cross thrown into them, after which young men dive into the waters to retrieve it.

The Western observance of Epiphany has centered on the figures of the Magi, popularly called the Three Kings. Their cult was especially strong at Cologne in the Middle Ages, for their supposed relics had been brought there in the twelfth century. The idea that the Magi were kings was derived from several verses of scripture (Ps. 71:10, Is. 60:3–6). The tradition that there were three of them was probably derived from the number of gifts mentioned in the biblical account of their visit (Mt. 2:1–12). The account of the visit of the Magi and of the miraculous star that guided them inspired several mystery plays during the Middle Ages. The story of their visit also gave rise to the custom of gift giving on Epiphany: in Italy gifts are given on that day by an old woman named Befana, and the feast is also an occasion for gift giving in Spanish cultures. ◆

"Now when Jesus was born in Bethlehem of Judaea in the days of Herod the king, behold, there came wise men from the east to Jerusalem, saying, Where is he that is born King of the Jews? for we have seen his star in the east, and are come to worship him."

King James Bible, Matthew 2:1–2

Fastelavn

DENMARK ● EARLY SPRING

Early in the morning of Fastelavn, children enter their parents' room wielding "Lenten birches" and whack their parents, crying, "I want buns! Give buns!"

astelavn, the Danish celebration of Shrovetide (the Monday before Ash Wednesday), usually happens between February 2 and March 8, and is a school holiday for children. Early in the morning, children come into their parents' room wielding "Lenten birches" (birch twigs covered with silk, crepe paper, or ribbon) and poke or whack their parents, crying, *"Boller vil jeg have!"* ("I want buns! Give buns!"). To put a stop to the beating, the parents hand over the traditional *Fastelavnsboller*, or Shrovetide buns.

Once the parents are awake, the buns are eaten or put to various festive uses. Sometimes a bun is suspended by a string from a rafter or chandelier, and children take turns trying to take a bite out of it—like bobbing for apples. In another similarity with Halloween, boys and girls dress up in costumes later in the day and go from door to door with their collection cups, chanting,

Fastelavn er mit navn,
boller vil jeg have,
hvis jeg ingen boller får,
så laver jeg ballade . . .

. . . .

Shrovetide is my name,
I want some buns.
If I don't get any buns
I will make a lot of trouble . . .

. . . .

Shrovetide is my name . . .
Buns up, buns down, I want buns . . .

118

Adults then give the little princesses, pirates, devils, and ghosts a treat of candy, coins, and more *Fastelavnsboller*.

Another game for the children is barrel-smashing with birch rods, known as "smashing the cat out of the barrel." All the children, dressed in their costumes, line up and take turns striking a barrel with a birch rod (similar to whacking at a piñata). The barrel may be filled with oranges or other treats and usually hangs from the ceiling or a tree limb, and is painted with the image of a black cat. The child who "knocks the cat out of the barrel" (breaks the barrel open) or, alternatively, knocks the last barrel stave to the ground, is made "king." The king can be a boy or a girl. The king then chooses a queen; they are given golden crowns made of paper, and they are rulers for the day.

The barrel-smashing is easier on cats than it was in the Middle Ages, when young men would strike at a barrel containing a live cat, and go on hitting till the animal died. This was done not to hurt the cat "personally," so to speak, but because black cats were (and often still are) believed to be carriers of evil spirits, or representatives of ills, evils, malevolent spirits, and possibly bad harvests. The ritual was similar to the ancient pagan practices of purging towns and villages of evil spirits on Walpurgis Night (May Day eve) and during the twelve days between Christmas and Epiphany. (It has been supposed that the beating with birch rods may derive from ancient purification rites, where people would lash one another with switches to drive out devils and witches.)

Although it is now almost entirely a holiday for children, Fastelavn was originally a feast day when villagers would gather to celebrate the coming of Spring. The feast was also the occasion of a mock battle between a figure dressed as Winter (often clad in furs or moss) and a likeness of Summer dressed in leaves and flowers. In *The Golden Bough*, Sir James George Frazer describes such contests as having taken place all over northern Europe. The Winter man would hurl ice and snow at Summer, trying to prolong his dominion, but Summer would always conquer the cold. The vanquished Winter would be thrown to the ground and his clothing stripped from him and burned in a great bonfire while the celebrants sang and chanted songs in honor of victorious Summer.

In addition to the battle of the seasons, the ancient Danish springtime feasts included foot races, pot-smashing competitions, and flogging with birch branches. The feast also featured

> The Winter man would hurl ice and snow at Summer, trying to prolong his dominion, but Summer would always conquer the cold.

ring riding—horseback riders trying to catch a tiny ring with a stick while galloping past—and costuming and barrel smashing. Today, although Fastelavn is milder—like a Danish Halloween in late winter—the holiday still carries reminders of its ancient origins, fragments that the adults may consider while the children enjoy their Shrovetide buns. ◆

Father's Day

Father's Day is holiday for expressing gratitude and appreciation for fathers. Many countries observe a special day for fathers, although the exact date varies from country to country. In the United States and Canada, Father's Day is celebrated on the third Sunday in June.

In 1909 Sonora Louise Smart Dodd of Spokane, Washington, heard a sermon about the value of mothers, which moved her to suggest to her minister that a day be set aside for honoring fathers. Her own father, Henry Jackson Smart, a farmer in western Washington, had raised six children on his own after his wife died in childbirth. After his daughter Sonora Louise became an adult, she understood the selflessness her father had shown to his family, and she sought some way to honor him and other fathers that was similar to Mother's Day. Henry Jackson Smart's birthday was on June 19 and his daughter proposed this date for Father's Day.

Smart Dodd worked to publicize her idea and soon the Spokane Ministerial Association and the local Young Men's Christian Association lent their support. Spokane celebrated it's first Father's Day on June 19, 1910. The idea caught on and over the next decade, cities across America began celebrating a day in honor of fathers. In 1924 President Calvin Coolidge announced to the American people his support of Father's Day and two years later a National Father's Day Committee was formed in New York City. In 1956 a joint resolution of Congress formally recognized Father's Day as a national day of observance. A decade later, President Lyndon B. Johnson signed a

1909 Sonora Louise Smart Dodd of Spokane, Washington, suggests to her minister that a day be set aside for fathers.

1910 Spokane celebrates the first Father's Day.

1924 President Calvin Coolidge announces his support for Father's Day.

1956 A joint resolution of Congress recognizes Father's Day as a national observance.

1972 President Richard Nixon establishes Father's Day as a permanent national observance.

Children express love for their fathers with flowers and hugs on Father's Day.

presidential proclamation declaring the third Sunday of June as Father's Day. President Richard Nixon finally established Father's Day as a permanent national observance in 1972, almost sixty years after Mother's Day had been so designated. By the end of the century, Father's Day had evolved into a day to honor not only fathers, but all men who act as father figures, including stepfathers, uncles, grandfathers, godfathers, and even adult male friends.

Few traditions have developed in association with Father's Day because it is a relatively new holiday. People generally honor their fathers in the same manner they honor their mothers on Mother's Day. Young children draw pictures or make cards for their fathers. They may also compose poems for their fathers or write special Father's Day songs. Many children also help with housework or yard work that their father usually does himself. When children grow older they may give gifts such as flowers, cigars, or ties to their fathers. Children who live far from their parents may call their father to show him they are thinking of him on Father's Day. ◆

Feast of
Our Lady of Guadalupe

The Feast of Our Lady of Guadalupe on December 12 commemorates the apparitions that Roman Catholics believe the Virgin Mary made in Mexico to an Aztec peasant with the Christian name of Juan Diego. Mexicans revere the Virgin of Guadalupe more than any other saint, as she is seen to have reached out to the native people of Mexico.

In the centuries following the Spanish conquest of Mexico, many Native Americans converted to Catholicism. The Catholicism that Native Americans practiced incorporated native beliefs, and Aztecs blended worship of their gods and goddesses with that of Catholic saints. However, Spanish influence had gutted the heart of Aztec religion, a cult of warfare and human sacrifice, and it had lost its focus. The appearance of the Virgin of Guadalupe to Juan Diego offered a new religious focus, and devotion to the Virgin flourished. Within several years, millions more Indians became baptized as Catholics in central Mexico.

According to legend, on December 9, 1531, Diego made his daily walk to mass, near what is now Mexico City. Hurrying over Tepeyac Hill he heard music and saw a cloud surrounded by many colors. A woman's voice called him to the top of the hill. There he saw a beautiful woman dressed in a decorated Aztec-style gown. Speaking in Diego's native language, the lady identified herself as the Virgin Mary and asked Juan to tell the bishop to build a church on that site. The lady called herself, in

"When he reached the summit, he saw a Lady, who was standing there and told him to come hither. Approaching her presence, he marveled greatly at her superhuman grandeur; her garments were shining like the sun; the cliff where she rested her feet, pierced with glitter, resembling an anklet of precious stones, and the earth sparkled like the rainbow. "

Narration of Juan Diego's vision by Antonio Valeriano, mid 1500s

123

On the Feast of Our Lady of Guadalupe, a highwire performer entertains the crowd gathered in the courtyard outside the new (left) and the old (right) cathedrals of Our Lady of Guadulupe in Mexico City.

Aztec, Tecoatlaxope, meaning "she will crush the serpent of stone." The Spanish version became Holy Mary of Guadalupe. Diego visited the bishop and told his story, but the bishop wanted proof. So Diego returned to the hill on December 12, and the lady directed him to roses blooming on the midwinter morning. He gathered the roses in his cloak and took them to the Bishop. When he opened his cloak, the fresh roses fell to the floor, and both men then saw an image of the lady imprinted inside Juan's heavy cloak. The Bishop believed Diego, and soon built a church on the site. In 1746 Our Lady of Guadalupe became the patron saint of New Spain, a region that reached from California to El Salvador. Pope Pius XII named Our Lady of Guadalupe the patroness of the Americas in 1945.

The Cathedral of Our Lady of Guadalupe in Mexico City is one of the most popular pilgrimage sites in the Western Hemisphere. The Feast of Our Lady of Guadalupe remains a religious occasion and is celebrated with prayer and devotions throughout Mexico and in parts of the southwestern United States. Guadalupe Day is one of Mexico's most important religious holidays. Processions of devotees parade in colorful Indian costumes to the church for mass.

In various parts of Mexico and New Mexico, in Hispanic villages as well as Native American pueblos, dancers called *matachines* celebrate the service of Our Lady of Guadalupe, performing on December 12 in front of or inside the local Catholic church. Groups of matachines each have a leader and two lines of six to twelve dancers. A girl dressed in white called La Malinche represents purity. A character called El Toro (The Bull) depicts evil, and a clownish character called El Abuelo (The Grandfather) adds comic relief and controls the pace of the dance. El Monarca (The Monarch) leads the dance. Dancers move to the music of fiddle and guitar, with an occasional accordionist, and shake gourd rattles in rhythm. They wear high decorative headdresses, kerchiefs on their faces, and colorful ribbons and aprons. The dance often terminates in a mock killing of El Toro, overcoming evil. "Los Matachines," as they are known in Spanish, have roots in Moorish Spain.

An old tradition in Arizona is the *velorio* (watch service) in which devotees set up an altar in someone's home and spend the night kneeling in prayer. They decorate the altar with white sheets, flowers, and a large picture of Our Lady of Guadalupe. The service begins on the eve of the holiday and lasts until dawn on the twelfth. Women recite prayers, sing Spanish hymns, and serve festive foods such as tamales.

As the Hispanic population throughout the United States has grown, Catholic churches in many areas celebrate Guadalupe Day. Many parishes hold special liturgies and feasts. A celebration may include an outdoor procession, a mass, and a dinner. Processions are led by members of the congregation carrying large banners of the image of Our Lady of Guadalupe, while everyone in attendance carries candles and recites the rosary. The green, white, and red colors of Mexico's flag and a huge banner of Our Lady of Guadalupe may decorate a parish hall where churchgoers enjoy an evening of dinner and dancing to mariachi music. Some churches organize groups of pilgrims to celebrate the feast day in Mexico City. ◆

As the Hispanic population throughout the United States has grown, Catholic churches in many areas celebrate Guadalupe Day.

Feast of Saint Francis of Assisi

October 4 is the Christian feast day of Saint Francis of Assisi. On that day or a day close to it, Roman Catholic priests and many Protestant ministers celebrate the saint's life by blessing animals in homes, at farms, in churches, or at community gatherings. The blessings commemorate the love of animals that Saint Francis was famous for.

Saint Francis was a man who became revered and legendary during his own brief life. He was born in medieval Assisi, Italy, in 1181 or 1182 as Giovanni Francesco Bernardone, the son of a wealthy merchant. Francis lived a comfortable life until he spent a year as a political prisoner after fighting in a battle between Assisi and Perugia. In prison, Francis suffered from a serious illness during which he began a religious conversion. When he returned to Assisi, in about 1205, Francis began helping lepers and restoring a church. By 1208 he was living a life of voluntary poverty in imitation of Jesus Christ. He preached, cared for outcasts, and lived in the woods. Francis soon attracted followers, and he formed the Franciscan order. He led his men to Rome to ask for papal approval and in 1210 Pope Innocent III approved the order. The group elected Francis as their superior. They maintained a small chapel in Assisi and lived as traveling preachers.

In 1225 Francis wrote "Canticle of the Sun," a poem praising the creation of God, in which he celebrated the beauty of "Brother Sun" and "Sister Earth." This poem added to the legend of Francis as a man so gentle that wild animals, particularly wolves and birds, would approach him. Francis died in 1226

"My little sisters, the birds, much bounden are ye unto God, your creator, and always in every place ought ye to praise him, for that he hath given you liberty to fly about everywhere, and hath also given you double and triple raiment; moreover he preserved your seed in the ark of Noah, that your race might not perish out of the world."

Saint Francis of Assisi, "Sermon to the Birds," c. 1220

On the Feast of Saint Francis of Assisi, people bring their pets (from mice to elephants) to be blessed at New York City's Cathedral of Saint John the Divine.

and was declared a saint by the Catholic church in 1228. The Franciscan order became one of the largest in the Catholic church, and included priests, nuns, and brothers. They dedicate their lives to teaching and caring for the poor and sick.

After his death, the church established a rite to bless animals in honor of Saint Francis. Through the centuries, Francis became a popular subject in art, often pictured surrounded by nature, animals, and little children. Pope John Paul II named

On the Feast of Saint Francis of Assisi, both Catholic and Episcopal churches in the United States host animal blessings that can be large, colorful, light-hearted events.

Francis as the patron saint of ecology in 1979 because of his respect for nature and love of animals.

Both Catholic and Episcopal churches are known in the United States for animal blessings that can be large, colorful, and lighthearted events. The service often includes a mass, special prayers, and a reading on creation from the book of Genesis of the Bible. The priest or minister then blesses the animals with holy water. At an annual service at the Cathedral of St. John the Divine in New York City, the feast is celebrated by a mass attended by up to 6,000 pet owners. After pets are blessed, the service ends with an exotic procession of creatures. In Washington, D.C., people bring real and stuffed animals to St. Patrick's Episcopal Church to be blessed.

Many Catholic elementary schools have students bring pets to school for the St. Francis blessing. Schools become noisy, joyful menageries of cats, dogs, birds, snakes, crabs, fish, turtles, iguanas, hamsters, chinchillas, and even horses or other farm animals. The priest usually asks the pet's name and then blesses it with holy water and a touch. The worship aims to encourage children to respect nature and practice responsible stewardship.

Some unique feast day events include churches teaming up with groups such as the Society for the Prevention of Cruelty to Animals to offer pets for adoption at a blessing ceremony or to have a blessing at an animal shelter. Pet stores often join the festivities, and some churches give special blessings for sick and aged animals. Near St. Louis, Missouri, a wolf sanctuary hosts an annual open house for Saint Francis Day.

In Italy, where the tradition of animal blessings started, many farmers have their animals blessed. Priests may even bless the machinery of the farmers. The town of Assisi, a destination for many pilgrims, especially celebrates the feast of Saint Francis. The town is lit up by oil lamps, and a special blessing by a representative of the pope takes place. Many people visit the great Basilica of St. Francis with its famous frescoes, one of which depicts Saint Francis preaching to the birds. ◆

Fiestas in Latin America

LATIN AMERICA ● VARIOUS DATES

Fiesta is a Spanish term whose meaning ranges from private celebrations to nationwide fetes, from saint-day parties to the commemoration of national independence. Community holidays, especially civic and religious celebrations, serve as an occasion for social interaction, political negotiation, historical lessons, and turning-the-world-upside-down mimicry. Above all, fiestas serve as an occasion for the enjoyment of family, friends, compatriots, and **coreligionists**. The most dramatic Latin American celebrations contain a popular element—drawn from the indigenous peoples, blacks, mixed-ethnic groups, and European traditions—that often overwhelms official, sanctioned affairs. Carnival, for example, has become a Brazilian cultural expression that long ago surpassed in popularity and participants the Ash Wednesday initiation of Roman Catholicism's Lenten period.

coreligionists: people who adhere to the same religion.

One description of fiestas in Latin America classifies them as civic, religious, and commercial holidays. Commemoration of independence serves generally as the most significant holiday in each of the region's nations (see the following list), although it might be joined by an additional political anniversary. Two examples of the latter are the Cinco de Mayo holiday that celebrates the victory of the Mexican army over invading French troops (May 5, 1867), and July 26, which marks Fidel Castro's first (and unsuccessful) revolutionary effort in 1953 to seize power in Cuba, provided the name of his **guerrilla** movement, and commemorates his fellow rebels who died in the effort.

guerrilla warfare: war carried out by irregular harassment, ambushes, and small-scale attacks.

Independence Fiestas

Haiti	January 1
Dominican Republic	February 27
Paraguay	May 14–15
Cuba	May 17
Venezuela	July 5
Argentina	July 9
Colombia	July 20
Peru	July 28
Bolivia	August 6
Ecuador	August 10
Uruguay	August 25
Brazil	September 7
Costa Rica	September 15
El Salvador	September 15
Guatemala	September 15
Honduras	September 15
Nicaragua	September 15
Mexico	September 15–16
Chile	September 18
Panama	November 3

acculturation: adaptation to the ways of life of another culture.

Because Roman Catholicism served as one instrument of conquest and **acculturation** in Latin America, church holidays of this religion have the most general participation. Jewish, Protestant, and African-derived religious holidays are also celebrated throughout the region. The most impressive celebrations during the colonial years occurred on Corpus Christi and Holy Week, climaxing with Easter services. In the last century the Christmas holiday has emerged as more popular, with the suppression of many public aspects of the Corpus Christi and Holy Week festivals. In the Antilles, the Caribbean, and Brazil, Carnival has generally emerged as one of the most significant holidays. Of special importance throughout Latin America are the celebrations of the manifestations of virgins and saints. The best-known and most widely celebrated of these are the Virgin of Guadalupe, the patron of Mexico, on December 12, and Santa Rosa de Lima, the first saint of South America, on August 30. Other feasts mark the church's holy days of obligation. Such fiestas include the Feast of Christ of Esquipulas, called the Black Christ festival, in Guatemala (January 15) and the festival of Santiago (Saint James the Greater), the patron saint of Chile (July 25).

Commercial and special fiestas include those holidays created to honor special groups, such as Mother's Day and Teacher's Day. Others are attempts to revive, expand, and popularize celebrations to promote tourism. For example, Mexico's Day of the Dead fiestas in Pátzcuaro, Michoacán, resulted from the deliberate plans of the national tourism department. Carnival in several Caribbean nations today has taken on the character of a spectacle intended primarily for tourists. However commercial these events, they demonstrate what government officials want outsiders to recognize as typical of their culture.

Associated with most Latin American fiestas are special customs, artifacts, foods, band music, dancing, and fireworks. Gifts have become associated with special holidays—helmets at Corpus Christi, *matracas* (rattles) during Holy Week, and candy skulls at the Day of the Dead. Holiday cuisine ranges from special meals (for example, *chiles en nogada*, a green, stuffed chili pepper in a white cream sauce with red pomegranate seeds that displays the colors of the national flag for Mexican Independence Day), to preparations for religious feasts (for example, the Virgin's Tears, made from beet juice, for Holy Week; special egg-yolk bread made for the Day of the Dead; Three Kings Bread, a kind of sweet bread eaten on January 6 that has a ring baked in it to bring good luck to the person who finds it), to special beverages for holidays (Noche Buena beer brewed only during the Christmas holidays; *cuba libre*, a rum-and-cola drink, for national independence day; *chicha*, hard cider made from apples or grapes; and wine for Chile's major holidays).

The parades and processions often display visual lessons in social prominence and hierarchy through the order of march, the inclusion of different groups, and the nature of floats. Individuals find it necessary to participate as members of a residential, occupational, ethnic, or religious group. Fiesta organization in the past reflected these same groupings, with perhaps the religious confraternities (*cofradías*) dominant in the colonial years, occupational and ethnic associations slightly superior in the nineteenth century, and residential groups emerging as more important in the twentieth century. Displaying these groups during fiestas, while portraying social hierarchy, demonstrates and reaffirms the solidarity of the society.

Certain gifts have become associated with particular fiestas: helmets at Corpus Christi, *maracas* (rattles) during Holy Week, and candy skulls on the Day of the Dead.

Fiestas also mark individual rites of passage, including birth, christening, saint day, *quinceañera* (fifteenth birthday for girls), marriage, and death. The nature of these fiestas varies from family to family and differs by religion. Nevertheless, the nature of the family holiday, its proper celebration, remains the province primarily of the leading (or centralizing) woman. ◆

Flag Day

On June 14, 1777, the Continental Congress approved a flag for the newly born United States, to replace the British Grand Union flag and the flags of the individual colonies. According to legend, the first flag was designed and sewn by Philadelphia seamstress Betsy Ross at the personal request of George Washington. There is little evidence that this story is true, although Ross was the official seamstress for the Continental Navy and perhaps sewed one of the sample designs.

The Congress established this pattern: 13 alternating red and white stripes, each representing one of the original states; plus 13 white stars representing the states' union, set in a blue background symbolizing the sky. Originally a new star and stripe were added for each new state, but the number of states grew so large that this design proved impossible. So the stripes were reduced to the original 13, and a new star was added for each new state on the Fourth of July following its admission. (The fiftieth star, for Hawaii, was added to the flag in 1960.)

In 1877 the one-hundredth anniversary of the flag's adoption, Congress declared that the flag should be flown over all public buildings on June 14. But there was no annual national holiday to honor the flag until 1916, when President Woodrow Wilson issued a proclamation establishing Flag Day as an annual day of observance. In 1949 President Harry S Truman signed the National Flag Day Bill, which officially established June 14 as Flag Day. With the memory of World War II still vivid, Truman declared that June 14 of each year should be des-

1777 On June 14 the Continental Congress adopts the stars and stripes as the United States national flag.

1877 The U.S. Congress declares that the flag shall be flown on all public buildings on June 14 to commemorate the 100th anniversary of the flag's adoption.

1916 President Woodrow Wilson proclaims Flag Day an annual national observance.

1949 President Truman signs the National Flag Day Bill, officially establishing June 14 as Flag Day.

Displaying the Flag

Many Americans express their patriotism on Flag Day by flying the national flag. The United States Flag Code, established in 1923, adopted by Congress in 1942, and amended many times, prescribes a detailed set of rules for handling and displaying the flag. The code does not impose penalties for not following these rules however.

According to the code, the flag can be displayed on any day of the year, but especially on certain designated holidays, including New Year's Day, Armed Forces Day, Flag Day, Mother's Day, Memorial Day, Independence Day, Labor Day, Veterans Day, and Thanksgiving Day. The flag should be displayed on or near the main building of any public institution, post office, public school, and polling place. The code calls for displaying the flag in public only from sunrise to sunset; if flown at night the flag should be lighted. The flag should not be flown during inclement weather, unless it is an all-weather flag. The flag should be hoisted briskly and lowered slowly. When flags of cities, states, or organization are flown on the same staff, the U.S. flag must be at the top. Flags of other countries should be flown on separate staffs at the same height as the U.S. flag. The flag should never be displayed with the blue field down, except as a signal of distress or danger. The flag should never touch anything beneath it, such as the ground, the floor, water, or merchandise. The flag may cover a casket, in which case the blue field should be over the deceased's left shoulder, near the head and heart; the flag should be removed before burial. The flag should never be used to cover or hold objects, and it should never be used for advertising or promotional purposes. When a flag becomes badly weathered or damaged, it should be destroyed in a dignified way, preferably by burning.

ignated a national day for displaying the flag on all government buildings, and for the public to acknowledge the anniversary of its adoption.

Flag Day is not a legal holiday, except in Pennsylvania where the Continental Congress met in 1777. Because the United States flag can be displayed by private citizens as well as the government, many people commemorate the day by placing flags outside of their homes. In 1966 Congress asked the president to proclaim the week of June 14 as National Flag Week and to encourage people to display flags for the entire week. Flag-raising ceremonies, parades, band concerts, and programs explaining flag etiquette also are common.

In 1980 a pause to recite the Pledge of Allegiance was held at the Star-Spangled Banner Flag House in Baltimore (where the flag was sewn that flew over Fort McHenry during an 1814 battle with the British, inspiring Francis Scott Key to write the national anthem). This tradition spread, and in 1985 President

Reagan signed a law urging people to recite the Pledge of Allegiance at 7:00 P.M. on June 14. At this time, the Pledge also is recited at national ceremonies held at the Fort McHenry National Monument and Historic Shrine. In addition to this recitation, the national ceremonies include a band concert, a presidential address, a display by precision jets, and fireworks.

Several other countries commemorate their own flags with a holiday, including Argentina (June 20), Australia (September 3), Canada (February 15), Denmark (June 15), Finland (May 19), Haiti (May 18), Panama (November 4), Paraguay (May 14), and Sweden (June 6). As in the United States, these celebrations usually include parades, flag raisings, and other patriotic ceremonies. ◆

An enormous United States flag covers the lawn in front of the Washington Monument in Washington, D.C., on Flag Day 1992.

Great American Smokeout

UNITED STATES ● THIRD THURSDAY IN NOVEMBER

Each third Thursday of November, smokers all over the United States attempt to quit smoking for at least twenty-four hours. On that day, the American Cancer Society (ACS) sponsors the Great American Smokeout (GASO). The society has hosted this day since 1977 to raise the awareness of smokers of the benefits of quitting smoking. According to the ACS, 390,000 American die from the effects of smoking each year.

American Indians first smoked tobacco during religious ceremonies, but Europeans picked it up as a habitual practice in the 1500s. Physicians warned of health risks from tobacco as early as the 1500s, but cigarettes were not widespread until the late 1880s, when machinery allowed them to be mass produced. The taboos against women smoking soon disappeared, and the number of women smokers rose through the mid-1900s. Popular images often portrayed smoking as glamorous and sophisticated. This image began to change in the 1960s when scientific research showed that tobacco, especially cigarette smoking, could cause lung cancer, heart disease, and other diseases. In 1964 the Surgeon General of the United States released a landmark report warning of the dangers of smoking. At that time, 53 percent of adult American men smoked and 32 percent of women did. The surgeon general's report marked a major turning point in attitudes about smoking. Many smokers began trying to quit, which could be difficult due to the addictive nature of nicotine, the active ingredient in tobacco.

In 1977 the ACS began sponsoring the Smokeout, which had sprouted up in various forms in several areas of the country. The day was promoted with a number of lighthearted activities as well as many promotional materials such as posters, flyers, and buttons. The ACS also offers suggestions on nonsmoking alternatives activities. Many people sign a pledge to give up smoking. Quitters are encouraged to invite a friend to "adopt" them to help them as they recover from their nicotine addiction. Businesses, hospitals, clinics, public welfare agencies, and schools became involved in the GASO. By the early 1990s, the numbers of smokers had dropped to 28 percent of men and 24 percent of women. The decline in smoking was a great American success story. However, by the late 1990s, cigarettes were still responsible for the death of more Americans than AIDS, alcohol, car accidents, murders, suicides, drugs, and fires combined.

In 1998 the Great American Smokeout focused on encouraging children and adolescents never to start using tobacco.

In 1997 the U.S. Centers for Disease Control and Prevention's (CDC) issued a report on the impact of the Great American Smokeout of 1996. The 1996 promotion for the GASO had included advertisements in magazines, newspapers, and television that reached an estimated 122 million adults. The percentage of smokers who either quit or reduced smoking for one day increased from 18 percent in 1995 to 26 percent in 1996. The CDC report concluded that advertisements to promote quitting smoking increased quitting attempts.

Through the years, health professionals became most concerned about smoking among adolescents. About 90 percent of all new smokers are age eighteen and younger, and the average smoker begins at age thirteen. Once a teenager starts smoking, he or she is likely to become addicted, giving tobacco companies a customer for life. In 1998 the Great American Smokeout focused on encouraging children and adolescents never to start using tobacco. The theme for the year was "You Smoke You Choke," and the day included a Great American Smoke-Scream. On November 19, 1998, kids across the nation gathered in their schools to scream out together against smoking.

The ACS also began targeting cigar smoking, which had shot up by 133 percent between 1989 and 1993. This increase stemmed from cigar manufacturers' marketing efforts that included celebrity endorsements of cigars and the portrayal of cigars as glamorous. Many people seemed unaware that cigar smoking causes cancers of the larynx, oral cavity, esophagus, and lungs.

In the late 1990s, tobacco companies became the target of numerous lawsuits by individuals and state governments attempting to recover money spent on health care costs from smoking-related illnesses. In addition, nonsmoking policies at many public facilities and private companies created a strong antismoking atmosphere in the United States. Some supporters of smoking protested against the antismoking movement. These people claimed that court cases against tobacco companies aimed to eliminate personal choice and responsibility. They sought to defend smokers' rights and to fight bans against smoking. They said smoking was an individual choice involving the right to control one's own body. ◆

Groundhog Day

Groundhog Day is one of the most lighthearted United States holidays. According to tradition, every year on February 2 the groundhog awakes from its winter **hibernation** and crawls out of its underground burrow. If the sun is shining and the groundhog sees its shadow, it becomes frightened and runs back into its burrow, thereby predicting six more weeks of winter. If the day is cloudy and the groundhog does not see its shadow, it stays outside and an early spring is predicted. According to a custom that began in 1887, a groundhog known as "Punxsutawney Phil," who resides in Punxsutawney, Pennsylvania, emerges from his den every year on Groundhog Day. An elaborate ceremony in Punxsutawney accompanies the groundhog's awakening, and journalists from around the world cover Punxsutawney Phil's forecast.

hibernation: an inactive state that some wild animals enter during the winter.

Despite its playful nature today, Groundhog Day is rooted in serious rituals from several cultures. For centuries, February 2 has been observed on the Christian calendar as Candlemas Day, the day when Mary was purified and Jesus was presented at the temple forty days after his birth. Candlemas was celebrated as early as the fourth century; a ceremonial lighting of candles is traditional. According to old Scottish and German proverbs, the weather on Candlemas predicts when spring will arrive. February 1 is Saint Bridget's Day in Ireland; on that date a hedgehog looks for his shadow. This holiday grew out of Imbolc, a pagan celebration marking the arrival of spring that honored Brigit, a Celtic goddess. The ancient Romans also celebrated the coming of spring in early February, and might have

Phil, the famous
goundhog from
Punxsutawney,
Pennsylvania, gives his
forecast to city officials
on Groundhog Day.

imported this ritual to Ireland. Before the modern (Gregorian) calendar was adopted, these holidays fell in mid-February, when farmers prepared to plant crops in many climates.

In Germany and France, the tradition was to watch for hibernating bears to awaken; after settlements spread and the number of bears dropped, the hedgehog became the symbol of approaching spring. When Germans popularly known as the "Pennsylvania Dutch" settled in Pennsylvania, they brought their tradition along, but since there were no hedgehogs in the area they substituted the similar-looking groundhog. The Delaware tribe in the eastern United States had a creation story in which hibernating animals emerged as human beings. They considered "Wojak" or "Oijik" to be the ancestor of their tribe; this being was the origin of the English word "woodchuck."

On February 2, 1886, the editor of the newspaper the *Punxsutawney Spirit*, Clymer Freas, published a humorous announcement that the groundhog had not seen his shadow. By February 2, 1887, Freas had proclaimed a group of local hunters the "Punxsutawney Groundhog Club," and they made the first trek to Gobbler's Knob, where the groundhog supposedly resided. Soon the groundhog had been given a name, Punxsutawney Phil, and an elaborate title, "The Seer of Seers, Sage of Sages, **Prognosticator** of Prognosticators, and Weather Prophet Extraordinary."

prognosticator: someone who predicts the future.

Other local residents helped to expand the legend as the years passed. Punxsutawney proclaimed itself the "Weather Capital of the World." Dr. Frank Lorenzo, who headed the Groundhog Club for almost fifty years, chartered trains to bring notables from around Pennsylvania to participate in the annual celebration. After Lorenzo died in 1952, his successor, Sam Light, decided that the dignitaries who announced Phil's predictions, called the Inner Circle, should wear silk tophats and formal cutaway coats. Light also managed to get television coverage for the event.

By the 1990s, the Punxsutawney Groundhog Day festivities had become a major tourist attraction and received extensive media attention. In 1993 the film *Groundhog Day* starring Bill Murray recreated the holiday events at Gobbler's Knob. Because Punxsutawney lacked major highway access, the film was shot in Woodstock, Illinois, which in turn lacked Pennsylvania's hills; Gobbler's Knob was replaced by a town square.

According to his handler, the Phil who participated in the 1998 ceremony weighed fifteen pounds and enjoyed eating dog food. The actual ceremony involves transferring Phil from his usual home, an air-conditioned enclosure in the children's library of Punxsutawney's Civic Center, to Gobbler's Knob. There he waits in a heated burrow underneath an artificial tree stump placed on a stage. There is an elaborate setup of lighting and wiring for television cameras, plus a public address system. Around 7:30 A.M. on February 2, Phil is pulled from his burrow by his handler to make his prediction, which is announced in a formally worded proclamation by the head of the Inner Circle. The "prediction" is written in advance of the event by members of the Inner Circle.

Between 1887 and 1998 Punxsutawney Phil saw his shadow 89 times and did not see it 13 times; there is no record for nine years. His predictions have been accurate less than 40 percent of the time.

Between 1887 and 1998 Phil saw his shadow eighty-nine times and did not see it thirteen times (there is no record for nine years). His predictions have been accurate less than 40 percent of the time. Nevertheless, the event remains popular; Phil has appeared on the Oprah Winfrey television program and at the White House, and his prediction is read into the Congressional Record. In 1998 Phil made his debut appearance on the Internet. ◆

Guy Fawkes Day

Guy Fawkes
was a Roman
Catholic convert
who became
involved in con-
spiring to blow
up Britain's
Houses of
Parliament in
revenge for
repressive penal
laws against
Roman
Catholics.

Jesuits: a Roman
Catholic order of priests
devoted to missionary and
educational work.

The British Parliament established November 5 as a national day of thanksgiving in 1606 to commemorate the foiling of what has come to be known as the Gunpowder Plot. A group of Catholic conspirators planned to blow up the king and the houses of Lords and Commons on the opening day of Parliament, November 5, 1605. The plot was exposed when one of the conspirators sent a letter warning a Catholic relative not to attend Parliament on the opening day, and the letter was intercepted. Thirty-six barrels of gunpowder were discovered hidden under wood and coal in a cellar beneath the House of Lords. Guy Fawkes (1570–1606) was not the ringleader, but he was caught after someone tipped off the government, and his was among the severed heads displayed on London Bridge.

Fawkes, a convert to Roman Catholicism, became involved with Robert Catesby and others conspiring to blow up the Houses of Parliament in revenge for repressive penal laws against Roman Catholics and for King James's deportation of **Jesuits** from England. Fawkes was arrested upon entering the cellar of the House of Lords on the night of November 4–5, 1605. Under torture he revealed the names of his fellow conspirators; the others were either seized and killed on the spot or imprisoned and executed. On January 31, 1606, Fawkes and seven others were beheaded; their heads were displayed along London Bridge as an example for any other would-be conspirators. The plot's discovery only worsened conditions for English Catholics.

Although the holiday is essentially English, in the nearly four hundred years since its establishment Guy Fawkes Day has spread all around the former British Empire. People in towns and villages prepare for Guy Fawkes Day and Bonfire Night by building up wood for a great bonfire—usually trying to outdo last year's best—and making **effigies**, or "guys," that will be tossed into the bonfire on Guy Fawkes night. For several days before the bonfire, the "guys" are displayed in the street, or may be carried by children as they go along the streets begging passersby, "a penny for the guy." (It's best to give more than a penny.) The begging is an old tradition, so police tend to look the other way. The money usually goes straight to the fireworks stand, for better lights and noise at the bonfire. The children compete with rhymes, and in some towns they can't expect a penny if they don't say it right from beginning to end. The following rhyme was recorded in Christchurch, New Zealand, in 1920:

effigy: a crude representation of a despised person.

> Please to remember the fifth of November,
> The gunpowder treason and plot.
> I see no reason why the gunpowder treason
> Should ever be forgot.
> Four and twenty barrels lain down below,
> Blow old England overflow.
> Happy was the night, happy was the day,
> See old Guy Fawkes going to his den
> With a dark lantern and a candle in his hand.
> Get out! Get out! you dirty ole man!
> Holla, Holla, boys, make the bells ring.
> Holla, Holla, boys, God Save the King.
> A pound of cheese to choke him,
> A bottle of beer to wash it down,
> A jolly good fire to roast him.
> Christmas is coming, the pigs are getting fat,
> Please put a penny in the old man's hat.
> If you haven't got a penny, a **hapenny** will do.
> If you haven't got a hapenny, God Bless You.

hapenny: a British half-penny coin.

One account of the chanting for pennies reports adults tossing hot pennies to the children in the streets below. Some mischievous souls would heat the pennies over a fire and toss them down, mixed with unheated coins, and laugh as the boys yelped with surprise, but kept grabbing for the money anyway.

The bonfire is a universal custom—one might even call it a human trait—used for various ceremonial purposes, that probably dates back to life in the caves. The English word *bonfire* comes from the Middle English *bone fire*, meaning exactly that: bones were often burned in great fires, as were wood, effigies, and even, in more barbarous times, human sacrifices.

The practice of burning the effigies began on the very first Guy Fawkes Day, in 1606, but for the first two hundred years the figure burned was not an effigy of Guy Fawkes, but of the Pope. It was around 1800 that people began burning effigies of Guy Fawkes, but even today some communities still burn likenesses of the Pope along with the guy.

> **Guy Fawkes Day was celebrated widely in British settlements in colonial American, from New England to the Carolinas.**

Guy Fawkes Day was celebrated widely in British settlements in colonial America, from New England to the Carolinas. In addition to effigies of Guy Fawkes and the Pope, American celebrants often fashioned likenesses of certain despised lords and governors, and usually the Devil, all of whom were thrown to the flames. But first, in what must have been a carnival-like atmosphere, the young men of the town would carry the effigies through the streets on a platform or rolling stage, and stop at the houses of prominent citizens and chant a rhyme, such as this one reported in Newburyport, Massachusetts, before 1775:

> God by his grace he did prevent
> To save both king and parliament.
> Happy the man, and happy the day,
> That catched Guy Fawkes in the middle of his play.
> . . . .
> Here is the pope that we have got,
> The whole promoter of the plot.
> We'll stick a pitchfork in his back
> And throw him in the fire.

The American colonists began leaving the Pope out of the bonfires around 1775, as the American Revolution was getting underway. Being at war with Britain, Americans needed good relations with the French, who, being predominantly Catholic, could not find much to appreciate in the mocking and burning of the Pope.

It seems to be a characteristic of festivals with political origins that, over time, the initial reasons for the celebration become obscured or forgotten. Is Guy Fawkes Day a celebration of patriotism or of **anarchy**? Perhaps the passage of time has obscured the original reason for the holiday—or maybe loyalty to the crown isn't what it used to be—for some of the young in England have innocently wondered whether they are celebrating the plot's failure, or honoring the conspirators' attempt to bring down the government. ◆

anarchy: a state of law-lessness.

Halloween

BRITAIN, IRELAND, AND NORTH AMERICA ● OCTOBER 31

H alloween, or All Hallows Eve, is a festival celebrated on October 31, the evening prior to the Christian Feast of All Saints (All Saints' Day). Halloween is the name for the eve of Samhain, a celebration marking the beginning of winter as well as the first day of the New Year within the ancient Celtic culture of the British Isles. The time of Samhain consisted of the eve of the feast and the day itself (October 31 and November 1). This event was a crucial seam in the social and religious fabric of the Celtic year, and the eve of Samhain set the tone for the annual celebration as a threatening, fantastic, mysterious rite of passage to a new year.

pastoral: of the country-side.

The religious beliefs of the Celts emphasized **pastoral** deities, and Celtic festivals stressed seasonal transitions. Beltene, the beginning of summer, was a holiday celebrated at the end of April and the beginning of May. Samhain signaled the commencement of winter and, together with Beltene, divided the year into cold and hot seasons. Samhain marked the end of preparations for winter, when flocks and herds had been secured and harvested crops had been stored.

The eve of this festival brought with it another kind of harvest. On this occasion, it was believed that a gathering of supernatural forces occurred as during no other period of the year. The eve and day of Samhain were characterized as a time when the barriers between the human and supernatural worlds were broken. Otherworldly entities, such as the souls of the dead, were able to visit earthly inhabitants, and humans could take the opportunity to penetrate the domains of the gods and

supernatural creatures. Fiery tributes and sacrifices of animals, crops, and possibly human beings were made to appease supernatural powers who controlled the fertility of the land. Not a festival honoring any particular Celtic deity, Samhain acknowledged the entire spectrum of nonhuman forces that roamed the earth during that period.

Children dress in scary costumes to go trick-or-treating on Halloween.

Given the upheaval of normal human activities and expectations on the eve and day of Samhain, it was also thought to be an especially propitious time for ascertaining information about the future course of one's life. Various methods of **divination** were used by individuals attempting to discover their fortunes, good or ill, and to foretell events such as marriage, sickness, or death.

divination: fortune-telling.

Samhain remained a popular festival among the Celtic people throughout the christianization of Great Britain. The British church attempted to divert this interest in pagan customs by adding a Christian celebration to the calendar on the same date as Samhain. The Christian festival, the Feast of All Saints, commemorates the known and unknown saints of the Christian religion just as Samhain had acknowledged and paid tribute to the Celtic deities. The eve of the Celtic festival was also christianized, becoming the Vigil of All Saints or Allhallows Eve (with special offices existing in both the Anglican and Roman churches). The medieval British commemoration of All Saints' Day may have prompted the universal celebration of this feast throughout the Christian church.

The customs of Samhain survived independently of the Christian holy day. Gradually, the eve of Allhallows (Halloween) lost much of its Celtic religious significance for the masses, and it became a secular observance, although many traditionally Celtic ideas continued to be associated with the evening. Divination activities remained a popular practice. Adults, dressed in fantastic disguises and masks, imitated supernatural beings and visited homes where occupants would offer tributes of food and drink to them. A fear of **nocturnal** creatures, such as bats and owls, persisted, since these animals were believed to communicate with the spirits of the dead.

nocturnal: active at night.

Halloween was celebrated only in the Celtic areas of Great Britain: Ireland, Scotland, Wales, and northern rural England. In non-Celtic England, many of the customs of Halloween were assimilated into a commemorative festival that arose in the seventeenth century as the celebration of Guy Fawkes Day (November 5). English Protestant settlers in the New World did not bring the custom of Halloween with them. Irish and Scottish immigrants introduced scattered Allhallows Eve observances to America, but it was only in the years after the massive immigration of the Irish to the United States during the potato famine (1845–46) that Halloween became a national event.

Modern Halloween activities have centered on mischief making and masquerading in costumes, often resembling otherworldly characters. Folk customs, now treated as games (such as bobbing for apples), have continued from the various divination practices of the ancient celebrants of this occasion. Supernatural figures (such as the ghost, the witch, the vampire, the devil) play a key role in supplying an aura of the mysterious to the evening, whether or not they originally had an association with the festival. Children are particularly susceptible to the imagery of Halloween, as can be seen in their fascination with the demonic likeness of a carved and illuminated pumpkin, known as the jack-o'-lantern. In recent times, children have taken up the practice of dressing in Halloween costumes and visiting homes in search of edible and monetary treats, lightly

Folk customs such as bobbing for apples derive from serious divination practices of the ancient celebrants of Halloween.

threatening to play a trick on the owner if a treat is not produced. There also has been renewed interest in Halloween as a
time when adults can also cross cultural boundaries and shed
their identities by indulging in an uninhibited evening of frivolity. Thus, the basic Celtic quality of the festival as an evening of
annual escape from normal realities and expectations has
remained into the twentieth century. ◆

A father helps his
daughter carve
jack-o'-lanterns on
Halloween.

Hanukkah

JEWISH ● KISLEV

anukkah, also spelled Hannuka or Chanuka, is the Jewish winter festival that falls on the twenty-fifth of the month of Kislev (usually December) and lasts for eight days. The Hebrew word *hanukkah* means *dedication*. It celebrates the victory of the Jewish forces led by Judah Maccabee over the forces of the Syrian tyrant Antiochus after a three-year battle in the second century B.C.E.

The major sources on the festival's origin are two **apocryphal** books, 1 Maccabees and 2 Maccabees. It is stated there that the altar in the Temple in Jerusalem was rededicated and the festival of eight days introduced because during the war with the Syrians the Jews were unable to celebrate the eight-day festival of Sukkot. Thus in the earliest period there is no reference to Hanukkah as a feast of lights. That it became such is due to the **Talmudic** legend that the Maccabees found only one small jar of oil for the kindling of the *menorah* (candelabrum) in the Temple. This was sealed with the seal of the high priest but contained only sufficient oil to burn for a single night. By a miracle the oil lasted for eight nights. It was consequently ordained that lights be kindled on the eight nights of Hanukkah. However, it is stated in the Talmud that two Jewish groups, the Shammaites and Hillelites, at the beginning of the present era, debated whether the lights were to be kindled in descending order (eight the first night, seven the second, etc.) or in ascending order (one the first night, two the second, etc.). If this statement is historically correct, it demonstrates either that the legend of the oil was already known at that time or

apocryphal: not included in the Jewish Old Testament.

Talmudic: relating to the Talmud, a collection of books containing Jewish law.

150

Potato Latkes for Hanukkah

According to the Talmud, when Jewish forces entered the Temple in Jerusalem after defeating the Syrians in 165 B.C.E., they found only one small jar of oil. The jar held enough fuel to light the Temple lamp for one day, but the oil lasted for eight days. Jewish families eat foods fried in oil on Hanukkah to commemorate this miracle. Fried potato pancakes called latkes are a Hanukkah favorite.

4 large potatoes	1/4 cup matzo meal or flour
1 teaspoon lemon juice	2 teaspoons salt
1 large onion, chopped	1/4 teaspoon pepper
2 large eggs, lightly beaten	About 1/2 cup vegetable oil

Peel the potatoes and grate them. Squeeze the grated potatoes by handfuls to get rid of excess liquid. Place potatoes in a bowl and mix in the lemon juice. Combine the chopped onion, eggs, matzo meal, salt, and pepper and mix well. Add to potatoes. Heat oil in a skillet until very hot. Drop potato mixture into hot oil a tablespoon at a time and fry until brown on both sides. Remove from pan and drain on paper towels. Serve hot with sour cream and apple sauce.

---

that, at least, there was an association of Hanukkah and light even at this early period.

According to some historians, the origin of the festival is to be found in pagan festivals of light in midwinter. The prayers for Hanukkah refer only to the victory, but in practice the kindling of the lights is the main feature of the festival.

It has long been the custom for each member of the household to kindle the Hanukkah lights in an eight-branched candelabrum frequently called a *menorah* (though the *menorah* in the Temple had only seven branches) but nowadays also known as a *hanukkiyyah*. The lights are kindled in the synagogue as well as in the home. The older practice was to use only olive oil, and this is still customary among the more pious, but the majority of Jews use candles for the Hanukkah lights. Rabbinical authorities have discussed whether electric lights may be used for this purpose, the consensus being to permit them. One light is kindled on the first night, two on the second night, three on the third night, and so on until all eight are lit. In order to avoid lighting the candles one from the other, an additional candle known as the *shammash* (retainer) is used to light the others. A declaration is recited:

We kindle these lights on account of the miracles, the deliverances, and the wonders which thou didst work for our ancestors, by means of thy holy priests. During all the eight days of Hanukkah these lights are sacred, neither is it permitted to make any profane use of them; but we are only to look at them, in order that we may give thanks unto thy name for thy miracles, deliverances, and wonders.

A popular Hanukkah hymn is *Maoz tsur* (O Fortress Rock), sung to a familiar melody said to have been originally that of a German drinking song.

A Jewish family lights a menorah on Hanukkah.

Medieval Jewish thinkers understood the Hanukkah lights as representing spiritual illumination. The festival is a time for intensive study of the **Torah** as well as for almsgiving. Hanukkah is consequently treated as a more "spiritual" festival than the boisterous Purim, so that although fasting is forbidden on Hanukkah, there is no special festive meal. The Torah is read on each day of the festival; the passages chosen are from the account of the gifts brought by the princes at the dedication of the **Tabernacle** and the command to kindle the light of the *menorah*. The prophetic reading on the sabbath of Hanukkah is from the vision of the *menorah* seen by the prophet Zechariah. An addition to each of the daily prayers thanks God for delivering the strong into the hands of the weak, the many into the hands of the few, the impure into the hands of the pure, and the wicked into the hands of the righteous.

It is nowadays customary for Hanukkah presents to be given to children. This practice is found in none of the early sources and seems certain to have been introduced to offset the giving of Christmas presents at this season of the year.

Children and some adults play a game with a spinning top (dreidel) on each side of which is a different letter representing a move in the game. These letters are the initial letters of the Hebrew words making up the sentence "A great miracle happened there." To the consternation of the more conventional rabbis, card playing is often indulged in on Hanukkah.

The Talmudic rabbis stress the need for proclaiming the miracle by kindling the Hanukkah lights outside the door of the home, but eventually this practice was discouraged because it could be misinterpreted by non-Jews as a desire to demonstrate Jewish reluctance to live among their gentile neighbors. The less obtrusive practice of kindling the lights near the door but inside the home became the norm. In modern Israel it is far from unusual to see a huge Hanukkah candelabra on top of public buildings and synagogues. ◆

Torah: the first five books of the Old Testament; the body of wisdom and law containing sacred Jewish writings and oral tradition.

Tabernacle: a sanctuary used by the Israelites during the Exodus.

Hiroshima Peace Day

JAPAN ● AUGUST 6

Hiroshima Peace Day (also called Atomic Bomb Day) is day of prayer and memorial services in Japan. It is observed on August 6, the anniversary of the dropping of the atomic bomb on Hiroshima in 1945 during World War II. On this day, the Japanese people remember and pray for those killed by the atomic blast and its deadly radiation, and they offer prayers for world peace. The ceremony has been held every year since 1947 in Peace Memorial Park in Hiroshima.

Peace Memorial Park is located at the hypocenter of the bomb explosion, the area on the ground directly below where the bomb exploded. The bomb, called "Little Boy," was detonated about 2,000 feet (600 meters) above Hiroshima at 8:15 A.M. on August 6 (August 5 in the United States), 1945. It instantly killed from 70,000 to 100,000 people and incinerated about five square miles (thirteen square kilometers) of the city. Thousands more died afterward from injuries sustained in the blast or from exposure to radiation. The only building in Hiroshima to survive the destructive fire of the bomb was what is now called the Atomic Bomb Dome, the former Prefectural Industrial Promotion Hall, a building made of reinforced concrete. Today its burned-out shell stands as a symbol of the world peace movement.

After a second atomic bomb was dropped on Nagasaki on August 9, Japan surrendered on August 14 and formally signed the official statement of surrender on September 2, 1945, bringing an end to World War II. The people of Japan then began the process of rebuilding their cities destroyed during the war.

"At this 50th anniversary of the end of World War II, it is important to look at the stark reality of war in terms of both aggrieved and aggriever so as to develop a common understanding of history."

Takashi Hiraoka, mayor of Hiroshima, 1995

A mother and daughter stand in Hiroshima's Peace Memorial Park beside a monument to Sadako, who died of leukemia in 1955 after folding hundreds of paper cranes. Today, people lay long strings of paper cranes at Sadako's monument.

The survivors in Hiroshima decided to rebuild their city as a place of tranquility with many flowers and trees, and they constructed the peace park near the epicenter of the blast.

Every year on Hiroshima Peace Day, the people of Hiroshima pause at 8:15 A.M. and pray for the atomic bomb victims. Survivors and families of victims later gather at the peace park and leave offerings of flowers and water before an altar in the park. Children come to the park and leave paper cranes on

"*Memory is where past and future meet. Respectfully learning the lessons of the past, we want to impress the misery of war and the atomic bombing on the generations of younger people who will be tomorrow's leaders.*"
Takashi Hiraoka, mayor of Hiroshima, 1995

the Children's Peace Monument. The monument was built after a girl named Sadako died of leukemia, a form of cancer caused by atomic radiation, ten years after the bomb blast. While trying to recover from her illness, Sadako began to busy herself with origami, the art of paper folding, in an attempt to heal herself. According to an old Japanese legend, anyone who folds 1,000 origami cranes will have his or her wish granted. The Japanese believe cranes bring good luck. Sadako folded 644 cranes before she died of leukemia in 1955. Her classmates finished the 356 cranes, which were buried with Sadako. They then raised money with students from around Japan and other countries to build the monument, a statue of a young girl holding a crane.

In the evening on Hiroshima Peace Day, thousands of paper lanterns inscribed with the names of loved ones who were killed by the bomb and its deadly radiation are lit and set adrift on all the rivers of Hiroshima. The lanterns represent the spirits of the dead who, while barely alive after the explosion, had sought relief in the rivers for their burning flesh. At the ringing of a Buddhist bell called "peace," hundreds of doves are released over the park. Many other ceremonies for world peace and against the use of atomic weapons also take place around the world in early August, including in the United States and Europe. ◆

Hogmanay

Hogmanay is the name for the last day of the year—also called Old Year's Day—celebrated primarily in Scotland, but also in parts of northern England and in Northern Ireland. Hogmanay appears to be native to the Highlands of Scotland. The origin of the name is uncertain; some say that *Hogmanay* derives from *Hoggu-nott*, or *Hogg-night*, the ancient Scandinavian name for the night before the feast of Yule. Another explanation is that the name comes from the French expression *Au gui l'an neuf* (To the mistletoe this New Year)—a reference to the ancient custom of gathering mistletoe (*gui*)—which may have metamorphosed into a single word *aguillanneuf*, and from there to *Hogmanay*.

Whatever the origin of the name, Hogmanay is an ancient and joyous door-to-door custom similar to what Americans know as trick-or-treating. On Old Year's Day, children wearing **pinafores** and sheets doubled up in front to form pouches go from house to house, especially to the homes of the wealthy, calling out "Hogmanay!" and singing songs and reciting traditional rhymes.

pinafore: a sleeveless garment fastened at the back and worn as a dress or apron.

> Hogmanay!
> Trollolay!
> Give us of your white bread
> And none of your grey.
>
> Get up, gude wife, and shake your feathers,
> And do not think that we are beggars.

For we are **bairns** come out to play
Get up and gie's our Hogmanay.

In return, each child is given the traditional gift of an oatmeal cake, or bannock (a flat round griddle cake, usually unleavened), or other cake. Because of the cakes, December 31 was also known as Cake Day.

Sir James George Frazer, in *The Golden Bough*, a classic study of ancient worship and rituals around the world, explains that, like Halloween, Hogmanay grows out of an ancient pagan custom called *calluinn*. In the Highlands of Scotland on Hogmanay it was the custom for a man to dress in a cow's hide and go from house to house, accompanied by a band of young men, each of whom carried a staff with a piece of rawhide tied to the end. The hide-covered man would run three times around the house *deiseal* (Scottish Gaelic = clockwise), so as to keep the house on his right hand, while the others pursued him, beating on the hide and on the outside of the house. Once the group was let in to the house, one of the men would invoke a blessing on the family: "May God bless the house and all that belongs to it, cattle, stones, and timber! In plenty of meat, of bed and body

---

Hogmanay Bannock

On Hogmanay children in Scotland go door to door singing songs and reciting hymns. In return, the children are given a type of round, flat cake called a bannock. People in Scotland, England, and northern Canada often eat bannocks on holidays. Traditional Scottish bannocks were dense, unleavened griddlecakes made with oats or barley. Canadian bannocks usually contain baking soda or yeast, making them lighter and similar to a scone or Irish soda bread. Many Canadian cooks add nuts, berries, or raisins to their bannocks. This following recipe makes Canadian-style bannocks.

2 cups flour
2 tablespoons baking powder
1 teaspoon salt
2 teaspoons sugar
1/2 cup butter or margarine
1 cup water or milk
1/2 cup raisins (optional)

Mix together flour, baking powder, salt, and sugar. Cut butter or margarine into dry ingredients. Add water or milk. Mix in raisins. Roll dough on a floured board to about 1/2 inch thick; cut into round cakes. Lay on a greased sheet and bake at 450° for about 15 minutes.

clothes, and health of men may it ever abound!" Each member of the group would then singe in the fire a piece of the hide tied to his staff, and would touch the singed hide to the nose of each member of the household and all their domestic animals. The touch of the hide was intended to convey protection to the people and animals from disease, misfortune, and especially from witchcraft in the coming year. This ceremony, called *calluinn* from the loud drumlike noise made in beating on the hide, was practiced in the Hebrides islands off the coast of Scotland as late as the second half of the eighteenth century and possibly into the nineteenth century.

An Irish variant of this custom called *coullin* was recorded on Rathlin Island, off the coast of County Antrim in Ulster, in 1851. This coullin also involved a sort of Hogmanay cake, in this case a scone. Led by a man wearing a dried sheepskin, whose back was also drummed with a stick, parties of young men numbering twenty or thirty would go around to the houses of their neighbors, crowd inside, and chant a traditional request for a scone, "and let it be well buttered." The family would give money, or food, or wool, or meal, knowing the collection was to be given to the poor. In return, a small piece was cut from the sheepskin and given to the woman of the house as an acknowledgment of her charity and as a wish for her good fortune in the new year. Then the group invoked a blessing on the house and moved on to the next house. ◆

In the Highlands of Scotland on Hogmanay it was the custom for a man to dress in a cow's hide and go from house to house, accompanied by a band of young men, each of whom carried a staff with a piece of rawhide tied to the end.

Holi

Holi is a popular North Indian festival noted for its Saturnalia-like excitement celebrated each year at the full moon in the lunar month of March–April. The ceremony is not found in South India, but a similar festival in honor of the Hindu god of love, Kama, takes place there at the same time. While there does not seem to be a direct link between the two rites, literary sources suggest that both occasions are examples of an age-old tradition of celebrating the arrival of spring.

People in northern India usually celebrate Holi during the few days after the full moon. However, in many places the festival starts before the full moon, sometimes as early as Vasanta (spring), the fifth day of the waxing moon in the lunar month of February–March, when the Holi fire is first prepared for lighting. At this time, people begin to collect and contribute wood and cowdung to pile up around a central pole; in addition, a pot is sometimes filled with seeds and buried beneath this pile. The main Holi ritual centers around a bonfire ceremoniously kindled at the time of the rising moon. Both men and women **circumambulate** the fire, into which they often throw coconuts or on which they roast new barley. Divinations of the coming harvest are cast by interpreting the direction of the flames (when the fire is burning) or by the state of the seeds in the buried pot (when the fire has gone out). People sometimes take embers from the fire to their homes in order to rekindle their own domestic fires; they also collect the ashes from the Holi fire for use as protection against disease.

circumambulate: walk around.

The Holi fire is also regarded as a funeral **pyre**, for it is understood to destroy a female demon commonly known as Holika. Certain through a **boon** she was granted that she was never to die by fire, Holika climbs the pyre taking in her lap Prahlada, a faithful devotee of the Hindu god Vishnu who is either her brother or the son of her brother Hiranyakasipu (Vishnu's enemy). Prahlada, who is sometimes identified with the central pole that rises out of the fire, survives the ordeal through his fervent devotion to Vishnu; Holika, the evil one, perishes in the flames.

This exemplary narrative does not really explain the erotic and occasionally violent mood of "playing Holi." People—usually members of the lower social strata—drench one another as well as powerful and prestigious members of the upper classes with water stained with various powders, cattle urine, and mud. Those victims of the various tricks and pranks played on them, including those men who during the festival have been beaten with sticks by women, must simply go along with their reversed status for the time being. The Holi celebration is marked by the selection of the King of Holi, and the hearty enjoyment of lewd singing and shouting.

During the Holi celebration, crowds of people splash and soak one another with buckets full of colored water.

pyre: a pile of wood for burning a dead body.

boon: a favor or blessing.

Anthropologists have been intrigued by these rites. McKim Marriott, for example, notes that "the dramatic balancing of Holi—the world destruction and world renewal, the pollution followed by world purification—occurs not only on the abstract level of structural principles, but also in the person of each participant." The negation of social status is, however, a limited one, and Holi does not involve the complete reversal of everyday norms. According to Hindus of northern and central India, the frenzy and **licentiousness** of the festival is merely a reenactment of the *lilas* of the Hindi god Krishna, the amorous and frolicsome "plays" that the god enjoys with cowherd boys and girls. Indeed, Holi is the "feast of love," and its excesses are clothed in the emotional feelings and motives of Krishna **bhakti** movements.

licentiousness: disregard for traditional moral and legal restraints.

bhakti: religious devotion.

In a Bengali variant of the festival, the burning of a human effigy is associated with the Krishnaite swing festival. In India, the swing carries erotic connotations and may be an element of a generalized marriage ritual. Although Krishna does not appear in all variations of the celebrations, the burning of a human or animal effigy is common and has gone on for years.

In Andhra Pradesh in Southern India, the festival to Kama mentioned earlier retains some of the frenzy of the North Indian Holi. Such ritual delirium does not appear to any significant extent in Tamil Nadu. Although a festival to Kama may take place here and there in orthodox temples dedicated to Siva, Hindu goddess of destruction and reproduction, Tamil celebrations usually involve only small local groups instead of entire villages. During the Kama festival an effigy of Kama is constructed while people recount his story. Assisted by the effects of alcohol, the participants dance wildly, some of them dressed like tribal women. The effigy of Kama is burnt in the fire in a ritual reenactment of a well-known tale in which Kama sends an arrow to Siva in order to distract him from his meditation long enough to allow the god to father a son. Enraged, Siva destroys Kama with a bolt of lightning from his third eye, reducing the Lord of Desire to ashes. However, the terrible **yogin** (Siva) himself becomes "Desire" for a short time and enjoys the pleasures of union with Parvati. For that moment Siva becomes, in effect, Kama. The theological reversal echoes the ritual reversal.

yogin: a person who practices the Hindu philosophy of yoga.

The element of *bhakti* does not appear in the South Indian festival, but here the ritual is more explicit. First, in conformity with the Hindu sacrificial context, the Kama rite focuses on the element of desire—its fulfillment and destruction. Although *kama* (the fulfillment of desire) may be the lowest of the four traditional goals of life (the others being *artha,* or prosperity; *dharma,* or religious duty; and *moksa,* or salvation) it is just as essential as the others, for no aspect of the other three goals can be met without desire. The **ascetic** Siva is also Kama, and thus sires Skanda, for the heroic son must eventually save the world by destroying the demons who are forever threatening the power of the gods. In addition, *kama*—desire without knowledge—is the goal attributed particularly to the *sudra,* the non-initiated, lowest order of Hindu society. In the springtime, the time of cosmic renewal, everyone ritually becomes a *sudra* in order to recreate the world. This temporary inversion of the social hierarchy and of the four goals of Hindu life is marked in the ritual when Kama, or Holi, is crowned king. ◆

ascetic: practicing strict self-denial as a measure of spiritual discipline.

Holy Week (Santa Semana)

CHRISTIAN ● SPRING

Santa Semana (Holy Week) is celebrated passionately throughout the Spanish-speaking world, which is largely Roman Catholic.

Holy Week is the week that precedes the Christian holiday of Easter and a time when Christians remember the final days in the life of Jesus. Easter is the most important Christian festival of the year, celebrating the Resurrection of Jesus after his crucifixion. It is celebrated on a Sunday between March 22 and April 25, making it a movable feast. In Eastern Orthodox churches, Easter may take place later due to different factors in calculating the date of the festival. Easter week begins on the Sunday before Easter, called Palm Sunday, which celebrates Jesus' entry into Jerusalem. Holy Thursday, the next important day, recalls the first occasion of the Eucharist. Good Friday mourns the crucifixion of Jesus, and Holy Saturday commemorates his burial. Holy Week ends the forty-day season of Lent, a time of spiritual discipline and renewal that begins with Ash Wednesday. Santa Semana is Spanish for Holy Week and is celebrated passionately throughout the Spanish-speaking world, which is largely Roman Catholic.

The Easter season corresponds with spring, and its celebration can be traced to ancient religions. In Greek legend, Persephone, daughter of Demeter, the goddess of earth, returned from the underworld to the light of day, symbolizing the resurrection of life in the spring. The Phrygians, ancients who lived in the region of modern Turkey, believed that their god went to sleep at the winter solstice, and they performed music and dances to awaken him at the spring equinox. Traditions associated with ancient festivals are the Easter rabbit, a symbol of fertility, and brightly colored eggs to represent the sunlight.

Several European languages call Easter some variation of the word *Pascha*, which comes from the Hebrew word *pesah*, meaning passover. Jesus was celebrating the Jewish festival of Passover before he was arrested and sentenced to death. Passover recalls the Jews' rescue from slavery in ancient Egypt. For Christians, Easter celebrates Jesus rescuing them from eternal death.

Observances of Holy Week took their present form in the late 300s, when Christians linked the final events of Jesus' life with the days on which these events were thought to have occurred. In Jerusalem, early Christians began celebrating Jesus' life by holding services at sacred sites in the city. Today, many of those sites are active during Holy Week. Since the Middle Ages, many places have performed Passion plays reenacting the Easter story. The most famous one, dating from 1634, occurs once a decade in Oberammergau, Germany.

Modern observances of Palm Sunday commemorate how the Jews spread palms and clothing in front of Jesus as he entered Jerusalem. During Palm Sunday services, churches bless and distribute palm boughs, sometimes woven into the shape of a cross. Greek Orthodox Christians receive branches of bay leaves that they use in cooking.

Men dressed in purple robes and white hoods carry a huge float over a sawdust carpet in Antigua, Guatemala, during Santa Semana.

During Maundy Thursday services, priests often wash the feet of twelve people in remembrance of how Jesus washed the feet of his twelve disciples.

Holy Thursday, or Maundy Thursday, commemorates the Last Supper, which is revered as the first occasion of the Holy Eucharist. The name Maundy comes from *mandatum*, Latin for "commandment," the first word of a song sung that day. Many churches re-create the Last Supper of Jesus in an evening liturgy that includes Holy Communion. During Maundy Thursday mass, Roman Catholic priests often wash the feet of twelve people in remembrance of how Jesus washed the feet of his twelve disciples at their last meal together.

Good Friday observes the sad event of Jesus' death on the cross. The day's name came from "God's Friday" and features penance, fasting, and prayer. Churches hold mourning services, some lasting from noon until 3 P.M. to symbolize three hours of darkness that occurred as Jesus suffered on the cross. Eastern Orthodox churches reenact Jesus being taken from the cross and placed inside a tomb. Good Friday is a legal holiday in most of Europe, in South America, in Great Britain and many parts of the Commonwealth, and in several states of the United States.

Holy Saturday is a day of solemn vigil. Services begin at nightfall as observance of the Resurrection approaches. Vigil services may include the baptism of new church members. A dramatic point in the service occurs when lights are put out, leaving the church in darkness. The priest then lights one tall candle, representing the risen Jesus. The flame from this candle is used to light other candles held by worshipers, symbolizing the spreading of God's light. In Eastern Orthodox Churches, the priest lights his candle exactly at midnight. After the light has returned, the people begin to celebrate the joy of Easter. Joyous music and Bible readings begin. Traditionally, newly converted Christians were baptized on this day.

Easter celebrates Christians' belief that they can attain life after death just as Jesus did by his Resurrection. Many churches begin the feast with outdoor sunrise services. The light of the rising sun reminds them of God's light and love returning to the world. Many churches also hold other services later in the morning.

Many Easter traditions can be seen throughout various countries. Exchanging and eating hard-boiled and dyed eggs is a popular custom. Easter eggs designed in Ukraine and Poland are decorated with complicated red, black, and white patterns. In many countries, children hunt for Easter eggs hidden around the home.

The common custom of wearing new clothes for Easter may have started with the old practice of newly baptized Christians wearing white clothes for the Easter celebration. New clothes represent the new life brought by the Resurrection. Easter promenades of people in new clothes are a tradition in many European towns and villages, sometimes led by a person holding a cross or an Easter candle. In New York City, thousands of people show off their new clothes in the Easter parade down Fifth Avenue.

The most elaborate and colorful Holy Week celebrations are seen among Spanish-speaking nations. In Spain, Santa Semana combines the spiritual and the profane, the pagan and the Christian. In Seville, men dressed in white hooded robes bear candles through the streets and members of religious brotherhoods shoulder floats with life-sized religious figures. In the town of Turuel, drummers beat until their hands bleed, proclaiming through the night the passion and death of Jesus. In Malaga, processions of floats are accompanied by grieving singers. In Murcia on Good Friday, men in large hats blow long horns that convey the suffering of Jesus. Throughout Spain, towns come alive with drumming and somber processions. Passion plays with ancient scripts are performed throughout the country.

As Spanish influence spread throughout Latin America and mingled with Indian customs, even more elaborate and colorful Santa Semana celebrations emerged. In Antigua, Guatemala, Palm Sunday vigils in churches are interspersed with processions featuring seventeenth-century carvings of Jesus atop huge floats, or *andas*, carried by the faithful. Artists work all night before Good Friday creating a carpet of flowers and brightly colored, hand-dyed sawdust, making images that include religious scenes and geometric Mayan designs. Before dawn on Good Friday, characters dressed as Roman soldiers ride through town proclaiming Christ's impending death. Starting just after sunrise, a procession bearing a sculpture of Jesus crucified parades across the carpets of art. The procession stops at the city jail, where two prisoners are chosen to shoulder heavy crosses. Later, they're allowed to go free. In the town of Santiago Atitlán, brilliantly dressed villagers carry an image of Christ together with San Simón, a saint who loves to smoke and drink. The image wears silk scarves, sneakers, and a hat. Villagers mob him to pour hard liquor down his throat or light his cigar.

On Easter morning in New York City, thousands of people show off their new clothes in the Easter parade down Fifth Avenue.

In Mexico, Santa Semana processions and Passion plays take place throughout the country. In the southern state of Chiapas, Mayan-descended villagers have their children baptized on Holy Saturday in a church whose pews have been replaced by pine boughs and needles on the floor. The town of San Cristóbal de las Casas features Holy Week parades through the narrow streets, complete with Roman soldiers whipping Jesus. On Saturday in San Cristóbal, effigies of detested politicians and Judas Iscariot, the apostle who betrayed Jesus, are set on fire. In towns from Aguascalientes in central Mexico to Merida in the Yucatan Peninsula, hooded celebrants walk in beautiful torchlight processions in total silence. Throughout the country, music, dancing, and fireworks add a festive note to religious observances.

Santa Semana in the eastern lowlands of Bolivia features Indian interpretations of Jesuit missionary teachings, creating an unusual mix of theatrics, processions, and fire bombs. In Quito, Ecuador, a huge Good Friday procession features men **flagellating** themselves and other men dragging crosses and being whipped by Romans. Throughout Peru, Santa Semana is a week of high drama. Quito, once the center of the Inca world, hosts an Easter Monday procession in which the faithful carry a statue of the Lord of the Earthquake through the city over a carpet of red flowers to plead with Jesus not to send earthquakes to the city. On Good Friday, effigies of Judas and hated politicians are hung and burned.

flagellating: whipping or striking.

In the Philippines, once a colony of Spain, the passion, death, and resurrection of Jesus are reenacted in dramatic detail. On Good Friday, women wail songs of sorrow, and Passion plays abound. Some people flagellate themselves with glass-spiked leather thongs.

Poland is another strongly Catholic country where Holy Week is very important, featuring elaborate processions on Palm Sunday and Passion plays in the week. On Maundy Thursday, villagers often hang effigies of Judas. They drag him from the village, flog him, and burn or drown him. On Good Friday the faithful visit mock caves that represent the tomb of Jesus. On Holy Saturday, everyone takes eggs, sausage, bread, and salt to church to be blessed. They eat the food on Sunday. ◆

Homecoming

Homecoming is an annual American celebration, usually taking place in the fall season, at which alumni return to their high school or college. The purpose of the reunion is to spark school spirit and unity, as well as to encourage the loyalty and patronage of alumni. For many alumni, Homecoming is a time for nostalgia and renewing ties with old friends and acquaintances.

Homecoming may last as little as a few days, but usually consists of a weeklong series of events, parties, and programs for returning alumni, current students, and their families. High school, college and university administrators, educators and current students—divided into distinct committees—organize the events surrounding Homecoming. Events vary dramatically from school to school, but usually include a football game, rally, dance, and other social and charitable activities.

Traditionally, the high point of the Homecoming week is a football game, often pitting the home team against a team from a rival school. In addition to the excitement of the game itself, elaborate halftime shows showcase marching bands, acrobatic stunts, and the crowning of the queen of the Homecoming court. Throughout the game, the team mascot—usually an animal or person dressed like a particular character meant to bring the team good luck—makes appearances.

The football game is usually preceded by a pep rally, in which cheerleaders and the team mascot drum up school spirit with traditional school songs and chants. Many alumni host tailgate parties—elaborate picnics served from the backs of

Traditionally, the high point of the Homecoming week is a football game, often pitting the home team against a team from a rival school.

169

The typical American Homecoming includes a football game, performances by the school marching band, and the election of a local boy and girl to be Homecoming King and Queen.

trucks, vans and cars, either in the parking lot of the football stadium or school. Many cars are decorated with banners, streamers, and other paraphernalia in school colors.

The Homecoming court is composed of ten or twelve women—often from the senior class—nominated by their peers. The nominees are presented during the football game halftime show, and the nominees usually appear in formal wear on the field. Based on popular vote, one is crowned Homecoming Queen. Sometimes a Homecoming King is also crowned.

Traditionally, one of the most well attended events is the Homecoming parade. In addition to the school marching band, elaborate floats created by student groups, classes and clubs proceed down a major street through campus or the town. The floats usually have a theme and are limited only by students' imagination; they are made of chicken wire, crepe paper, lumber, and many other materials. At the Georgia Institute of Technology, tradition challenges students to build "ramblin' wrecks," motorized contraptions assembled with used car parts, machinery and almost anything else. Winning floats are usually announced during the football game halftime show.

After the football game, the school, as well as student organizations such as clubs and fraternities, sponsor Homecoming dances and parties. Other events may include bonfires, fireworks displays, competitions, shows, contests for pie-eating or lip-syncing, and charity or fund-raising events. Recently the University of Missouri at Columbia broke the world's record for the largest peacetime blood drive on a college campus during Homecoming week.

Several universities claim to have "invented" Homecoming. The University of Illinois traces its Homecoming tradition to 1910, when students and administrators developed the idea in order to rekindle alumni loyalty and generate excitement. According to tradition at the University of Missouri at Columbia, the first Homecoming took place on its campus in 1911. For the first time in its twenty-two-year history, the Missouri Tiger football team would play its arch rival, the University of Kansas, in Columbia rather than in Kansas City. Students and administrators feared that alumni and fans wouldn't travel to Columbia for the game, so in order to add some excitement to the already legendary rivalry between the two teams, the director of athletics issued a call to all alumni and fans of Missouri to "Come Home" for the game and a celebration, which included a parade and a rally. Over 9,000 fans attended.

Whatever its origins, by the 1920s and 1930s, other universities, colleges and secondary schools had begun celebrations of their own. Today Homecoming is celebrated in nearly every educational institution across the nation. ◆

Several American universities claim to have "invented" Homecoming.

Id al-Adha (Feast of Sacrifice)

MUSLIM ● DHU AL-HIJJA

pilgrimage: a journey to a
sacred place.

Id al-Adha is the Muslim Feast of Sacrifice that marks the culmination of *hajj*, Islam's major **pilgrimage**, which is made to Mecca, Saudi Arabia. Hajj means "voyage to a sacred place," and is one of the five religious duties — the Five Pillars of Islam — taught in the Koran, the holy book of Islam. All adult men and women who are physically and financially able must perform the hajj at least once in their lifetime. Pilgrims only make the hajj during the first two weeks of the Islamic month of Dhu al-Hijja, which corresponds to the last month of the lunar year. Because Islam's calendar follows the lunar cycles, the time is different every year.

To make the hajj (pronounced "haj," and sometimes spelled hadj), pilgrims must put themselves in a state of purity before they reach Mecca by performing ritual bathing and wearing the *ihram*, a white seamless shroud. They keep the shroud for the rest of their lives to be their burial garb. While in the state of purity, the pilgrim does not engage in certain activities, such as sexual relations.

The Kaaba, the most sacred shrine of Islam, is in Mecca and is the main goal of the pilgrimage. Pilgrims carry out a set of rites that culminates in their circling the Kaaba seven times. This is called the *tawaf*, and the scene of thousands of white-clad Muslims circling the large cube-shaped building near the center of the Great Mosque is one of the world's most extraordinary and beautiful sights. A famous Black Stone, enclosed in a silver ring, rests in the eastern corner of the Kaaba. According to Muslim tradition, the Kaaba was originally built by Abraham and Ishmael, and the Black Stone was given to Abraham by the angel Gabriel. Pilgrims run and walk around the Kaaba seven times, praying and reciting verses from the Koran. They touch or kiss the stone to end the ceremony.

Other rituals of the hajj include the crossing back and forth between two hills, Safa and Marwa, seven times. Groups of pilgrims stop on a hill in the valley of Arafat from noon until sunset. They also participate in a symbolic stoning of the devil in the valley of Mina.

The pilgrimage concludes with the Festival of Sacrifice, called the "major feast" of the religious year, as opposed to the Breaking of the Fast at the end of Ramadan, which is the lesser feast. Muslim pilgrims celebrate the Festival of Sacrifice in the valley of Mina, near Mecca, by ritually slaughtering a sheep or larger animal—often a goat or camel. This killing reenacts the sacrifice that God demanded Abraham to make of his son. Muslims who are not making the hajj in a particular year slaughter an animal at home. People at home usually give the meat to the poor, and the hide to a charitable organization. People believe that the animal they slaughter will carry them to Paradise. In the largely Hindu country of India, where cows are sacred, the slaughter of animals by Muslims has caused riots in some years. During the Festival of Sacrifice Muslims visit family, friends, and neighbors. They wear their best clothes and exchange gifts.

More than one million Muslims annually make the pilgrimage to Mecca. Muslims believe a person who makes the hajj secures great religious merit, and such a person is called a hajji and held in esteem. Mecca is the birthplace of Muhammad, and Muslims believe it is the place where God's will was revealed to Muhammad. Saudi Arabia considers itself the birthplace of Islam, and Muslims revere Mecca as their most sacred city. Every day, five times a day, the billion Muslims around the world face Mecca to pray. In the Arab world, they are called to prayer from the minarets of mosques. Mecca is set in a rugged landscape consisting mostly of solid granite, with rocks sometimes reaching 1,000 feet above sea level. It is enclosed by the Valley of Abraham, which is surrounded by two nearby mountain ranges to the east, west, and south. Only Muslims are allowed to enter Mecca. ◆

Muslim pilgrims celebrate the Festival of Sacrifice in the valley of Mina, near Mecca, by ritually slaughtering a sheep or larger animal—often a goat or camel. This killing reenacts the sacrifice that God demanded Abraham to make of his son.

Id al-Fitr
(Feast of Fast Breaking)

MUSLIM ● SHAWWAL

Each day's fast begins when "the white thread of dawn appears to you distinct from the black thread" according to the Koran. The fast ends immediately at sunset.

Id al-Fitr is the Muslim Feast of Fast Breaking that marks the end of Ramadan. Ramadan is the holy month of fasting that all adult Muslims are obligated to participate in, according to the Koran, Islam's holy book. Id al-Fitr is a three-day time of feasting and gathering with family and friends.

Ramadan is a time of worship, spiritual reflection and renewal, and charity. It also marks the time that Muslims believe the Koran was "sent down from heaven." Ramadan takes place in the ninth month of the Islamic year, the month during which Muhammad received the first of the Koran's revelations. Because the Islamic calendar is lunar, Ramadan falls at different times of the year.

Fasting during Ramadan is the fourth of the five Pillars of Faith, the chief religious duties of a Muslim. All Muslims of sound mind who have reached puberty must fast. People who are exempt include the sick and the elderly, pregnant or nursing women, and travelers. Some other circumstances allow people to break the fast, but they must make up the missed days at a later time. A Muslim who deliberately breaks the fast must atone by fasting for two continuous months or feeding the poor.

Each day's fast begins when "the white thread of dawn appears to you distinct from the black thread" according to the Koran. The fast ends immediately at sunset. During the day's fasting, Muslims are not supposed to eat, drink, smoke, or engage in sexual activity. Believers may not even swallow their

Muslim women in Baghdad, Iraq, buy sweets at the market in preparation for Id al-Fitr.

own saliva. The daily fast is broken by a light meal, preferably dates and water, called the *iftar*, followed by the evening prayer. Muslims often gather with friends, neighbors, or family at home or at the mosque to partake in the *iftar*. The nights are often devoted to special prayers and to recitations from the Koran. A predawn meal called the *suhoor* is also eaten. The last ten days of Ramadan are the most blessed and people commit themselves to intense devotions and prayers. Some Muslims seclude themselves in a mosque for full-time religious contemplation. The night between the 26th and 27th days of Ramadan is called the Night of Determination, during which, according to the Koran, God determines the course of the world for the following year.

The sign of the end of Ramadan is the new moon on the last night of the month of fasting. Muslims wait for the official sighting of the new moon and then begin the Feast of Fast Breaking. They joyfully celebrate Id al-Fitr with special prayers and festivities. The breaking of the fast celebrates a return to normal daily life. People feel spiritually refreshed and grateful. Muslim cities and villages take on a festive look and feel as people step out in their best clothes. They meet on the street or in mosques, hugging, kissing, and greeting each other with congratulations on completing their fast. A common greeting is "Id mubarak" (Happy Id). Turkish Muslims call Id al-Fitr *Seker Bayrami*, which means Sugar Feast, after the custom of giving out sweets. People make special morning prayers on Id al-Fitr and make a contribution to charity. Id al-Fitr is called the lesser feast, as opposed to the greater Feast of Sacrifice.

Muhammad, Islam's main prophet, introduced fasting in the 600s as a way to achieve piety, celebrate the glory of God, and thank God for the Koran. The Koran is made up of revelations, that, according to Muslim beliefs, Muhammad received from Allah, or God. The number of Muslims has grown faster than any other religion in the United States, and many American Muslims gather in mosques or in each other's homes to celebrate Id al-Fitr. Some congregations of Muslims offer special events to share their religious heritage with fellow Americans. These events feature speakers to answer questions about Islam and presentations of characteristic ethnic food. ◆

Independence Day

UNITED STATES ● JULY 4

Independence Day (also known as the Fourth of July) is by far the most important patriotic holiday in the United States. On July 4, 1776, the Continental Congress representing the thirteen British colonies approved the Declaration of Independence and agreed to band together as a new country free of British rule.

This document was composed after a year of war that began with the battles of Lexington and Concord. In June 1776, the Congress met in Philadelphia and appointed a committee of five men—John Adams, Benjamin Franklin, Thomas Jefferson, Robert R. Livingston, and Roger Sherman—to write a draft of the Declaration. Jefferson, who was a skilled writer, probably wrote most of it.

On July 2, the Congress voted to become independent and the draft of the Declaration was presented to the delegates, who debated its wording for two days. One topic that provoked argument was whether to include a passage banning slavery in the new country. This passage was removed from the final document, paving the way for the Civil War almost a century later. On July 4, nine of the thirteen colonies agreed to adopt the revised document and one delegate, John Hancock, signed it. (The official document was not signed until a month later; fifty-six delegates eventually signed it.)

The first Independence Day celebration took place on July 8, 1776, when the Declaration of Independence was read publicly for the first time in Philadelphia's town square. A large bell, known as the Province Bell and later renamed the Liberty

> "We, therefore, the representatives of the United States of America, in General Congress assembled, appealing to the Supreme Judge of the world for the rectitude of our intentions, do, in the name and by the authority of the good people of these colonies solemnly publish and declare, That these United Colonies are, and of right ought to be, FREE AND INDEPENDENT STATES"
>
> From the Declaration of Independence, July 4, 1776

177

The Fourth of July parade in Cody, Wyoming, is typical of parades that take place in cities and small towns across America on Independence Day.

Bell, was rung after the reading. The residents lit bonfires, and church bells rang throughout the night in celebration. But people outside of Philadelphia did not know that they were part of an independent country until the news slowly spread. On July 9 the Declaration of Independence was read to George Washington's army, which was camped in New York. Boston residents heard the news on July 18; cannons and rifles were fired thirteen times (once for each colony) near the Massachusetts State House. Bostonians also destroyed statues and portraits of the despised British King George III.

The following year, 1777, marked the first official celebration of Independence Day. After some debate about what the permanent date should be (July 2 when the colonies agreed to become independent, or July 4 when the declaration was adopted), July 4 was chosen. In Philadelphia, the celebration included bonfires and fireworks, which soon became an Independence Day tradition. The new country was still at war during the first official Fourth of July celebration. Washington's troops celebrated with an extra ration of rum.

In 1783 the war ended; five years later, the United States constitution took effect, and a huge Independence Day celebration was held in Philadelphia, now the nation's capital. Parades and speeches also became part of this holiday's traditions. By a strange coincidence, three early U.S. presidents died on July 4: John Adams and Thomas Jefferson, drafters of the Declaration of Independence, both died on July 4, 1826 (the fiftieth anniversary of its adoption); and James Monroe died on July 4, 1831.

As pioneers moved westward in the 1800s, they carried the Independence Day holiday with them, and it was celebrated

Every year on July 4, Washington, D.C., puts on a spectacular fireworks display.

throughout the new states and territories. However, during the Civil War celebrations stopped in the Confederate states that had seceded from the United States. In 1876 the reunited country celebrated the centennial of the Declaration of Independence. More than ten million people came to the Centennial Exposition in Philadelphia and saw two wonderful exhibits: Alexander Graham Bell's first telephone and the original Declaration of Independence. (Because of its frail condition, the Declaration now is kept in Washington, D.C., in the National Archives Building, where it can be protected from damage by light, heat, and humidity.)

In 1941 the United States Congress formally established July 4 as a permanent federal holiday. Today, Independence Day is a legal holiday in all states and territories of the United States. Congress moved the official dates of several federal holidays to a Monday beginning in 1971, but celebration of Independence Day was kept on July 4. In addition to parades, patriotic speeches, and fireworks displays held throughout the country, many people spend the day at outdoor gatherings with friends and family. Some of the more unusual local celebrations include a Native American powwow in Flagstaff, Arizona, and annual games held above the Arctic Circle by Alaskan Eskimos.

On the 200th anniversary of the signing of the Declaration in 1976, major festivities were held nationwide. Several million people went to New York City, where they could view 212 tall ships that had sailed from around the world to honor the nation's bicentennial celebration. In Philadelphia, descendants of the original signers of the Declaration softly tapped the Liberty Bell, which could not be rung because it is cracked. Two million people watched a huge fireworks display in Washington, D.C., that evening.

Ten years later, another major celebration was held, honoring the hundredth birthday of the Statue of Liberty in New York Harbor. The statue had been closed to the public for several years while it was being renovated, and it was reopened and relit on July 4, 1986. Once again there were huge fireworks displays, and a new group of tall ships sailed into New York Harbor. Millions of people participated in this "Liberty Weekend," both in New York City and in local celebrations around the country. Some people even built replicas of the statue.

Because so many present-day countries once were colonies of other countries, versions of Independence Day are celebrated in at least 100 countries worldwide. For example, Dominion

1776 The Continental Congress adopts the Declaration of Independence.

1783 The Revolutionary War ends.

1826 Thomas Jefferson and John Adams die on July 4, 50 years after the adoption of the Declaration of Independence.

1876 The United States celebrates the centennial of its independence.

1941 The U.S. Congress declares July 4 a permanent federal holiday.

1976 Major festivities take place around the country for the bicentennial of the adoption of the Declaration of Independence.

1986 The Statue of Liberty is reopened on July 4 after several years of renovation.

Day (July 1) commemorates the day in 1867 when Canada was granted dominion status by the British Commonwealth. This allowed Canada's residents self-rule, even though they still acknowledge the king or queen's sovereignty. Mexico's Independence Day (September 16) honors the priest Father Hidalgo (Miguel Hidalgo y Costilla), who in 1810 urged the Mexican people to revolt against Spanish rule. His plea for independence, the "Grito de Dolores," is still recited at ceremonies today. And Liberia, originally a group of settlements of freed slaves from the United States who returned to Africa, celebrates its Independence Day on July 26. On that day in 1847 Liberia adopted a Declaration of Independence and became the first independent black African republic. ◆

Janmashtami (Birthday of Krishna)

Janmashtami (also called Krishnastami) is the Hindu celebration of the birth of Krishna, the human incarnation of the Hindu god Vishnu, the preserver of the Universe. It falls on the new moon day of the Hindu month of Bhadrapada, which occurs in August and September. Janmashtami is one of the most important Hindu festivals and a national holiday in India.

> *"Whenever the Law declines and the purpose of life is forgotten, I manifest myself on earth. I am born in every age to protect the good, to destroy evil, and to reestablish the Law."*
>
> *Bhagavad Gita*
> 4.7–8

According to sacred Hindu writings, Krishna was born about 5,000 years ago in Mathura to the sister and brother-in-law of the wicked king Kamsa. Kamsa had imprisoned the couple after a voice from the sky warned him that the eighth child of his sister, Devaki, would one day destroy him. The enraged Kamsa killed the first seven of Devaki's children. Before the birth of the eighth child, a divine voice told the father, Vasudeva, to exchange his newborn with his friend's child. On the night of Krishna's birth, Vasudeva escaped the prison, traveled through a great storm, and exchanged his son for his friend's newborn girl. After he returned to the prison with the baby girl, the evil Kamsa grabbed the baby and threw her into the air. The infant, who was actually a goddess, flew out of sight while a voice scolded Kamsa and warned him that his destroyer was indeed alive.

Krishna then grew up among the cowherds of Gokulam, developing a fondness for milk and butter. One day, he did slay the wicked Kamsa and saved people from all sorts of disasters.

182

During Janmashtami in India young men form human pyramids in an attempt to reach pots full of butter and curds suspended above them.

He became the unchallenged hero of his times, protecting the good and destroying the wicked. Despite his remarkable triumphs, Krishna mingled freely with people from all walks of life. He was loved dearly by all who knew him. Aside from his remarkable feats of heroism, one of Krishna's most important contributions to the world was the sacred work called the *Bhagavad-Gita*, which means *Song of God*. In this philosophical dialogue, Krishna reveals the paths to divine salvation.

In southern
India, the floor
of the house
from the door to
the meditation
room is marked
with a child's
footprints made
of flour and
water to signify
Krishna's
entrance into
the house.

Because of all his great contributions to mankind, Krishna is now one of the most worshiped deities in the Hindu faith, and his birthday is celebrated with great joy in India. The main centers of the celebration take place in Agra, Bombay, and Mathura, the place of Krishna's birth. Preparations for the celebration begin eight days before Janmashtami, when there are many recitations of sacred works. All the Hindu temples and homes are also decorated in anticipation of the event.

On Janmashtami, many Indians begin their day with baths in sacred waters and with prayers. Many fast until the new moon appears at midnight, the time of the Lord's birth. At that time, the idol of the baby Krishna is bathed and placed in a silver cradle. The blaring of conches, ringing of bells, chanting of hymns in praise of Krishna, and shouts of "Victory to Krishna!" accompany the sacred bath. During the worship of Krishna, there may also be offerings of flowers, waving of lights, and readings about the birth of the Lord Krishna. Some people bring toys to the temples to present to Krishna. Some areas display scenes depicting Krishna's mischievous childhood pranks. Villagers may also act out the scenes, delighting in the antics of their beloved Krishna. Devotional songs and dances are also performed at temples in parts of India. Many women make offerings of sweets prepared with milk. In southern India, the floor of the house from the door to the meditation room is marked with a child's footprints made of flour and water, signifying Krishna's entrance into the house.

People in some areas also play games that reflect stories from Krishna's youth. In the Indian state of Tamil Nadu, greased poles are set up with pots of money on top. Boys dressed as Krishna compete with each other, trying to shinny up the poles while others squirt water at them. In the state of Maharashtra, pots filled with butter and curds are suspended high above the ground. Groups of boys form human pyramids, trying to reach the pot and break it. Whichever group reaches the pot gets the money tied to the rope above the pot. These games are based on scenes from Krishna's childhood, when Krishna would try to steal butter and curds in earthenware pots tied up beyond his reach.

In Nepal, people dressed in fine clothes and covered with garlands of flowers carry images of Krishna through the streets. Musicians and people carrying banners join in the procession, shouting "Krishna is God!" Women also take part in traditional dances around the temples devoted to Krishna. ◆

Juneteenth

UNITED STATES ● JUNE 19

On January 1, 1863, President Abraham Lincoln issued the Emancipation Proclamation, which freed the slaves then in Confederate-held territory. But since the state of Texas remained under rebel control until the end of the Civil War, the proclamation had little or no practical impact there during the conflict.

According to tradition, the slaves of Texas did not even hear of Lincoln's decree until June 19, 1865, when Union major general Gordon Granger arrived in Galveston and proclaimed: "The people of Texas are informed that in accordance with a Proclamation from the Executive of the United States, all slaves are free." This set off a round of celebrations in East Texas, where the great majority of the former slaves resided. In some places, solemn thanksgiving services were held; in others, the just-freed slaves held more raucous celebrations, such as drilling holes in trees, filling them with gunpowder, and enjoying the resulting fireworks.

Since then, African Americans in Texas have celebrated June 19 as emancipation day. At some point, at least as far back as the 1920s, blacks dubbed the day "Juneteenth." In Texas it became an unofficial holiday on which African Americans were excused from work. The holiday was celebrated much as the majority of Americans celebrated the Fourth of July, with family reunions, picnics, parades, dances, baseball games, speeches, and readings from historical documents.

Juneteenth spread beyond the borders of Texas to the nearby states of Arkansas, Louisiana, and Oklahoma. As black

> *"The people of Texas are informed that in accordance with a Proclamation from the Executive of the United States, all slaves are free."*
>
> Major Gordon Granger, 1865

Texans emigrated from their state, Juneteenth was also observed in places as far away as California. It became the most widely observed of the various African-American Emancipation Days celebrated on various days in different localities around the nation.

After World War II, the popularity of Juneteenth declined. Many local governments in the South had co-opted the holiday so that it became associated with segregation; the cities of Dallas, Fort Worth, and Houston, for example, disregarded its segregation ordinances on that one day, a practice that was regarded as insulting by the growing number of blacks influenced by the civil rights movement of the postwar era. Also, as the civil rights struggles of the 1950s and 1960s aroused hopes of imminent equality, many African Americans came to resent aspects of the Juneteenth celebration—such as drinking, eating watermelon, and dancing—as reinforcing stereotypical images of subservient blacks. As a consequence, Juneteenth was abandoned by many urban and middle-class blacks.

Juneteenth experienced a revival after black representatives in the Texas legislature won recognition for June 19 as an official state holiday in 1979. All state agencies and many businesses observed the day. During the 1980s it flourished in Texas and many other states in connection with blacks' growing appreciation of their cultural and historical heritage. Juneteenth celebrations from Houston to San Francisco, from Dallas to Buffalo, began to incorporate such things as Buffalo soldier reenactments, dramatizations of the Underground Railroad's operation, African fairs and storytelling, and film festivals, sometimes stretched over a period of weeks.

While an official holiday only in Texas, by the late 1990s it was celebrated in some thirty states. In 1995 the U.S. Senate approved a resolution, sponsored by both the majority and minority leaders, establishing June 19 as "Juneteenth Independence Day" and encouraging (although not legally establishing) the national observance of the day. ◆

During the 1980s Juneteenth celebrations flourished in Texas and many other states in connection with African Americans' growing appreciation of their cultural and historical heritage.

Junkanoo

Junkanoo, a joyous, colorful carnival-like parade celebrated primarily in Nassau, the capital city of the Bahamas, and in Jamaica, on Boxing Day (December 26) and January 1, contains elements of ancient tribal rituals of Africa, **mummers**' parades, and Mardi Gras. Africa is particularly evident in the masks, costumes, music, and dancing. Junkanoo (also spelled Jonkonnu, in Jamaica, and John Canoe) once flourished all along the coast of the Carolinas and in parts of the English-speaking Caribbean at Christmastime, but is now observed almost exclusively in the Bahamas and Jamaica. The biggest celebration is in Nassau, home to half the Bahamian population, on the island of New Providence. The festival is held on Boxing Day and New Year's Day because, in the days of slavery, these two days and Christmas were the slaves' only holidays.

mummers: actors, usually masked and costumed, who perform during festivals.

Nassau, The Bahamas. The festival usually begins at three or four in the morning and runs till nine or ten A.M. Simply and elaborately costumed dancers step in the Afro-Bahamian rhythm called Goombay—one step forward, two steps back—accompanied by music (or, if not music, noise will do) from goatskin drums, congos, bongo drums, cowbells, **lignum vitae** sticks, pebble-filled "shik-shaks," horns, whistles, conch shells, shakers, steel drums, cans, and even saws. The main thing is to make noise, dance well, and have a good time.

lignum vitae: a hard, heavy wood from trees that grow in tropical America.

The parade is composed of different gangs, or groups, that used to run in a joyous frenzy up and down Bay Street in Nassau. More recently the processions have become more organized and stately, and move at a slower, more refined pace, one reason

A costumed dancer does the limbo during the Junkanoo parade in Nassau, Bahamas.

being that there are contests in which groups are judged according to the elaborateness of their costumes and the quality of their music and dancing. Present-day revelers wear masks, but probably in the old days they simply painted their faces, as their ancestors had done in Africa. The masks and costumes typically take months to prepare, but the emphasis, whether in costuming or music or dancing, is on fun, not prizes. Many costumes are made of cardboard, flour paste and crepe paper (sponges, too, were used in earlier times), and many masks are made of crepe paper and painted wire screens. Towering, elaborate African-style headdresses are also common.

Jamaica: Roots and Fancy Dress. In Jamaica, Jonkonnu is not limited to Boxing Day or New Year's Day; the dancing and costuming are part of Independence Day celebrations and sometimes appear at political rallies. Jamaicans have two kinds of Jonkonnu parades, "Roots" and the more sedate "Fancy Dress" troupes. In a Fancy Dress procession, elegantly dressed Courtiers are followed by a King and Queen; the King and Queen are often preceded by a Flower Girl. Courtier-style costumes are usually composed of a short, stiff skirt over laced, mid-calf pants, and a blousy shirt. Fancy Dress processions also feature a Sailor Boy who keeps the audience in line by threatening to use his whip; an East Indian cowboy, called Babu, who carries a cattle prod; and a raggedy character called Pitchy Patchy.

Roots Jonkonnu culture is associated mostly with "peasant" or "lower class" origins—"closer to the earth" might be a more polite way of saying it—and partly for this reason the music and parades exude a vitality and exuberance not found in the more "Creole" Fancy Dress parades. (It is from Roots culture that reggae music and the **Rastafari** religion arose.) Instead of the Flower Girl found in Fancy Dress parades, Roots processions feature Whore Girl, who flashes her skirts to excite the crowd, or Belly Woman, who charms onlookers with her belly dance movements. In keeping with its rural origins, a Roots parade has Cowhead, Horsehead, and other animal characters; Cowhead, equipped with actual horns, keeps the crowd in line by butting (or threatening to butt) anyone standing too close to the parade. Horsehead, a frightening figure, is made of a mule's skull and equipped with a movable jaw attached to a pole.

Rastafari: relating to a black nationalist and religious movement among Jamaicans that advocates the return of blacks to Africa.

The African origins of Junkanoo have been traced back to eighteenth-century Axim on the west coast of Ghana near the Ivory Coast. The festival also has English and Creole elements, however, dating from plantation days. While the masks have an African look to them, the Courtier style of clothing is European, and the vegetal Jack-in-the-Green look of Pitchy Patchy, with strips of paper or leaves attached to his body, is similar to mummers' costumes in Britain.

Until fairly recently, Junkanoo was a festival for the poor and working classes, but in more recent times, tourism has broadened the involvement. Junkanoo became the main winter tourist attraction in the Bahamas and fed the tourist industry's boom. ◆

Kathin

monsoon: a season of wind and heavy rain.

monastic: of monks and the monastery.

Kathin is a Buddhist celebration during which monks are given new robes and other items necessary for their way of life in the forthcoming year. It follows a period of retreat known as the Buddhist Lent, which begins in about July at the start of the **monsoon** season in Southeast Asia and ends three months later in October. Kathin is observed in East Asian countries where Theravada Buddhism is practiced. Buddhists in Burma, Cambodia, India, Laos, Sri Lanka, and Thailand follow the Theravada school, which places importance on the historical life of the Buddha and the virtues of **monastic** life. Theravadists follow the teachings of the Buddha written in ancient scriptures called the *Tripitika*.

During the Buddhist Lent, monks remain in their monasteries to study and meditate. The practice of the three-month retreat stems from the earliest days of Buddhism, when monks wandered the countryside, only stopping during the monsoon season, when traveling was difficult. Another reason for holding the retreat at this time was so that the monks would not trample on young, tender rice plants as they walked across fields. The founder of Theravada Buddism is said to have made such a retreat. He was an Indian prince named Siddhartha Gautama who became known as *Gautama Buddha*, the Enlightened One. The day before the retreat is said to commemorate Buddha's first sermon to his disciples after he attained enlightenment.

Today, most monks live more settled lives in monasteries, but they still have spiritual retreats during the rainy season. In Burma and Thailand this period is called *Waso*, *Wasa*, or

190

Phansa; in Laos it is called *Vatsa*; and in Cambodia and India the period is known as *Vassa*. Buddhists in northern Asia, including parts of China, Japan, and Korea, also celebrate the Buddhist Lent at this time, though they do not experience the same rainy season. Everywhere Waso is celebrated, people bring food and supplies to the monasteries to help the monks through their long retreat. Many also offer financial assistance.

In Thailand, young laymen take vows for temporary ordination during Waso. It is considered customary for all young men to get such spiritual training at some point in their lives. For this retreat, they have their heads shaved and washed with **saffron**, and they dress in yellow monastic robes. As with all Buddhist monks, they take vows of poverty and spend their retreat meditating and studying. For many others in Thailand, Waso is a time of abstinence and religious instruction.

saffron: the orange aromatic dried stigmas of the purple-flowered crocus.

The end of the Waso is marked with great rejoicing and thanksgiving to the monks. It represents the time when the Buddha returned to earth after giving his mother instruction in heaven. He journeyed to see her to share the wisdom that he had attained during enlightenment.

Throughout Asia, the most common ceremony tied to the end of Waso is Kathin, the presentation of robes and alms to Buddhist monks. The new robes replace the old ones that became soiled during the rainy season. In Thailand, colorful processions fill the rivers and streets as people bring robes to the monks. Bangkok, the capital of Thailand, hosts a spectacular Kathin ceremony in which the king of Thailand travels in a procession of elaborate golden royal barges along the Chao Phraya River to present new robes to the monks at the famous Wat Arun Temple. The first royal presentation of robes by boat took place during the rule of the Thai kingdom of Ayutthaya, which lasted from about 1350 to 1767.

In Laos, monks leave the wat to embark on pilgrimages. In addition to new robes, Laotians offer the monks alms bowls and sleeping mats for their pilgrimages. At home, a festive atmosphere takes hold as people decorate their homes and clean them to rid the environment of the evil spirits who roam during the rainy season. Boat races are also held near riverside towns in Laos and Cambodia at this time.

In Burma, the Festival of Lights marks the end of the Buddhist Lent. This festival predates Buddhism in Burma. It began as a celebration of the God of Lights, and it coincided with the time when the moon was at its brightest. It was also a time to

Bangkok, the capital of Thailand, hosts a spectacular Kathin ceremony in which the king of Thailand travels in a procession of elaborate golden royal barges along the Chao Phraya River to present new robes to the monks at the Wat Arun monastery.

honor the Hindu god Vishnu with offerings of incense, food, and lights. Buddhists later gave the festival a different meaning. According to one legend, Siddhartha's mother had a premonition about her son's intention to become a monk. So she spent the night weaving robes for him so that he would have them in the morning. Today's robe-weaving events reflect the Buddhist legend. At the Shwe Dagon pagoda in Yangon, formerly Rangoon, young, unmarried women stay up all night weaving robes to offer to images of Buddha at the pagoda and to monks.

During the Festival of Lights, people also traditionally illuminate the countryside with lanterns and fire balloons, which are large bamboo frames covered with paper made from local tree bark. Torches are set under the balloon, which is tethered to a wooden platform. The balloon rises as it fills with hot air and the tethers are cut, sending the balloon shooting into the air. Sometimes fireworks are attached to the balloon as well. ◆

Kumbha Mela

The Kumbha Mela is a Hindu pilgrimage fair that occurs four times every twelve years, once in each of four locations in North India: at Haridvar, where the Ganges River enters the plains from the Himalayas; at Prayag, near Allahabad, at the confluence of the Ganges, Yamuna, and "invisible" Sarasvati rivers; at Ujjain, in Madhya Pradesh, on the banks of the Ksipra River; and at Nasik, in Maharashtra, on the Godavari River. Each twelve-year cycle includes the Maha (great) Kumbha Mela at Prayag, which is the largest pilgrimage gathering in the world.

These *melas* (fairs), also known as Kumbha Yoga or Kumbha Parva, occur during the conjunctions of celestial beings who performed important acts in the myth that forms the basis of the observance. In one version of the story, the gods and the antigods had concluded a temporary alliance in order to churn *amrta* (the nectar of immortality, ambrosia) from the milky ocean. Among the "fourteen gems" they churned from the ocean was a pot *(kumbha)* of *amrta*. One of the gods, Jayanta, took the pot and ran, chased by the antigods. For twelve divine days and nights (the equivalent of twelve human years) they fought over the *amrta*. The Moon protected it from "flowing forth," the Sun kept the pot from breaking, Jupiter preserved it from the demons, and Saturn protected it from fear of Jayanta. During the battle, drops of *amrta* fell at eight places in the inaccessible worlds of the gods and four places (Haridvar, Prayag, Ujjain, and Nasik) on the earth.

> **For twelve divine days and nights (the equivalent of twelve human years) the gods fought over the nectar of immortality.**

Millions of Hindu pilgrims congregate in Haridvar in India to bathe in the Ganges River during the Kumbha Mela festival.

The Kumbha Mela is celebrated at the four earthly points where the nectar fell, during the conjunctions of planets (*graha*) with astrological houses (*rasi*) that are characters in the story—for example, at Haridvar when Jupiter (Guru) is in Aquarius (Kumbha) and the Sun (Surya) is in Aries (Mesa). It is popularly thought that a ritual bath (characteristic in all Hindu pilgrimages) at the Kumbha Mela confers extraordinary merit, not only by cleansing the pilgrim of "sin" (*papa*), but also by immersing him in waters infused with *amrta*. Major baths are done at different times in each of the four Kumbha Melas, chiefly on new-moon and full-moon days.

The historical origin of the Kumbha Mela is an open and indeed almost uninvestigated question. The authenticity of its purported mention in the *Atharvaveda* has been challenged, although certain *khila* verses of unknown date in the *Rgveda* demonstrate familiarity with some of the sites and relevant astrological conjunctions. The Chinese Buddhist pilgrim Hsuan-tsang visited Prayag in the seventh century, but there is no evidence that he witnessed a Kumbha Mela.

Traditions regarding the determination of the time of the Kumbha Mela are not unanimous. This is partly due to the absence of a single, authoritative scripture sanctioning the *mela*. It is mentioned only in late texts, notably the *Skanda Purana*, which has several notoriously inconsistent **recensions**. Thus there are occasional disagreements between those who say that the Kumbha Mela should be held every twelve years and those who claim that, in exceptional instances, the precise astrological conjunction may occur in the eleventh year. Matters are complicated by the fact that Haridvar and Prayag have traditions of *ardha* (half) Kumbha Melas, which occur six years after the Kumbha Melas. Nevertheless, there is at present a rough consensus of learned opinion regarding the appropriate times of its occurrence.

> **recension**: revision to a text.

Kumbha Melas are popularly understood to be not only pilgrimage fairs at which sins can be cleansed and merit gained but also religious assemblies at which doctrine is debated and standardized and Hindu unity affirmed. This is perhaps an apt characterization of present-day Kumbha Melas, but historical evidence indicates that in centuries past they were the scenes of bloody battles, chiefly between the militant sections of rival orders of Hindu monks. The main object of contention in these battles, which occurred as recently as 1807, was the right to bathe in the most auspicious place at the most powerful instant. The conflicts were so fierce that indigenous and British courts finally had to establish and enforce specific bathing orders at the various sites of the Kumbha Mela. The *sais*, processions of monks to the bathing place, are still focal events in the Kumbha Melas.

With the advent of modern transportation and communications, contemporary Kumbha Melas are sometimes attended by several million people in a single day. The government of India provides safety, order, sanitation, and preventive inoculations for this multitude, which besides innumerable devout Hindus includes merchants, representatives of religious organizations, casual tourists, groups of monks, and others. Many of those who attend the Kumbha Mela hope to gain some specific "fruit," such as a job, a son, success in studies, and so on. The special power of the Kumbha Mela is often said to be due in part to the presence of large numbers of Hindu monks, and many pilgrims seek the *darsan* (Sanskrit, *darsana*; "auspicious mutual sight") of these holy men. Others listen to religious discourses, participate

> With the advent of modern transportation and communications, contemporary Kumbha Melas are sometimes attended by several million people in a single day.

in devotional singing, engage brahman priests for personal rituals, organize mass feedings of monks or the poor, or merely enjoy the spectacle. Amid this diversity of activities, the ritual bath at the conjunction of time and place is the central event of the Kumbha Mela. ◆

Kupalo

Kupalo, a Ukrainian festival celebrated on June 24—Midsummer's Day and Night—is an ancient celebration dating back to pagan days. Kupalo was a mythical being, a god of summer and fertility who slept all winter beneath a tree, or down among its roots. Each spring Kupalo would awaken and shake the tree, making the seeds fall as a sign of the harvest to come. The festival of Kupalo is primarily celebrated by young unmarried men and women, and boys and girls. During the day and night of the celebration, boys and girls decorate a young tree with flowers, seeds, and fruits, and name it Kupalo. Around the decorated sapling they dance (as around a maypole) and sing songs honoring the god of summer and praying for good weather and a bountiful harvest.

In other Kupalo customs that celebrate the coming of summer, and indicate the power of fertility possessed by the spirit, young women gather flowers to make a wreath. Each young woman then tosses her wreath into the stream or river; the spot where the wreath comes ashore indicates the family she will marry into. The girls and young women also make an effigy of Marena, the goddess of death and winter. After singing ceremonial songs, they burn or drown the effigy of Marena so that her power in the coming winter will be weakened.

Legend has it that the young men, each equipped with a knife, a white powder, and a special cloth, would go into the forest to seek a special fern that blooms only on Midsummer Night. If one finds the fern (and if he's strong enough to resist the enticements of wood nymphs), he must draw a circle on the

Each young woman tosses her wreath into the river; the spot where the wreath comes ashore indicates the family she will marry into.

ground with the white powder, and then sit within the magic circle and wait for the fern to bloom. When the fern blooms, he cuts the blossom with his knife and folds it away in the special cloth. The fern will give him power and good fortune, but only if he never tells anyone he found it.

In *The Golden Bough*, Sir James George Frazer describes a custom that takes place on the Eve of St. John, or Midsummer Eve. Villagers make a figure of Kupalo out of straw and dress the effigy in women's clothes, a necklace, and a crown of flowers. Then they cut down a tree, decorate it with ribbons, and set it up in a chosen spot. This tree is (or represents) Marena; beside her they place the straw figure and a table set with food and drink. Then a bonfire is lit, and young men and women jump over the fire in couples, holding hands and carrying the straw figure with them. On the next day, Midsummer Day, they strip the tree and the effigy of their ornaments and throw them both into a stream.

Midsummer Day and Night, occurring around the time of the summer solstice (about June 21), has been associated with solar ceremonies and fertility rituals since time immemorial. All around Europe (including the Ukraine and parts of Russia) bonfires and merrymaking have been part of the celebrations of summer and fertility rites. It is likely that Midsummer's importance to love and lovers survives from ancient fertility rites, something Shakespeare understood when he wrote the romantic comedy *A Midsummer Night's Dream.* ◆

Kwanzaa

UNITED STATES ● DECEMBER 26 THROUGH JANUARY 1

In 1966, at the height of black self-awareness and pride that characterized the Black Power movement, black political activist Maulana Karenga created the holiday of Kwanzaa. Karenga, who later became a black studies professor, wanted the holiday to help blacks connect with their African heritage and to unify black families and communities. He based Kwanzaa on harvest festivals that are seen throughout much of Africa. Karenga believed that black people outside Africa should set aside time to celebrate their African cultural heritage and affirm their commitment to black liberation.

Karenga's philosophy, called *Kawaida*, formed the ideological basis of Kwanzaa. Karenga theorized that, by exposure to their cultural heritage, black Americans could undergo a revolutionary change. Many blacks have embraced the holiday as an opportunity to reaffirm their commitment to their families, their community, and their struggle for equality.

The name *Kwanzaa* comes from a Swahili phrase, *matunda ya kwanza*, that means "first fruits of the harvest." Karenga used Swahili because it is a hybrid East African language—of Arabic and Bantu—that is tied to no particular tribe. Kwanzaa is also not tied to any religious tradition or political movement. One aim of Kwanzaa was to provide a nonmaterialistic alternative to Christmas, so it is celebrated from December 26 through January 1. Each of the seven days of Kwanzaa is devoted to one of the seven principles on which Kawaida is based. The principles are *umoja* (unity), *kujichagulia* (self-determination), *ujima* (collective work and responsibility), *ujamaa* (cooperative econom-

> *"Kwanzaa takes place during a time, as the Ashanti say, when the edges of the year meet, when the old year is going out and the new year is coming in. And for us as African people, this has historically been and remains a time of turning inward, sober assessment of ourselves and community and recommitment to our highest values in heart, mind and practice."*
>
> Kwanzaa founder Maulana Karenga, 1994

199

Fried Okra for Kwanzaa

The Kwanzaa feast features traditional African-American dishes using foods brought to the Americas from Africa, such as yams, sesame seeds, black-eyed peas, collard greens, and hot peppers. The okra plant is indigenous to west Africa and its edible pods have become a standard part of the Kwanzaa meal. There are many ways to prepare okra. The pods can be boiled, added to soups and stews, or coated in batter and fried as in the recipe below.

40 fresh okra pods	2 teaspoons baking powder
2 cups buttermilk	1 teaspoon salt
1 1/4 cups flour	1/4 teaspoon cayenne pepper
1/2 cup yellow cornmeal	vegetable oil

Wash the okra pods and pat them dry. Trim the stems from the okra and place the pods in a large bowl. Pour the buttermilk over them. In a separate bowl, combine the flour, cornmeal, baking powder, salt, and pepper. Roll the okra pods in the flour mixture until they are completely coated. Heat the vegetable oil to about 375° in a large flat skillet. Place the okra pods in the hot oil and fry for 3 minutes. Turn the okra pods over and fry for 3 minutes more, or until lightly browned. Remove the okra from the skillet and place on paper towels to drain.

ics), *nia* (purpose), *kuumba* (creativity), and *imani* (faith). These seven principles are collectively named *Nguzo Saba*, and they serve as guides for meditation and daily living.

The attempt to honor communal heritage through ceremony is central to Kwanzaa. Celebrants greet each other with the Swahili phrase "Habari gani." This means "What is the news?" and the response is the principle of the day, such as "Umoja" on December 26. On each evening of Kwanzaa, family and friends gather to share food and drink and to perform the candle-lighting ritual. Hosts adorn their table with the symbols of Kwanzaa, explaining their significance to guests. A *mkeka* (straw mat), representing the African-American heritage in traditional African culture, is laid out. A *kinara* (candleholder) is placed upon the mat. It has seven candles, called *mishumaa*, in memory of African ancestors. Each of the candles represents one of the seven values being celebrated and is lit on the day that value is celebrated. The first is lit on Unity Day and is black, symbolizing black unity. The rest alternate between green and red. Red represents the blood of the people's struggles, and green represents past victories, all life, and hope for the future. Included in the candle-lighting rituals are the acknowledgement of ancestors and readings of poetry. On the last day, Imani, all candles blaze.

A *kikomba* (communal cup) is placed on the mat to symbolize the unity of all African peoples. An elder fills the cup with wine, juice, or spirits and passes it around for all to drink. *Mazao* (tropical fruits and nuts) are laid out to represent the yield of the first harvest. Each day, *zawadi* (gifts) are exchanged that represent the theme of the day. Gifts are meant to be uplifting and educational. Typical gifts include books written by or about Africans, dolls and crafts, or educational games and toys. Also laid out are *vibunzi* or *muhindi* (ears of corn), one for each child in the household, representing new life. Kwanzaa ceremonies often include drumming or other musical selections, readings from sacred literature, and reading of the seven principles.

The main feast of Kwanzaa is *karamu*, which is held on the last evening of Kwanzaa, December 31. Families and friends gather in rooms decorated with symbols of Kwanzaa and celebrate the festival's closing. They pray, sing, dance, and toast their ancestors. The feast is meant to inspire celebrants to go forth and maintain the principles of Kwanzaa through the year. Traditional African dishes are served at karamu, especially ones

An African-American family celebrates Kwanzaa in their home.

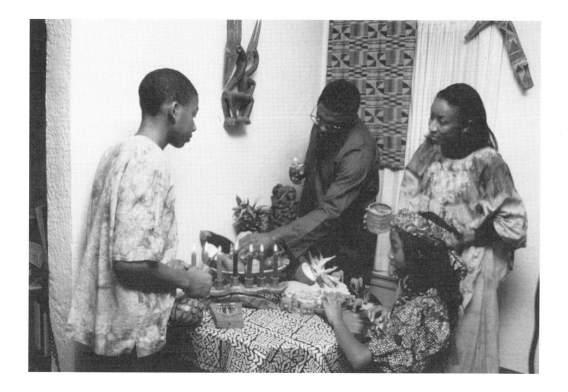

that Africans brought to the Americas, such as yams, sesame seeds, collard greens, and hot peppers. Other popular Kwanzaa foods are those of the Caribbean islands. Rice is often the grain served to symbolize the harvest, and many people eat black-eyed peas, a cultivated breed of cowpeas that grow wild in Africa. The *Black Family Pledge*, written by African-American poet and author Maya Angelou, is often recited during the karamu. Each stanza may be read by a different family member, with the pledge at the end recited in unison. The pledge recalls the suffering of the African-American people and renews their commitment to each other.

> "We are especially reminded during Kwanzaa that our culture comes with its own special way of being human in the world and that this particular African way of being human in the world provides a pathway to the universal. For it represents African peoples' way of engaging the fundamental concerns of humankind."
>
> Maulana Karenga, 1996

By the late 1990s, an estimated twenty million people in the United States, Canada, Great Britain, the Caribbean, and Africa celebrated Kwanzaa. However, it gained its widest acceptance and popularity among African Americans. Although Kwanzaa was at first limited in practice to cultural nationalists, the holiday gained wider and more mainstream acceptance as more African Americans came to heightened awareness and appreciation of their African heritage. Increasingly, many interracial churches, schools, and communities create a Kwanzaa celebration or acknowledgement in order to share the spirit of the holiday and to honor the African-American community. Although some families replace Christmas with Kwanzaa, most black families still celebrate Christmas. Many families combine the two holidays. The majority of African Americans are Christian because their ancestors were slaves owned by Christians. For that reason, many church leaders support Kwanzaa as filling a need of black Americans for a cultural holiday that is their own.

Each year, Kwanzaa takes on more commercial aspects in the United States. Card and gift shops sell cards and other items devoted to the holiday. Many African Americans buy clothing with the Kwanzaa colors of black, red, and green. Some merchants point to the increasing popularity of Kwanzaa as having contributed to some Christmas traditions becoming more Afrocentric, such as blacks decorating Christmas trees with brown-skinned angels and ornaments inspired by African culture. Many stores carry as many black Santa Claus figures as white Santas. Kwanzaa has contributed to the development of positive imagery in the African-American community, adding to a trend of more African-American-owned companies that offer items specifically meant for African-American consumers. In 1997 the U.S. Postal Service released a Kwanzaa stamp. ◆

Labor Day

Labor Day is an occasion to honor the contribution of all working people in America. Although workers' holidays had been observed for centuries in Europe, the United States did not have it's own Labor Day until May 1882, when Peter J. McGuire, leader of a carpenters' union, proposed that the New York City Central Labor Union observe a workers' holiday. The following September 5, up to 250,000 people turned out to watch between 10,000 and 20,000 New York workers march from lower Broadway to Union Square on Fourteenth Street. In the years immediately following, the celebration of Labor Day in early September spread throughout the country. In 1887 Oregon became the first state to establish Labor Day as an official holiday.

Two years later the American Federation of Labor (AFL), which was replacing the Knights of Labor as the leading union federation in the United States, proposed May Day, or May 1, as a day for commencing a campaign for an eight-hour day. Months later, on July 14, 1889, a congress of socialists and other radicals gathered in Paris to mark the 100th anniversary of the storming of the Bastille. The congress resolved that workers everywhere should demonstrate on the same day in favor of the eight-hour workday, and the gathering selected May 1 since it had already been chosen by the AFL.

For a time, both May Day and Labor Day were observed by workers in the United States. But since May Day was linked to European radicalism from the start, Congress wished to discourage American workers from celebrating it. Therefore, in 1894 it

Nineteenth-century Labor Day celebrations featured massive parades to show organized labor's strength to the public at large. Some parade banners bore radical slogans asserting that labor created all value and should be the new ruling class.

The Jerry Lewis Labor Day Telethon

The Jerry Lewis Muscular Dystrophy Association Telethon is a 21^1/$_2$-hour Labor Day fund-raising broadcast watched by millions of Americans. The MDA is a voluntary agency that works to stamp out 40 neuromuscular diseases. The organization sponsors research, medical services, and professional and public health education. It was created in 1950 by a group of people interested in the problem of muscular dystrophy, a crippling genetic disease involving gradual muscle loss. The Jerry Lewis Labor Day Telethon began in 1966 with a broadcast that aired on one New York City station. It was the first such fund-raising event to raise more than $1 million in pledges. By 1970, 65 stations nationwide carried the Telethon, and it became the MDA's single most important source of donations. By the late 1990s the 21^1/$_2$-hour broadcast aired on nearly 200 stations. In 1998 the Telethon reached up to 75 million Americans in 30 million homes and also became the first worldwide telethon. Over the years, countless entertainers, athletes, and leaders in business, government, and civic affairs have participated in the Telethon. Jerry Lewis has become synonymous with the MDA, serving as the Telethon's host and the MDA's national chairman. He and the Telethon depend on a network of about two million volunteers nationwide.

passed a bill, signed by President Grover Cleveland, that recognized the first Monday of September as Labor Day, a legal federal holiday. By then, thirty-one states had already followed in Oregon's footsteps and established Labor Day as a legal state holiday. After the turn of the twentieth century, only unions dominated by radicals paraded on May 1.

Large cities in the east and midwest and cities with strong labor movements began celebrating Labor Day in the 1880s and 1890s, while many smaller cities and towns in the west and south did not have significant observances until the twentieth century. The nineteenth-century celebrations featured massive parades to show organized labor's strength to the public at large and to win public support. Some of the parade banners bore radical slogans asserting, for example, that labor created all value and should be the new ruling class. There also were floats representing the various crafts and trades; few industrial workers belonged to unions at the time and so were underrepresented in the parades. The parades often ended with a mass rally at which Democratic and Socialist party candidates competed for votes. Then came labor picnics aimed at creating solidarity among the workers.

After 1900 the celebration began to change. Tens of thousands of workers came out to march when Labor Day coincided

with major strikes or other matters of importance to labor. But with the wages of workers increasing, thanks in part to the successes of the trade unions, many workers no longer saw an urgent need to march. They preferred to observe the day as one of rest or to spend their spare cash on individual or family recreational activities of their own choice. To attract working people to Labor Day celebrations, union leaders decided to shorten them by dropping either the parade or the picnic. To make the picnics more appealing, a wide variety of entertainment and athletic activities was organized.

Don Breckenridge hosts the Jerry Lewis Labor Day Telethon in Los Angeles, California.

The era between the end of World War I and the early 1930s was a very conservative one. Membership in the AFL, by now the overwhelmingly dominant force in the labor movement, fell from 4.1 million in 1920 to 2.1 million in 1933, and unions were widely suspected as representing an alien, radical presence in America. Under these conditions, the AFL unions were careful not to offend the public. Radical messages were barred from Labor Day parades. To dilute the parades' class character, organizers sometimes invited business and other middle-class groups to participate in the marches, and political officeholders of all stripes—not just those who were pro-labor—were also asked to participate. In Atlanta, for example, the Chamber of Commerce, the Lions Club, Bible school students, and members of a local opera club participated.

During the 1930s, Labor Day observances changed substantially with the onset of the Great Depression and the creation of the Congress of Industrial Organizations (CIO) to organize production workers. The number of Labor Day parade participants grew as organized labor revitalized itself. But because of the antipathy between the craft-oriented AFL and industry-oriented CIO, two parades were held in most cities. In the parades of the CIO, whose left-leaning leadership stood in sharp contrast to AFL conservatism, women for the first time marched together with the men instead of in separate units. Also, the CIO parades, reflecting the composition of the industrial workforce, included many unskilled laborers, African Americans, and immigrants. Their causal attire clashed sharply with the more prosperous appearance of AFL marchers.

The CIO parades did not, however, mark a return to the radicalism of the early marches. The CIO events did not include revolutionary sloganeering. And like the AFL's parades, those of the CIO featured bands, attractive women on floats, and patriotic imagery, all of which was in alignment with, not against, middle-class culture. Also, the CIO did not revive the Labor Day picnics that were once held to promote a separate working-class consciousness.

Post–World War II prosperity made Labor Day demonstrations seem unnecessary and outdated to many workers. Most of them joined their fellow Americans in observing Labor Day as part of a generic three-day holiday of rest and relaxation. Also, the movement of many factories and other businesses to the suburbs made it more difficult to gather workers into urban areas for large-scale Labor Day events. Finally, the proportion of workers represented by the trade unions fell almost one-third in the 1950s to 15 percent at the end of the century; this meant that union leaders had fewer troops to call on for Labor Day celebrations.

As a consequence, Labor Day parades were organized only occasionally during the second half of the twentieth century. Still, when trade unions felt that they or their members were especially threatened, they could still turn out large numbers of marchers. During a recession in 1959, 115,000 workers paraded

1882 Peter McGuire proposes that the New York City Central Labor Union observe a workers' holiday.

1887 Oregon becomes the first state to establish Labor Day as an official holiday.

1894 The U.S. Congress passes a bill that recognizes the first Monday of September as Labor Day.

1959 During a recession, 115,000 workers stage a Labor Day march in New York City calling for higher wages.

uptown on Fifth Avenue in midtown Manhattan, many carrying banners calling for a higher minimum wage and higher wages in general. In 1982, the 100th anniversary of Labor Day, a high national unemployment rate of nearly 10 percent, and what the trade unions saw as President Ronald Reagan's pro-rich, antipoor, and antiunion policies all combined to spark large Labor Day parades. In New York City some 150,000 workers from 250 labor organizers marched up Fifth Avenue from 26th Street to 52d Street. Many of the marchers' banners specifically attacked the administration. The parade also featured 125 floats and over 200 marching bands. Local trade union councils organized parades in Denver and Indianapolis for the first time in forty years and in Chicago for the first time in thirty years. In Racine, Wisconsin, workers marched wearing black armbands with the number 250,000, representing the total of unemployed in the state. During the 1980s and 1990s Labor Day parades were held more frequently than in the immediately preceding decades, but their occurrence remained sporadic. ◆

Lupercalia

ANCIENT ROME ● FEBRUARY 15

Some people believe that the Lupercalia festival is the forerunner to Valentine's Day.

Lupercalia is an ancient Roman religious festival that was celebrated every year on February 15 near a cave called Lupercal, located in the southwest corner of Palatine hill in Rome. The Latin word *lupercal* is related to the word *lupus*, which means *wolf*. According to Roman myth, a wolf in the cave had nursed Remus and Romulus, the legendary founders of Rome, when they were infants. The Lupercalia festival involved young men called Luperci. The Luperci were divided into two groups: the Luperci Quinctiales and the Luperci Fabiani; the former bound themselves to Romulus, the latter to Remus. The Luperci appeared naked or wearing only a loincloth, which brought to mind a precivilized state and according to the ancient Roman writer Cicero, they constituted a "truly savage brotherhood."

The Luperalia ceremony began with a sacrifice of a goat in the cave. According to the ancient Roman writer Plutarch, the Luperci also sacrificed dogs. The Luperci then began running through crowds of people carrying lashes called *februa*, made from the hides of goats, with which they struck the spectators, especially women, in order to ensure their fertility. The word *februa* is related to the word *februatur*, which means *purification*, so the lashing was also apparently a purification rite by which evil spirits were symbolically driven from the body. Plutarch also writes that during the ceremony young people from noble families were led forth; some touched their foreheads with bloody knives while others smeared their bodies with wool soaked in milk. Ancient Roman writers report that after they had been smeared with blood or milk, the young people would begin laughing.

Some people believe that the Lupercalia festival is the forerunner to Valentine's Day. According to legend, the Lupercalia festivities also involved a custom by which the names of young unmarried girls were put in a jar. Each boy drew a name from the jar and was paired off for the remainder of the festival, or the entire year, with the girl whose name he drew.

Scholars are uncertain about the meaning of many elements of the Lupercalia festival. For example, no one knows what divinity was the patron of the feast, although the Roman poets Virgil and Ovid both designate the Greek god Pan as the patron. Pan, who was believed to be half man and half goat, was the god of woods and pastures and the protector of shepherds and farmers. ◆

Mardi Gras (Shrove Tuesday)

Mardi Gras, also called "Shrove Tuesday" or "Fat Tuesday" is a flamboyant Carnival celebration that most Americans associate with the city of New Orleans. The exact date for Mardi Gras varies from year to year, but it always falls on the Tuesday before Ash Wednesday, forty-one days before Easter.

Mardi Gras has roots deep in pagan rites of ancient Greece, and is the "climax day" of a whole season of festivities—balls, parties, parades—that begins on Twelfth Night, or Epiphany (January 6). Although the festival is associated with New Orleans, the first American Mardi Gras was celebrated in Mobile, in present-day Alabama, in the 1830s (except it was really New Year's Eve). Mardi Gras is still celebrated in Mobile, as well as in other southern Louisiana towns and cities such as Baton Rouge, New Roads, and Lafayette.

"Fat Tuesday," the culmination of over a month of celebrations, is the great day when the parades of New Orleans's Zulu Social Aid and Pleasure Club and a society called the Krewe of Rex roll down oak-lined St. Charles Avenue into downtown New Orleans, where thousands of people are lined along Canal Street, the widest downtown street in America. When the great floats arrive, masked captains and parade marshals, dressed in robes of medieval royalty, throw beads and other gifts to the spectators. People yell, "Throw me somethin', mister!" and reach up in a joyous frenzy for the colorful beads, cups, doubloons, and the famous painted Zulu coconuts. Though the big parades don't go into the Vieux Carré (old quarter) anymore,

Mardi Gras King Cake

One of the most flavorful Mardi Gras customs in New Orleans and elsewhere in southern Louisiana starts at the very beginning of the Carnival season, on January 6—also known as Epiphany and formerly known as King's Day. The Epiphany commemorates the day when the three kings, or magi, first beheld the infant Jesus and presented him with treasures. Twelfth Night cakes, with a bean or coin hidden inside, are a centuries-old tradition in Europe. The person receiving the slice with the bean would be designated King (or Queen) of the Bean and would receive special honors during Twelfth Night festivities, including the right to choose his or her royal partner.

In New Orleans and other southern American cities, there is an old tradition of hosting king cake parties, beginning on the first Friday after Epiphany and continuing till the Friday just before Mardi Gras. The New Orleans–style king cake is usually a simple, ring-shaped cake made of sweet dough, flavored with cinnamon, then braided and covered with green-, purple-, and gold-colored icings. Purple, green, and gold—the colors of the house of Romanoff—have been the traditional colors of Mardi Gras since the grand duke of Russia, Alexis Romanoff, visited New Orleans during Carnival in 1872. Green represents faith, gold is power, and purple is justice. Some king cakes are filled with cream cheese, and somewhere inside the cake a small plastic baby, representing the Christ child, has been hidden. King cake parties are usually held on a Friday, either at someone's home or in the workplace. Each guest is given a slice of cake, and whoever "bites the baby" must host the next party, on the following Friday. The parties continue each week until the end of Carnival, or Mardi Gras day.

the crowd swells across Canal into the French Quarter: sometimes a million people are crowded together on land that is five to ten feet below sea level, a quarter mile from the Mississippi River.

Mardi Gras or Shrove Tuesday's pagan origins are best traced to the ancient Roman Lupercalia festival, though the roots go even deeper, into fertility and purification rites in Greek **Arcadia** some five thousand years ago, as recorded by the Roman poet Ovid. He describes a springtime purification and fertility rite practiced by Greek shepherds in Arcadia about five thousand years ago in hopes of winning good crops and remission of sins. Priests known as *luperci* would sacrifice a goat, eat its flesh, and cut its hide into strips. As the sun was setting on the day of the rite, the *luperci* would appear, their faces smeared with the goat's blood, and brandishing the goathide whips. The *luperci* ran through the fields or lanes of the town, chasing and lashing the men and women. This ritual was later introduced to

Arcadia: a region of ancient Greece famous for the simple, contented life of its people.

Rome, where it developed into a riotous festival known as the Lupercalia.

Around 200 B.C., the Romans began to worship Cybele, the Great Mother, a fertility goddess with roots in Asia Minor, and embraced the cult of Cybele's son, Attis. The springtime rituals for fertility and purification that became known as the Lupercalia followed a week of fasting; the festival was a two-day frenzy of drunken abandon accompanied by music of trumpets and flutes and cymbals. For two days, all social order was cast aside as priests would wear women's clothes (if they liked); patrician masters and mistresses consorted with slaves; and masks, costumes, and cross-dressing were common among both priests and the laity. The Lupercalia continued as an annual custom for at least seven hundred years.

Naturally, the early Christian church was horrified by the disorder. Saint Gelasius I, the bishop of Rome (that is to say, the Pope) from 492 to 496, forbade Christians from participating in the Lupercalia and transformed the festival into the feast of the Purification of the Virgin. By this time, however, the Lupercalia had spread from Rome and Ostia into the provinces, especially in Gaul and Africa. In Gaul, or present-day France, Druid

Thousands of spectators watch colorful floats as they parade through New Orleans's French Quarter during Mardi Gras.

Spectators reach up to catch beads, coins, and other trinkets thrown from parade floats during Mardi Gras in New Orleans, Louisiana.

priests had long celebrated a Fête du Soleil (Festival of the Sun) in which a young bull dressed in garlands of leaves and flowers was led through the town, then sacrificed. The bull appears today as the Boeuf Gras, symbolizing the last meat permitted before Lent, at the head of the Rex parade on Mardi Gras day.

In 325 the Council of Nicea established a method for reckoning the date of Easter, the celebration of Christ's resurrection

This New Orleans Mardi Gras celebrant wears a stylized version of an American Indian costume.

from the dead. It was decided that Easter Sunday would be on the first Sunday after the next full moon following the vernal equinox (March 21). The forty days before Easter, beginning with Ash Wednesday, were the period of penance, prayer, and fasting known as Lent. The last possible day before Lent to enjoy earthly pleasures, then, was the Tuesday we know today as Mardi Gras.

In the French territory they called "la Louisiane," the two principal settlements were Mobile and "la Nouvelle-Orléans." The French and Spanish Creoles who had lived in New Orleans since the 1700s had loved music and theater from their earliest days; a fine ball or opera was always more important than money or business. (New Orleans had two opera houses before any other American city had one.)

One of the earliest mentions of a Mardi Gras procession (not an organized parade, as would appear later) appears in a *Picayune* of 1838: "In the procession [of young Creole gentlemen] were several carriages superbly ornamented—bands of music, horses

People in New Orleans dress up in extravagant and colorful costumes for Mardi Gras.

richly caparisoned—personations of knights, cavaliers, heros, demigods, chanticleers, and punchinellos, all mounted. Many of them were dressed in female attire, and acted the lady with no small degree of grace."

Although they developed an elaborate culture of masked balls and fêtes, the French did not originate the Carnival parades as we know them today. To the Creoles' horror and disgust, it was those vulgar *Américains* on the other side of Canal Street who began the tradition of parades with decorated floats through the streets of New Orleans. In December 1856, at a time when New Orleans was at its pinnacle of prosperity, six young men who had moved to New Orleans from Mobile, and had been among that city's New Year's Eve revelers calling themselves the Cowbellions, formed a society, which they called "The Mystick Krewe of Comus," after the hero in John Milton's poem *Comus*, a sorcerer and a **hedonist**, the son of Bacchus and Circe. On Mardi Gras night of 1857, Comus's inaugural parade through the Garden District was a pair of carriages bearing the masked krewe members, preceded by brass bands

hedonist: one who believes that pleasure should be the chief goal of life.

Although New Orleans hosts the largest and best known Mardi Gras festival, many smaller cities and towns throughout the Deep South celebrate the holiday. This Cajun Mardi Gras party took place in Mamou, Louisiana.

and surrounded by a ring of torches. It was a spectacular procession of pageantry and theater, and no one could stop talking about it. After the debut of Comus in 1857, elaborate parades became the centerpieces of Carnival.

Mardi Gras received a great boost of refinement and popularity in 1872 when the krewe of Rex gave its first parade, coinciding with a visit to New Orleans by Alexis Romanoff, the grand duke of Russia. During his tour of the United States, Grand Duke Alexis had become enchanted by a musical-comedy performer in the New York production of *Bluebeard*: the actress-singer Lydia Thompson's singing of "If Ever I May Cease to Love" was widely reported as having caught the Grand Duke's heart. Therefore the newly assembled krewe of Rex promoted the song, and decorated the city with the colors of the house of Romanoff, green (for faith), gold (power), and purple (justice). These three colors have since been adopted as the official colors of carnival. In addition to introducing the colors, the krewe of Rex added several other elements that have become integral to Carnival: Rex, the king of Carnival (there was no king before Rex), the Boeuf Gras, and the anthem, "If Ever I May Cease to Love." Rex introduced a grandeur to the madness, as shown in this Proclamation from the King of Carnival in 1934:

Greeting: The Lord High Chamberlain of His Majesty's household announces that the King will pay his annual visit to His beloved Capital City of New Orleans on the great fête day of Mardi Gras on the 13th day of February 1934. . . . It is ordained that good weather shall prevail, and the City of Flowers in its Festive array promises abundant pleasure to all within her gates.

The original krewes were social clubs of wealthy and powerful gentlemen, and most of them still are today. But anyone can form a krewe (a variant spelling of *crew*), as the following names may attest: the Knights of Momus, the Order of Druids, the High Priests of Mithras, and the krewes of Rex, Bacchus, Endymion, and the Zulu Social Aid and Pleasure Club. More recent additions include Iris, Isis, the Krewe de Vieux, the gay Krewe of Petronius, and the Krewe of Barkus (for dogs).

Mardi Gras is not a moneymaking opportunity in the ordinary sense, unless one owns a hotel, restaurant or a liquor wholesale supply company. Costumiers and maskmakers can do a good business, but the best ones are not "in it for the money." The parades are free, they are not sponsored by any company, and (one hopes) they never will be. There is a clear hierarchy of participation in the festival, but the Carnival is for everyone, a mingling of the poor and the wealthy and everyone in between. Carnival is a release from all the cares of dollars and deals; imagination and good cheer are infinitely more important than anything money can buy—although a hotel room with a bathroom near Canal Street is always highly valued.

It is not an exaggeration to say that to the people of New Orleans, Mardi Gras is bigger than Christmas; even a hundred years ago, Carnival was the biggest show in town, and Christmas, while a holy day, was not nearly the huge commercial or nostalgic juggernaut it has become during the twentieth century.

The police on horseback move in a phalanx down Bourbon Street, sweeping the crowds onto the narrow sidewalks, telling everyone to go home, the party is over. The police are serious. Lights are going out, people are walking home, or trying to find where they parked, and some are taking aspirins to ward off tomorrow's hangover. Lent has come; time to sacrifice, to put aside certain pleasures for forty days, till Easter. But already the krewes are planning balls and parades, and all across town the Mardi Gras Indians are threading their needles for next year's costume. ◆

Martin Luther King Day

Martin Luther King Day marks the birthday of the pre-eminent leader of the civil rights movement of the 1950s and 1960s. Although King's actual birthday was January 15, 1929, the holiday is observed each year on the third Monday in January.

A Baptist minister, Dr. King led the successful Montgomery bus boycott against segregated seating on Montgomery, Alabama, buses in 1955 and 1956. In 1957 he founded the Southern Christian Leadership Conference, a major civil rights organization, and served as its president. The King-led demonstrations against segregation in Birmingham, Alabama, in 1963 sparked passage of the Civil Rights Act of 1964, and reaction to the voting rights protests that he led in Selma, Alabama, in 1965 helped pass the Voting Rights Act that year. For his commitment to social change and nonviolence, King won the Nobel Peace Prize in 1964.

King's life was brought to a sudden and tragic end on April 4, 1968, when he was assassinated by gunfire in Memphis, Tennessee, where he had come to support striking black sanitation workers. Beginning the next year and continuing at an accelerating pace, many African-American workers spontaneously stayed home on January 15, King's birthday, and some businesses closed down. During the 1970s some unions succeeded in obtaining January 15 as a paid holiday. During the same decade, some states made the civil rights leader's birthday a legal holiday.

Meanwhile, on April 8, 1968, just four days after King's assassination, black U.S. Representative John Conyers of

"I have a dream that one day on the red hills of Georgia the sons of former slaves and the sons of former slave owners will be able to sit down together at the table of brotherhood."

Martin Luther King Jr., 1963

Michigan introduced a bill to make January 15 a federal holiday. The measure did not get far. But support for a federal King holiday grew in the 1970s, manifested by petitions to Congress, demonstrations, and other forms of pressure. Congress held its first serious hearings on the subject in 1975. Four years later, the House of Representatives came close to passing a bill designating January 15 as a national holiday. The final congressional debate on a federal holiday for King came in 1983. Supporters of a holiday bill argued that passage would give recognition to the achievements of King and the civil rights movement. Most of the measure's opponents gave as their reason the cost in terms of lost productivity. A few brought up old, unsubstantiated charges that King was pro-Communist. These included North Carolina senator Jesse Helms, who staged an unsuccessful filibuster against the bill.

The House passed the measure on August 2, 1983, by a vote of 338–90. The Senate followed with a 78–22 vote on October 19. President Ronald Reagan signed it on November 2. Under the terms of the legislation, King's birthday would be celebrated as a federal holiday on the third Monday of January, beginning in 1986.

This group of young people in Long Beach, California, celebrates diversity and racial tolerance on the birthday of Martin Luther King Jr.

1929 ▶ Martin Luther King Jr. is born in Atlanta.

1955 ▶ King leads a boycott of the segregated bus system in Montgomery, Alabama.

1957 ▶ Kings helps establish the Southern Christian Leadership Conference.

1964 ▶ Kings wins the Nobel Peace Prize.

1965 ▶ King leads protests in Alabama to draw attention to the denial of the voting rights of African Americans.

1968 ▶ King begins the Poor People's Campaign.

1968 ▶ King is assassinated in Memphis; Congressman John Conyers introduces a bill to make King's birthday's a national holiday.

1983 ▶ President Ronald Reagan signs a bill establishing King's birthday as a federal holiday.

1986 ▶ The first official Martin Luther King Day observances take place.

During the 1980s the states felt growing pressure to recognize King's legacy. By 1988 a legal King holiday had been established (in most cases on the third Monday of January) by the District of Columbia and all states but Hawaii, Idaho, Montana, Wyoming, North Dakota, South Dakota, New Hampshire, and Arizona, none of which had significant black populations. Arizona created a King holiday in the 1980s but repealed it later in the decade. A national boycott of Arizona launched after the reversal cost the state significantly in convention and tourist revenues. In 1993 Arizona and New Hampshire, the last two holdouts, finally joined the others (although in New Hampshire the holiday was named Civil Rights Day).

In some of the southern states the King holiday brought with it ironic historical twists. Alabama, Arkansas, Mississippi, and Virginia celebrate King's birthday along with that of Confederate general Robert E. Lee, and Virginia added another Confederate general, Thomas "Stonewall" Jackson, to the birthday commemoration. This aroused the displeasure of many African Americans in those states.

In the late 1990s the Reverend Jesse Jackson conducted a campaign to persuade brokerage houses to hire more members of disadvantaged groups. The financial world, to show its good will, closed down Wall Street in 1998 for the first time in honor of King's birthday.

Probably the most extensive celebrations of the holiday have been held in King's hometown of Atlanta, Georgia. By 1990 the city was observing a full King Week, featuring dinners, speeches, receptions, exhibits, concerts, and forums. The observance took on the likeness of a fair or carnival outside the Ebenezer Baptist Church, where King's father and King himself once preached, and the Martin Luther King Jr. Center for Social Change, run by the King family.

The King holiday is celebrated in many other ways around the country. In 1995 Chicago schoolchildren wrote and performed a radio play about a childhood experience of King. In Houston, workshops, speeches, children's performances, and concerts marked the holiday in 1997. In Michigan, 130 different celebrations were counted in 1998; they covered a wide range of activities from parading to political rallies, and from gospel singing to educational programs.

With many blacks moving from the inner cities to the suburbs in the 1980s and 1990s, the observances spread with them. For example, the commemorations moved from Detroit into such nearby towns as Westland, Wayne, and Inkston. In suburban Prince George's County, Maryland, near Washington, D.C., the 1998 festivities featured color guards, marching bands, and drill teams parading for two miles on Martin Luther King Jr. Highway.

Martin Luther King Day became a focus for announcing or initiating measures of interest to blacks. During the 1990 celebrations in Massachusetts, a number of Boston's most powerful banks announced a $400-million investment plan to assist in the revitalization of the inner city. On the King holiday in 1996, Black Entertainment Television started up BET on Jazz, an all-jazz cable network. In 1998 Bill Lann Lee, assistant attorney general for the Civil Rights Division of the Justice Department, went to Detroit on Martin Luther King Day to speak to that city's civil rights groups about hate crime issues, and also to announce that the White House would request an additional $86 million for the civil rights enforcement budget.

In the spirit of the holiday's namesake, some use King Day as a time for social protest. After the official commemoration of the holiday at the University of Michigan in Ann Arbor in 1995, about 300 mostly black students gathered on the lawn of the university president's official residence. The students protested what they believed was the university's failure to deal adequately with the needs of black students and its slow pace in expanding black student enrollment. Two years later upwards of 400 students rallied at Indiana University to demand new cultural and academic programs for minority groups. ◆

In the spirit of the holiday's namesake, some use Martin Luther King Day as an occasion for social protest.

Masquerades in Africa

AFRICA ● VARIOUS DATES

articulated: having joints or hinges.

exegesis: explanation or interpretation.

A masquerade is a ceremony in which performers wear masks to represent spirits, ancestors, or societal authority. The mask may also serve as a symbol for some mysterious aspect of the natural world, or it may symbolize some type of secret knowledge. Many African societies have long and rich traditions of masquerades. In the fourteenth century Ibn Battuta, an Arab geographer, commented upon the use of **articulated** bird masks in the court of the Mali Empire. In 1738 Frances Moore was one of the first Europeans to give an account of an African masquerade, which he encountered in the Senegambia in west Africa. From the mid nineteenth century through the early decades of the twentieth century many travelers, missionaries, and colonial officials published descriptions of masquerades from diverse regions in Africa. Throughout the twentieth century African masks and the masquerade rituals and ceremonies within which they appear have been the focus of study and **exegesis** by anthropologists and others.

Throughout Africa masks take many forms and include a variety of carved wooden constructions, as well as those that are made entirely from bark, animal skins, plant fibers, and woven cloth. Masquerades may be owned collectively by communities, lineages, initiation and other voluntary associations, or by individuals. With few exceptions, women are excluded from direct participation in masquerading.

In the late twentieth century masquerades continue to be used by many groups living in west Africa, including the Dogon, Bamana, Mossi, Senufo, Mende, Dan, Yoruba, Igbo

(Ibo), Ijaw, Ibibio, Efik, Idoma, Mambila, and Bamileke. Numerous central African groups, including the Chokwe, Kuba, Luba, Hemba, Teke, and Lega, among many others, also utilize masks. By contrast, masquerades are much less significant among groups living in northern, eastern, and southern Africa, although they are performed by some Berber peoples living in Morocco, as well as by the Makonde in Tanzania and the Chewa in Malawi.

In many societies masquerades are the visible manifestation of spirits. These spirits may be ancestral or powerful bush, forest, or water spirits. Among the Yoruba of southwestern Nigeria, Egungun ritual society masquerades are embodiments of ancestral spirits. Ancestral spirits also appear as important masquerades among the Okpella and the Igala of Nigeria and among the Chokwe of Zaire. Forest and bush spirits among the Senufo and Dan of Côte d'Ivoire and the Igbo of Nigeria are made visible through the vehicle of masquerades. In Ijaw communities in Nigeria, water-spirit masquerades are performed in annual public ceremonies that are intended to honor and propitiate these powerful beings.

In a number of African societies masks were formerly used in a **regulatory** capacity and played a central role in the governance of the community. Masquerades were used as strategies for social control by warrior associations among the Bamileke in Cameroon and in the Cross River area in Nigeria. Among the Dan of Côte d'Ivoire and the Igala, Idoma, and certain Igbo groups in Nigeria, a masked figure sat in judgment of criminals, levied and collected fines, and presided over cases involving land disputes. Among the Bamana of Mali, the Komo men's association and its masquerade were charged with eradicating witchcraft.

Masks play central roles in chieftaincy rituals. In contemporary rural Malawi, spirit masks of the Chewa Nyau society perform at the installation of village headmen. This modern ritual, which has its origins in precolonial rituals for the installation of divine kings, conjures up images of a heroic past, but also reflects and reconfigures current political realities. In the twentieth century among the Bamileke, regulatory societies have been transformed into prestigious titled societies and the distinctive beaded elephant mask has been incorporated into chieftaincy rituals. In Côte d'Ivoire among the Dan, a chief may own several old and important masks. These old masks are no longer used in performance, but are laid beside the chief in ritual con-

regulatory: serving to bring under the control of law or authority.

texts as a validation of his political authority. Pectoral and hip masks have been a long-standing part of leadership regalia and are still worn today by the *oba* of Benin and the *attah* of Idah in Nigeria as symbols of political authority.

Masquerades are often material symbols of secret knowledge and serve as ritual separators between various segments of the community, such as men and women, initiated and noninitiated, community members and strangers. Among the Lega of Zaire (Congo), for example, different ranks within the Bwami initiation association own and use a variety of masks. Miniature wooden and ivory masks are the property of several of the highest ranks within the association. These masks might either be worn on the body or carried by members during various ceremonies, and function as **mnemonic** devices alluding to the **esoteric** knowledge that is the purview of each specific rank. Leaders of the men's Poro association in Liberia and Sierra Leone often own small miniature versions of larger-scale spirit masks to which they have titular rights. These personal masks validate a man's right to sit at Poro counsels and to participate in decision making. They also serve as a means of identification and a validation of authority for **itinerant** Poro leaders.

Throughout Africa masquerades play a central role in coming-of-age ceremonies. During these rituals, the separate realms of bush and village, living and dead converge. First, the novices are sequestered for a period of time outside of the village, in the bush, the domain of the spirits. During this period, the initiates are symbolically reborn as adults under the watchful eye of masked spirits. Masks are often used to orchestrate the training in esoteric knowledge, and in the closing ceremonies of initiation, spirit masks appear in public ceremonies when the young people are presented to the community as adults. Among the Chokwe, masked spirits control the boy's initiation camp and bar women from entry into the ceremonies. Among the Gola, Bassa, and Vai of Liberia and the Mende, Bullom, and Temne of Sierra Leone, the water-spirit guardian of the women's Sande association takes the form of a masquerade. The spirit presides over the initiation camp, protects young girls during their seclusion, participates in their training, and appears with them during their reentry into the community as adult women.

Death produces a dangerous rupture in the social fabric, and it is carefully managed through a variety of rituals. In the clos-

mnemonic: intending to assist memory.

esoteric: known or understood by only a small group of people.

itinerant: traveling from place to place.

ing phase of many societies' funeral ceremonies, including those of the Dogon of Mali, the Mossi of Burkina Faso, the Dan of Côte d'Ivoire, and the Chewa of Malawi, masks play an important role. Among the Hemba of Zaire, the final phase of the funeral marks the end of mourning for the bereaved and the return of the village to a normal social life. In the ritual, the *so'o* mask, an allegorical figure of death, is used in two performances. The first performance emphasizes the state of disorder caused by death; the second performance restores order to the village. Among the Kuba and Kuba-related peoples of Zaire, many of the masks that play a critical role in men's initiation appear at the funerals of titled elders. Their use in performance reinforces distinctions in power between titled and nontitled men and between men and women. The masks validate the institution of title-taking and reinforce the authority invested in senior title-holders.

Masks and the performances in which they are used often embody important forms of symbolic classification and the ordering of social experience. Among the Dogon of Mali the towering vertical form of the *sirige* mask represents the multi-storied family house, and the graphic motifs engraved and painted on this mask symbolize the history of generations within Dogon communities. The masker's symbolic gestures reenact fundamental episodes of the Dogon creation myth.

In several Berber communities in Morocco, masquerades are performed between the Sunni Muslim feast of sacrifice and the celebration of the New Year. In these masked rituals, characters parody and contest central values, which the Muslim feast of the sacrifice sanctifies.

In Zaire the Teke *kidamu* mask, carved in the shape of a flat disk with clearly articulated **bipolar** divisions, is symbolically rich. This mask type, first created around 1860, has been continually modified in the twentieth century, reflecting a history of shifting and evolving relationships between two competing segments within the Teke political organization. The mask's primary symbolism and its use in performance express the essential nature of Teke society and highlight relationships the Teke have had with their neighbors over the centuries.

In Côte d'Ivoire some Dan spirit masks are defined as entertainers. In Mali, youth-association puppet masquerades, which are performed by Bamana, Bozo, Somono, and Maraka troupes, are defined by the participants as play, although the content of

Masks and the performances in which they are used often embody important forms of symbolic classification and the ordering of social experience.

bipolar: expressing two opposite images or ideas.

A group of Dogon dancers performs in a masquerade in Mali, West Africa.

iconography: a traditional system of symbols used to represent objects and ideas.

these masquerade performances is often quite serious and explores the nature of society and people's relationship with powerful spirit entities.

Multiple masking traditions may exist parallel to one another in a single society. Moreover, every masquerade tradition has its own history, which may be marked by periodic transformations in the material repertoire (the masks and their costumes), in the context of use, and in the universe of interpretations assigned to them. Spirit masks among the Dan operate in a variety of contexts. Many are central to boys' initiation, while others act as messengers, debt collectors, adjudicators, and entertainers. Throughout its life history an individual Dan mask from any of these contexts might acquire prestige as it ages and subsequently its behavior, role, and interpretation is modified accordingly.

Among the Bamana of Mali the Chiwara men's association performs paired male and female antelope masquerades in annual rites that inaugurate the farming season. The form, **iconography**, and performance of these paired masquerades embody the virtues that the Bamana associate with farming. Chiwara is the mythical antelope who introduced farming to the Bamana and the pairing of the male and female mythical antelopes recreates the essential conditions for agricultural fertility symbolizing the union of the sun, the male principle, and the earth and water, the female principle. Today, in those Malian communities where the Chiwara men's association is now defunct, these same antelope masquerades are often incorporated into festivals that the community defines as entertainments. The interpretation of the masquerades in their new performance context clearly resonates with meanings emergent in the older context. However, in many multiethnic communities today these same Chiwara masquerades evoke a distinctive Bamana ethnic identity based on participants' sense of a shared history and a group investment in an agricultural life.

Masquerades have undergone repeated transformations over time and new forms and contexts of use are continually emerging in Africa. In Sierra Leone in the 1950s Ode-Lay masked associations, which were multiethnic and urban, grew up in Creole neighborhoods in Freetown as a response to disruptive social change. The inspiration for the Creole Ode-Lay associations, however, is to be found in Yoruba secret societies that were established in Sierra Leone by Yoruba immigrants after 1807. The Ode-Lay masked performances draw heavily upon Yoruba hunters' association and Egungun society rituals. Other key elements have been borrowed from Mende and Limba masking traditions. The Ode-Lay masquerades are militant and during the performances participants perform martial arts games with each other or with members of competing troupes. By the 1970s members of Sierra Leone's ruling party served as patrons for Freetown's various Ode-Lay associations and, as a way of extending their influence and consolidating their authority outside of the capital, they encouraged the establishment of Ode-Lay associations in more rural areas. Elsewhere in Mali, Zaire (Congo), Nigeria, and Côte d'Ivoire masquerades have been incorporated into the repertoire of national dance troupes and stand as valued examples of artistic and cultural **patrimony**. Other masquerades, like those still performed today at Dogon funerals, are now occasionally performed for tourists. In Mali the Chiwara antelope mask has been adopted as a national cultural symbol and is used on the masthead of *Jamana*, a Malian cultural publication. The mask is also used as an emblem for Bamako, the capital city. ◆

patrimony: something inherited from one's ancestors.

Mawlid

Mawlid is an Arabic word that literally means the time and place of a birth, but the word is used in particular for the birth of the prophet Muhammad (*mawlid al-nabi*) and refers to festivals observing his birth. In some Islamic countries it also refers to the festival days of local saints (*walis*). The actual birth date of the prophet Muhammad is unknown, but the anniversary of his birth is celebrated on 12 Rabi I of the Islamic lunar calendar, a day prior to the anniversary of his death (in 632 C.E.).

Muhammad is portrayed in the Koran as a messenger of God who was an ordinary mortal in other respects. Only in later centuries did many Muslims begin to assert a higher sanctity for his person. The first recorded celebrations of his birth occurred during the latter part of Fatimid rule in Egypt (909–1171). As Shiah Muslims who held descendants of the Prophet in particularly high esteem, the Fatimid elite similarly observed the mawlids of Muhammad's son-in-law, Ali, his daughter, Fatimah, and the reigning **caliph**. Palace dignitaries and religious notables held daylight processions and delivered sermons, a practice briefly prohibited but later revived. The Sunni majority in Egypt took no part in these ceremonies.

The first popular mawlid occurred in 1207. Muzaffar al-Din Kokburu, brother-in-law of the famed Salah al-Din (Saladin), arranged for a festival in Arbala, a town near Mosul in present-day northern Iraq. As described by the historian Ibn Khallikan (d. 1282), a native of the town, the mawlid became an elaborate annual event, attracting scholars, notables, preachers, and

caliph: a successor to Muhammad as the head of Islam.

228

poets from throughout the region. The deeds and person of Muhammad were celebrated in religious poetry and songs and culminated on the eve of the mawlid in a torchlight procession led by the prince. Followers of Sufi orders were also prominent in the celebrations, and gifts were lavishly distributed to participants.

Some aspects of early mawlids appear to have been influenced by Middle Eastern Christian traditions of the period, such as lavish entertainments and nighttime processions in honor of saints. Even as mawlids also developed for saints and other holy persons, especially in Egypt, the Prophet's mawlid continued to be the most elaborate. Mawlids quickly became highly popular occasions associated with mysticism, during which Sufi orders congregated in public, reciting rhythmical chants in praise of God and in some cases entering into trance. From Egypt, mawlids spread to many other parts of the Islamic world.

The popularity of mawlids met initial resistance from some theologians. Ibn Taymiyah (d. 1328) and others condemned the Prophet's mawlid as a harmful innovation. After considerable discussion, most theologians, except those precursors of the later Wahhabi movement, who espoused Islam in its most idealized and fundamental form, tolerated the mawlid as a praiseworthy innovation, since it inspired reverence for the Prophet. The central activity of mawlids is the recital of long **panegyrical** poems and legends commemorating Muhammad and his deeds, recitations so popular that they are repeated on festive occasions throughout the year.

panegyrical: expressing formal and elaborate praise.

The acceptance of popular practice by theologians shows the Islamic principle of consensus at work. A key doctrinal tenet in Islam is that the community of believers cannot agree upon error. The legal opinions of religious jurists appear to have had minimal influence in reducing the popularity of mawlids, so that most jurists were encouraged to accommodate theological doctrine to social realities.

As with other Islamic celebrations and rites of passage, mawlids show considerable differences throughout the Islamic world. In some contexts, the mawlid is minimally distinguished from other festive occasions; elsewhere, it is one of the most important annual religious events. In nineteenth-century Cairo, mawlid celebrations started on the first day of Rabi I. Large tents were pitched in one of Cairo's quarters and decorated with lamps and Koranic inscriptions. Each night

Sufi orders carried their banners in procession to their tents, where they chanted the name of God, recited poems in praise of Muhammad, and provided refreshments to guests. In the daytime, dancers, clowns, and storytellers entertained the audience in a carnival atmosphere. Festivities climaxed on the eleventh and twelfth evenings of the month, with elaborate poems and songs in praise of Muhammad that continued until morning. In recent times government restrictions against large public gatherings sought to curtail these events. Nonetheless, the Prophet's mawlid and to a lesser extent those for local saints continue to be large communal festivals attracting hundreds of thousands of people in Egypt's larger towns.

Elsewhere in the Islamic world, religious orders play a less central role in mawlid festivities. In Morocco, the month in which the Prophet's birthday occurs is popularly known as *mulud*, the local pronunciation of mawlid. Children born during this month are considered especially fortunate and are often named after it, and it is a good time to circumcise boys. Celebrations last a week, culminating with recitations of panegyrics of Muhammad in decorated and illuminated community mosques. On the final night, recitations continue until daybreak.

henna: a reddish-brown dye obtained from the leaves of the henna plant.

Some families offer a feast and distribute food to the poor; women decorate their hands and feet with **henna** and visit cemeteries. In Java, a feast is offered for the mawlid, which is one of the two most important ceremonies in a region given over to elaborate festival cycles. A popular Javanese belief is that the giving of feasts for the Prophet's birthday and the end of Ramadan distinguishes Muslims from non-Muslims and humans from animals; this view of the importance of the occasion is not necessarily shared by those Javanese who have a more elaborate understanding of Islamic doctrine and ritual.

The symbolism of the mawlid is especially highly developed among Swahili-speaking East African Muslims. In the town and island of Lamu, located off the northern coast of Kenya, most Muslims hold that the prophet Muhammad, created of dust, like all other persons, carried "light" to the earth in this month. The discipline of fasting during the month of Ramadan emphasizes the separation of nature and culture and the distance between actual human society and the Islamic ideal. Likewise, the month of Muhammad's birth is regarded as a joyous occasion that emphasizes life as lived here and now, combined with belief in the Prophet's willingness to intervene on behalf of his people and to accept them in full recognition of their individual shortcomings. It is said that during this month the Prophet lives on the earth like a human being and loves and hates just as they do.

The first twelve days of the month are marked by processions, singing, and the music of tambourines and flutes. Intense competitions are held on successive evenings in the mosques and religious associations of the various quarters in Lamu. Each quarter vies in enthusiasm to praise Muhammad's life and deeds in song and prose and to show its love for the Prophet. *Sharifs,* descendants of Muhammad, are especially honored in Lamu during this period.

Sharifs are invited to recite poems in praise of Muhammad in most of the nineteen mosques of Lamu town. In beautiful performances on successive evenings, assemblies of young boys from mosque schools and musicians perform songs and poems that have been rehearsed for months. Brightly colored tunics, donated by wealthy Muslims, are worn for the ceremonies. The freeborn and the ex-slaves, members of two important local social categories, compete with one another during these celebrations to express a willingness to use earthly wealth—the offer of food and refreshments to guests—and talent to show their love for the Prophet. If not enough effort is put into the preparations for quarter festivities, the *sharifs* are said to participate with less enthusiasm and to attract fewer blessings for the quarter.

Love of the Prophet is said to join together the world of nature and the world of culture. Ceremonies include the sacrifice of cows, highly valued on the island, visits to cemeteries, and the distribution of rose water by *sharifs* to symbolize Muhammad's ability to cleanse his followers of their sins. Until the 1970s distinctions between freeborn and ex-slave and *sharif* and commoner remained significant for many East African Muslims, although in recent years such distinctions have been eroded under pressure from reformist Muslims. ◆

The month of Muhammad's birth is regarded as a joyous occasion that emphasizes life as lived here and now, combined with belief in the Prophet's willingness to intervene on behalf of his people and to accept them in full recognition of their individual shortcomings.

May Day

May Day is the only major festival of pre-Christian Europe that was not adapted by the Christian church for its own purposes. Part of a yearly cycle that includes midwinter and harvest celebrations, it stands midway between the long, cold nights of winter and the days of plenty at summer's end, with symbolism and ceremony that reflect its pivotal position.

Across Europe the key symbol of the day is fresh spring growth, and the general hope is for **fecundity**. Traditionally, youths spent the eve of May Day in neighboring woods and awoke the villagers the next morning by visiting each house, singing a traditional carol and bearing garlands of fresh leaves and flowers. Or they might disguise one of their number as Jack-in-the-Green by enshrouding him with a portable bower of fresh greenery. Jack and his followers danced around the town collecting money from passersby for later feasting. In many villages these young people also cut down trees, which they then erected as maypoles in the village centers. Each pole served as a gathering place for community dances and activities. Dancers circled the maypole holding the ends of ribbons secured to its top. As they danced they wove the ribbons around the pole.

Traditional dramas enacted on May Day in many European countries commemorated the triumph of summer over winter, while in England the focus was on dancing and pageantry. Youths elected a king and queen of the May to preside over the day's proceedings; sometimes they were dressed as Robin Hood

fecundity: fertility.

Traditionally, youths spent the eve of May Day in neighboring woods and awoke the villagers the next morning by visiting each house bearing garlands of fresh leaves and flowers.

and Maid Marian, with members of their entourage represent-ing Friar Tuck, Little John, and Robin's other merry men.

Although the origins of May Day are unknown, what is known of its history is suggestive. The festival is not based on a magical ritual to secure the fertility of the crops, as once thought, but instead is a community expression of hope and joy. The emphasis has always been social solidarity, and not the supernatural or the metaphysical.

In modern times, people in many Western countries con-tinue to celebrate May Day as a lighthearted spring holiday. May Day festivities are often elaborate in Europe, but May Day has never been a major holiday in the United States because early American Puritans disapproved of the secular frivolity and exuberance of traditional May Day festivities. Nonetheless, children in many American towns and cities celebrate the day by wearing flowers in their hair and singing and dancing around a maypole. In many parts of the country, children make little May Day baskets, fill them with candies and other sweets, and present them to their friends and neighbors.

During the late 1800s May 1 began to be observed in many countries as a day to honor workers, similar to the September

Young girls and boys dance around the maypole during the May Day celebration at their school in New Haven, Connecticut.

This photo of the 1964 May Day parade through Red Square in Moscow shows Soviet leaders reviewing a convoy of tanks outside of the Lenin Museum.

Labor Day in the United States. A May Day of this type has been an especially important holiday in communist and social-ist countries. The former Soviet Union used the occasion to display its military strength during its annual May Day parade in Red Square in Moscow. The traditional May Day parade has continued in Russia since the Soviet Union dissolved in 1991, but its tone has become less militant. ◆

Medieval Festivals in Europe

EUROPE ● VARIOUS DATES

Activity occupying one-third of a lifetime must be culturally significant. While conditions varied with the country and the century, the medieval Christian calendar generally mandated fifty-two Sundays of enforced leisure plus, from the twelfth century on, at least forty saints' days. To these holidays could be added unlimited local church feasts averaging more than thirty, creating an astonishing 126 or more days per year on which work was not allowed. Englishmen added celebrations of St. Swithin's Day, the weather on which portended fine or failing crops; Canterbury townsfolk honored by holiday not only St. Thomas Becket but also Saints Alban, Dunstan, Ethelreda, and Edward the Confessor. Universities had their own holidays; fourteenth-century Montpellier's seventy-seven, plus Sundays, totaled 133 yearly festivals. Moreover, many holidays were not limited to twenty-four hours. No matter how hard a person's labors, holidays and festivals prevented existence from being entirely dour and dreary. Traditional costumery, song, dance, divination, drama, feasts, and revelry were as likely accompaniments to holidays as pious prayer, contrition, and acts of penance.

This quantity of church-enforced leisure in western Europe had social and commercial effects. Crops in harvest, buildings under construction, and shiploads of perishables could not be neglected for holiday rest without loss of product or workers' wages. Account ledgers suggest that employers with weekly salaried workers suffered financially when recompensing half a week's labor with full pay. Those paying only for rendered

> No matter how hard a person's labors, holidays and festivals prevented existence from being entirely dour and dreary.

235

Stuffed Dates for Winter Feasts

The date palm tree is native to the dry desert regions of north Africa and the Middle East, where its fruit has been a dietary staple for thousands of years. Moors from northwestern Africa brought dates to Spain in the 8th century, and they were eventually carried to other parts of Europe. Dried dates can be stored for many months, so during the Middle Ages they were available when other fruits were out of season. Dates stuffed with various cheeses, meats, and herbs were a popular delicacy on winter holidays.

1 pound pitted dried dates
1 cup dried bread crumbs
1/4 cup fresh sweet basil or 2 tablespoons dried basil
1/2 teaspoon salt
3 eggs, hard-boiled
1/2 pound ricotta cheese
1/2 cup beef broth

Cut a slit along one side of each date, then set aside. Mix together bread crumbs, basil, and salt. Mash the hard-boiled eggs. Add eggs to crumb mixture. Stir the ricotta into the beef broth, then add to egg and crumb mixture. Fill each date with about 1/2 teaspoon of the egg and cheese mixture.

services complained of holiday interference with productivity and profit, and employees lamented lost pay. Ecclesiastics such as John Gerson condemned the multiplicity of required holidays as an unfair burden upon farmers and the laboring poor. Local laws often compromised between clerical demands for holiday leisure dedicated to Christian godliness and contrary to **ecclesiastical** and mercantile insistences that human sustenance was the necessary precursor to contemplating divinity. Some jurisdictions alternated year by year, or month by month, celebration of holidays necessitated by God's calendar and their noncelebration as required by man's.

Forms of festivity also worried critics of holidays. Clerical or civil control over the **decorum** of celebrations required people's presence in church, chapel, or hall, and some coercion thereafter, lest revelers return from holiday unfit for serious work. While condemnations of celebratory excess may be ascribed to moralistic exaggeration of festal drinking and gambling, nevertheless holiday jubilation might easily deflect attention from piety to sensual pleasure. Furthermore, observant clergymen visiting church communities, such as thirteenth-century Bishop Eudes of Rouen (Odo Rigaldus) and other church

ecclesiastical: relating to the church as a formal institution.

decorum: propriety and good taste in conduct and appearance.

reformers, condemned riotous revelments of priests, chaplains, monks, and nuns. As Chaucer asked, "If [clerical] gold rusts, what will [the common folk] iron do?"

The most startling quality of seasonal holidays and festivals was their reconciliation of Christian custom and earlier pagan fertility rites. Solar solstice observances were rededicated to Christian purpose. Bonfires, originally bone-fires of animals sacrificed to the ancient **druidic** god Bal or Bel, glorified St. John the Baptist on Midsummer Eve. Such stamping dances as morris dances, Twelfth Night oxhorn rounds, and maypole dances originated in pagan reminders to winter-slumbering earth spirits to reawaken and assure spring crops and summer abundance. Augustine and Gregory the Great agreed that what Christianity could not eliminate, it must adapt.

druidic: relating to an ancient Celtic priesthood.

This pagan heritage for the games, songs, dances, and foods of calendar festivals (originally not entertainments, but stimulators and **propitiators** of fertility gods) partially explains their persistence and their identity in form among people of nearly all ages, degrees of education, wealth, and social status. Castle and cottage ceremonies differed in detail but not in basic structure. Merrymaking around a maypole was ritualistically patterned, whether the shaft was elegant, strung with gold and silken streamers, and crowned with jeweled wreaths, or rude, wrapped with rope and topped by daisies. Knights and carpenters similarly enjoyed Midsummer Eve plays with St. George's customarily terrifying "dragon," either an expensive marvel of machinery with mechanical wings and bellowing smoke, or a homespun dragon-shaped kite held aloft by shepherds' sticks and strings.

propitiator: one who attempts to pacify or make another less angry.

The Christian celebrations in western Europe of the tenth through fifteenth centuries necessarily included political fetes such as public honorings of royal crownings, marriages, births, and funerals; war and peace commemorations; kings', queens', and prelates' visitations and progresses; and other festive occasions. Banquets and entertainments upon these occasions were affirmations of power. They introduced classical, historical, and moral allusion in their subtleties and illusion foods, as well as in their pageants, **tableaux**, farces, and pantomimes. King Charles V of France regaled Emperor Charles IV in 1378 with a grand dinner spectacle simulating the crusaders' capture of Jerusalem in 1099, complete with battling knights scaling ladders beside a turreted castle and a rigged ship on the waters. Indoor or outdoor mock bowers, fountains, and grottoes looked up to theatrical clouds and heavenly gates where classical divinities, epic

tableaux: a scene presented by silent, motionless actors in costume.

heroes, or allegorical figures declaimed, chastised, or smiled upon the delighted audience. Horse-drawn cars moved Victory and the Virtues in triumph through archways erected at dramatic vantage points on parade routes.

Banquet courses crafted to stimulate the festive mood were interrupted by huge, edible, allegorical devices, such as the Four Ages of Man, edifying first spirit, then palate. John Russell's fifteenth-century *Boke of Nurture* describes such subtleties: a young man called Sanguinus or Spring, joyously loving, singing, and piping, standing on a cloud; an angry man of war, Colericus or Summer, standing in flames; a tired, sluggish, fat man, wielding a sickle and standing in a river, Fleumaticus or Harvest; and last, feeble, old, envious, sad Melencholicus or Winter, gray-haired and sitting on a hard, cold stone. Refined noblemen performed as rustics or wildmen dressed in grass and straw costumes. In 1393 the infamous Ball of the Flaming Ones, the *bal des ardents*, nearly incinerated King Charles VI of France when an inquisitive torchbearer ignited the antic players. Disasters notwithstanding, such occasional holidays, sometimes for a vast public, sometimes more private, were ornamental to the traditional holiday procession from January to December. Twelve calendar festivals typify that yearly ritual cycle.

A major January holiday was Twelfth Night, the eve of Epiphany. Concluding the twelve days of Christmas, Twelfth Night observances were ritual contests between good and evil. Star-led Magi in dramas outsmarted wicked King Herod to find the marvelous child in his manger. Traditional country actors, called mummers in England, performed St. George and the Dragon plays in which the saint overcame an evil knight. Team games such as Oranges and Lemons ended with a tug-of-war between representatives of winter and spring. The necessary winner was the triumphant new season.

Food rites also assured a bountiful rebirth of the land after its winter deadness. **Wassailing** toasts of spiced and herbed ales and wines were drunk and offered to the trees. Wassailing fruit trees in country orchards, or symbolically in a hall, was accompanied by loud, jubilant, stamping dances such as the oxhorn rounds. Revelers capped by "oxhorned" headdresses joyously circled the wassail tree, their earth-pounding, ankle-belled feet rhythmically signaling spring awake. Also derived from rural fertility practices were Twelfth Night fires, rings of twelve small fires set around a larger one in grainfields, originally to stimu-

King Charles V of France regaled Emperor Charles IV in 1378 with a grand dinner spectacle simulating the crusaders' capture of Jerusalem in 1099, complete with battling knights scaling ladders beside a turreted castle, and a rigged ship on the waters.

wassail: an early English toast to someone's health.

late harvests, or recreated indoors by circles of twelve candles centered by a thirteenth; Christianized, these flames represented the twelve days of Christmas or the twelve apostles, and the thirteenth signified the Virgin Mary or Christ. Honored guests at the Twelfth Night high table were the king and queen of the bean. They were selected by their finding the Twelfth Night luck amulet, a bean—in poor farm kitchens a dried vegetable; in castles a precious gold, porcelain, or jeweled favor—baked into the twelfth-cake, otherwise known as kings' cake or *gâteau des rois* or *galette des rois*.

A February feast for St. Valentine's Day paid tribute to Love, seemingly more closely related to the classical Venus and Cupid than to the deeds or deaths of the several second- and third-century Christian saints named Valentine. Love lanterns, hollowed and pierced vegetable candleholders, lit the hall while stimulating love music, often raucous and discordant, called the shivaree, regaled people garbed in love sleeves (stylish arm covers separable from garments for exchange with a beloved) and love jewelry, such as a gold or fabric love knot, symbolizing eternal affection, or a crowned *A*, standing for *amor vincit omnia* (love conquers all). Foods of love were thought to stimulate affection. To these were added symbolic edibles such as plum shuttles, oval cakes for "weaving" love into the "fabric" of life, and cherry or pomegranate "heart" cakes for heartfelt emotions.

Diversions included Valentine pairing games such as selections by lot of **nonce** lovers, required to serve one another in affection—jocularly, not truly—for the day or a year. Divinations revealed true loves or false. Hemp seed thrown over the shoulder fell in a readable pattern. The vitality of sprigs of yarrow, eryngo, and southernwood, known also as lad's-love or boy's-love, signaled durable affection; fading or wilting leaves told of doomed love. Secret love messages were sent in **rebus** writing and signed "your valentine." A wonderful valentine note exists in the fifteenth-century *Paston Letters*.

> **nonce**: only for the extent of the festival.

> **rebus**: a message made up of symbols or pictures of objects whose names suggest the intended words.

Easter Sunday was the central holiday in a seventeen-week cycle calculated to begin nine weeks earlier, on Septuagesima, and to end eight weeks afterward, on Trinity Sunday. Between, such holidays as Quinquagesima, Shrove Tuesday, Ash Wednesday, Mothering Sunday, Carlings (Care) Sunday, Palm Sunday, Maundy Thursday, Good Friday, Rogation Sunday, Ascension, Pentecost, and Whitmonday were celebrated in the most observant ecclesiastical centers. But considering the potential disruption of agricultural and mercantile enterprise, secular rules often countervailed to emend or ignore parts of the Easter cycle.

The name Easter derived from the pagan goddess of dawn and spring, Eostra or Eostre, or from Eostur, the Norse word for spring, and the Easter rituals pertained to the rising of the sun and to the triumph of ascending spring over winter. Christian sermons and liturgies easily adapted these earlier sun **sanctifications** to lauding the Son's ascent to heaven, revealing the light of understanding and the day of salvation and promising victory over death. Pace-egging was a popular Easter entertainment. From the Hebrew word *pesaḥ,* whence Passover and paschal, hard-boiled pace-eggs were splendidly painted and decorated, exchanged as gifts, rolled in contests, or given in recompense to itinerant mummers or to morris dancers. While the name morris came from the Moorish dancers of Spain, the dances themselves were traditional spring fertility observances, with wooden taps on shoes and belled ankles stamping to insistent music of cymbals, pipes, and **tabors**, and vigorous leaps for inspiring grain to grow tall, flocks to multiply, and folk to thrive. Mystery plays dramatized Christ's crucifixion and resurrection. Others retold such Old Testament stories as that of Noah and the Flood, which as *The Deluge,* from the English town of Chester, prefigured the Easter themes of rebirth, renewal, and restoration.

An April festival of All Fools' Day sometimes was united with the church holiday the Feast of Fools, often a January feast, in which the ordered world was portrayed upside down. Festivities were directed by the Lord of Misrule, and boy bishops conducted holy services, called whiddershins, in reverse. In Rouen and Beauvais the Feast of Asses was commemorated with playlets on adventures of the biblical prophet Balaam and his wondrous talking donkey. Ennoblings of Folly and ludicrous antics were indirect reaffirmations of order and restraint.

May Day customs, costumes, decorations, dances, and symbolic spring green foods indirectly saluted earlier pagan spirits of trees and woodlands. Most European towns had festive equivalents of the English maypoles, Maying-round-the-maypole, crowning the Queen of the May, hoop rolling, and athletic contests, and verdant foods such as peppermint rice, and the lime-glazed gingerbread man called Jack-in-the-Green or Jack-in-the-Bush.

sanctification: the act of making something sacred.

tabor: a small drum.

Similarly identifiable pagan vestiges were canonized in the June festivals of Midsummer Eve and St. John's Eve. Beltane bonfires from May Day were reconsecrated to St. John, and the plants St.-John's-wort, St.-John's-bread, and St.-John's-fern were used for country **divinations**. Circular, clockwise pagan sun worship processions were transformed into Christian **rogations** around churches, marketplaces, and great halls.

> **divination**: fortune-telling.
>
> **rogations**: solemn prayers of supplication, usually chanted.

July holidays usually honored fruitfulness—and rain. Weather on St. Swithin's Day, named after the ninth-century English bishop of Winchester, was thought to predict wet or drought for forty days thereafter, and therefore the proper time to make sun and star measurements for weather almanacs determining planting, harvesting, and traveling. In August grain harvests and bread were generally celebrated. The geometrically shaped, many-colored, whimsically devised loaves baked on Lammas Day) (from the Anglo-Saxon "loaf mass") in England were typical of European ecclesiastical grain blessings and thanks for God's bounty at high summer, before the agricultural year reached its end.

Michaelmas (St. Michael's feast, September 29) gave its name to the fall season, Michaelmastide, a quarterly rent payment, the autumn term in schools and universities, and important merchandise markets and fairs. Michaelmas was the busy season for lawyers and magistrates of the Pie Powder courts (from French *pieds poudres*, dusty feet) adjudicating market larcenies and crimes of the fairs' travelers and merchants. October concluded with Halloween, the eve of All Hallows' or All Saints' Day, honoring all Christian saints, followed by All Souls' Day, solemnized by prayer for the souls of the dead in Purgatory. Summer's end, Samhain in the Celtic calendar (coincident with All Hallows' Eve), was the year's finale; its customs included candle and torchlight processions, apple-bobbing contests, nut-cracking divinations, and the masked "soulers" begging for soul cakes for wandering spirits.

May Day customs, costumes, decorations, dances, and symbolic spring green foods indirectly saluted earlier pagan spirits of trees and woodlands.

Catherning (Cathern or St. Catherine's Day, November 25) honored one of the most famous women saints: noble, intelligent, learned Catherine of Alexandria, martyred, according to legend, on a spiked wheel of torture before being beheaded in the fourth century. Patron saint of lawyers, wheelwrights, rope makers, carpenters, and others, she was particularly revered by working women as guide and guardian of lace makers, spinners, unmarried women, and women students. Catherings were often specifically women's feasts. Commemorating the instrument of her death, Catherine wheels decorated windows, walls, costumes, and jewelry. The serving of Catherine cakes, spike-shaped currant, orange, and caraway biscuits, preceded entertainments with Catherning candle circles, for jumping over or through, and radiant catherine-wheel fireworks.

Christmas Day introduced the twelve winter holy days culminating in Twelfth Night. Called Time of the Twelves, these twelve days in the twelfth month, alluding also to the twelve apostles, required twelve ritual gifts given and got, twelve wassailings to the celebrants' health, and twelve kisses exchanged beneath the Christmas bush (a mistletoe, holly, and evergreen decoration, ornamented with ribbons, small sculptures, and fruits, suspended from the ceiling). Household festivities began only after an entertainer called First Foot or Lucky Bird crossed the symbolic Christmas threshold, allowing good fortune and Christmas joy to be "let in" the dwelling. Christmas also was Time of the Bee. Just as bees produced sweetness and light, by means of honey and beeswax candles, so, according to St. Ambrose, in the hive of life, the church, faithful Christians ceaselessly labored for the sweetness of Christ's teachings and the light of Christian understanding, which qualities were affirmed in Christian customs. Sweet plum pudding, **frumenty**, **posset**, honeyed gingerbread Yule dolls, and hot elderberry wine were eaten by the light of the Yule candles and the Yule log blazing on the hearth.

frumenty: wheat boiled in milk, then flavored with sugar and spices.

posset: a hot drink of sweetened, spiced milk curdled with wine or ale.

Wassailing with the Milly was a Christmas parade with children singing, collecting gifts, and carrying a small shrine with the Virgin and Child. Other pageantry included a boar's head procession and a play of the Three Shepherds. Typical was the charming fourteenth-century Christmas playlet from Rouen, incorporating the so-called *Quem quaeritis* Latin trope. Two midwives ask the shepherds, "Whom do you seek in the manger, shepherds? Tell us." As they draw back the curtains protecting the Christ child, the shepherds gasp in wonderment and triumphally, and worshipfully cry, "Alleluia!"

Such dramas, symbolic foods, decorations, ceremonies, and rites of the calendar year occupied more than a third of the lifetime of townsmen, country folk, and castle dwellers. In addition to the usual amateur mummers and morris dancers, professional actors, jugglers, jesters, acrobats, mimes, magicians, minstrels, composers, jongleurs, raconteurs, comedians, puppeteers, ventriloquists, animal trainers, and masters of revels worked their way through the seasons, individually or in troupes, from marketplace to fair to festival. Wealthy houses augmented entertainment by household artists with itinerant acts, the total productions coordinated by a surveyor of ceremonies or professional dance master, often politically powerful and an arbiter of cultural taste. In the yearly round of holidays and festivals, play beautifully balanced life's work. ◆

Memorial Day

UNITED STATES ● LAST MONDAY IN MAY

1866 The first memorial day for the dead of the Civil War takes place in Waterloo, New York.

1868 The first national Decoration Day observance is held at Arlington National Cemetery in Washington, D.C.

1873 New York becomes the first state to proclaim May 30 as Decoration Day.

1882 The Grand Army of the Republic suggests changing the name of the holiday to Memorial Day.

1971 Congress passes a law making Memorial Day a permanent federal holiday.

Memorial Day is a holiday officially established to honor all Americans who have died in war and to pray for permanent peace. It also is popularly recognized as the beginning of the summer season. Originally called Decoration Day and celebrated on May 30, the holiday can be traced back to the end of the Civil War in 1865. About twenty-five communities, in states that fought on both sides in that war, have claimed to be the first to hold Memorial Day ceremonies. For example, in Boaltsville, Pennsylvania, women decorating their relatives' graves in 1864 supposedly agreed to meet again the next year. In 1866 the widows of Confederate soldiers in Mississippi, Georgia, and Virginia reportedly placed flowers on the graves of soldiers from both armies.

A century later, Congress finally declared the official birthplace of the holiday to be Waterloo, New York, where a ceremony was held on May 5, 1866, to honor local soldiers who had died during the Civil War. The first national observation of "Decoration Day" was held at Arlington National Cemetery on May 30, 1868. The ceremony included speeches, prayers, hymn singing, and the placing of flowers on the graves of soldiers. The ceremony was organized by John A. Logan, commander-in-chief of the Grand Army of the Republic, an organization of Union veterans. He had issued a proclamation setting aside May 30, "for the purpose of strewing with flowers or otherwise decorating the graves of comrades who died in defense of their country during the late rebellion"—in other words, a day to honor only Union soldiers.

Poppies on Memorial Day

The poppy, a small flower that grows in many parts of the world, has become associated with holidays that commemorate wars. People lay wreathes of poppies at war memorials and military cemeteries on Veterans Day and Memorial Day in the United States, Anzac Day in Australia and New Zealand, and Remembrance Day in Canada and Great Britain. In addition, veterans' organizations raise money by selling poppies, both real and artificial, and many people wear them on these holidays as a symbol of remembrance.

The tradition began in May 1915 during World War I when Canadian army surgeon John McCrae wrote a poem describing the red poppies growing in a military cemetery near the town of Ypres, in the Flanders region of Belgium. It begins:

> In Flanders fields the poppies blow
> Between the crosses, row on row . . .

These flowers thrive when the soil is stirred up, and the shell craters and trenches of the front, as well as the newly dug graves of fallen soldiers, produced an abundance of poppies during the war. McCrae's poem was published in December 1915 in the British magazine *Punch*, moving people to embrace the poppy as a symbol for the sacrifices made during battle. After the war, organizations such as the American Legion and Veterans of Foreign Wars began to sell poppies to raise funds for disabled veterans and for the widows and children of soldiers who had died. Recitations of McCrae's poem have become a traditional part of Veterans Day, Memorial Day, Anzac Day, and Remembrance Day ceremonies. In 1998, during a ceremony marking the eightieth anniversary of the end of World War I, 55,000 poppy petals were scattered in the military cemetery in Ypres—one petal for each of the unmarked graves.

In 1873 New York became the first state to officially proclaim May 30 as Decoration Day. Many northern and western states later joined New York in establishing Decoration Day as a state holiday, but southern states that had belonged to the Confederacy chose other dates to honor their own dead. In 1882 the Grand Army of the Republic, a society of Civil War veterans, suggested that the name of the holiday be changed to Memorial Day. Many states observed Memorial Day, a Confederate holiday, or both; there was no federal holiday until 1971, when Memorial Day was first officially observed on the last Monday in May. The holiday now serves as a remembrance of all Americans who have died in war, and as a day to pray for peace.

Today, many southern states continue separate observances of holidays dedicated to the memory of Confederate soldiers. For example, Confederate Memorial Day is celebrated in Alabama (fourth Monday in April); Georgia (April 26);

On Memorial Day flags fly at half-mast on all public buildings and on U.S. naval vessels stationed around the world.

Louisiana (June 3, also celebrated in some southern states as Jefferson Davis's birthday); Mississippi (last Monday in April); North Carolina and South Carolina (May 10); and Virginia (May 30). Tennessee celebrates June 3 as Confederate Decoration Day. In Texas, January 19 is known as Confederate Heroes Day.

Memorial Day is commemorated with a combination of patriotic and religious ceremonies. Many towns and cities across the country hold parades. Flags on public buildings fly at half-mast, as they do on U.S. naval vessels stationed around the world. At the site of the 1863 Civil War battle in Gettysburg, Pennsylvania, children place flowers on the graves of soldiers during a memorial service. While the holiday officially honors those who have died in war, many people choose this day as a time to visit the grave of any friend or relative who has died.

At the heart of the national Memorial Day observance is a ceremony held at the Tomb of the Unknowns in Virginia's Arlington National Cemetery. This tomb, originally built to hold the remains of an unidentified soldier from World War I, later also became the resting place of the remains of unidentified soldiers from World War II and the Korean conflict. On Memorial Day in 1984 the remains of an unidentified soldier from the Vietnam War were placed in the tomb. Although the war had ended in the early 1970s, it took a decade to locate a set of unidentifiable remains among the more than 58,000 American soldiers who had died in Vietnam.

As always with this war, however, controversy arose. Michael Blassie was a pilot who had been shot down near Cambodia in 1972, near the end of the war. In 1998 DNA testing requested by his family revealed that the soldier in the tomb was Blassie. Skeletal remains found by a search party in 1973 had been tentatively identified as Blassie's, but for unknown reasons, the Army later declared that the remains belonged to an unknown soldier and then selected them for burial in the tomb. Blassie's remains were removed from the tomb and in July 1998 were reburied in a military cemetery in St. Louis. ◆

Mexican Independence Day (*Fiesta Patrias*)

MEXICO ● SEPTEMBER 15 AND 16

Mexican Independence Day (*Fiesta Patrias*) is celebrated on September 15 and 16. The celebration marks a September 16, 1810, rebellion of Mexican peasants against their Spanish overlords led by Father Miguel Hidalgo y Costilla. Fiesta Patrias is Mexico's most important political holiday.

Spaniards had conquered Mexico in the 1500s and put in place a colonial government led by a Spanish viceroy. The population of New Spain, as Mexico was then called, was made up mainly of Native Americans, *criollos* (Spaniards born in the New World), and *mestizos* (people of mixed Indian and Spanish ancestry). These groups all held lesser status than the Spanish nobles, church leaders, and soldiers to whom the government of Spain had granted large tracts of land. Spaniards and *criollos* used Indians and *mestizos* as laborers.

By the beginning of the 1800s, the resentment of *criollos*, Native Americans, and *mestizos* grew into a brewing political rebellion. Some Catholic priests had tried to help the oppressed peoples, and one of these was Miguel Hidalgo y Costilla, a priest in the small village of Dolores. Hidalgo helped his villagers toward economic self-sufficiency, and he also stockpiled weapons. When Spanish soldiers learned of Hidalgo's guns, the rebellion erupted in September 1810. Hidalgo rang the church bells and issued the famous "El Grito de Dolores" (The Cry of Dolores), a call to arms to end serfdom and class inequalities.

1810 Encouraged by Hildalgo y Costilla, Mexican peasants rebel against the Spanish.

1811 Spanish forces execute Hidalgo.

1821 Mexico becomes formally independent when the last viceroy of Spain accepts the Treaty of Cordoba.

247

Young girls in traditional dresses dance on Independence Day in Puerto Vallarta, Mexico.

Hidalgo assembled his parishioners and delivered a passionate speech calling for an overthrow of Spanish rule. That speech inspired the people to attack Spanish colonialists the next day, September 16, 1810, launching an eleven-year liberation struggle.

The peasants held their own, but royalist forces finally captured and shot Father Hidalgo at Chihuahua in 1811. Another priest, José María Morelos y Pavón, took leadership of the liberation movement. He convened a congress that proclaimed Mexico an independent republic in 1814. But a year later, royalist forces defeated Morelos and his army. The revolution continued under Vicente Guerrero, who headed a small army. Guerrero met with New Spain's top general in 1821, signed an agreement, and the two combined forces. Their agreement, known as the Plan of Iguala, set forth three guarantees: Mexico would become an independent country, the Roman Catholic church would be the state church, and all inhabitants would receive equal rights and privileges. The last viceroy of New Spain accepted a Treaty of Córdoba in July 1821, formally beginning Mexican independence.

Mexicans celebrate Fiesta Patrias the greater part of a week, with the climax happening at 11 P.M. on September 15. That is when the president of Mexico appears on the balcony of the National Palace to shout the famous El Grito de Dolores (Cry of Dolores). The "Grito," as it is often called, repeats the call to freedom that the Hidalgo shouted to rouse the peasants to fight for their independence. The crowd in front of the National Palace shouts "Viva Mexico" (Long Live Mexico) followed by shooting guns, fireworks, and partying. Throughout Mexico, towns and cities also perform the ritual, with local mayors or other officials shouting the Grito at precisely 11 P.M. The following day, September 16, Independence Day features fireworks, ringing church bells, and military parades. The national lottery has become a major part of the celebration, and the drawing is held that day.

Many Mexican Americans celebrate Mexican Independence Day. The celebrations are often held on a weekend if September 16 falls on a weekday. Mexican Americans cherish the day as a time to maintain their cultural traditions and celebrate their homeland. Many Americans join their Hispanic friends in the festivities, as the occasion is similar to the Fourth of July in spirit and offers a chance to celebrate the freedom of both countries.

Cities with large Mexican communities that celebrate Fiestas Patrias include Denver, Houston, Chicago, and Los Angeles. Denver features an annual Mexican fiesta that draws crowds of thousands for music, food, dancing, and arts and crafts in several locations throughout the city. Mariachis play and Aztec dancers perform in bright, beaded costumes and feathered headdresses. In Chicago's Little Village neighborhood, famous for its Mexican culture, cries of "Viva Mexico" and Mexican flags fill the streets as thousands of people gather to watch the parade celebrating Mexican Independence Day. Dozens of folk dancers and mariachi bands, bedecked in colorful traditional Mexican costumes, stroll with the parade. In Houston, a Fiesta del Grito features a large outdoor concert, an evening fireworks display, and the traditional "Grito" shout of independence by the consul general. In suburbs and towns throughout the United States, wherever there are Mexican residents, people celebrate Mexican Independence Day with parades and picnics featuring favorite Mexican foods. Catholic churches often celebrate Mass as part of the celebration.

Chicano student groups at universities in such states as California host Independence Day celebrations to share their cul-

> **El Grito de Dolores (the Cry of Dolores) repeats the call to freedom that Hidalgo y Costilla shouted in 1810 to rouse the peasants to fight for their independence.**

tural heritage. Such celebrations often feature mariachi music, traditional Mexican food, speeches, and dancing. For many Hispanic Americans, Fiestas Patrias celebrates all of Latin America's independence from Spain, which began with Mexico's declaration in 1810. They use the occasion to commemorate the independence of such countries as Belize, Chile, Costa Rica, El Salvador, Guatemala, Honduras, and Nicaragua. ◆

Mother's Day

UNITED STATES ● SECOND SUNDAY IN MAY

Mother's Day is a holiday for remembering, honoring, and expressing love and gratitude to mothers. People in many countries celebrate a Mother's Day, although the exact date varies from country to country. In the United States, Mother's Day is observed on the second Sunday in May.

The tradition of honoring mothers can be traced back to an ancient Greek festival, held annually in the spring, to honor the goddess Rhea. Rhea was the female counterpart of Cronus, ruler of the race of deities called Titans. According to Greek myth, Rhea was the mother of the goddesses Demeter, Hera, and Hestia, as well as the gods Hades, Poseidon, and Zeus.

During the 1600s, Christian families in England began celebrating a day called "Mothering Sunday" on the fourth Sunday day of Lent, a forty-day period of fasting and repentance before Easter. On Mothering Sunday, children who had left home to work as apprentices or servants would return to their family home. They referred to this excursion as "going a-mothering." On the first Sunday of their visit home, the children would attend church services with their families and offer flowers and other gifts to their mothers and the church. Families often baked a special cake, called "a mothering cake," to mark the occasion. Mothering Sunday gradually changed in nature to become a day to honor the "Mother Church." The term Mother Church referred to the particular church where one was baptized, and also the Christian church in general, which people recognized as having the power to nurture and protect them like

1872 Julia Ward Howe suggests establishing June 2 as Mother's Day in the United States.

1907 Anna Jarvis begins a national campaign to set aside a day to honor mothers.

1908 Church services honoring mothers are held in Philadelphia and Grafton, West Virginia.

1914 President Woodrow Wilson signs a congressional resolution recommending the observation of Mother's Day.

1915 Wilson proclaims Mother's Day an annual national observance.

Anna Jarvis envisioned a Mother's Day marked by church services, home-cooked meals, and small tokens of filial piety.

a mother. Over time, people began honoring both their mothers and the mother church on Mothering Sunday.

European immigrants to the United States carried the Mothering Sunday tradition with them, but it was not until after the Civil War that a movement began in the United States to formally designate a day to honor mothers. In 1872 writer and reformer Julia Ward Howe suggested establishing June 2 as Mother's Day in the United States. For several years Howe held an annual Mother's Day meeting in Boston, and people in a few American cities responded to her suggestion. A schoolteacher named Mary Towles Sasseen began conducting Mother's Day celebrations in Kentucky in 1887. Frank E. Hering of South Bend, Indiana, began a local campaign for the observance of Mother's Day in 1904. However, Julia Ward Howe's proposal did not gain widespread acceptance until 1907, when Anna Jarvis, a West Virginian who had migrated to Philadelphia, was moved by the death of her mother two years earlier to begin a national campaign to celebrate the image of the old-fashioned mother. Jarvis envisioned a day marked by church services, home-cooked meals, and small tokens of filial piety. The following year on May 10, 1908, church services in which mothers were honored were held in Philadelphia and in Grafton, West Virginia, where Jarvis's mother had taught Sunday school. At the end of the service in Philadelphia, Jarvis presented a carnation, her mother's favorite flower, to each mother and child in attendance. Jarvis worked diligently for many years to popularize her idea; she wrote hundreds of letters to congressmen, governors, mayors, journalists, and church and business leaders. Jarvis's idea proved widely compelling and many churches, towns, and cities began unofficial Mother's Day celebrations. By 1912 Mother's Day was observed in every state. Finally, in 1914 President Woodrow Wilson signed a joint congressional resolution recommending the establishment of Mother's Day as a national day of observance. The next year, congress authorized President Wilson to proclaim Mother's Day a permanent annual national observance.

Today Mother's Day is one of the most widely celebrated holidays in the United States. Children honor their mother by giving her flowers, boxes of chocolates, and other gifts. Children also write poems and songs, draw pictures, and make special cards for their mother. Many children offer to cook for their mother or to help her with housework. Most churches in the United States have special Mother's Day services, and many children take their mother to a restaurant for a Mother's Day brunch after the service. Children who live far from their mother will call her on the telephone or send a Mother's Day card. Many people still wear carnations on the second Sunday in May in honor of their mother. According to tradition, people whose mother is alive wear a red or pink carnation, while people whose mother has died wear a white carnation.

Through the years Mother's Day has become highly commercialized and Americans respond to advertisers by spending millions of dollars every year buying Mother's Day flowers, cards, and gifts. Anna Jarvis herself strenuously disapproved of the commercialism of the holiday, which she had hoped would always be a quiet, simple observance with the church and home at its center. ◆

Moussem

MOROCCO ● VARIOUS DATES

While some moussems are not much more elaborate than a typical market day, others feature animal sacrifices, dancing, offerings of gifts, and special events such as camel races.

Moussems are festivals celebrated at various times during the year in the towns and cities of Morocco in honor of local patron saints. Muslim worshipers make a pilgrimage to the shrine of the local saint at the time of the Moussem, which often coincides with the birthday of the saint. The exact date of the moussem is set by the cadis, the local ruler. Moussems are the main social and religious festivals of Moroccan culture. While some are not much more elaborate than a typical market day with the addition of special prayers, others feature animal sacrifices, offerings of gifts to obtain the saint's blessing, dancing, and special events such as the camel races of the Goulimine moussem. The importance of the moussem depends on the importance of the saint. Most moussems are held during the summer and some last for several days.

Moussems offer a view of the rich variety of Moroccan folklore and customs. They reflect the customs of the region, although some moussems have come to take on a national character and some have become tourist attractions rather than religious pilgrimages.

The most important moussem, and Morocco's most important religious holiday, is the Moulay Idriss moussem celebrated in the third week of September. This moussem originated in the small city of Moulay Idriss in north central Morocco near Meknes, the burial place of Idriss I, the founder of the Moroccan state. This city is Morocco's most important pilgrimage center and during the moussem thousands of pilgrims come to visit Idris's mosque. Moulay Idriss is also celebrated in Fès, the capital of Morocco, as it is something of a national holiday. The moussem in Fès features processions of merchants and crafts people through the streets. Large, decorated candles and sacrifices of cattle and oxen are offered in honor of the patron saint. The festivities continue throughout the day and into the night in the squares and marketplaces with traditional dancing and music.

Another moussem of note is Moulay Ibrahim, one of the largest moussems in all Morocco, which is celebrated in Asni in the scenic beauty of the high Atlas range sometime between June and July. Moulay Yacoub celebrated in the province Oujda in the autumn is also a harvest festival as well as an occasion to honor the patron saint Yacoub. The largest moussem in the province of Marrakech is Zaouia-Tassaft, which lasts for three days. The moussem of Imilchil takes place in Bel Maati in the province of Tafilalet during the third week of September and is also known as the engagement festival. These are just a few of the many moussems that are celebrated in each Moroccan province. ◆

Music Festivals in America

UNITED STATES ● VARIOUS DATES

Music festivals commemorate anniversaries, celebrate religious or ethnic traditions, or offer music of a composer, period, or type; they can range from a single event to many events encompassing days or even a season. The earliest festivals in the United States date from the eighteenth century and had religious, social, or **pedagogical** functions. The first were associated with singing schools, to promote the singing of psalms according to established rules and order. Folk music began in the eighteenth century in the form of fiddlers' contests, many expanding to several days and involved instrumental music and community audiences. Several large events took place beginning in the middle of the nineteenth century. In 1856 the Boston Handel and Haydn Society presented three major choral works—Haydn's *The Seasons*, Handel's *Messiah*, and Mendelssohn's *Elijah*. In 1869 the bandmaster Patrick S. Gilmore arranged a National Peace Jubilee in Boston comprising 20,000 instrumentalists. During the 1876 centennial of independence, Philadelphia sponsored a major music festival. Worcester, Massachusetts, in 1858 and Cincinnati, Ohio, in 1873 inaugurated festivals that have continued to the present day. Four festivals that came out of the tradition of singing schools continued into the twentieth century: the Messiah Festival in Lindsborg, Kansas (1882), the Big Singing Day in Benton, Kentucky (1884), the Ann Arbor May Festival (1894), and the Bethlehem, Pennsylvania, Bach Festival (1900).

Festivals proliferated in the twentieth century. Many occur in rural settings during summer months and feature classical

pedagogical: intending to educate.

music, jazz, folk, bluegrass, country, cajun, and light or pops. Commercial motives and entrepreneurial talent have been a significant force in their promotion. Major symphony orchestras that employ musicians year-round include summer seasons that have become virtual festivals. Beginning in 1936 the Chicago Symphony Orchestra has played in Ravinia Park north of Chicago. Tanglewood, in the Berkshire Hills of western Massachusetts, has been the summer home of the Boston Symphony Orchestra since 1936; in 1940 its former music director Serge Koussevitzky opened the Tanglewood Music Center. Meadowbrook became the summer home of Detroit's orchestra in 1964; the Blossom Music Center between Cleveland and Akron became the summer residence of the Cleveland Orchestra in 1968. The Philadelphia Orchestra has given free concerts at the Mann Music Center in Philadelphia and since 1966 has performed at Saratoga Springs, New York. In that year the annual Mostly Mozart Festival became a major offering of the Lincoln Center for the Performing Arts in New York City.

Many of these summer centers have expanded to offer jazz, folk, and rock music. Smaller festivals have grown out of centers that specialize in the study of particular styles of music. The Marlboro School in Vermont has stressed chamber music since 1950. The National Music Camp at Interlochen, Michigan, has offered a variety of musical programs since 1928. The Brevard Music Center in western North Carolina has sponsored festivals since 1936. A number of festivals center on opera. Since 1920 the Cincinnati Summer Opera Festival has offered a series of productions, while Santa Fe (1957) has featured little-known operas. Beginning in 1975 the Seattle Opera offered Richard Wagner's *Ring* cycle, first in German, then in English, in an event that has become the Pacific Northwest Festival. Contemporary or new music is offered in programs in California—Ojai since 1947 and Cabrillo since 1963. New Music Across America began as a festival in New York in 1979 and has emphasized works by composers using new techniques and new instruments; in 1992 the festival took place simultaneously in many sites across the country.

Festivals of indigenous or folk music have similarly increased in the twentieth century. Building on the tradition of fiddlers' contests, the Old Time Fiddler's Convention began in North Carolina in 1924. The National Folk Festival first took place in St. Louis in 1934 and in 1971 moved to Wolf Trap Farm Park southwest of Washington, D.C. The Kool Jazz Festival,

Many music festivals occur in rural settings during summer months and feature classical music, jazz, folk, bluegrass, country, cajun, and pops.

founded in 1954 as the Newport Jazz Festival in Rhode Island, moved to New York City in 1972, and, on the Pacific coast, the Monterey Jazz Festival began in 1958. Rock music promoters staged big events in the 1960s, notably the 1967 Monterey International Pop Festival in California and the Woodstock, New York, Music and Arts Fair in 1969, which was the biggest rock concert ever organized, attracting about 400,000 representatives of the counterculture of the decade. The Woodstock event took on **iconic** status for many and was commemorated in 1994 by a second concert.

During the 1990s annual touring festivals of rock and pop music became popular. One of the largest was Lollapalooza, which began in 1991 and continued every summer until 1997. Lollapalooza showcased new bands and performers from all genres of popular music. Lilith Fair, a popular summer tour featuring new music by women, began in 1997. ◆

iconic: serving as a symbol of a movement or era.

Navaratri

Navaratri (nine nights), also known as Durgotsava (festival of the goddess Durga), is a festival celebrated twice each year in India and Nepal at the time of the vernal and autumnal equinoxes. The nine nights are followed by a festival known both as Dasara, (or Dasahara, destroying the ten [sins]) and as Vijayadasami (victory on the tenth [day]). Although the festival of the vernal equinox is not celebrated in all regions of India, it appears in modified form in local festivals dedicated to the Goddess. The great autumnal Navaratri, which takes place during the nine nights following the new moon in the lunar month of Karttika (October–November), is pan-Indian and is regarded as an important rite performed to benefit a variety of aspects of Hindu life.

The religious and sociological meaning of Hindu female deities, particularly the goddess Durga, find expression during Navaratri. The festival is based on the *Devimahatmya,* which means "glorification of the goddess," a section of a sacred Hindu text called *Markandeya Purana.* According to that text, the demons *(asuras)* at one time overcame the gods, and Mahisasura, the Buffalo Demon, took the place of the king of the gods. From the palpable anger of the gods was formed the body of the Goddess, known variously as Mahamaya (great illusion), Candi (the cruel), Durga (unattainable), and by other names. The Goddess, incarnate at the energy *(sakti)* of the gods, obtained weapons from the gods and in her various forms fought against the multifarious *asuras,* whose **archetype** is Mahisa.

archetype: the original pattern or model.

259

When she is regarded as a virgin, as distinct from any male consorts, or as the supreme deity, the Goddess in India is depicted as a fearsome and terrible deity who demands blood sacrifices. From the defeated Buffalo Demon springs a *purusa*, a "man" who when sacrificed becomes a devotee of the Goddess. Navaratri is thus closely associated with sacrificial themes, although in most regions vegetable substitutes now take the place of sacrificial animals in the ritual. The many forms and aspects of the Goddess and of the *asuras* correspond with the various interests and evils of this earth, for the continuation of which she manifests herself. What is more precisely at stake in the story of the *Devimahatmya*, however, is Mahisasura's usurpation of the gods' power over the world. Hence it follows that the Goddess's close relationship with the king is a crucial element for the preservation of the Hindu cosmos–social order and for the prosperity of the kingdom as well.

The Navaratri is more complex in some regions of India than in others. In some areas it is primarily a festival marking the growing season. In others, it centers mostly around the worship of a local goddess, who may be thought of as the spouse of an untouchable. It may also be a highly ceremonialized and intricate festival, as in the former princely states, where the king was required to perform the Buffalo Sacrifice.

The main Navaratri ritual consists of installing an image of Goddess in the home and in the temple throughout the nine nights of the ceremony. In Tamil Nadu the Goddess is seated among many other images in a royal audience and is visited daily by women singing devotional songs; there, the ninth night is consecrated to the worship of Sarasvati, the goddess of learning, and to *ayudhapuja*, the worship of weapons and tools. In other regions young girls are worshiped as embodiments of the virgin Goddess. In Mysore (modern-day Karnataka) and Bastar the nine nights were a time of **ascetic** practices for the king.

In Bengal, the installation of the Goddess in a royal temple is an elaborate life-giving rite. The night between the eighth and ninth days serves as the climax to the ceremony as a whole. Navaratri is also an important popular festival in which the Bengalis build huge, richly decorated images of the Goddess. These icons of Devi are destroyed during the Vijayadasami rites. Large and excited crowds of people (who at times transgress the norms of conduct) parade the many images of the Goddess to bodies of water, where they are immersed.

The main Navaratri ritual consists of installing an image of the Goddess in the home and in the temple throughout the nine nights of the ceremony.

ascetic: practicing strict self-denial as a measure of spiritual discipline.

Vijayadasami concerns primarily the *ksatriya* caste. In royal states and in Nepal the king performs *ayudhapuja*, officiates at parades of soldiers astride horses and elephants, and symbolically conquers the world by throwing arrows to the four directions. Ritually crossing the boundaries, the king goes toward the northeast to perform *samipuja*, the worship of the *sami* tree, traditionally associated with the sacred fire. This appears to be a ritual restatement of an event recounted in the *Mahabharata* in which the heroes of the epic retrieve the weapons they had hidden in that tree. Seated in a royal audience, the king receives the renewed allegiance of his subjects.

In some regions there are dramatic enactments of the victory of Visnu's incarnation as Rama over Ravana, the demon-king of Sri Lanka. In former times, the end of Navaratri, which coincides with the end of the monsoon, marked the time for kings to return to their wars. Moreover, the close association between the *asura*-slayer, Devi, and the kingdom, which is under her protection, symbolically restores prosperity to everyone in the domain. ◆

Nawruz

IRAN ● MARCH

Nawruz (new day) is the Iranian national festival that celebrates the arrival of spring. A festival of renewal, hope, and happiness, Nawruz begins on the first day of Farvardin, the first month of the Iranian solar calendar, at the spring equinox (approximately March 20), and continues for twelve days. It is the most widely celebrated, the longest, and the most colorful of Iranian festivals, and though inherited from Zoroastrian Persia, it is the only festival that is not confined to a single religious group.

The origins of Nawruz are obscure. In popular legend its institution is associated mostly with Jamshed, the mythical Iranian king. In Persian writer Firdawsi's epic poem the *Shah-na-mah* (completed about 1000 C.E.), it is said that the feast commemorates Jamshed's ascent into the skies in a chariot built by the demons whom he had subdued and forced into the service of mortals. Nawruz appears, however, to have been originally a pagan **pastoral** festival that marked the transition from winter to summer; rites of fertility and renovation can be easily recognized in some of its customs.

Zarathustra (Zoroaster), the ancient prophet of Iran, probably **reconsecrated** Nawruz to his religion. In any event, like Mihragan, the festival that marked the end of summer, Nawruz continued to be observed in Zoroastrian Iran with full vigor; the two celebrations formed the festive poles of the Iranian calendar year. Nawruz was immediately preceded by Hamaspath-maedaya, a major religious feast that fell on the thirtieth day of the last month of the year (March 20) and was dedicated to the

pastoral: of the countryside.

reconsecrate: to make sacred again.

spirits of the departed, the *fravashis*. These spirits were thought to come down to the earth during this period to visit their abodes and to dwell with their families. In anticipation of the *fravashis'* arrival, houses were cleaned, and food and drink were laid out for them. Nawruz thus had a sober and commemorative prelude, informed by the remembrance of the departed family members, ancestors, and pious believers. Among the Zoroastrians the two festivals eventually merged, and the Farvardigan holidays came to comprise both.

In Zoroastrian Iran, Nawruz proper began at dawn as the *fravashis* withdrew and the old year faded away. For the Zoroastrians the festival also celebrated the creation of fire and its celestial guardian, Artavahisht. On the first day of spring, prayers were offered to Rapithwan, a helper of the powerful deity Mehr (Avestan, Mithra). Rapithwan, who personified noon, the ideal time, would withdraw underground during the winter months to protect the roots of plants and springs of water from frost, a creation of the demons. At Nawruz, he would appear above ground to usher in the summer season.

The Achaemenid kings (559–330 B.C.E.) celebrated Nawruz above all at Persepolis, their capital, and some scholars have hypothesized that the parade of gift-bearers from various nations depicted in the **bas-reliefs** of the palace walls represent Nawruz ceremonies. Under the Sasanids (226–652 C.E.), Nawruz, together with Mihragan, was to some extent **secularized**. Contemporary accounts as well as reports in early Islamic sources attest to the Sasanid kings' lavish celebration of Nawruz and its colorful ceremonies and customs. Some of these tended to observe the number seven: for instance, seven kinds of seeds were grown in small containers as part of the festival rites and decoration, a custom still observed in the few remaining Zoroastrian villages in Iran. Furthermore, it is said that at Nawruz seven kinds of grain, twigs from seven different trees, and seven silver coins were placed before the king. Today an essential and cherished decoration of Nawruz is a collection of seven items whose names begin with the letter *s* in Persian (*haft sin*). Of ambiguous or obscure origin, these are most often apple, vinegar, sumac, garlic, silver coins, sorbapple, and fresh grass.

Stripped of its Zoroastrian connotations, Nawruz survived the advent of Islam and continued as the Iranian national festival. The Shiah Muslims of Iran, however, came to associate important religious events with Nawruz. Muhammad Baqir

bas-relief: sculpture in which the image stands out only slightly from the background

secularize: to transfer from religious to nonreligious use.

Majlisi quotes a number of traditions from the Shiah imams (in *Bihar al-anwar*, vol. 14, the section on *nayriz*), who report that it was on Nawruz that Adam was created, that God made a covenant with humankind, that Abraham destroyed the pagan idols, that the prophet Muhammad took his young son-in-law, Ali, on his shoulders to smash the idols in Mecca, and, most important of all, that he chose Ali as his rightful successor. The Muslim rulers of Iran, continuing the Sasanid tradition, celebrated Nawruz with pomp and circumstance. The ceremonies generally included the recitation of congratulatory **panegyrics**, feasting, the reception of dignitaries, music and dance, and the exchange of gifts. From about the middle of the sixteenth century, when Iran came into the possession of firearms, the onset of Nawruz was announced in larger cities by the firing of cannons.

panegyrics: poems or songs expressing formal and elaborate praise.

As a religious feast, Nawruz apparently began as a one-day celebration, but calendar reforms, combined with the popular tendency of observing the festivals according to the old calendar, seem to have stretched it first to six days, with its division in Sasanid times into Lesser Nawruz (the first day) and Greater Nawruz (the sixth day), and eventually to its present length. In or about the year 1006, the first of Farvardin fell on the first day of spring, and a calendar reform, in which the poet 'Umar (Omar) Khayyam participated, fixed the date of the feast on the first of Farvardin and arranged for keeping it constant by intercalating one day before the New Year festival every four years.

Preparations for Nawruz begin well in advance of the holiday. Although there are local variations, some practices are fairly general. A week or two before the New Year, grains of wheat or lentils are soaked in water and, after they germinate, are spread over a dish to grow. The resulting fresh mass of green blades (*sabzeh*) is an essential and symbolic decoration of the festival. In addition to the *sabzeh* and the *haft-sin*, the Nawruz table is adorned with a mirror, a copy of the holy book of the household's faith, a bowl of water in which green leaves or flower petals may float, and colored eggs, as well as fruits, fresh herbs, cakes, and candies. The "turn" of the year is awaited with eagerness and excitement, particularly by the young. A few moments before the solemn announcement of Nawruz, the members of the family, by this time all bathed and clad in new or clean clothes, gather around the table, ready to embrace and exchange greetings and gifts. The visiting of relatives and friends is a common Nawruz activity. In villages young men often engage in wrestling and other athletic games.

On the thirteenth day of Nawruz, the ceremonies are brought to an end with a picnic in the countryside. The *sabzeh* must now be taken out and thrown into running water, which is thought to take away with it any bad luck of the previous year. Wishes are made, especially by young girls, for a happy future. The Parsis of India, who left Iran in the tenth century in order to preserve their Zoroastrian faith, also continue to celebrate Nawruz (*jamshedi Navroz*) as a major feast. ◆

Ncwala (Newala, Incwala)

The first three days of the Ncwala ceremony are marked by displays of the Swazi king's weakness.

Ncwala is a first fruits ceremony celebrated at the new year in Mbabane, the capital of Swaziland, a small country in southern Africa. This ceremony, the most important holiday in Swaziland, shares common traits with other first-fruit ceremonies that are central to many traditional African religions. The essence of the first fruits ceremony is the ritual honoring of the ancestors by making an offering, usually by the leader of the tribe or clan, of the first taste of the harvest. Once the ancestors have received this offering the community can then enjoy the fruits of the harvest. The Swazi ritual also has significance as a rite of kingship. The ritual expresses the dominance of the king and the unity of Swazi society. Another element of the Ncwala ceremony is breaking with the old year and making a clean beginning in the new year.

The celebration lasts for a month and culminates in six days of rituals. The exact dates of Ncwala are strongly linked to the lunar calendar. Little Ncwala begins at the new moon of the month prior to Ncwala. At this time special officials, "priests of the sea," collect water from the ocean and certain rivers for the ritual purification of the king. The main Ncwala ceremony begins on the night of the full moon and roughly coincides with the winter solstice. The first three days of the ceremony are marked by demonstrations of the king's weakness. Like the sun, which at its furthest point from the earth is at its weakest, the king's powers are considered diminished and in need of strengthening before he will have the vitality required to taste the first fruits.

The Ncwala ceremony is performed within a special enclo-sure, the sibaya, which is cleared of all non-Swazis by the sea priests. The young warriors collect green **acacia** branches for the king's revitalization. On the following day the warriors sacrifice a black bull, pieces of which are then used in medicines to strengthen the king. The warriors then drive into the enclosure another black bull that the king rides as a demonstration of his virility. At several points in the first three days of Ncwala the *simeno* is sung. This mournful song describes the people's rejec-tion of the king.

acacia: a species of small trees in the pea family.

On the fourth day, the culmination of Ncwala, the king appears naked before the people and the women weep at the sight of their diminished king. The royal clan sings of its desire to leave the people. The king is forced into his hut to be later lured out with taunts about his weakness. Finally, the king emerges in an elaborate costume with a headdress of black plumes. In this powerful guise the king performs a dance that depicts his reluctance to rejoin the people. The warriors per-form a vigorous, frantic dance that culminates with the king throwing a green gourd, called a *luselwa*, that the warriors catch in their shields. The taboo on eating the fruits of the harvest has now been lifted.

The next day the king spends in seclusion as he is deemed too potent to be seen. The people also seclude themselves in solidarity with their king. On the final day of Ncwala the para-phernalia from the rituals are burned, symbolizing the destruc-tion of the filth of the past year. The fire is extinguished by the rain, which is said to be the blessing of the ancestors, and the clean beginning of the new year.

Ncwala has been celebrated in this manner since the found-ing of Swaziland by the Dlami clan in approximately 1750. Today the ceremony not only celebrates the vitality of the king and the unity of the nation but also the folklore of the Swazi people. ◆

New Year's Day

JANUARY 1

Many people regard the commencement of the new year as an opportunity to make a fresh start, and some make resolutions to do better in the new year than they did in the old.

New Year's Day celebrates the beginning of the calendar year. Though some cultures celebrate the new year based on the lunar calendar, most people around the world observe January 1 as the start of the new year. There is no other holiday that is so widely celebrated around the world. For most people, it is a festive time for visiting friends and relatives, sending greeting cards, and warmly greeting others with a joyous cry of "Happy New Year!" Many people also regard the commencement of the new year as an opportunity to make a fresh start, and some make resolutions to do better in the new year than they did in the old. To aid them in this effort, many cultures have traditions meant to bring people good luck. For many, it is also a time to attend a religious service.

The celebration of New Year's Day goes back more than 5,000 years. One of the earliest known celebrations took place in the ancient region of Babylonia in what is now southeastern Iraq, where the new year started with the new moon nearest the spring equinox, typically mid-March. The date of the new year's start changed over time as the calendar and its connection to the seasons evolved.

In ancient Roman times, the calendar year began on March 1, which coincided with spring. Julius Caesar changed the beginning of the year to January in 46 B.C.E., but the Julian calendar was always slightly off, and after hundreds of years, it no longer matched the seasons. In 1582 Pope Gregory XIII changed the calendar to match the seasons. We observe the Gregorian calendar to this day.

Hoppin' John on New Year's Day

In the southern United States people serve a dish called hoppin' John on New Year's Day. Hoppin' John is made from black-eyed peas and rice, and according to tradition eating it on the first of January will ensure good luck and health for the rest of the year. There are many stories to explain the name of the dish. Some say that "hoppin' John" is a corruption of an African or a French word. Others explain that "hoppin' John" refers to an old New Year's tradition of having children hop around the dinner table before eating. Another explanation, perhaps the most plausible, is that the name describes the way the beans hop around the pan as they cook.

1 cup dried black-eyed peas	1 cup uncooked rice
1/4 pound diced salt pork	1 tablespoon butter
1 green bell pepper, chopped	cayenne pepper
1 onion, chopped	black pepper
water	salt

Soak peas overnight, drain. Put peas in a deep skillet along with salt pork, green pepper, and onion. Cover with water and simmer for about 2 hours or until peas are tender. Add more water if necessary. Cook rice according to package directions. When peas are done and water has cooked very low, add rice, butter, a pinch of cayenne pepper, black pepper, and salt. Cover and cook over low heat until liquid is absorbed.

Ancient celebrations of the new year included bonfires and purification rituals. The pagan Roman festival of Saturnalia—which honored Saturn, the Roman god of agriculture—fell at the end of the year, and included dancing, feasting, and gift giving. To distance Christians from such abhorrent pagan activities that took place around January 1, the Christian Church linked the new year to March 25, the celebration of The Annunciation—the announcement of the angel Gabriel to Mary that she would be the mother of Jesus. For Christians, New Year's Day became a time to repent, pray, and attend services. To this day, many Christians begin New Year's Day with a religious service.

When the Gregorian calendar was adopted in the sixteenth century, most western nations observed January 1 as the start of the new year. The Church retained the significance of New Year's Day as a holy day by establishing January 1 as the Feast of Christ's Circumcision.

Today, New Year's Day is full of customs, rituals, and symbols, both old and new. The tradition of using a baby to symbolize the new year goes back to the ancient Egyptians, for whom a baby symbolized rebirth. The Church later adopted this image as a symbol of the baby Jesus. The custom of making noise at the stroke of midnight on New Year's Eve is a sound of revelry as well as an ancient practice of frightening away the evil spirits. Many countries set off fireworks at midnight. In Canada and the United States, church bells ring out, and people bang pots and pans and blow whistles and horns. In Denmark, children smash damaged pottery against people's doors.

Many customs are meant to bring people good luck. In parts of Great Britain, the first person to enter the home on New Year's Day is known as the "first footer." Good luck comes to the home if this person is a man with coal for the fire, bread for the table, and whiskey for the head of the household. It is also a tradition to leave the back door open until midnight to let the Old Year out, and then lock it to keep the luck of the New Year in the house.

Many people make special foods intended to bring good luck part of their New Year's celebration. In Europe, a roast pig is often served on New Year's Day. According to tradition, the pig is a symbol of good luck because it roots in a forward direction, making it a symbol of a "fat future." In Spain and Portugal, at midnight on New Year's Eve, everyone eats exactly twelve grapes,

These revelers join millions of people to celebrate New Year's Eve in 1995 in New York City's Times Square.

one for every stroke of midnight. This practice is said to bring good luck in every month of the coming year.

A common practice in Western society is to hold a party on New Year's Eve to await the arrival of the new year, while the next day is spent resting, visiting friends, and in the United States, watching football on television. Time Square in New York City holds a notable public celebration on New Year's Eve. There, crowds gather to count down the seconds to the first of the year. A huge ball rigged with lights and strobes drops from a flagpole exactly at midnight, when it spins and sends light beams dancing over the crowd. ◆

Oktoberfest

GERMANY ● AUTUMN

Oktoberfest is an annual beer festival held in Munich, Germany. It runs for sixteen days, beginning on the second to last Saturday in September. Each year, about six million people attend Munich's Oktoberfest and consume more than five million liters of beer.

The history of the festival begins with the marriage of the Crown Prince Ludwig of Bavaria, who later became King Ludwig I, to Princess Therese of Saxony-Hildburghausen in October 1810. The citizens of Munich were invited to attend the royal event, which was held on the fields in front of the city gates. These fields soon became known as the *Theresienwiese* (Therese's fields) in honor of the princess, and to this day they still serve as the grounds for the festival. Horse races were held at the close of the prince's party, and the decision to repeat the horse races the following year gave rise to the annual tradition of the Oktoberfest.

In 1811 an agricultural show was added to the festivities. By 1818 performers, a carousel, and beer stands were an integral part of the festival. In 1896 the first beer tents replaced the beer stands. Over the years, more fair rides and activities were added to the festivities. The horse races were discontinued in the early 1900s, but many other events continued, including the agricultural show, which is now held every third year. The celebration of the Oktoberfest was eventually moved to September to ensure better weather for the event.

Today Oktoberfest begins with a parade of the mayor and brewers in carriages, the horse-drawn beer carts of Munich

1810 Prince Ludwig of Bavaria marries Princess Therese of Saxony-Hildburghausen in October, and a great festival is held in Munich.

1811 An agricultural show is added to the Oktoberfest.

1818 Performers and beer stands have been added to the fest.

1846 German immigrants in Milwaukee, Wisconsin, hold their first German fest.

1896 Large beer tents replace the traditional beer stands.

breweries, beer-hall waitresses on floats, the beer-tent bands and other performers, and many men, women, and children in traditional Bavarian costume. The parade makes its way through the city center to the Schottenhammel tent, the oldest private tent at the fest, where the mayor of Munich taps the first keg of beer by jamming a bronze spout with a wooden hammer into the keg. The mayor's pronouncement of "*o'zapft is!*" (It's been tapped!) officially signals the start of the Oktoberfest.

Dancing, regional folk performances, a parade of riflemen, and many carnival rides and activities are all part of the festivities. One of the most popular competitions is the "Hau den Lucas," which resembles the activity of splitting wood. Players swing a massive wooden hammer down on a wooden block, sending a projectile up a vertical track that measures one's strength. The strongest players are able to hit the bell at the top of the track.

The most significant event of the Oktoberfest takes place in the beer halls, which serve only beer brewed at one of Munich's major breweries. German bands play traditional music and set the tone of the festivities in the tents, where revelers, many wearing traditional German costumes, eat thick

Oktoberfest revelers in traditional German costumes enjoy special Oktoberfest beer during the annual festival in Munich.

sausages and other German specialities and drink liter-sized glass mugs of specially brewed Oktoberfest beer served by costumed beer "maidens."

German immigrants began festivals modeled on the Oktoberfest in other parts of the world. The German Fest of Milwaukee, Wisconsin, is one of the oldest festivals of its kind. It started in 1846. Many such festivals offer a variety of German foods, beer, music, and crafts. ◆

Passover

Passover is the joyous Jewish festival of freedom that celebrates the Exodus of the Jews from their bondage in
Egypt. Beginning on the fifteenth day of the spring
month of Nisan, the festival lasts for seven days (eight days for
Jews outside Israel). The Hebrew name for Passover, Pesah,
refers to the paschal lamb offered as a family sacrifice in Temple
times, and the festival is so called because God "passed over"
(*pasah*) the houses of the Israelites when he slew the Egyptian
firstborn. The annual event is called Hag ha-Pesah, the Feast of
the Passover, in the Bible. Another biblical name for it is Hag
ha-Matsot or the Feast of the Unleavened Bread, after the command to eat unleavened bread and to refrain from eating
leaven. The critical view is that the two names are for two originally separate festivals, which were later combined. Hag ha-
Pesah was a pastoral festival, whereas Hag ha-Matsot was an
agricultural festival. In any event, the paschal lamb ceased to be
offered when the Temple was destroyed in 70 C.E., and although
the name Passover is still used, the holiday is now chiefly
marked by the laws concerning leaven and, especially, by the
home celebration held on the first night—the Seder (order,
arrangement).

    Prohibition on Leavening. On the night before the festi-
val the house is searched thoroughly for leavened bread. Any
found is gathered together and removed from the house during
the morning of 14 Nisan. This is based on the biblical injunction that not only is it forbidden to eat leaven, but no leaven
may remain in the house. On Passover observant Jews do not

> *"For the Lord will
> pass through to
> smite the Egyp-
> tians; and when
> he seeth the blood
> upon the lintel,
> and on the two
> side posts, the
> Lord will pass
> over the door, and
> will not suffer the
> destroyer to come
> in unto your
> houses to smite
> you. And ye shall
> observe this thing
> for an ordinance
> to thee and to thy
> sons for ever."*
>
> King James
> Bible, Exodus
> 12:23–24

275

employ utensils used during the rest of the year for food that contains leaven. Either they have special Passover utensils or they remove the leaven in the walls of their regular utensils by firing or boiling them in hot water. Only food products completely free from even the smallest particle of leaven are eaten.

In many communities, rabbis supervise the manufacture of packaged Passover foods to verify that they are completely free from leaven, after which they attach their seal of fitness to the product. There was at first considerable rabbinical opposition to machine-made **matsah** on the grounds that pieces of dough might be left in the machine and become leaven. Nowadays, with vastly improved methods of production, the majority of Jews see no objection to machine-made *matsah*.

matsah: thin unleavened bread.

The biblical reason given for eating unleavened bread and refraining from eating leaven (*hamets*) is that during the Exodus the Israelites, having left Egypt in haste, were obliged to eat unleavened bread because their dough had had insufficient time to rise. *Matsah* is therefore the symbol of freedom. A later idea is that leaven—bread that has risen and become fermented—represents pride and corruption, whereas unleavened bread represents humility and purity.

Great care is consequently taken when baking *matsah* for Passover. The process is speeded up so that no time is allowed for the dough to rise before it is baked. The resulting *matsah* is a flat bread with small **perforations** (an extra precaution against the dough's rising). Some Jews prefer to eat only round *matsah*, because a circle is unbounded, representing the unlimited need to strive for freedom.

perforations: small holes.

Synagogue Service. The synagogue liturgy for Passover contains additional prayers and hymns suffused with the themes of freedom and renewal. On the first day there is a prayer for dew; the rainy season now over, supplication is made for the more gentle dew to assist the growth of the produce in the fields. The scriptural readings are from passages dealing with Passover. On the seventh day, the anniversary of the parting of the sea, the relevant passage is read; some Jews perform a symbolic reenactment to further dramatize the event. On the Sabbath in the middle of Passover, the Prophetic reading is Ezekiel's vision of the dry bones. On this Sabbath, too, there is a reading of the Song of Songs (interpreted by the rabbis as a dialogue between God and his people), in which there is a reference to the spring and to the Exodus.

The Seder and the Haggadah. The Seder, celebrated in the home on the first night of Passover (outside Israel, also on the second night), is a festive meal during which various rituals are carried out and the Haggadah is read or chanted. The Haggadah (telling) is the traditional collection of hymns, stories, and poems recited in obedience to the command for parents to tell their children of God's mighty deeds in delivering the people from Egyptian bondage. The main features of the Haggadah are already found in outline in the **Mishnah** with some of the material going back to Temple times. It assumed its present form in the Middle Ages, with a few more recent additions. The emphasis in the Haggadah is on God alone as the deliverer from bondage. It is he and no other, neither messenger nor angel, who brings his people out from Egypt. Even Moses is mentioned by name only once in the Haggadah, and then only incidentally, at the end of a verse quoted for other purposes.

A special dish is placed on the Seder table upon which rest the symbolic foods required for the rituals. These are three *mat-*

Two women wash a man's hands as part of the Passover ritual.

Mishnah: a part of the Talmud, a collection of books containing Jewish law.

sot, covered with a cloth; *maror*, bitter herbs that serve as a reminder of the way the Egyptian taskmasters embittered the lives of their slaves; *haroset*, a paste made of almonds, apples, and wine, symbolic of the mortar the slaves used as well as of the sweetness of redemption; a bowl of salt water, symbolic of the tears of the oppressed; parsley or other vegetables for a symbolic dipping in the salt water; a roasted bone as a reminder of the paschal lamb; and a roasted egg as a reminder of the animal sacrifice, the *hagigah* offered in Temple times on Passover, Shavuot, and Sukkot. During the Seder, four cups of wine are partaken of by all the celebrants, representing the four different expressions used for redemption in the narrative of the Exodus. Since in ancient times the aristocratic custom was to eat and drink while reclining, the food and drink are partaken of in this way as a symbol of the mode of eating of free men. Some medieval authorities held that since people no longer recline at meals, there is no longer any point in the symbolic gesture, but their view was not adopted.

benediction: a short blessing.

The Seder begins with the Qiddush, the festival **benediction** over the first cup of wine. The middle *matsah* is then broken in two, one piece being set aside to be eaten as the *afiqoman* (dessert), the last thing eaten before the Grace after Meals, so that the taste of the *matsah* of freedom might linger in the mouth. It is customary for the grown-ups to hide the *afiqoman*, rewarding the lucky child who finds it with a present. The parsley is first dipped in the salt water and then eaten. The youngest child present asks the Four Questions, a standard formula beginning with "Why is this night different from all other nights?" The differences are noted in four instances, such as, "On all other nights we eat either leaven or unleaven, whereas on this night we eat only unleaven." The head of the house and the other adults then proceed to reply to the Four Questions by reading the Haggadah, in which the answers are provided in terms of God's deliverances. When they reach the section that tells of the ten plagues, a little wine from the second cup is poured out to denote that it is inappropriate to drink a full cup of joy at the delivery, since in the process the enemy was killed. This section of the Haggadah concludes with a benediction in which God is thanked for his mercies, and the second cup of wine is drunk while reclining.

The celebrants then partake of the meal proper. Grace before Meals is recited over two of the three *matsot* and a benediction is recited: "Blessed art thou, O Lord our God, who has sanctified us with thy commandments and commanded us to eat *matsah.*" The bitter herbs (horseradish is generally used) are then dipped in the *haroset* and eaten. There is a tradition that in Second Temple times the famous sage Hillel would eat *matsah,* bitter herbs, and the paschal lamb together. In honor of Hillel's practice, a sandwich is made of the third *matsah* and the bitter herbs. In many places the first course is a hard-boiled egg in salt water, a further symbol of the tears of the slaves in Egypt and their hard bondage.

At the end of the meal the *afiqoman* is eaten, and the Grace after Meals is recited over the third cup of wine. The Hallel (consisting of Psalms 113–18) and other hymns of thanksgiving are then recited over the fourth cup of wine. Before the recital of Hallel, a cup is filled for the prophet Elijah, the herald of the Messiah, who is said to visit every Jewish home on this night. The door of the house is opened to let Elijah in, and the children watch eagerly to see if they can notice any **diminution** in Elijah's cup as the prophet quickly sips the wine and speeds on his way to visit all the other homes. At this stage there is a custom dating from the Middle Ages of reciting a number of **imprecations** against those who oppressed the Jews and laid the Temple waste. Nowadays, many Jews either do not recite these verses or substitute prayers more relevant to the contemporary situation, such as prayers for freedom to be established for all people.

diminution: lessening in the amount.

imprecations: curses.

The Seder concludes with the cheerful singing of table hymns, most of them jingles for the delight of the children present, such as *Had Gadya* (One Kid), constructed on the same lines as *This Is the House That Jack Built*, the cat devouring the kid, the dog devouring the cat, and so on until the Angel of Death devours the final slaughterer and then God slays the Angel of Death. Commentators to the Haggadah have read into this theme various mystical ideas about the survival of Israel and the ultimate overcoming of death itself in eternal life. All join in singing these songs, for which there are many traditional melodies. This night is said to be one of God's special protection so that the usual night prayers on retiring to bed, **supplicating** God for his protection, are not recited since that protection is granted in any event. ◆

supplicate: to ask humbly for something.

Patriots' Day

> *"By the rude bridge that arched the flood, Their flag to April's breeze unfurled, Here once the embattled farmers stood, And fired the shot heard round the world."*
>
> Ralph Waldo Emerson, "Concord Hymn," 1837

Patriots' Day, a holiday celebrated only in Massachusetts and Maine, commemorates the date of the battles that launched the Revolutionary War in America. On April 15, 1775, the military governor of Massachusetts, General Thomas Gage, was ordered by the British government to destroy military supplies that rebel colonists had hidden in Concord. Around midnight on April 19, several hundred British soldiers secretly began to travel from Boston to Concord. However, the rebels had been watching the soldiers' movements, and soon Paul Revere began his famous ride from Boston to warn that the British were coming. Contrary to the legend, he was captured by the British just outside of Boston and two other men, William Dawes and Samuel Prescott, actually completed the ride.

When the British soldiers reached the Lexington Green around dawn, they were met by a group of armed farmers. After a short battle in which men on both sides were killed, the farmers escaped into nearby woods and the British continued on to Concord. They were met there by another group of farmers at the Old North Bridge; this time the rebels were more successful, and the British were forced to retreat. As Ralph Waldo Emerson later wrote in his poem "Concord Hymn," the colonists had fired "the shot heard round the world." At the time, only a minority of the colonists wanted to break away from Britain, but with the battles at Lexington and Concord the American Revolution had begun.

A monument to the battle was dedicated in Concord in 1837, at which Emerson's hymn was sung; lines from the hymn are engraved on the monument. But there was no official holiday to commemorate the occasion until 1894, when the Massachusetts legislature passed a bill doing away with "Fast Day," an annual day of fasting and prayer, and establishing Patriots' Day as a legal state holiday. The day was to be recognized as "the anniversary of the birth of Liberty and Union" and was to be dedicated to "solemn religious and patriotic services." In 1907 Maine likewise replaced its "Fast Day."

In 1968 Patriots' Day was moved from April 19 to the third Monday in April, following the example of the federal "Monday Holiday Law" that moved several federal holidays to Mondays. The major celebrations take place in eastern Massachusetts, where there are parades in many towns. "Paul Revere" rides a horse along the route from Old North Church in Boston to the battlegrounds in Lexington and Concord. On the Lexington Green and at the Minuteman National Historical Site in Concord (where the Old North Bridge is a major attraction), people dressed as colonial and British soldiers gather at dawn and recreate the 1775 battles.

The most widely known Patriots' Day celebration, however, has little connection to the historical events. Since 1897 the Boston Marathon road race has been held on Patriots' Day. The course runs along major streets from the suburb of Hopkinton eastward to Boston, not along the battle route. The oldest annual marathon, it attracts international champions; the starting field of 38,708 runners at the 100th running in 1996 was the largest ever recorded for a marathon. ◆

Potlatch

NATIVE AMERICAN ● VARIOUS DATES

Potlatches were major feasts held at various times of the year by the Indians of the Pacific Northwest of North America. Potlatches were given by people of high rank and social status. The feast lasted several days, during which the host fed the guests and gave them valuable gifts. The Potlatch was associated with the transfer or inheritance of hereditary titles and their associated rights, privileges, and obligations. Potlatches are characterized by the reenactment of the sacred family histories that document the legitimacy of the claimant to the rank, by ritual feasting, and by the formal distribution of gifts by the host group to its guests, each according to his rank. Though the wealth distributed at a potlatch may be quite substantial, the amount distributed is much less important than the requirement that it be distributed according to the correct social protocols and moral prescriptions.

Potlatches have traditionally occurred at times of social stress accompanying any part of the process of ascension or succession to rank: **investiture** into a new name; the building of a house; erecting of a totem pole or other emblem of hereditary **prerogative**, such as a marriage or a child's coming of age; or alternatively as a funeral feast for a previous rankholder, as a means of acquiring prestige; and sometimes even as a means of discrediting rival claimants. The legitimacy of the rankholder's claims is proved by his dual ability to command the allegiance of his family group in putting together such a complicated ceremony and to perform correctly the formal display of his family's origin myths and ceremonial objects. The acceptance of

investiture: a ceremony formally giving power or authority to someone.

prerogative: a special privilege.

282

gifts by the guests signals their acceptance of the validity of his claim.

Anthropologists have focused on the secular, social aspects and functions of the potlatch—on the way in which potlatches maintain social equilibrium, consolidate chiefly power over commoners, provide for the orderly transfer of wealth and power, provide a measure of group identity and solidarity, redistribute surplus wealth and level economic imbalances, provide outlets for competition without recourse to violence, and provide an occasion for aesthetic expression and dramatic entertainment. Irving Goldman has suggested in his *The Mouth of Heaven* (1975) that, since in northwest coast philosophy all status, power, and wealth are considered to be a gift from the beneficent supernatural beings who provide the materials that humans need to survive, the potlatch is inherently a religious institution, fundamentally endowed with a sacramental quality.

Each of the family origin myths, whose retelling is such an important part of the potlatch, tells of how one of a particular family's ancestors was able to make a covenant with a supernatural being. In return for the right to collect food of a specific type at a specific location, to possess an aristocratic name, to

Native American dancers from the Tsimshian Eagle clan perform at a potlatch in Metlakatla, Alaska, in 1994.

covenant: a formal pledge between two parties to perform some action.

impersonate (and thus become) the supernatural being in ceremonies, and to invoke the aid of that being in times of distress, the ancestor accepted the responsibility of performing the rituals that would ensure the reincarnation of that supernatural being. This **covenant** expresses the mutual dependency of human and supernatural, and the potlatch is the ceremony through which the aristocrat fulfills his responsibilities to the supernatural being.

The chief is the representative of his house to the spirits and in his person are brought together all the historical, social, and spiritual aspects of his group's identity. He is the being who links the spiritual world to the social world, and his costume and behavior at potlatches clearly state the duality of his role as spirit in human form. Indeed, since chiefs are the representatives of particular supernatural beings, the distribution of wealth to other chiefs at potlatches can be seen as a metaphorical distribution by one supernatural being to others, and as such it represents the flow of substance throughout the entire universe.

The potlatch, obviously a rite of passage for human beings, a death of an old identity and a rebirth into a new one, is also a rite of passage for the supernaturals. The supernatural beings sustain human beings not only by giving them power and knowledge, but by being their food—when supernatural beings come to the human world, they put on costumes that transform them into animals. The objects displayed, transferred, or distributed in potlatches are manifestations of the bodies of supernatural beings: the flesh and skins of animals (which, since they are thought to be the animals' ceremonial costumes, imply that humans survive by ingesting the ceremonial, spiritual essence of their prey); the coppers (large, ceremonial plaques that represent repositories of captured souls awaiting reincarnation); and the feast dishes (which are the coffins for the animal substance before the humans who partake of that substance begin the process of its reincarnation). Potlatches, in a sense, are funerals for the supernaturals and inherently involve the reaffirmation of the eternal moral convenants between mankind and the other inhabitants of the universe. As animals sacrifice their flesh that humans may eat it and live, so humans must sacrifice themselves or their wealth, which is a symbol of themselves, that the dead may be reborn.

In northwest coast thought, moral order and spiritual purity are achieved through acts of self-sacrifice, and the giving away of possessions places humans in harmony with the moral order of the universe. The universe is imagined to have been originally a place of self-interest and possessiveness, that is, until culture heroes started the process of distribution. Northwest coast peoples believe that the universe will collapse back into the primordial chaos of selfishness unless humans continually reaffirm their willingness to disburse their possessions, to pass out wealth to their fellow men, and to pass on rank to their children. The potlatch provides the ceremonial realization of that commitment to the cosmic moral order and is a reaffirmation by all its participants—hosts, guests, ancestors, the unborn, and supernatural beings—of the system of moral covenants and mutual dependencies that lie at the basis of northwest coast society. The potlatch reenacts myth, and then, through redistribution, recreates its processual nature, thereby becoming a graphic representation of the continuing reality and salience of those myths, linking the past to the present, the dead to the living, the sacred to the mundane, the human to the supernatural, the local to the cosmic, and the momentary to the eternal.

It should be noted that the potlatch underwent substantial change during the nineteenth century. Heavy governmental and missionary pressures contributed to the abandonment or secularization of many northwest coast Indian rituals. Potlatches and all other native ceremonies were illegal in Canada between 1876 and 1951, and though some ceremonies were carried out in secret, northwest coast religion was irreparably altered. The potlatch and other ceremonies have played an important role in the native renaissance of the 1960s, 1970s, 1980s, and 1990s, but few studies of the potlatch in contemporary Indian life have been conducted, and very little can be said of the particulars of its role in Indian society today. ◆

> **Potlatches and all other native ceremonies were illegal in Canada between 1876 and 1951, though some ceremonies were carried out in secret.**

Presidents' Day

Presidents' Day was created by combining the February birthdays of two great United States presidents, which traditionally had been celebrated as separate holidays: Abraham Lincoln's birthday on February 12 and George Washington's birthday on February 22.

In 1968 Congress passed the "Monday Holiday Law," which permanently moved the date of several federal holidays to Mondays. Celebration of Washington's Birthday was set on the third Monday in February. Lincoln's Birthday had been celebrated in most northern and western states, but in many southern states the century-old memory of the Civil War lingered, and the birthdays of notable Confederate figures were celebrated instead. Because of this resistance, and also because the two holidays fell so close together, most states now celebrate only the third Monday in February. The holiday is usually called Presidents' Day, but in some states it is known as Washington–Lincoln Day or Washington's Birthday.

George Washington was born in 1732; the date was actually February 11, but the English calendar was changed during his lifetime and his birthdate moved to February 22. Washington's birth date was not officially changed until 1790, however; this caused so much confusion that, long after his death, celebrations were held on both dates.

In 1778, while the colonial army led by General Washington was suffering through a winter encampment at Valley Forge, Pennsylvania, troops honored his birthday by playing fife and drum music. Washington went on to serve as the first

"It will be happy for us both, and our best reward, if, by a successful administration of our respective trusts, we can make the established Government more and more instrumental in promoting the good of our fellow citizens, and more and more the object of their attachment and confidence."

George Washington, annual message to Congress, 1790

United States president (1789–97). In 1791 plans were made to build a national capital city named for him, and a military parade was held in his honor in Philadelphia, which was then the United States capital. Since Washington had led the army in rebellion against Great Britain's monarchy, it was ironic that the United States followed the British tradition of publicly celebrating the current king or queen's birthday by celebrating Washington's birthday during his lifetime.

A man dressed as George Washington greets visitors at Virginia's Mount Vernon, the first president's home and burial place, on Washington's birthday.

Washington died in 1799 and was buried at Mount Vernon, his family estate in Virginia. February 22, 1800, was designated a national day of mourning by Congress. Major celebrations of his birthday were held on its centennial in 1832. In 1848 construction began on the Washington Monument in Washington, D.C.; the monument took almost four decades to build, and was finally dedicated in 1885. The bicentennial of Washington's birth in 1932 was celebrated by the issuance of commemorative stamps and by ceremonies at historic locations throughout the United States.

Born in 1809, Abraham Lincoln served as president during the Civil War that threatened to destroy the United States before it had survived its first century. Lincoln was inaugurated in March 1861, the war began only a month later, and he was assassinated in April 1865, only a few days after the Confederate Army surrendered. Not surprisingly, no public celebrations of Lincoln's birthday occurred during his presidency. The year after his death, there were local commemorations of his birthday, such as the meeting of New Jersey's "Lincoln Association." The first statue of Lincoln in Washington, D.C., was erected ten years later.

In 1892 Lincoln's birthday was finally established as a state holiday in his home state of Illinois; other states soon followed, but not those that had fought on the side of the Confederacy. In those states, celebrations were held instead on the birthdays of Robert E. Lee, head of the Confederate Army (January 19) or Jefferson Davis, president of the Confederacy (June 3). Today these holidays still are celebrated in much of the South, where Lincoln's birthday was never observed on a large scale. However, on his birthday in 1914, ground was broken for the Lincoln Memorial in Washington, D.C.; the memorial was dedicated on his birthday in 1922.

Today celebrations of Washington and Lincoln's birthdays include parades, plays about their lives, and ceremonies at the Washington Monument and Lincoln Memorial in Washington, D.C. A wreath is laid at Washington's grave at Mount Vernon, and at Valley Forge the encampment of the colonial army is reenacted. A popular holiday dessert is cherry pie, linked to the legend that George Washington, an honest child, could not lie to his father about chopping down a cherry tree.

The three-day holiday weekend that includes Presidents' Day is also eagerly anticipated for reasons having nothing to do with the historical figures it commemorates. In many places, automobile dealers run sales on this midwinter weekend when business would otherwise be slow. Presidents' Day is also the beginning of a school vacation week for many public school students. ◆

> *"With malice toward none, with charity for all, with firmness in the right as God gives us to see the right, let us strive on to finish the work we are in, to bind up the nation's wounds, to care for him who shall have borne the battle and for his widow and his orphan, to do all which may achieve and cherish a just and lasting peace among ourselves and with all nations."*
>
> Abraham Lincoln, second inaugural address, 1865

Purim

Purim (Hebrew for lots) is a minor Jewish festival (one in which work is not prohibited) that falls on the fourteenth day of Adar (February to March). It celebrates the deliverance, as told in the Book of Esther, of the Jews from the designs of the Persian minister Haman, who cast lots to determine the date of their destruction. According to some historians, the events recorded in Esther are fictitious, the festival probably having its origin in a Babylonian festival. But there is evidence that Purim was celebrated as a Jewish festival from the first century B.C.E. Purim was observed also as a reminder to Jews that God often works "behind the scenes" in order to protect his people. Medieval thinkers found a basis for this idea in the absence of God's name in Esther, the only book in the Hebrew Bible in which the divine name does not appear.

The central feature of Purim is the reading of the Megillah (scroll), as the Book of Esther is called, in the form of a **parchment** scroll, written by hand and occasionally profusely illustrated. This public reading takes place on the night of Purim and again during the morning service in the synagogue. During this service the passage in the Torah concerning the blotting out of the name of Amalek, enemy of Israel, is read because Haman was a descendant of Amalek. Based on this is the practice, frowned upon by some Jews, of making loud noises with rattles and the like whenever the name of Haman is mentioned during the reading of the Megillah.

Esther 9:22 speaks of sending portions to friends and giving alms to the poor. Hence the rabbinic rule is that each person

parchment: sheep- or goatskin prepared for writing on.

must send a gift of at least two items of food to a friend and give at least one donation to two poor men. From the reference in Esther 9:17 to "days of feasting and joy," the rabbis further established the Purim festive meal, at which there is much imbibing of wine. A **Talmudic** statement has it that a man must drink until he is incapable of telling whether he is blessing Mordechai or cursing Haman.

Talmudic: relating to the Talmud, a collection of books containing Jewish law.

As part of the Purim jollity, undoubtedly influenced by the Italian Carnival, people dress up, and children, especially, produce Purim plays in which they assume the characters mentioned in the Megillah. Rabbis objected to men dressing up as women and vice versa since this offends against the law in Deuteronomy 22:5, but Meir of Padua in the sixteenth century defended the practice as a harmless masquerade. In some communities it is the practice to appoint a "Purim rabbi" whose duty it is frivolously to manipulate even the most sacred texts.

The Jews of Shushan celebrated Purim on the fifteenth day of Adar. To pay honor to Jerusalem, it was ordained that cities that, like Jerusalem, had walls around them in the days of Joshua should celebrate Purim on the fifteenth. Consequently, the citizens of Jerusalem today keep the festival and read the Megillah on Shushan Purim, the fifteenth of Adar, while for other Jews Purim is on the fourteenth of the month. ◆

Quinceañera

The quinceañera is a Mexican rite of passage for young women as they reach age fifteen. It is celebrated by Hispanics in some Latin American countries and the United States. The ceremony has its roots in the Aztec culture and is similar in aim to coming of age ceremonies seen in many cultures throughout the world. The quinceañera represents a girl's passage to adulthood and reaffirms cultural and community ties. It is accompanied by religious observances, and some families celebrate it with a party that reaches the proportions of a wedding.

In pre-Columbian Mexico, Aztec girls age twelve to thirteen entered one of two schools. Girls who entered the Calmacac school received training for a lifetime of religious service, and the Telpucucali school prepared girls for marriage. The girls underwent initiation rites in which they vowed chastity, truthfulness, and obedience. Following Spain's conquest of Mexico, Native Americans blended their religious practices with those of Catholicism. The age of female initiation eventually became fifteen, and the ceremony received the name *quinceañera*, from the Spanish words *quince* (fifteen) and *anos* (years). In traditional Latino families, a girl did not date, dance, or wear makeup until her quinceanera.

As with weddings, quinceañeras usually reflect the social and economic well-being of a family. While some families celebrate with a modest birthday party, other families plan far ahead and spend large amounts of money for the quinceañera. Parents bear the primary cost of the event, but the girl's godparents also

> The quinceañera represents a girl's passage to adulthood and reaffirms cultural and community ties.

A Mexican-American father escorts his daughter during her quinceañera party in Miami, Florida.

contribute. Invitations may be sent out, and relatives often travel to attend the event.

A central piece of the quinceañera is the dress, a formal gown as lush and ornate as a wedding dress. The girl also wears a crown made of rhinestones, pearls, or flowers and carries a bouquet. From among her friends, the family selects her *damas*, female attendants, and *chambelanes*, male escorts. These people form her *Corte de Honor* (honor court), fourteen couples who together with the girl and her *chambelan* (escort) *de honor* make fifteen couples, one for each year.

Catholic clergy welcome the quinceañera as an opportunity to strengthen ties with the faith. A priest often meets with the family to plan the ceremony and to review the spiritual aspects of the occasion. The Catholic sacrament of confirmation marks passage into adult spiritual life, and many churches will not perform the quinceañera for girls until they have been confirmed. Mandatory confirmation classes educate young people about the church.

Beginning the ceremony, the girl follows her court in procession down the church aisle with her parents at her side. The priest says mass, during which he advises the girl about her role and the model of Mary, the mother of Jesus. The girl's godparents present her with a rosary, a ring with her birthstone, and a prayer book. They will have already presented her with a *medalla de oro* (gold religious medal) signifying Our Lady of Guadalupe, Mexico's patron saint. During the ceremony, the girl recites a prayer of dedication to God and presents flowers to the statue of Mary.

After the service, the quinceañera party is held at a festively decorated hall or home. The court makes a grand entrance, and the father dances his daughter's first waltz with her, first placing a pair of high-heeled shoes on her to symbolize her new adulthood. He then steps aside for the chambelan de honor to dance with her. Dance music may include waltz, salsa, merengue, rock, or pop. There may be a mariachi band or a DJ. Festive foods such as fajitas or special dishes made from *cabrito*, goat meat, may be served. Other favorites are tamales; *posole*, a hominy dish; *polle en mole*, chicken with a special sauce; and the typical tortillas, beans, and rice. A large birthday cake, similar to a wedding cake, creates a centerpiece, and the girl is presented with a symbolic *última muñeca* (last doll) when the cake is cut.

Many Hispanic families fit the quinceañera to their own tastes, finances, or regional traditions. Some feature a court of only damas, only chambelanes, or neither. Often a quinceañera takes place at a convenient time after the girl's actual birthday. Some churches combine several ceremonies or hold them at Sunday mass. While many Mexican girls wear white dresses, Central American, Cuban, and Puerto Rican girls wear pink or pastel colors. El Salvadorans call the quinceañera *Mi fiesta rosa* (My Pink Party), and the girls wear pink. Cubans may celebrate with a fancy ball, featuring choreographed dances and lavish dresses, but no mass. In some areas, such as border towns of Texas, photos of quinceañera celebrants are published in the social pages of newspapers. ◆

While many Mexican girls wear white dresses on quinceañera, Central American, Cuban, and Puerto Rican girls usually wear pink or pastel colors.

Rosh ha-Shanah and Yom Kippur

JEWISH ● TISHRI

Rosh ha-Shanah and Yom Kippur, holy days prominent in the Jewish religious calendar, mark the beginning of the new year and set off the special period traditionally designated for self-scrutiny and repentance. They are referred to as Yamim Noraim (Hebrew for "days of awe"), the time when the **numinous** aspect of Judaism comes into its own.

numinous: spiritual, supernatural.

Rosh ha-Shanah. Rosh ha-Shanah (head of the year, i.e., New Year) is the name given in postbiblical times to the biblical festival of the first day of the seventh month (counting from the spring month of the Exodus from Egypt) and described in the Old Testament as a day of blowing the horn. The postbiblical name is based on **Talmudic** teachings that on this day all mankind is judged for its fortunes in the coming year. For this reason Rosh ha-Shanah is also called Yom ha-Din (day of judgment).

Talmudic: relating to the Talmud, a collection of books containing Jewish law.

Biblical scholars, exploring the origins of the festival, have noted the parallels with ancient Near Eastern agricultural festivities in the autumn and the enthronement ceremonies of the king as the representative of the Canaanite god Baal or the Babylonian god Marduk. According to the critical view, references to the festival occur in sections of the **Pentateuch** known as the priestly code, which could well have been influenced by Babylonian practices. Such theories remain, however, conjectural. In Nehemiah 8:1–8 there is a vivid description of the dramatic occasion when the Israelites who had returned from

Pentateuch: the first five books of the Old Testament.

Babylonian captivity renewed their convenant with God. Ezra read from the Torah on this first day of the seventh month; the people, conscious of their shortcomings, were distressed at hearing the demands of the Law, but Nehemiah reassured them: "Go your way, eat the fat, and drink the sweet and send portions unto him for whom nothing is prepared; for this day is holy unto our Lord; neither be ye grieved, for the joy of the Lord is your strength." These are the antecedents of the festival as it later developed (held on the first and second days of the autumnal month of Tishri), a day of both joy and solemnity. The day also became known as Yom ha-Zikkaron (day of remembrance) because on it God remembers his creatures.

A man blows a shofar (made from ram's horn) during Rosh ha-Shanah services.

The themes of God as king and judge of the universe and the need for repentance all feature prominently in the Rosh ha-Shanah liturgy. The special additional prayer consists of three groups of verses and prayers: (1) *malkhuyyot* (sovereignties, in which God is hailed as king), (2) *zikhronot* (remembrances, in which God is said to remember his creatures), (3) *shofarot* (trumpet sounds, which refer to the blowing of the horn). A popular medieval interpretation of these three is that they represent the three cardinal principles of the Jewish faith: belief in

God, in reward and punishment (God "remembers" man's deeds), and in revelation (the horn was sounded when the Law was given at Sinai, as stated in Exodus 19:16).

Another prayer of the day looks forward to the **messianic** age, when the kingdom of heaven will be established and all wickedness will vanish from the earth. In a hymn recited on both Rosh ha-Shanah and Yom Kippur, continuing with the judgment theme, God is spoken of as the great shepherd tending his flock. He decides on Rosh ha-Shanah, and sets the seal on Yom Kippur, "who shall live and who shall die; who shall suffer and who shall be tranquil; who shall be rich and who poor; who shall be cast down and who elevated." At various stages in the liturgy of Rosh ha-Shanah and Yom Kippur there are prayers to be inscribed in the Book of Life, based on a Talmudic passage stating that the average person whose fate is in the balance has the opportunity during the period from Rosh ha-Shanah to Yom Kippur to avert the "evil decree" by repentance, prayer, and charity. These days, including Rosh ha-Shanah and Yom Kippur, are consequently known as the Ten Days of Penitence, the period for turning to God and for special strictness in religious observances. The verse "Seek ye the Lord while he may be found" is applied especially to this time of the year.

The central ritual of the Rosh ha-Shanah festival is the ceremony of blowing a horn called a shofar. Although the shofar may be fashioned from the horn of several kosher animals, a ram's horn, reminiscent of the ram sacrificed by Abraham in place of Isaac, is preferred. Many attempts have been made to explain the significance of the rite. Maimonides, an important Jewish philosopher of the Middle Ages, explained:

> Although it is a divine decree that we blow the shofar on Rosh ha-Shanah, a hint of the following idea is contained in the command. It is as if to say: "Awake from your slumbers, you who have fallen asleep in life, and reflect on your deeds. Remember your Creator. Be not of those who miss reality in the pursuit of shadows, who waste their years seeking vain things that neither profit nor deliver. Look well to your souls, and improve your actions. Let each of you forsake his evil ways and thoughts. (*Code of Law*, Repentance 3.4)

The shofar is sounded a number of times during the synagogue service. The three basic notes are *teqiah* (a long, drawn-out note, signifying hope and triumph), *shevarim* (a broken set of short notes), and *teruah* (a set of even shorter notes that, like

messianic: relating to the belief in a future king or deliverer of the Jews.

The central ritual of the Rosh ha-Shanah festival is the ceremony of blowing a horn called a shofar.

shevarim, represents weeping). First, the *teqiah* suggesting firm commitment to God's laws is sounded followed by the two weeping sounds as man reflects on his sins and failings, and finally a second *teqiah* is blown signifying confidence in God's pardon where there is sincere repentance.

At the festive meal on Rosh ha-Shanah it is customary to dip bread in honey and to eat other sweet things while praying for "a good and sweet year." In some places the celebrants eat fish to symbolize the good deeds they hope will proliferate like fish in the sea in the year ahead. An ancient custom is to go to the seaside or riverside on the afternoon of the first day of Rosh ha-Shanah, there to cast away the sins of the previous year. This is based on Micah 7:19, a verse that speaks of God casting away the sins of the people into the depths of the sea.

Yom Kippur. Yom Kippur (day of **atonement**) is the culmination of the **penitential** season, the day of repentance and reconciliation between man and God and between man and his neighbor. It is the most hallowed day in the Jewish year and is still observed by the majority of Jews, even those who are otherwise lax in religious practices. During a period of Jewish history when religious life was centered on the Jewish Temple in Jerusalem, elaborate sacrificial and purgatory rites, described in Leviticus 16, were carried out. The high priest entered the Holy of Holies in the Temple, where no other person was allowed to enter under pain of death, to make atonement for his people. A whole section of the Talmud describes in greater detail the Temple service on Yom Kippur. After the destruction of the Temple in 70 C.E., the day became one of prayer and worship. The reference to "afflicting the soul" on this day is understood as an injunction to fast. No food or drink is taken from sunset on the ninth of Tishri until nightfall on the tenth. Other "afflictions" practiced are abstaining from marital relations, from wearing leather shoes, and from bathing.

The ninth of Tishri, the day before Yom Kippur, is devoted to preparation for the fast. On this day, festive meals are eaten both for the purpose of gaining strength for the fast and to celebrate the pardon Yom Kippur brings. In Talmudic teaching, Yom Kippur does not bring atonement for offenses against other human beings unless the victims have pardoned the offenders. It is the practice, consequently, for people to ask forgiveness of one another on the day before the fast. The custom of *kapparot* (atonements) is carried out in the morning. The procedure is to take a **cockerel**, wave it around the head three times, and recite

atonement: reparation for wrongdoing.

penitential: relating to expressions of sorrow for doing something wrong.

cockerel: a young rooster.

"This shall be instead of me," after which the cockerel is slaughtered and eaten. Many medieval authorities disapproved of the practice as a pagan superstition, but it is still followed by some Jews. Others prefer to use money instead of a cockerel, and then to distribute it to the poor. Another custom still observed by some is that of *malqot* (flagellation), in which the beadle in the synagogue administers a token beating with a strap as atonement for sin. Many pious Jews, in preparation for the fast, immerse themselves in a *miqveh* (ritual bath) as a purification rite. Before leaving for the synagogue, as the fast begins, parents bless their children.

In the majority of synagogues, services are several hours long on Yom Kippur night, and continue without pause during the day from early morning until the termination of the fast. The evening service begins with the Kol Nidrei (all vows), a declaration in Aramaic to the effect that all religious promises that will be undertaken in the year ahead are hereby declared null and void. This was introduced as a means of discouraging such vows since a promise made to God had dire consequences if broken. Throughout the day hymns and religious poems composed over many centuries are chanted. These consist of praises, supplications, **martyrologies**, and, especially, confessions of sin.

martyrology: a catalog of martyrs with brief information about their lives.

A prominent feature of the additional service (Musaf) is the remembering of the Temple service on Yom Kippur. At the stage that relates how the high priest would utter the divine name and the people would then fall on their faces, the members of the congregation kneel and then prostrate themselves. This is the only occasion nowadays when there is prostration in the synagogue. At the late-afternoon service, the story of the Old Testament prophet Jonah is read as a lesson that none can escape God's call and that he has mercy even on the most wicked if they sincerely repent. The day ends with Neilah (closing), a special service signifying that the gates of heaven, open to prayer all day, are about to close. At this particularly solemn time of the day, the worshipers make an urgent effort to be close to God, many standing upright for the hour or so of this service. As the sun sets, the congregation cries out aloud seven times: "The Lord he is God." Then the shofar is sounded to mark the termination of the fast.

White, the color of purity and mercy, is used on Yom Kippur for the vestments of the scrolls of the Torah and the ark in which the scrolls are kept as well as for the coverings in the synagogue. Traditional Jews wear white robes; in fact, these are shrouds to remind man of his mortality. This tradition serves a main theme of Yom Kippur: human life is frail and uncertain, but one can place trust in God and share in God's goodness forever. Since the festival of Sukkot falls a few days after Yom Kippur, it is advised that as soon as the worshipers return home from the synagogue and before breaking the fast, they should make some small preparation for the erection of the Sukkot booths and so proceed immediately after the day of pardon to do a good deed. ◆

Saint Patrick's Day

Saint Patrick's Day, observed on March 17, commemorates Ireland's patron saint. Born in Celtic Britain about C.E. 389, Patrick became a Roman Catholic bishop. Around 431 he went to Ireland where he established Christianity as the religion of that island. The legend that he drove the snakes out of Ireland probably refers symbolically to his ridding the land of pagans. The shamrock is associated with Saint Patrick's Day because he used the three-leaf plant as a teaching tool for explaining the Holy Trinity.

In Ireland the day has traditionally been commemorated quietly as a religious holiday observed in church. In the twentieth century a Saint Patrick's Day parade was introduced in Dublin, Ireland's capital, although as much to satisfy tourists as for any other reason. And although "drowning the shamrock," or pub crawling, became part of the holiday for some, it remained a mostly solemn saint's day holiday. Although Ireland is the only country in which Saint Patrick's Day is a legal holiday, most of the celebrating, especially of the more boisterous kind, occurs in the places around the world where Irish emigrants have settled, especially in New York City, Chicago, and Boston.

The first celebration of the holiday in North America occurred in 1684 in New York City. The first observance outside of a church seems to have been in Boston in 1737. The initial Saint Patrick's Day parade in New York City was held in 1766 by an Irish military unit recruited by the British to serve in the colonies. Until the mid-nineteenth century, however,

Although Ireland is the only country in which Saint Patrick's Day is a legal holiday, most of the celebrating occurs in the places around the world where Irish emigrants have settled, especially in New York City, Chicago, and Boston.

300

Who Was Saint Patrick?

The man honored on Saint Patrick's Day was a Christian Briton sent by his church as a missionary bishop to Ireland. Although there are numerous traditions and legends about Patrick, historians are dependent on two documents, his *Confessions* and *Letter to the Soldiers of Coroticus*, for information about his life. Patrick was apparently born and raised in Britain around 389 C.E., when the region was under the control of Rome. His father was a Roman citizen, a wealthy landowner, and an official of the British Christian church. About 406, when Patrick was sixteen, Irish raiders captured him and took him to Ireland to work as a herdsman. The hardship of enslavement was traumatic, yet the experience kindled in young Patrick a strong religious faith. After six years, Patrick fled his captors and made his way back to his family in Britain. He spent the next several years training for the clergy in monasteries in Britain, and perhaps also in France.

Sometime in the 420s, Patrick dreamed that his former Irish captors were calling him back. During his slave years he had learned the Irish language and now felt drawn by God to return and convert the Irish to Christianity. The British church concurred with Patrick's calling, appointed him bishop, and around 431 sent him and some assistants to Ireland. He traveled to the northeast of Ireland, was welcomed by the regional king, and probably made his headquarters at Armagh, near the king's estate. Amid the traditional Irish religion of the druids and among the unlettered Irish, Patrick's work was typical of a fifth-century missionary bishop. He made friends, preached, celebrated mass, baptized thousands of people, founded numerous monasteries and churches, and trained and ordained clergy. Patrick's ministry in Ireland lasted about thirty years, until his death around 460. Details of Patrick's travels and work in Ireland are not available, but legends about him attest to the love and respect he must have garnered. After his death, the Irish church that he helped found contributed substantially to the evangelization of Scotland, northern England, and western Europe.

the number of marchers was only in the hundreds, consisting mostly of Irish militiamen and Irish benevolent societies. The major form of celebration took the form of evening banquets held by Irish fraternal and charitable societies. These groups consisted of well-to-do Irish Catholics and Protestants, and their dinners were genteel in tone. The first group to hold these banquets regularly was the Society of the Friendly Sons of Saint Patrick's in New York City, founded around 1784. Its large meals were followed by a multitude of toasts to Ireland and the United States.

The Irish famine of the 1840s drove great numbers of the island's poor Catholics into exile, which in turn changed both the form and content of Saint Patrick's Day observances in the Irish diaspora. The great number of new Irish Americans could

A man wears a green suit decorated with shamrocks, a symbol of Ireland, on Saint Patrick's Day in Chicago.

not be accommodated at the traditional banquets, and parades replaced them as the major form of celebration. By 1870 the New York City parade consisted of around 40,000 marchers watched by several hundred thousand bystanders. The parades around the country became strictly Catholic in composition and anti-British in tone. They were dominated by Irish nationalist groups who supported the struggle for Irish independence from Britain; in New York City the most important organization in the parade was the nationalistic Ancient Order of Hibernians. Sometimes Anglo-American nativists clashed violently with the Irish-American marchers.

In the twentieth century the size of Saint Patrick's Day parades continued to increase. By the 1980s the number of marchers in New York City had grown to 150,000, with perhaps as many as a million spectators. There, as elsewhere, "wearing of the green" (sporting at least one item that matched the color of Ireland, the Emerald Isle) was an essential part of the holiday for marchers and many spectators. The New York parades had the additional distinction of moving up Fifth Avenue along a center line painted green for the day. The marchers moved past St. Patrick's Cathedral (across Fifth Avenue from Rockefeller

Center), from which the archbishop of New York emerged to greet them. The processions included contingents of Irish-American policemen and firemen; Irish-American auxiliaries and societies; high school fife and drum corps; bagpipe marching bands; and the United Irish Counties Association, with members from each of the thirty-two Irish counties marching behind their own banners. Leading political officeholders normally regarded attendance as a political necessity.

Parades in other cities had their own distinguishing characteristics. In Dublin, attempts to make the parade more lively began in 1996 by including, in addition to the usual bands and floats, dance groups illustrating Irish customs; currachs (small Celtic boats of ancient times); and, as the modern element, air corps jets flying overhead. Some 3,500 marched and 350,000, many of them foreigners, watched. New Orleans parades, influenced by the Mardi Gras tradition, included many floats. Those on the floats threw cabbages, carrots, onions, and other vegetables to onlookers. The St. Louis parade, 5,000 strong, includes giant helium balloons. Most U.S. celebrations became associated with practices frowned upon by traditionalists as frivolous, such as drinking green-dyed beer and wearing green buttons saying "Kiss Me, I'm Irish."

A bagpipe band marches in the New York City's Saint Patrick's Day parade.

389 Patrick is born in Britain.

431 Patrick travels as a missionary to Ireland.

1684 Irish immigrants in New York City observe Saint Patrick's Day in North America.

1737 Irish immigrants in Boston celebrate Saint Patrick's Day outside of the church.

1766 New York City hosts first Saint Patrick's Day parade.

Since Northern Ireland remained under British control, the parades retained a nationalist component into the 1990s, with some marchers carrying signs demanding the incorporation of the northern counties into the Irish Republic, established earlier in the century. During the 1980s controversy erupted when an alleged member of the violent Irish Republican Army was selected as the grand marshal of the New York City parade. Additional political controversy emerged in the early 1990s when gay and lesbian Irish Americans sought to participate in the Boston and New York City marches under their own banners. In 1995 the U.S. Supreme Court settled the issue by ruling that march organizers had the right, as a matter of free speech, to decide which groups and messages to allow into the parades. In 1998 the Dublin parade became embroiled in controversy when its organizers, the city corporation and the Irish Tourist Board, called upon participants and onlookers to dress as "witches, warlocks, and wizards"; some Catholics protested, saying this would turn Saint Patrick's Day into a pagan rather than a Christian celebration.

A prominent feature of late-twentieth-century Saint Patrick's Day celebrations occurr after the parades are over. Many of the marchers, along with nonmarching sons and daughters of Erin, retire to Irish pubs to eat, drink, and listen to Irish folk music. A pub in Atlanta normally seats only fifty but uses its parking lot for a Saint Patrick's Day party for 3,000. Some pubs are tributes to Ireland in themselves, reflecting the nostalgic feelings of Irish-Americans for their ancestral home. A pub in Coral Cables, Florida, for example, boast a Waterford crystal chandelier from Ireland, a mahogany bar installed by Irish laborers imported for the job, and a 150-year-old maple floor from a Dublin church.

The foods served includes Irish favorites like corned beef, soda bread, Irish stew spiked with Guinness and Port, shepherd's pie, mashed potatoes with green onion and butter, and lamb shank. The heavy drinking of alcohol is common, a favorite drink being black and tan, consisting of one part Guinness stout and one part lager. Not all entertainment is in the pubs; Carnegie Hall in New York City, for example, has an annual Irish folk concert on Saint Patrick's night. ◆

Sallah

Sallah is the name given by the Hausa of northern Nigeria and southern Niger to the Muslim holiday, Id al-Adha, which is celebrated on the 10th day of Dhu'l-hija. The exact date of the holiday coincides with the new moon. Dhu'l-hija, the last month of the Islamic calendar, is the month during which Muslims make their pilgrimage to Mecca. This holiday, also known as the Feast of Sacrifice, commemorates Abraham's willingness to sacrifice his son with the ritual sacrifice of an animal. It is one of the most important festivals in the Islamic calendar and Muslims all over the world sacrifice an animal on this day.

The celebration of Id al-Adha in Hausaland in northern Nigeria not only commemorates Abraham's sacrifice but also honors the emir, the regional ruler. The Hausa, the largest ethnic group in Nigeria, were conquered by the Muslim Fulani during the Fulani jihad, or holy war. In 1808 the Fulani captured the seven Hausa city-states, Katsina, Kano, Rano, Daura, Zaria, Gabir, and Zamfora. A Fulani emir, essentially a governor, was installed as the ruler of each city-state and this system of governance remains in place today.

Like other Id al-Adha ceremonies, the Hausa celebrate Sallah by sacrificing a ram, if it is within their means. The other important rite of Sallah is the procession in honor of the emir. Both the Fulani and Hausa are natural horsemen and much of the procession takes place on horseback. On the evening before Sallah, the horses of each district head are brought to the city with an entourage of ornately robed riders accompanied by

> On the evening before Sallah, horses belonging to the head of each district are brought to the city with an entourage of ornately robed riders.

During the Sallah celebration in Niger, ornately robed Hausa riders parade from the palace of the emir to the prayer grounds.

recorder and drum music. In the morning the procession from the palace of the emir to the prayer grounds takes place amid great pomp and circumstance.

The emir and his entourage, the district heads and their entourages, and hundreds of riders, each riding a stallion with silver and gold ornamented bridles and saddles and each wearing a rich costume of velvet and brocade, join in the procession. When the procession arrives at the prayer ground, the riders, who remain mounted, are led in prayer by the Imama. The procession then returns to the palace through the streets lined with people who eagerly await the appearance of the emir. The procession is a jubilant affair with the music of pipes, drums, flutes, horns, and the rhythmic jingle of ankle bells worn by dancers. Women, who usually observe the restrictions imposed by purdah, join in this public celebration.

When the procession returns to the grounds of the emir's palace a crowd gathers to watch the culmination of the Sallah festivities, the durbar. This elaborate salute to the emir is an affirmation of his power and demonstration of the proud heritage of Hausaland. First to arrive are horsemen in European-style uniforms who bear the flag of the city-state. They are followed by marching bands, playing Sousa-type marches, and bagpipe players. Next to arrive are the emir's armed guard, who are attired in traditional chain mail vests worn beneath blue robes and blue turbans. The emir's personal bodyguards immediately precede the emir and they wear European red coats and white turbans. Their white horses are decorated with red ribbons. Finally, the emir arrives on a white stallion, dressed in white robes and a white turban.

The durbar commences. Each group of riders gallops up to the seated emir. They rein in their horses at the last minute so that their horses rear up on their hind legs. The men raise their clenched fists in salute and the emir responds by raising his sword. The sallah procession and the durbar embody the mixed European and traditional heritage of Hausaland, as demonstrated by the styles of dress and music. The tradition of the Sallah procession dates back to the beginning of the Fulani empire. Although the tradition was broken during the British colonial reign, the Sallah procession has been reinstated since independence. ◆

San Fermin Festival

SPAIN ● JULY 6 TO 14

The most famous event of the San Fermin Festival, which takes place in the city of Pamplona in the Basque region of northern Spain, is the running of the bulls. This 400-year-old festival has far outgrown its namesake in fame. Little can be said of Saint Fermin, Pamplona's patron saint and the town's first bishop. But the festival, which takes place during the first two weeks of July, draws people from around the world.

The Fiesta de San Fermin begins at noon on July 6, the eve of the saint's feast day, when a rocket is fired from the balcony of the town hall and the mayor shouts, "Viva San Fermin!" From that moment until midnight on the 14th, the nonstop party includes fireworks, musical bands, and dancing in the streets. Other festivities include bullfights, **jai alai** matches, and singing contests. There are also parades of papier-mâché giants, ceremonial presentations of colorfully dressed matadors, and crowded cafes and restaurants.

jai alai: a game similar to handball.

A running of the bulls takes place each day of the festival. Each morning, the event is signaled with a parade of bagpipers while runners gather in the town hall square. At 8 A.M., a rocket is shot from the town hall, and six to a dozen bulls are released from a corral and goaded to run for a winding half mile through cobblestone streets toward the bullring. Runners sprint ahead of the bulls, and can only carry a rolled up newspaper for protection. Those who fall must cover their heads and lie motionless until the bulls pass. Many runners leap up on barricades to escape the bulls.

The most dedicated runners are called *aficionados*. These are local residents who wear traditional Basque white pants and shirts with red scarves at their neck and waists. These men often dare to taunt the bulls and leap in front of them. Many amateurs run with the bulls, including some women. Slow runners may be crushed by other runners or maimed by a bull. Successful runners reach the bullring safely and, once in the ring, dare to slap bulls as they run past. Each afternoon, bullfights are held.

The fiesta began in 1591 when young men began running alongside the bulls as they were driven through town to the bullring. At the turn of this century, butcher boys of Pamplona ran in front of bulls as they were driven from the rail station to the Plaza de Toros. The Pamplona run gained worldwide fame from Ernest Hemingway's 1926 novel *The Sun Also Rises*, becoming famous as a test of *machismo*, or masculine vitality.

By the 1990s July 6–14 in Pamplona had become a world-famous party, drawing many Europeans, Australians, New Zealanders, South Africans, and Americans. Revelers gather to drink sangria—a Spanish wine punch—and dance until dawn before the morning bull run. Pamplona's population doubles or triples during the festival, and the number of runners can reach

Men and bulls race through the streets of Pamplona, Spain, during the Festival of San Fermin.

3,000. Each year, a number of injuries occur. In 1995 a twenty-two-year-old American man was gored to death. He was the first person killed in fifteen years and the thirteenth runner to be killed since 1924. Pamplona officials said the American fell and then stood up again rather than lying still. After that, the city published guidelines for visitors on how to run the race.

In 1996 a minor political incident occurred when the Basque Fatherland and Liberty (ETA) group raised a large banner saying "ETA Wishes You a Happy Festival" in the city hall plaza during festivities. The ETA have fought for the independence of Spain's Basque region, and had allegedly killed some 800 people since 1968. The crowd chanted anti-ETA obscenities and tried to tear down the banner, while the Basque rebels fought back with sticks. ◆

San Juan Bautista Day (Feast of Saint John the Baptist)

CHRISTIAN ● JUNE 24

San Juan Bautista Day is a Christian holiday celebrated on June 24 in honor of Saint John the Baptist. John, known in Spanish as San Juan Bautista, is considered by Christians the last Jewish prophet and the forerunner of Jesus Christ. John predicted the imminent appearance of the messiah. He baptized his followers and baptized Jesus, his cousin. John was eventually executed by the Roman authorities.

On the Roman Catholic calendar the Feast of Saint John the Baptist, also called John's Day, or San Juan Bautista Day, commemorates John's death (unlike most saint's days, which celebrate the nativity of the saint). It replaced and incorporated the Midsummer's Day of pre-Christian Europe, which marked the summer solstice with the lighting of bonfires that symbolized the strength of the sun.

San Juan Bautista Day has special significance for the island of Puerto Rico in the Caribbean. Columbus landed on the island on November 19, 1493, and named it San Juan Bautista. Early in the sixteenth century its name was changed to Puerto Rico (Rich Port), but shortly thereafter the capital was named San Juan, and San Juan Bautista has since been its patron saint.

In the centuries of Spanish rule, San Juan Bautista Day was celebrated as a Catholic holiday with religious processions and feasts. Symbolic bathing was associated with the holiday, based

> San Juan Bautista Day has special significance for the island of Puerto Rico; Columbus landed on the island in 1493 and named it San Juan Bautista.

on the episode in the Bible in which John baptized Jesus. Celebration was restricted largely to San Juan.

The celebration of San Juan Bautista Day changed sharply after the United States took control of Puerto Rico following the Spanish-American War of 1898, and especially after the island gained commonwealth status in 1953. The vast influx of tourists from the U.S. mainland during the second half of the twentieth century was a key influence in the transformation; especially significant was the mainlanders' use of Puerto Rico's beaches for sun tanning and swimming. Traditionally, Puerto Ricans did not use beaches for recreational or celebratory purposes, and it has been estimated that at mid-century, less than 20 percent of Puerto Rican adults knew how to swim. But over the next five decades, the impact of tourism on Puerto Rican culture changed that. One consequence is that San Juan Bautista Day has become a beach-centered and more secular holiday that is much more widely and intensively celebrated than before the 1950s.

The San Juan Bautista Day beach celebration climaxes at midnight when everyone walks backward into the water three (or sometimes seven) times.

Many Puerto Ricans leave work during the afternoon of the day preceding the June 24 festival (although neither day is a legal holiday). Then, families carrying food and drink get into their cars or whatever vehicles are available and head to the coastal beaches. (Puerto Ricans who do not live near the coast celebrate at other natural bodies of water or around swimming pools.) There, on the evening of June 23, barbecues are started up. Young people intending to stay all night pitch tents. Decorative lights and platforms for musicians are set up. The musicians play loud salsa music. In a more traditional mode, the beachgoers light bonfires, continuing a practice going back to Midsummer's Day. The beach celebration climaxes at midnight, when everyone walks backward into the water three (or sometimes seven) times. This immersion has largely lost its religious symbolism and is now simply considered a way of ensuring *suerte*, or good luck over the next year. The beach parties continue through the night, along with concerts and street dancing. At dawn, church services are held. This is just the beginning of a week of celebration, which features religious processions, secular parades, and music.

Puerto Ricans on the U.S. mainland also commemorate San Juan Bautista Day. In Camden, New Jersey, for example, the annual parade includes beauty queens, salsa dancers, and floats carrying children dancing La Plana. It is followed by a picnic at which folk dancers perform the traditional *tuna* and *cumbia*. Parents value the festivities as a way of passing down Puerto Rican traditions to their children. The weeklong celebration is also marked with a banquet and an art exhibit. In Jacksonville Beach, Florida, the holiday is oriented more to adults and seeks to draw tourists with a variety of professional bands and orchestras playing salsa, meringue, and reggae music. Hartford, Connecticut, celebrates on the Saturday nearest June 24. Featured are Puerto Rican foods and bands playing Puerto Rican music using traditional instruments. Some 15,000 people, Puerto Ricans and others, attend. Other Latino groups in the United States also celebrate the day, in particular Chicanos in California. ◆

Saturnalia

In Roman mythology, Saturn presided over the Golden Age, an era of peace, happiness, and prosperity at the beginning of the world.

Saturnalia was an ancient Roman festival that celebrated Saturn, the Roman god of agriculture. Saturnalia began on December 17 and lasted a week, until the 23rd. The Saturnalia may have begun as a celebration after the winter planting, but became a time of general merrymaking.

Saturn held the same position as the Greek god Cronus and as such was the husband of Ops, the goddess of the plentiful harvest. Saturn was also the father of Jupiter, Ceres, Juno and many others. In Roman mythology, Saturn presided over the Golden Age, an era of peace, happiness, and prosperity at the beginning of the world. War, crime, and injustice were unknown in this era, and the earth bore abundant fruits.

Saturnalia fell on the dates associated with the winter solstice, the shortest day of the year. The solstice was December 25 in the Roman calendar, though it is December 21 on the modern calendar. The month leading up to the first day of January was dedicated to Saturn as well as other gods, creating an extended holiday season. Each year, Saturnalia celebrated the memory of the Golden Age. For seven days, people attempted to recreate that time of happiness. All business was suspended, and executions and military operations were postponed. People showed goodwill and spent their time in banquets and the exchange of visits and gifts.

The Saturnalia was the most popular holiday and one of the major events of the Roman year. The festival began with a formal sacrifice at the temple of Saturn. The woolen bonds were untied from the statue of Saturn and then a festive banquet was held. Dress codes were relaxed during Saturnalia, and at home people took it easy. The social order was inverted, and a key event was the master waiting on slaves at meal times. A tradition of choosing a mock king to preside over the festival included each household choosing a Master of the Saturnalia who ordered others to do his bidding.

Friends exchanged gifts such as small pottery dolls and candles. Wax candles, which signified the calling of light on the longest night of the year, were a luxury, as people could usually only afford oil lamps or firelight. Other gifts included holly twigs with small treats tied to them. During the holiday, moral restrictions were loosened. Gambling was allowed in public, and slaves did not have to work. People drank wine and ate generously. Women worshipers drank and celebrated licentiously and engaged in ritual obscenities. The festival eventually became a week of **debauchery**.

debauchery: excessive indulgence in sensual pleasures such as eating and drinking.

The festival of Saturnalia resembled celebrations in other parts of the ancient world that took place during December, many of which have echoes today. Common elements of winter solstice celebrations throughout Europe included evergreen decorations, mainly holly and pine, as well as mistletoe, a ceremonial plant associated with immortality. The lavish dinner as well as such holiday foods as special fruits, pastries, and cider or mulled wine come down to us from Saturnalia. The practice of slaves and masters exchanging places occurs today when military officers serve the enlisted or managers serve employees at Christmas dinners. The mock king has survived in such characters as the Lord of Misrule seen at modern Carnival and Twelfth Night celebrations.

In 336 C.E., Christians moved Christ's birthday to December 25 to fit the holiday season already in place with Saturnalia and the winter solstice. This season has survived in Christmas and New Year's Day, even starting with Thanksgiving, our harvest festival. A modern religious movement known as neopaganism has revived some of the ancient rituals. Many Neopagans celebrate the winter solstice and some celebrate adapted versions of such festivals as Saturnalia. ◆

Shavuot

JEWISH ● SIVAN

Pentateuch: the first five books of the Old Testament.

theophany: the appearance on earth of a deity.

Torah: the first five books of the Old Testament; the body of wisdom and law contained in sacred Jewish writings and oral tradition.

S
havuot, or Pentecost, is the Jewish festival that falls on the sixth day of the month of Sivan (May or June, and also on the seventh day, outside Israel). In the **Pentateuch** the festival is called Shavuot (weeks) because it falls after seven weeks (forty-nine days) have been counted from the "morrow of the Sabbath" of Passover. In the Talmudic literature a debate is recorded between two ancient Jewish groups, the Sadducees and the Pharisees: the former understood the word *Sabbath* in the verse to mean literally the Sabbath of Passover (so that, for them, Shavuot always fell on Sunday), while the latter, whose view is accepted, understood "the Sabbath" to be the first day of Passover. It is difficult to know what doctrinal issues really lie behind these two opinions, since, if the report is accurate, it is unlikely that the debate was purely exegetical.

In the Pentateuch the festival appears to have been a purely agricultural one. The rabbinic name for the festival, Atseret (assembly), the term used in Numbers 29:35 for the additional festival of Sukkot, suggests that originally the festival was no more than an adjunct to Passover. But beginning no later than the second century C.E. a vast transformation of the festival took place. The arrival at Mount Sinai of the people coming from slavery in Egypt occurred in the third month from the Exodus (the month of Sivan, as it came to be called). Through examination of the texts, a view developed that the **theophany** at Sinai had taken place on the sixth of Sivan, and Shavuot was then celebrated as the anniversary of the giving of the **Torah**. (Although the passage speaks only of the Decalogue being

316

given at Sinai, later Jewish tradition held that the whole of the Torah was given to Moses at that time.)

The liturgy of the day contains references to the Torah and the 613 commandments (the rabbinic figure for the sum total of positive precepts and negative injunctions of the law). A feature found only on this festival is the recital of an Aramaic hymn on the first day in praise of the Torah. It is generally held that these hymns are vestiges of introductions in Aramaic to the Targum, the Aramaic translations of the texts that, in ancient times, were always read in the synagogue. The Pentateuchal reading is from the Sinai narrative, and the Prophetic reading from Ezekiel 1, the vision of the heavenly chariot. The link between the two is that of revelation, to the people as whole and to the individual prophet. The Book of Ruth as well is read in the synagogue. Ruth, the prototype of the righteous **proselyte**, took upon herself the observance of God's laws, as did the Israelites at Sinai.

proselyte: a new convert to Judaism.

There are no special Shavuot rituals, in view of the late origin of the festival in the form in which it is now celebrated. However, there are a number of customs, such as decorating the synagogue with plants and flowers (because beautiful plants are said to have flowered on the barren mountain when the Torah was given) and eating dairy dishes at the festive meal (because, like milk, the Torah nourishes young and old). The sixteenth-century mystics of Safad introduced the all-night vigil on Shavuot night, a practice that has been widely adopted by all Jews. During this night an anthology of readings from all the classical sources of Judaism is studied. ◆

Sol

KOREA ● JANUARY OR FEBRUARY

According to Korean tradition, on Sol a ghost called Yagwangi visits houses and tries on everyone's shoes.

Sol is the Korean lunar new year. It is celebrated by Koreans in many parts of the world on the first day of the first lunar month, which occurs in late January or early February. Sol is one of the biggest holidays of the year in Korea and everyone takes off work to celebrate it. Some Koreans also celebrate the new year on January first.

Sol is a time for family gatherings and ancestral worship. Families traditionally gather at the eldest male's house for the holiday. Very early in the morning, families may hang a mesh dipper or sieve called a *pokjori* on the wall. Before the commercial production of rice, this dipper was used to separate the straw and weeds from rice grains. People believed it would bring good luck. The hanging of the *pokjori* is tied to Korean folklore concerning a ghost called *Yagwangi*. On Sol, *Yagwangi* visits houses and tries on everyone's shoes. He steals them if they fit, and the owner of the stolen shoes is considered unlucky. But if a *pokjori* is hung outside the house, Yagwangi will forget to try on shoes because he is busy counting the holes in the sieve.

On the morning of Sol, everyone wears their best clothes, which they believe brings good fortune. Many dress in traditional Korean clothing. Traditional male clothing consists of baggy pants and shirts. Women and girls don a short jacket closed with two long ribbons; a shirt with long, full sleeves; and a full-length, high-waisted skirt. The traditional clothes are believed to ward off evil spirits and bring good fortune in the new year.

The families then observe a ritual of ancestor worship called *Charyei*. The ritual is held at a household shrine or in the living room. During the ritual, all the males in the family make formal bows to show their respect for the ancestors. They also make offerings of rice cakes, fruit, meat, and wine to the ancestors. Children and grandchildren then perform a ceremonial bow to their family elders. The elders bless the children and wish them good health and good fortune during the year. Some children also receive money. The young then go out to extend New Year's greetings and pay respects to other relatives and friends in the neighborhood. The formal greetings to elders continue for ten days. It is considered an important part of a young person's education in good manners.

A large breakfast feast is part of the Sol morning. The meal includes dishes that were offered during the *Charyei* ceremony. One of the most popular parts of the Sol holiday feast is *ddokguk* (also spelled *ttokkuk* or *duggook*), a rice cake soup prepared with bits of meat, soy sauce, green onion, and sticky rice disks. The custom of eating white rice cake on New Year's Day comes from beliefs that the first day of the year should be clean. According to Korean tradition, eating one bowl of *ddokguk* on Sol makes a person one year older.

The day also includes a visit to an ancestor's grave. There, families hold a memorial service and praise the virtue of their ancestor. Traditional offerings are always left for the spirit of the ancestor.

After the more serious events of the morning, there is time for games on Sol. Many people enjoy *yut*, a board game in which players try to be the first to move their "men" completely around a square of twenty dots. The move is determined by a throw of four *yut* sticks, which are rounded on one side and convex on the other. On Sol, the sound of clattering *yut* sticks can be heard all over Korea. Children also enjoy competing in kite-fighting on Sol. The fighting kites have glass powder or ceramic slivers glued to their strings so that the strings are sharp. Children use their body weight to tug and pull the kites in different directions and make them "fight" other kites. The object of the contest is to cut the strings of other people's kites. The last person left flying a kite wins.

A traditional game for girls is jumping on seesaws. The traditional seesaw was made of a long wooden plank balanced on a rolled up bale of straw. A girl stood on each end of the plank and jumped on the end, making the plank move up and down. Originally, when young Korean girls were not allowed outside the family courtyard, it is said that jumping on seesaws was a way that Korean girls could bounce into the air to see the world beyond the courtyard and perhaps also get a glimpse of boys. ◆

Songkran

THAILAND ● APRIL

Songkran is the celebration of the Thai New Year. It occurs in mid-April, around April 13, and lasts for three days. Songkran, also known as Pi Mai, is a holiday devoted to the family, but it includes both public festivities and religious ceremonies. Songkran is an old festival that dates back at least 1,000 years. It is celebrated throughout Thailand and among Thai populations elsewhere in the world. Certain peoples in Laos, Burma, Cambodia, and Vietnam also celebrate Songkran. The word *Songkran* comes from the Sanskrit words meaning *new year*.

Preparation for the festival may begin with scrubbing of houses clean and discarding of worn-out clothing. According to traditional belief, anything old and useless will bring bad luck in the new year. On the morning of the first day of the festival, people dress in new clothing so that they may face the new year with a fresh start.

There are many different activities associated with the holiday. Throughout the festival, music is often played on the streets and in the wats, and children and families visit and play many traditional Thai games. One of the most important religious activities is the offering of food to monks at the local wat, a Buddhist temple-monastery. People also present food and other items to elderly relatives on this day. Another important religious activity is the ceremonial bathing of sacred altars and images of Buddha in rose-scented water. This respectful bathing takes place in all the homes and temples. Many children also bring colored sand to their local wat and build miniature stupas, dome-shaped Buddhist monuments.

Songkran is also known as the water festival because the celebration includes throwing water on other people.

321

Many people release fish in bowls and caged birds from captivity during Songkran. Animals are specially sold in the market just for this occasion. The practice of releasing animals into the wild is believed to come from the days when central Thailand was flooded during the summer rainy season. After much of the flood water drained away, small pools were left in various places, leaving baby fish trapped. Farmers used to catch the fish and keep them until Songkran, when they released them into large waterways. Freeing the fish was a way of doing something positive for their fellow creatures and it also helped preserve one of their main sources of food.

Songkran is also known as the "Water-Throwing Festival" because the celebration includes throwing of water on other people. The young line the streets with buckets, cups, squirt-guns, and hoses, waiting to douse an unsuspecting passerby. The Thai people enjoy this activity because Songkran takes place during the hottest season of the year and the splashes of water are refreshing. The custom of throwing water may come from an ancient belief in mythical serpents called the Nagas, which

A group of women in Chiangmai, Thailand, throw buckets of water at passing motorcyclists during the Songkran festival.

brought rain by spouting water from the seas. Throwing water on Songkran may be an old tradition for making rain.

In Chiang Mai, a city well known for its robust celebration of the holiday, there are also parades and a beauty contest, from which the "Queen of the Water Festival" is chosen. The Ping River, which runs through the city, is typically overflowing with wading people on Songkran, each filling buckets of water to toss on neighbors.

Though the water throwing is fairly indiscriminate, elders, monks, and policemen are treated with respect during these raucous times and are not targets of water pistols and hoses. Instead, in a ritualistic show of respect, children pour rose-scented water into the hands of elders and parents, seeking their blessing. In the past, the young actually bathed their elders and presented them with new clothing. In some areas, whole neighborhoods line up to pour water over the hands of the community's two oldest members and to give and receive blessings for the coming year.

In southwestern China, an ethnic group known as the Tai—distant relatives of today's Thai people—also celebrate New Year's Day by dressing up in traditional costumes and going to the temple to bathe the Buddha. They then splash one another like their relatives to the south. To the Tai, the water represents happiness and it washes away the demons of the past year. ◆

Sukkot

tabernacle: a sanctuary used by the Israelites during the Exodus.

Sukkot is the Hebrew name for the Jewish autumnal festival, also called the Festival of Booths, or **Tabernacles**. Sukkot begins on the fifteenth day of the month of Tishri (September–October) and lasts for seven days, followed by an eighth day called Atseret (possibly meaning "assembly"). (Outside Israel, Atseret is observed also on the ninth day.) Thus, according to Jewish tradition, there are really two distinct but interconnected festivals: Sukkot proper and Shemmini Atseret (eighth day of Atseret). The Sukkot rituals are carried out only on Sukkot proper; two are essential. The first is to dwell in booths or tabernacles (*sukkot*; sg. *sukkah*) as a reminder of the dwellings in which the Israelites lived at the time of the Exodus from Egypt. The second is derived from the biblical verse regarding four plants: *lulav* (palm branch), *etrog* (citron), *aravot* (willows), and *hadassim* (myrtles). It is traditionally understood that these four plants are to be ritually held in the hand. Sukkot, as the culmination of the three pilgrim festivals, is the season of special rejoicing and is referred to in the liturgy as "the season of our joy."

The Sukkah. The main symbol of the festival is a hut, having at least three walls, no roof, but covered with leaves or straw. During the seven days of the festival, all meals are eaten in the *sukkah*. Many Jews, especially those living in warm climates, sleep there as well. In addition to the biblical reason, medieval thinkers saw the command to dwell in the *sukkah*, a temporary dwelling, as a reminder to man of the transient nature of material possessions, and an exhortation that he

should place his trust in God. According to the mystics, the *sukkah* is visited on each of the seven days by a different biblical hero—Abraham, Isaac, Jacob, Moses, Aaron, Joseph, and David. It is the custom among many Jews to recite a welcoming formula to these guests *(ushpizin)* as if they were real persons visiting the *sukkah*.

Worshipers in Jerusalem circle the Torah scrolls on Sukkot; each carries a citron fruit and a palm, willow, and myrtle branch.

The Four Species. The rite of the four plants consists in taking them in the hand during the synagogue service and waving them above and below and in the four directions of the compass. The stated reason is to dispel harmful "winds" and to acknowledge God as ruler over all. Various interpretations have been given of why it is commanded to take these four plants. For example, it has been said that they represent man's backbone, heart, eye, and mouth, all of which must be engaged in the worship of God. Moses Maimonides (1135/8–1204) treated these as homiletical interpretations and suggested as the true reason a means of thanksgiving to God for the harvest.

The harvest motif is also observed in the custom of having a procession in the synagogue while holding the four plants on each day of Sukkot. During the procession the Hoshanah (save now) prayer for a good harvest in the year ahead is recited. On

There is a folk belief that if a man sees his shadow without a head on the night of Hoshanah Rabbah, he will die during the year.

the seventh day there are seven processions, hence the name of the day, Hoshanah Rabbah (great Hoshanah). At the end of the service on this day, the ancient custom of beating bunches of willows on the ground follows. On Shemini Atseret a special prayer for rain is recited. In a later development within Jewish tradition, Hoshanah Rabbah is seen as setting the seal on the judgment made on Yom Kippur, so that the day is a day of judgment with prayers resembling those offered on Yom Kippur. There is a folk belief that if a man sees his shadow without a head on the night of Hoshanah Rabbah, he will die during the year.

Shemini Atseret. The last day of the festival has acquired a new character from medieval times. The weekly Torah readings—from the beginning of Genesis to the end of Deuteronomy—are completed on this day and then immediately begun again, so that the day is both the end and the beginning of the annual cycle. The day is now called Simhat Torah (rejoicing of the Torah). In the Diaspora, Simhat Torah falls on the second day of Shemini Atseret. In Israel, Simhat Torah coincides with the one-day celebration of Shemini Atseret on 22 Tishri, the day also observed by Reform Jews, who no longer observe the additional second day of festivals traditionally observed by Diaspora Jews. The person who has the honor of completing the reading is called the "bridegroom" of the Torah, and the one who begins the reading again is the "bridegroom" of Genesis. On this joyful day the scrolls of the Torah are taken in procession around the synagogue, and the "bridegrooms" invite the congregation to a festive repast. ◆

Sun Dance

NATIVE AMERICAN ● VARIOUS DATES

Sun Dance is one of the most important religious ceremonies of the Indian tribes of the North American Great Plains. The Sun Dance was originally performed as a means of thanking the Sun, which represented the Supreme Being, and petitioning the Sun for protection and good fortune in the future. Almost all Great Plains tribes perform the Sun Dance, but the details and meaning of the ceremony vary from tribe to tribe and have changed over time. For most tribes the ceremony includes fasting and gazing at the sun while dancing. In some tribes, especially in former times, the Sun Dance included infliction of ritual torture. In all tribes however, the Sun Dance includes the construction of a ceremonial structure referred to as a lodge, which is built around a designated tree. Each tribe has its own term for the Sun Dance ceremony. The Shoshoni and Crow, for example, refer to the Sun Dance as the Thirst Lodge, or Thirst Standing Lodge; for the Cheyenne it is the Medicine Lodge; and for the Sioux peoples it is known as the Dance Gazing at the Sun.

The rich diversity of Sun Dance traditions in some thirty distinct tribal groups can hardly be encompassed within a brief essay. Judicious selection must therefore be made of essential elements across a fair sampling of tribal groups. Attention will also be given to contemporary movements among many Native American peoples for revitalization of traditional sacred values and practices. Indeed, it is primarily the Sun Dance that, as its popularity increases, is acting as model and stimulus for traditionalist movements extending even to non-Plains tribes and to

Most Sun Dance celebrations take place in late June or early July when "the sage is long" and "the choke-cherries are ripe."

disenchanted non–Native Americans who are seeking examples of what true religious traditions really are.

General Description. The major Sun Dance celebrations take place for all the tribal groups in late June or early July, "when the sage is long" and "the chokecherries are ripe," or, as some put it, in "the moon of fattening." In the times when these peoples were **nomadic**, the grasses of the prairies would during these months be sufficient to feed the great herds of horses belonging to the tribal bands, who often were joined in the circles of camps with allied tribes. These springtime ceremonies (in the past they may have been held earlier than June) were actually the climax of an annual cycle of minor rites and meetings of many types. Among the Crow, for example, "prayer meetings" take place regularly at the time of the full moon; among all the tribes, groups of singers meet periodically around their drums in order to practice and to instruct younger singers in the extremely difficult and subtle Sun Dance songs, many of which have been faithfully transmitted from ancient times. There are also contemporary songs that have come out of an individual's sacred experiences or that have been learned from other tribes. However, all songs that are used in the Sun Dance lodge must accord with particular styles and rhythms, since clear distinctions are made between ceremonial and social dance songs.

Given the complex logistics of the Sun Dances, with encampments of large numbers of people, many people volunteer or are selected during the year to fulfill a wide range of duties. Usually a sponsor coordinates the many details and materials for the construction of the sacred lodge or the provision of the feast at the end of the ceremonies, both of which are accomplished at considerable expense and sacrifice. The most important person however, is the spiritual leader, a "medicine person," who is guardian of the sacred lore and who usually has received special powers through the vision quest (or who may have received the authority to lead the ceremonies from a retiring elder who has passed on his sacred powers). These spiritual leaders have traditionally been recognized as holy people, for they know and live the sacred traditions and have powers for curing those who are ill in body or spirit. Such **shamanic** figures have been greatly respected as leaders within the tribe, or they have been feared because of the great strength of their mysterious powers.

nomadic: having no fixed residence but moving from place to place seasonally.

shamanic: relating to the religion of some Indian tribes of north Asia and North America.

Wild Rice

Wild rice is not really rice, but a tall grass that grows in shallow lakes, marshes, and streams in the north central United States and south central Canada. The grain that grows at the top of the plant's stock was a staple in the diet of the Sioux, the Cheyenne, and other Great Lakes and Great Plains Indian tribes, and wild rice was served on tribal feast days and other special occasions. The Indians cooked wild rice by boiling it in water, after which it was eaten plain, seasoned with herbs, or mixed with nuts, seeds, berries, and other native American foods. Warm wild rice mixed with milk, sunflower seeds, and blueberries, then sweetened with honey, makes a hearty breakfast cereal.

To cook wild rice, rinse 1 cup of rice in a colander. Place the rice in a large, heavy saucepan and cover with 4 cups of water. Bring the water to a boil. Reduce heat to a low boil, cover the pan loosely, and simmer for 50 to 60 minutes, until the rice is softened and puffed. Remove from heat, drain excess water, and fluff with a fork.

Those who participate in the actual ceremonies within the sacred lodge are often individuals who were previously in situations of extreme danger, perhaps as members of the armed forces in wars the United States has conducted overseas, and who vowed that if they should survive they would participate in the next Sun Dance upon returning home. Paradoxically, their experiences in foreign wars have acted as a stimulus for the continuation, and indeed intensification, of the Sun Dance traditions into the present.

To those sacrificing in the lodge for the first time are assigned mentors who are experienced in the Sun Dance rituals and who—having known the suffering of being without food or water for a period of three or four days—are able to counsel and give support to the novice in the lodge. Other camp duties are taken care of by special "police" who see that proper conduct and respect for sacred matters are observed, functions once fulfilled by the warrior societies. A camp crier is also named, who has the responsibility of encircling the camp on horseback in the very early mornings and in the evenings, of chanting instructions to the people, or of giving useful information concerning the day's activities. On occasion such criers might relate humorous incidents, intending to bring great laughter from the circles of lodges, or from the wall tents used today.

Lodge Construction. Once the Sun Dance encampment has been established at an appropriate place where there is good

The ceremonial tree represents the major themes of the Sun Dance, which involve the alternations of dry and moist, ignorance and wisdom, and death and life.

water and pasturage, the first ritual act is to select a special cottonwood tree with branches forking at the top. The tree is then cut in a ceremonial manner, the first blow of the ax often being given by a young woman who has been chosen for her virtue and purity. The tree must be felled in a specific direction and is not allowed to touch the ground; it is then carried on poles, with songs, ritual acts, and prayers performed along the way. The cottonwood tree is finally placed in a hole prepared at the center of what will be the sacred lodge, which is itself at the center of the encampment. The selected tree is now understood as the axis at the center of the world. It links heaven and earth, thus giving the people access to spiritual realities and conveying the images of the center and the heavens above, together with their larger implications. For most peoples who practice the Sun Dance, this special tree is understood as a "person." In a way akin to human participation in the sacrifice, the tree transmits to those who sacrifice in the lodge the cooling powers of the moisture it has gathered from the stream near which it grew, and then it dies.

The tree thus recapitulates the major themes of the Sun Dance, which involve the alternations of dry and moist, ignorance and wisdom, and death and life—for if there is to be life there must also be death. Once the tree has been ceremonially raised, offerings are placed at its base, and in its fork is put a nest of cherry or willow branches in which may be placed sacred offerings or, often, rawhide effigies. Colored ribbons, signifying heaven and earth, may be tied high on the tree's forking branches. Each tribal group has its own color symbolism and specific manner of dressing the tree. Among the Crow, for example, the head of a bull buffalo is placed, facing east, on the tree, and in the branches there is an eagle, both symbols recapitulating the theme of heaven and earth. Around the tree as spiritual center the circular lodge is then constructed in accord with symbolical variations specific to each of the tribal groups.

The general architectural design for most tribal Sun Dance lodges is the central tree around which are twenty-eight vertical, forked poles associated with the twenty-eight days of the lunar month. This circle of forked poles is then joined together by horizontal poles laid into the upright forks. In addition the Shoshoni, Crow, and Arapaho lodges have twenty-eight very long poles extending from the forks at the circumference and then all laid into the crotch high on the central tree, a structure that resembles a spoked wheel. The Sioux lodges do not have poles radiating out from the center; a distinctive feature of their lodge, in accord with their ceremonial usage, is the construction of a continuous overhead shade arbor around the inner periphery of the lodge. All styles of lodges, however, have entryways facing the east, the place of the rising sun, and brush is usually placed loosely around the outer walls for the greater privacy of the participants within.

For all tribal groups, the lodge is not merely understood as a "symbolic model" of the world, but rather it *is* the world, universe, or created cosmos. Since construction of the lodge recapitulates the creation of the world, all acts in this process are accompanied by prayers and powerful songs associated with ancient myths of origin and creation. The occasion, reminiscent of a primordial time, is solemn, dignified, and of great beauty.

Around the sacred lodge in concentric circles the camps of family units are set up in accord with long-established protocol. At Sun Dance encampments the doorways of many tipis or wall tents are not toward the east, as is customary in daily usage, but rather toward the sacred lodge and tree at the center of the circle. To the west of the sacred lodge there are usually special tipis in which private ceremonies take place exclusively for those who will sacrifice in the lodge. Sweat lodges are also set up, but apart from the camp circle, so that those who have made their vows may be purified before entering the lodge.

Typical Performances. Even though there are many commonalities in all Plains Sun Dance ceremonies, there are also tribal variations that are of great importance to the peoples concerned. For the Sioux, there are at least two distinctive and central sacrificial elements, one of which is described by the Lakota Sioux term for the Sun Dance, *wiwanyag wachipi* (dance gazing at the sun). Here, during one complete daylight cycle, the dancers, who are also observing a total fast, move periodically around the inner periphery of the lodge in sunwise manner so that they are always gazing at the sun—a cause, no doubt, of intense suffering.

A second Sioux emphasis, also involving sacrificial elements, is the practice of certain dancers, in accord with earlier vows, to have the muscles of the chest pierced by the presiding spiritual leader, who inserts wooden skewers by which they are tied with rawhide thongs to the central tree. These people then

> All styles of Sun Dance lodges have entryways facing the east, the place of the rising sun.

1875 The Crow abandon the practice of Sun Dancing.

1881 The U.S. government attempts to ban all Sun Dances.

1904 The U.S. Commissioner of Indian Affairs rigorously enforces the ban.

1934 The Indian Reorganization Act spurs a new enthusiasm for the Sun Dance among Native Americans.

1941 Shoshoni leader John Truhujo brings the Sun Dance back to the Crow.

dance, encouraged by the drums and the songs of warriors (brave songs), pulling back on the thongs until the flesh and muscles tear loose. In addition to elements of self-sacrifice, there are spiritual implications of being physically tied to and thus identified with the tree as sacred center. A similar theme is also expressed by the ceremony wherein individuals have skewers inserted into both sides of the shoulders and into the muscles of chest and back. The thongs are then attached to posts set up to represent the four directions. The individual is thereby identified with the center in relation to the four horizontal directions of space.

Such sacrificial acts are not just of former times, but are in increasing use today among a number of Sioux peoples. In distinction from prevailing traits and themes of the Sioux Sun Dance, which are strongly reminiscent of elements from earlier military complexes, the Arapaho, the Cheyenne, and the tribes of the Blackfeet Confederation place emphasis on rites of world and life renewal, employing ritual objects that include sacred medicine bundles whose contents have reference to the origins of the tribes.

In 1881 the United States government attempted to ban all Sun Dances, believing that they were "demoralizing and barbarous." It was not until 1904, however, that the dances were rigorously prohibited by the Commissioner of Indian Affairs. However, because these ceremonies were central to spiritual needs, they continued to be practiced in secret or in modified forms by almost all the Plains tribes with the exception of the Crow, who had already abandoned the ceremonies in 1875. One of the still continuing modified Sun Dances was that of the Wind River Shoshoni, whose version spread to the Northern Ute in 1890, to the Fort Hall Shoshoni and Bannock in 1901, and to the Shoshoni of Nevada in 1933. With the Indian Reorganization Act of 1934, however, open practice of the dances commenced, but now in forms that gave greater emphasis to spiritual elements rather than to the extreme tortures associated with the earlier military societies.

In 1941 the charismatic Shoshoni Sun Dance leader John Truhujo brought the Sun Dance back to the Crow through the support of the tribal superintendent Robert Yellowtail. A tradition that had been abandoned for more than sixty-six years was thereby reinstated. In January of 1985 Truhujo died at the age of approximately 105, having transferred his sacred powers to

Thomas Yellowtail, brother of the former superintendent. It is the Sun Dance in this particular form, faithfully led by Thomas Yellowtail to the present time, that has become for the Crow, as well as for many other tribes, an example and stimulus giving continuity and viability to the essentials of the spiritual heritage of the Plains peoples.

In this Shoshoni/Crow Sun Dance the dancers take positions in arbors that surround the inner periphery of the lodge, with the presiding spiritual leader, or "medicine man," always at the west. Women, who are allowed within the lodge to fast, take places slightly to the north of the east-facing entrance. The large ceremonial drum and the alternating teams of drummers and singers have their place a little to the south of the entrance, and they are surrounded by strong-voiced older women who help to sing the sacred songs. The dance's spiritual force resides in the movements of the fasting participants, who for the three or four days' duration of the ceremony are always oriented to the central tree, toward which they dance as often or as little as they wish. They blow on eagle-bone whistles tipped with eagle down, as if they themselves were eagles; then they dance backward to their stalls, still facing the central tree. The rhythmic movements of the dancers are dignified, and their concentration on the tree is continual and intense; for them this is the center and source of life, and the lodge symbolizes the totality of creation. In the course of the ceremonies, participants often receive sacred visions; when they sleep—never for more than a few hours at a time—dreams of special meaning may come.

An especially powerful and beautiful ceremony central to the Sun Dance takes place every morning just before sunup, when all the dancers, under the direction of the group's spiritual leader, face the direction of the rising sun, moving slowly to the beat of the drum and blowing softly on eagle-bone whistles. As the sun rises the drum and the sunrise greeting song come to a crescendo. Eagle plumes tied to the wrists of the dancers are held out to the sun's first rays and are then touched to parts of the body so that the dancer may receive purifying blessings. Once the sun is above the horizon, the dancers sit wrapped in their blankets while very ancient sacred songs are sung and communal prayers are offered.

On the second or third day of the dance, people who are ill come into the lodge and stand at the sacred tree to receive help from the spiritual leader, who prays over them and often draws

In 1881 the United States government attempted to ban all Sun Dances, believing that they were "demoralizing and barbarous."

out the illness with the aid of an eagle-wing fan. Accounts of cures are legion. At the conclusion of the Sun Dance, water that has been blessed is ceremonially passed around among the participants, who have taken no food or water since they first entered the lodge. Thereafter, many people from the camp bring valuable gifts into the lodge, sometimes even horses loaded with blankets and beadwork, which are given away to particular persons who are called forward to receive them. The dancers themselves usually complete the ceremonies with a purifying sweat bath at a nearby creek or river, and in the evening there may be a special feast for all.

The power of sacred traditions of primal origin cannot be compromised by time, place, or number of participants, for in themselves the values and realities concerned are of timeless and universal validity. Though a world of other priorities ignores or neglects such values they may nevertheless be redis-covered as still enduring, even increasing in meaning into the present day. The history of the Plains Sun Dance is continuing witness to this reality. ◆

Take Our Daughters to Work® Day

Take Our Daughters to Work® Day is an occasion for parents and friends to bring girls aged nine to fifteen into their work world. The day takes place on the fourth Thursday in April. The aim of the event is to support girls in their ambitions and goals through adolescence, a time when many girls lose self-confidence and focus on their looks rather than their abilities.

The Ms. Foundation for Women started the Daughters to Work® Day in 1993 in New York City. Interest in the event soon caught on nationally. The Ms. Foundation began producing organizing packets, T-shirts, buttons, and other materials to help participants. In 1997 over 48 million Americans reported that their company or their spouse's company participated.

Many companies organize a schedule of activities for the girls that resembles a typical day in the company, which may include helping the girls create a product typical of the company. For example, newspapers have allowed girls to write articles and publish a small paper. One year, at United Nations headquarters in New York City, 800 girls took over the General Assembly Hall and heard from the U.N.'s first female Deputy Secretary General and women ambassadors from several countries. In Dallas the mayor's office allowed a group of girls to participate in running one of the nation's largest cities. At American Airlines offices around the country, girls flew airplanes by simulator and helped customers.

> One year, at the United Nations headquarters in New York City, 800 girls took over the General Assembly Hall and heard from the UN's first female Deputy Secretary General.

335

In response to the huge success of Take Our Daughters to Work® Day, many parents wondered why boys could not be included, and public commentators debated the issue. Many people pointed to the need for boys to see their parents at work. The Ms. Foundation responded to the criticism by clarifying that Take Our Daughters to Work® Day was not a career day. It is meant to be a day to deal with the unique issues girls face at adolescence. The foundation stated that young boys have developmental needs of their own and that the daughters' day was not designed to meet those needs. They discouraged people from including boys in Take Our Daughters to Work® Day, and they helped develop materials for boys to use in the classroom while the girls were gone. They encouraged others to develop a special day for boys.

The Ms. Foundation founded Take Our Daughters to Work® Day in response to research in the early 1990s showing that, as adolescence begins, girls often show a significant drop in self-esteem and become insecure about their own judgments and emotions. Girls focus heavily on their physical appearance and how boys view them instead of planning for their own futures. Through ages thirteen and seventeen, girls develop

A young girl goes to work with her mother on Take Our Daughters to Work® Day.

negative views of science and are less likely than boys to enroll in important classes such as precalculus or physics. Furthermore, statistics showed that although women made up 46 percent of the workforce in the late 1990s, women in American corporations held just 2 percent of highly paid, highly responsible positions. Founders of the Take Our Daughters to Work® Day hoped a day watching women in the workplace would help heighten girls' aspirations.

The Ms. Foundation for Women is a fund founded in 1972 to support the efforts of women and girls to govern their own lives and influence the world around them. The Foundation assists women's self-help organizing efforts and promotes organizations involved in women's economic security, women's health and safety, and women in leadership. The Ms. Foundation oversees grants and funds to support girl-focused organizations that expand the impact of Take Our Daughters to Work®. These organizations range from Chicago community-based organizations providing after-school mentoring, athletics, and education to the Northern Cheyenne Reservation in Montana and the Rosebud Reservation in South Dakota where girls are linked with elders who can pass on cultural knowledge and traditions. ◆

Tet

Tet marks the beginning of spring and the start of the new year, and it is a time for family reunions, renewal of friendships, and the practice of ancient Vietnamese traditions.

Tet is the Vietnamese New Year. It is celebrated throughout Vietnam and by Vietnamese in other parts of the world on the first to the seventh days of the first lunar month, which falls between late January and early February. Tet is the most important Vietnamese holiday. It marks the beginning of spring and the start of the new year, and it is a time for family reunions, renewal of friendships, and practice of ancient traditions. The word *Tet* is an abbreviation for *Tet Nguyen-Den*, which means *first day*.

There are many traditions associated with the holiday, and activities vary from day to day. One of the more important customs throughout the holiday is the practice of setting the proper tone for the new year by being cheerful, polite, and optimistic. People dress in their best clothing or wear new clothing. Vietnamese houses are cleaned and painted, and everyone tries to pay off debts. Many homes are also decorated with such signs of spring as a flowering peach tree branch or a small kumquat tree.

On the eve of Tet, people set up a high bamboo pole called *Cay Neu* in front of their home. The pole is decorated with red paper because red signifies good fortune. A square of woven bamboo placed on top of the tree is said to ward off evil spirits. A small basket of betel nuts—palm nuts chewed as a stimulant—may also be placed on the top of the pole as an offering for good spirits. The pole is not taken down until the seventh day.

When the new year's first full moon appears, many Vietnamese make special offerings to Buddha and invite their

Moon Cakes for Tet Trung-Thu

After Tet Nguyen-Den, the second most important holiday in Vietnam is Tet Trung-Thu (tet-troong-thoo), also called the Mid-Autumn Festival or the Full Moon Festival. People in Taiwan, China, and some other Asian countries also celebrate this holiday. On the lunar calendar, the festival falls on the fifteenth day of the eighth month (late September or early October) when the first full moon nearest the autumn equinox rises in the sky, appearing larger and brighter than at any other time of the year. People eat small round confections called moon cakes during the Mid-Autumn Festival. Like many traditional foods, moon cakes are made differently in different places, and every family has its own favorite filling.

2 cups glutinous rice (available at Asian grocery stores)
3/4 cup coconut cream
1 teaspoon sugar
1/2 teaspoon salt
fillings such as sugar, peanuts, almonds, diced bananas, raisins, and other dried fruits

Put the rice in a 2-quart saucepan. Cover with hot tap water and soak for one hour. Drain well. Mix coconut cream, sugar, and salt into the rice. Cook over medium heat for about 10 minutes, stirring frequently. The rice should be only half cooked. Remove from heat and let cool. When rice is cool, take a handful and shape into a ball. Make a hold or pocket in the center with your thumb. Put in about 1/2 teaspoon of filling of your choice. Then press rice together so that filling is hidden in the middle of the ball. Wrap each rice ball in aluminum foil. Place in a steamer. Steam over boiling water for about 40 minutes or until the rice is soft.

deceased ancestors to join the celebration. At midnight, families usher out the spirits of the old year and Taoists give a warm welcome to the Spirit of the Hearth, who has been to visit the Jade Emperor, the supreme Taoist being. The Spirit of the Hearth goes to the Jade Emperor before Tet to report on the people of the household. Drums, gongs, and firecrackers sound off at the beginning of the new year to welcome the Spirit of the Hearth and to frighten off the devil, who fears bright light and loud noises.

The first visitor to visit the house on the morning of Tet is considered symbolic of what will come to pass over the next year. Some Vietnamese try to arrange for the first visitor to be a person of wealth, good spirit, and high social standing. During the day, Christians visit their local church and Buddhists visit their local pagoda to pray for good fortune and happiness. Much of the rest of the holiday is spent visiting friends and family. Flowers are often presented to friends to wish them a long, happy life and prosperity. Traditional two-line poems called *cau doi* are also used to convey good wishes at Tet. Families may visit their ancestors' graves several times and make offerings of special holiday foods. They hope that the ancestors will reside with them and protect them from evil. The ancestors are said to return to heaven on the fourth day, and on that day, most people return to work.

As with every festival around the world, there are special holiday treats. On Tet, a favorite food is *banh chung*, a sticky rice bundle made with beans, rice, meat, and spices and wrapped up in leaves. Candied fruits, lotus seed candy, bean cakes, and other sweets are also prepared at this time of the year.

Tet became notorious around the world in 1968 when North Vietnam and the Vietcong launched a major offensive against cities in South Vietnam on January 30 at the start of the Vietnamese New Year during the Vietnam War (1957–75). The

A Vietnamese man carries a flowering plum branch to decorate his home during Tet.

U.S. embassy in Saigon was held for six hours by the Vietcong, stunning television audiences around the world at the ferocity of the attack. The United States and South Vietnam quickly recovered from the attack, but many Americans became skeptical of U.S. efforts in the region and antiwar sentiments increased significantly after Tet. The incident forced President Lyndon Johnson to change his policy toward the Vietnam War, and he subsequently cut back on bombing and troops in the region and sought peace talks. Johnson also declared his intention not to seek reelection after the incident. ◆

These Vietnamese vendors in San Francisco are selling special Tet sweets to the local Vietnamese community.

Thanksgiving Day

UNITED STATES ● THIRD THURSDAY IN NOVEMBER
CANADA ● SECOND MONDAY IN OCTOBER

When Europeans began exploring and settling in North America, they brought with them a long-standing custom of observing harvesttime festivals of thanksgiving.

Thanksgiving Day is celebrated annually in the United States and Canada to offer gratitude for one's family, friends, fortune, health, and other good things. Americans observe Thanksgiving on the fourth Thursday of November. In Canada, Thanksgiving Day falls on the second Monday in October.

Autumn festivals of thanks after a bountiful harvest had been common for centuries in many parts of the world. The ancient Greek harvest festival of Thesmophoria was a type of thanksgiving, as is the Jewish festival of Sukkoth. When Europeans began exploring and settling North America, they brought with them a long-standing custom of observing harvesttime festivals of thanksgiving. It is difficult to pinpoint exactly when the first Thanksgiving feast occurred in the Americas. According to tradition, the holiday can be traced back to 1621, when William Bradford, governor of Plymouth Colony, initiated a three-day period of feasting and prayer to give thanks to God for a bountiful harvest. The colonists invited about ninety Native Americans to the feast, including Squanto (Tisquantum), who had taught them how to hunt local game, where to find edible wild plants, and how to raise indigenous crops. The first Thanksgiving meal consisted of meats, fruits, and vegetables that are native to North America, such as geese and turkeys, deer, pumpkins, Indian corn, and berries. The food was cooked over open fires and the feast was held outdoors.

Who Were the Pilgrims?

The people we call the Pilgrims were a group of English Protestants who sailed from England in 1620 on the *Mayflower* and founded Plymouth Colony in America. The leaders of the Pilgrims were separatist Puritans who had broken away from the Church of England and established their own congregation at Scrooby, England, in 1606. By 1608 about one hundred members of the Scrooby group had fled England to avoid religious persecution; they eventually settled in Leyden in the Netherlands. After a few years, however, many members of the Leyden community had become dissatisfied, in part because they felt they were losing their English identity. Forty-one of them, including William Brewster and William Bradford, decided to leave the Netherlands and attempt to establish a colony in America. The Leyden Pilgrims arranged the financial backing of English businessmen and took on an additional sixty-one people, including Miles Standish, in England. Originally the Pilgrims planned on sailing to America in two vessels, the *Speedwell* and the *Mayflower*. The *Speedwell* proved to be unseaworthy and they proceeded on the *Mayflower* alone, crossing the Atlantic in the early fall of 1620. After an uneventful voyage, they sighted Cape Cod on November 19. They scouted the nearby coast and decided to stay at what became Plymouth, landing there on December 26. Their first winter in America was difficult and forty-four people had died by April 1621. Their fortunes improved as summer approached, and the Pilgrims celebrated their first Thanksgiving feast that fall.

The colonists celebrated a second day of thanks two years later, in gratitude for rain that fell after a long drought. By 1630 an annual Thanksgiving feast came to be observed in Plymouth Colony after the harvest, and other New England colonies gradually took up the practice, although no standard date was established for the holiday.

During the course of the Revolutionary War, the Continental Congress recommended eight days be set aside to give thanks for various victories. In 1784 Congress decreed a special day of thanks for the return of peace. On October 3, 1789, President George Washington issued the following proclamation, setting aside the upcoming November 26 as a day to give thanks for the establishment of the new United States government:

> Whereas it is the duty of all nations to acknowledge the providence of Almighty God, to obey His will, to be grateful for His benefits, and humbly to implore His protection and favor; and Whereas both Houses of Congress have, by their joint committee, requested me "to recommend to the people of the United States a day of public thanksgiving and prayer, to be observed by acknowledging with grateful hearts the many and signal favors of Almighty God, espe-

1621 The Pilgrims of Plymouth Colony celebrate a festival of thanksgiving after a good harvest.

1784 The U.S. Congress decrees a day of thanks for the return of peace after the Revolutionary War.

1789 George Washington proclaims November 26 as a day to give thanks for the new government.

1815 President James Madison proclaims a day of thanksgiving at the end of the War of 1812.

1830 New York state adopts Thanksgiving as an annual holiday; other northern states soon follow.

1855 Virginia adopts Thanksgiving as an annual holiday; other southern states soon follow.

1863 Abraham Lincoln begins the practice of proclaiming an annual national day of thanks.

1941 The U.S. Congress permanently establishes the fourth Thursday in November as Thanksgiving Day.

cially by affording them an opportunity peaceably to establish a form of government for their safety and happiness":

Now, therefore, I do recommend and assign Thursday, the 26th day of November next, to be devoted by the people of these States to the service of that great and glorious Being who is the beneficent author of all the good that was, that is, or that will be; that we may then all unite in rendering unto Him our sincere and humble thanks for His kind care and protection of the people of this country previous to their becoming a nation; for the signal and manifold mercies and the favorable interpositions of His providence in the course and conclusion of the late war; for the great degree of tranquility, union, and plenty which we have since enjoyed; for the peaceable and rational manner in which we have been enabled to establish constitutions of government for our safety and happiness, and particularly the national one now lately instituted' for the civil and religious liberty with which we are blessed, and the means we have of acquiring and diffusing useful knowledge; and, in general, for all the great and various favors which He has been pleased to confer upon us

And also that we may then unite in most humbly offering our prayers and supplications to the great Lord and Ruler of Nations and beseech Him to pardon our national and other transgressions; to enable us all, whether in public or private stations, to perform our several and relative duties properly and punctually; to render our National Government a blessing to all the people by constantly being a Government of wise, just, and constitutional laws, discreetly and faithfully executed and obeyed; to protect and guide all sovereigns and nations (especially such as have show kindness to us), and to bless them with good governments, peace, and concord; to promote the knowledge and practice of true religion and virtue, and the increase of science among them and us; and, generally to grant unto all mankind such a degree of temporal prosperity as He alone knows to be best.

The United States government proclaimed occasional days of thanks over the next several decades. In 1815, for example, President James Madison asked for the nation to give thanks for peace after the War of 1812. But the holiday had not yet become established as an annual observance. By 1830 the state of New York had adopted Thanksgiving as an annual state holiday, and other northern states followed its lead. In the South the custom did not appear until 1855, when it was adopted by Virginia, and thereafter by the other southern states.

A family sits down to a traditional Thanksgiving feast.

In 1863, in the midst of the American Civil War, President Abraham Lincoln began the practice of issuing an annual presidential proclamation decreeing a national day of thanks. Lincoln fixed the fourth Thursday (later in the 19th century it came to be regularly the last Thursday) in November for Thanksgiving. Lincoln's first Thanksgiving proclamation (actually written by his secretary of state, William Seward) reads:

> The year that is drawing towards its close, has been filled with the blessings of fruitful fields and healthful skies. To these bounties, which are so constantly enjoyed that we are prone to forget the source from which they come, others have been added, which are of so extraordinary a nature, that they cannot fail to penetrate and soften even the heart which is habitually insensible to the ever watchful providence of Almighty God. In the midst of a civil war of unequalled magnitude and severity, which has sometimes seemed to foreign States to invite and to provoke their aggression, peace has been preserved with all nations, order has been maintained, the laws have been respected and obeyed, and harmony has prevailed everywhere except in the theatre of military conflict; while that theatre has been greatly contracted by the advancing armies and navies of the Union.

Needful diversions of wealth and of strength from the fields of peaceful industry to the national defence, have not arrested the plough, the shuttle, or the ship; the axe had enlarged the borders of our settlements, and the mines, as well of iron and coal as of the precious metals, have yielded even more abundantly than heretofore. Population has steadily increased, notwithstanding the waste that has been made in the camp, the siege and the battle-field; and the country, rejoicing in the consciousness of augmented strength and vigor, is permitted to expect continuance of years with large increase of freedom. No human counsel hath devised nor hath any mortal hand worked out these great things. They are the gracious gifts of the Most High God, who, while dealing with us in anger for our sins, hath nevertheless remem-

Macy's department store in New York City ushers in the Christmas shopping season with an annual Thanksgiving Day parade. The parade features gigantic balloons of popular cartoon characters.

Thanksgiving Cranberry Sauce

The first Thanksgiving feast consisted of foods native to the Americas, such as squash, leeks, and berries. The meal may have included cranberries, which grow wild in Massachusetts and other cool regions of the northern United States. For centuries before the Pilgrims arrived, the Indians of the northeast had been eating the tart berries fresh, mixed with cornmeal, or baked into bread and cakes. The Indians also made a simple sauce by cooking cranberries with water until they burst, then sweetening them with honey or maple sugar. Today, cranberry sauce remains an essential accompaniment to the Thanksgiving and Christmas turkey. Traditional recipes, like the one below, include only cranberries, water, and sugar, but many cooks enhance the sauce with other ingredients, such as lemon juice, cinnamon, and cloves.

4 cups fresh or frozen cranberries
1$\frac{1}{2}$ cups sugar
2 cups water

Combine all ingredients in a large saucepan and cook over medium heat, stirring occasionally, for 10 to 15 minutes, or until the berries burst. Transfer to a bowl and let cool, then chill in the refrigerator.

---

bered mercy. It has seemed to me fit and proper that they should be solemnly, reverently and gratefully acknowledged as with one heart and voice by the whole American People.

I do therefore invite my fellow citizens in every part of the United States, and also those who are at sea and those who are sojourning in foreign lands, to set apart and observe the last Thursday of November next, as a day of Thanksgiving and Praise to our beneficent Father who dwelleth in the Heavens. And I recommend to them that while offering up the ascriptions justly due to Him for such singular deliverances and blessings, they do also, with humble penitence for our national perverseness and disobedience, commend to his tender care all those who have become widows, orphans, mourners or sufferers in the lamentable civil strife in which we are unavoidably engaged, and fervently implore the interposition of the Almighty Hand to heal the wounds of the nation and to restore it as soon as may be consistent with the Divine purposes to the full enjoyment of peace, harmony, tranquillity and Union.

Annually thereafter, the president would issue a formal proclamation decreeing the last Thursday in November as Thanksgiving Day. President Franklin D. Roosevelt upset the tradition in 1939, 1940, and 1941 by setting Thanksgiving on the third Thursday in November, one week earlier. Roosevelt hoped to invigorate the American economy during the Great Depression by lengthening the shopping period before Christmas. Many state governors refused to bend tradition for the sake of business and held to the customary date, although a few states actually authorized the celebration of both dates. To avoid further disagreement, Congress enacted a resolution in 1941 permanently establishing the fourth Thursday of November as Thanksgiving Day.

In the United States schools, businesses, and government offices are generally closed on Thanksgiving Day and the following Friday, so people can travel to their family home for a reunion. Most families hold an elaborate meal on Thanksgiving Day, featuring many of the same traditional American foods that the Plymouth colonists ate during the first Thanksgiving feast. The Thanksgiving meal is usually centered around a roast turkey, an indigenous American bird. Other foods traditionally served on Thanksgiving include cornbread, beans, cranberries, squash, and pumpkin pie.

Many Americans consider Thanksgiving a religious holiday and they attend church services on Thanksgiving morning to give thanks to God. Some cities hold Thanksgiving Day parades to usher in the Christmas shopping season. One of the most famous is the annual Macy's Thanksgiving Day parade in New York City, which features gigantic balloons of popular cartoon characters that float over thousands of spectators lining the streets. ◆

Thesmophoria

ANCIENT GREECE ● AUTUMN

The Thesmophoria was an annual women's festival widely celebrated in ancient Greece. In most areas it took place in autumn, at the season of plowing and sowing, and it was held in honor of the grain goddess Demeter and her daughter, Persephone. Fertility of crops and of women was evidently the essential theme.

Demeter was a prominent figure in the mythology and cultic life of ancient Greece. She was originally a fertility goddess associated primarily with plants grown for food, especially grain. With Zeus as father, Demeter gave birth to a daughter, Persephone. When Persephone became a young woman, Hades, god of the underworld, fell in love with her and received Zeus's approval of his wish to marry her. Demeter refused to give her consent, however, so one day, while Persephone was gathering flowers in the company of friends, Hades appeared and snatched her away. Demeter, distraught by the abduction, wandered over the earth so grief-stricken that she appeared age-old, so inattentive to her ordinary responsibilities that no crops would grow and the human race was threatened with starvation. Unable to appease her in any other way, Zeus gave in and ordered Hades to release the maiden. The reunion between mother and daughter was joyous, but Persephone had eaten several pomegranate seeds, a symbol of marriage, while in the underworld. As a result, she was considered married to Hades and was required to spend a third of each year with him. The annual separation caused Demeter to grieve, and during this time the earth was

Distraught by the abduction of her daughter, Demeter wandered over the earth so inattentive to her ordinary responsibilities that no crops would grow and the human race was threatened with starvation.

Athenian: of Athens, a
city in ancient Greece.

barren and no crops grew. When mother and daughter were reunited, the earth became fertile.

The **Athenian** form of the ritual is the best known of the Thesmophoria festivals. Here the festival occupied three days. On the first day the women went up to the sacred grove of Demeter Thesmophoros, set up an encampment there, out of sight of all males, and made some preliminary sacrifices. On the second day they fasted, sitting humbly on the ground, as Demeter was said to have fasted in grief over the abduction of her daughter. This abstinence was probably understood as a kind of purification in preparation for the main ceremonies. The third day featured pomegranates to eat, obscene jesting, and perhaps flagellation—all things associated with fertility. Piglets were slaughtered, and parts of them, it seems, were cooked and eaten; substantial portions, however, were thrown into *megara*, deep holes in the earth, together with wheat cakes shaped like snakes and an otherwise unknown goddess, Kalligeneia, whose name means "fair birth," was invoked.

At some stage—perhaps the night before—certain women who had for three days observed purity restrictions climbed down into the hole, and while others clapped, brought out the decayed remains of the previous year's offerings. These were ceremoniously carried out of the camp and set forth on altars. (The Thesmophoria itself took its name from this "bringing of the deposits.") If a farmer took a little portion of the remains and mixed it in with his seed corn, he was supposed to get a good crop. This element of primitive agrarian magic suggests that the Thesmophoria's origins lay in a remote past. ◆

Timquat (Timkat)

Timquat is the Ethiopian Orthodox Church celebration of the Epiphany, or the baptism of Jesus. The holiday is celebrated on January 19, two weeks after the Orthodox Christmas, Genna. It is the most important holiday in the calendar of the Orthodox Church and begins on the eve of the 18th and carries over into the 20th, when the Feast of St. Michael is celebrated.

Although Timquat has a festive quality and is a day for games and feasting, its religious significance is of primary importance. The focal point of the Timquat celebration is the procession of the tabot. The tabot is a replica of the tablet that bore the commandments handed down to Moses from God. It is housed in the center of the church, called the holy of holies, which can only be entered by those ordained in the church. The presence of the tabot is what makes a building a sanctified place of worship in the Orthodox tradition. Thus the procession of the tabot through the community is a sacred event.

Timquat is a day of community celebration. Children are given new clothes and all the adults' shammas, traditional Ethiopian white robes, are washed for the occasion. On the eve of Timquat everybody puts on new or clean clothes and attends a church service. The people then follow the procession of the tabot. The church deacons and lesser priests precede the tabot carrying long prayer sticks and perform a slowly accelerating dance that according to Ethiopian lore was handed down from King David. Some carry the gorgeous, fringed umbrellas that are part of all Ethiopian Orthodox ceremonies. The priest

A priest carries the tabot on his head during a Timquat procession in Ethiopia. He is accompanied by other priests and deacons carrying fringed umbrellas.

dressed in colorful robes carries the tabot on his head under the cover of an embroidered drapery. Hymns are sung affirming God's covenant with man and rhythmic dances are performed to the accompaniment of traditional percussive instruments.

The riotous procession ends at an open space near water, often a field or public park. Here, as the sun sets, the covered tabot is placed in a simple tent and the people gather for a night of prayer. A mass is performed at 2:00 in the morning and dabo (a whole wheat bread) and talla (a barley beer) are consumed. At dawn, the priest performs the baptism ceremony sprinkling water from the stream or pool on the people. Some people immerse themselves completely in the water that has been sanctified with a golden cross and lighted candles. At noon the people, who have gone home to rest, return to the ritual site and follow the procession of the tabot back to the church. When the tabot has been returned to the holy of holies, the people return to their homes for the Timquat feast.

Timquat is a day of freedom for Orthodox women, whose lives are usually restricted by the customs of the Orthodox Church, and a day of courtship for young women, who wear their finest clothes for Timquat and, if they can afford it, jewelry and perfume. Young men look for suitable brides during the celebration and will make inquiries of young women's families. In many ways Timquat unifies the Orthodox community and is a cornerstone of Ethiopian cultural life. ◆

Twelfth Night

Twelfth Night (January 5), the night before Epiphany, is the end of the Christmas season. According to the Christmas story, the Epiphany (Greek = showing, manifestation) is the day when the Magi, the Three Wise Men guided to Jerusalem by a star, beheld the infant Jesus in the manger, twelve days after he was born to Joseph and Mary. And they brought him gifts of gold, frankincense, and myrrh.

"Twelfth Night" is perhaps best known as the title of a romantic comedy by Shakespeare, though the play is not about the festival. As suggested in *William Shakespeare: The Complete Works*, the play was titled *Twelfth Night, or What You Will*, because Twelfth Night, being traditionally a time of revelry and topsy-turvydom, was thought appropriate to a comedy about a servant aspiring to win his mistress's love.

The festive events of Twelfth Night celebrate the visit of the three Magi to the Christ child, but also include vestiges of ancient winter solstice rituals marking the new year. In Denmark and other parts of Scandinavia, January 5 is the night when the Christmas tree is lit for the last time; the Christmas season is over for another year. Twelfth Night pageants often feature elaborate masked figures and traditional dances, with music performed by costumed musicians. The end of the Christmas season and the beginning of the new year combine in revelries, games, masking, and dancing.

There is an old custom of baking a sugary, well-decorated Twelfth Night cake, or twelfth cake, to be served at the festivities. The cakes were probably simple at first, but over time,

> *"Foolery, sir, does walk about the orb like the sun; it shines everywhere."*
>
> William Shakespeare, *Twelfth Night*

twelfth cakes became elaborate enough to shame a wedding cake. (In *A Christmas Carol*, Charles Dickens mentions "immense twelfth-cakes" in the vision of Plenty when Ebenezer Scrooge visits the Ghost of Christmas Present.) In each cake was a hidden bean (and often a pea). The man who got the slice containing the hidden bean and the woman getting the pea were chosen as king and queen to preside over the festivities. The king was known as the King of the Bean, or Lord of Misrule. (In New Orleans during the Mardi Gras season, sugar-sprinkled "king cakes" contain a tiny plastic baby; whoever gets the baby gives the next party.)

In *The Golden Bough*, a study of ancient customs and rituals around the world, Sir James George Frazer mentions that in parts of Europe "the mystic twelve days" between Christmas and

Shakespeare's *Twelfth Night, or What You Will*

Although Twelfth Night is not widely celebrated in modern times, the holiday is well known as the title of a romantic comedy, *Twelfth Night, or What You Will*, by William Shakespeare. Scholars believe the play was probably first performed in England around 1600 as part of that year's Epiphany celebrations, although it was not published until 1623. Shakespeare's play is not about the holiday, but its story of trickery, mistaken identity, and misdirected love is appropriate to a holiday marked by rule breaking and role reversals.

The play concerns a nearly identical twin sister and brother, Viola and Sebastian, who become separated during a shipwreck. Viola finds herself stranded in a country called Illyria, which is ruled by the duke Orsino. She disguises herself as a man, calls herself Cesario, and becomes a page to the duke. The duke, who is enamored of a beautiful countess named Olivia, sends Cesario to woo the countess for him. The countess, however, spurns the duke and falls madly in love with Cesario, who she thinks is a young man. Viola, meanwhile, has fallen in love with the duke, who doesn't know she is a woman. The romantic intrigue is complicated by a host of meddling comic characters including the foolish but wise clown Feste, the bumbling nobleman Sir Andrew Aguecheek, Olivia's pompous steward, Malvolio, her clever housemaid Maria, and her drunken uncle, Sir Toby Belch. Sir Andrew, who wants to marry Olivia, buys food and drink for Sir Toby to gain his support. Sir Toby and Sir Andrew cooperate with Maria in tricking Malvolio, whom they dislike, into believing that Olivia harbors a secret passion for him, especially when he wears yellow stockings and smiles continually. When Viola's brother, Sebastian, turns up in Illyria alive and well, everyone mistakes him for Cesario, causing further confusion all around. In the end all identities and relationships are sorted out: Viola marries Orsino, Sebastian marries Olivia, and Maria marries Sir Toby. The well-known saying "Some are born great, some achieve greatness, and some have greatness thrust upon them" is uttered by Malvolio.

Epiphany were a "witching time," like Walpurgis Night (May Day's eve), a time for expelling witches. In Switzerland, for example, in the village of Brunnen along the Lake of Lucerne, boys would go around on Twelfth Night in a procession carrying torches and making as much noise as possible with horns, bells, and whips to frighten away Strudeli and Strätteli, two spirits of the wood. It was believed that if the villagers did not make enough noise to drive away the witches, there would be little fruit in the next year's harvest.

Frazer observes that "a conspicuous feature of the Carnival is a **burlesque** figure personifying the festive season," which, after a glorious but brief career of gaiety and dissipation, is publicly burned or otherwise destroyed, "to the feigned grief or genuine delight of the populace." In the old days, such was the fate of the King of the Bean on Twelfth Night; often an effigy of the lord of the revels would be tossed onto a bonfire.

There has been some confusion whether Twelfth Night should be on the fifth of January (also known as Epiphany Eve, and Twelfthtide) or on the sixth; January 5 is the twelfth night after Christmas Eve, and January 6 is the twelfth day after Christmas *Day*. The holiday is often observed on the night of Epiphany rather than the night before. On whichever day it is celebrated, Twelfth Night traditionally closes the Christmas season in many European and Latin American cultures. But the celebrations need not stop: Twelfth Night also marks the first night of the Carnival season. In New Orleans and other places where Mardi Gras or Shrove Tuesday is celebrated (about two months later), Twelfth Night begins the series of balls, parties, and parades that culminate in "Fat Tuesday." ◆

burlesque: broadly humorous mockery.

United Nations Day

INTERNATIONAL ● OCTOBER 24

U nited Nations Day is celebrated around the world to commemorate the formation of the United Nations on October 24, 1945, and to raise awareness of the United Nation's role in promoting peace, economic development, and human rights. United Nations Day is also an occasion for people to learn about history, arts, food, and customs of the 185 countries that form the organization.

President Franklin Delano Roosevelt devised the name "United Nations" during World War II to designate the alliance of twenty-six countries at war against the Axis powers (Germany, Italy, Japan, and their associates). On January 1, 1942, the United States and twenty-five other countries issued a document called the "United Nations Declaration," in which they pledged to an all-out war against the Axis countries. They also pledged to support the principles of the Atlantic Charter, which called for disarming aggressor nations until a permanent peace system could be established. A total of forty-six nations eventually signed the United Nations Declaration.

Subsequently, many of the conferences between Roosevelt and the heads of other Allied countries dealt with the creation of some form of future peacekeeping organization. Two conferences in particular were organized to prepare for such an organization. The first, held at Bretton Woods, New Hampshire, in July 1944, dealt with methods of international economic cooperation after the war. The second, held at Dumbarton Oaks near Washington, D.C., from August to October 1944, addressed the details of the postwar peacekeeping system. The Allied coun-

"In every corner of the world – in every village and city and community – the United Nations is a living testament of hope. The United Nations lives in the heart and mind of every citizen striving to end violence and promote tolerance; advance development and ensure equality; protect human rights and alleviate poverty."

UN Secretary General Kofi Annan, address on United Nations Day, 1997

Villagers of the Yap Islands in Micronesia celebrate United Nations Day by marching through town carrying flags from around the world.

tries formed an agency called the United Nations Relief and Rehabilitation Administration (UNRRA) to supply immediate aid to the people and countries as they were freed from the grip of enemy forces in the last phases of World War II. From 1943 to 1947, the UNRRA distributed millions of dollars worth of food and equipment in countries that had been devastated by Axis invasion during the war. The UNRRA foreshadowed the United Nations' future mission to provide humanitarian aid to refugees and victims of war.

On April 25, 1945, representatives from fifty countries, including the forty-six that had signed the original United Nations Declaration, convened in San Francisco, California, to draft a charter to formally establish the United Nations. On June 26, 1945, all fifty nations present at the conference voted to accept the charter. It went into effect on October 24, 1945. The goal of the United Nations, as stated by the charter, is "to save succeeding generations from the scourge of war, which twice in our lifetime has brought untold sorrow to mankind," and "to reaffirm faith in fundamental human rights, in the dignity and worth of the human person, in the equal rights of men and women and of nations large and small."

The United Nations Charter outlined the role and organization of the United Nations, and called for six chief organs including the General Assembly, the Security Council, and the Secretariat. The General Assembly includes every member nation; each nation has one vote on any General Assembly question. The General Assembly meets once a year, but it may be called into special session in case of emergency. Its chief task is to recommend solutions to international problems and to suggest ways for member nations to preserve peace. The Security Council includes fifteen nations: five permanent members (the United States, Russia, the United Kingdom, France, and China) and ten nonpermanent members elected to two-year terms by General Assembly vote. The Security Council is in continuous session. Its main task is to handle threats to world peace immediately as they arise; to investigate disputes between nations; and, when necessary, to take action to settle disputes between nations. The Secretariat is the administrative branch of the United Nations. Headed by the Secretary General, the Secretariat is responsible for carrying out the directives of United Nations councils, as well as accomplishing the routine work of the organization. The United Nations Economic and Social Council, the Trusteeship Council, and the International Court of Justice are the remaining core bodies of the United Nations. The United Nations headquarters are located in New York City on land that is officially United Nations territory.

Since World War II, the United Nations has helped end a number of conflicts around the world through the negotiation of cease-fires and peace agreements, and the deployment of special international military forces. The United Nations and its agencies also work throughout the world to protect human rights; promote arms control; encourage the protection of the environment and the peaceful uses of nuclear energy; advance the rights of women and children; fight epidemics, famine, and poverty; assist refugees and victims of war; deliver food aid and expand agricultural production; and make loans to developing countries to help stabilize financial markets.

In 1947 the United Nations General Assembly adopted a U.S.-sponsored resolution declaring October 24, the anniversary of the UN's formation, as United Nations Day. United Nations Day is now an official day of observance in most countries. The holiday is especially important in parts of the world where people have benefited from United Nations services. Many cities hold a parade in honor of the United Nations on

1942 During WWII, the United States and 26 nations issue the United Nations Declaration; 21 other nations sign later.

1944 Representatives of Britain, China, the Soviet Union, and the United States hold a series of meetings at Dumbarton Oaks near Washington, D.C., to discuss the organization of the UN.

1945 Delegates meeting in San Francisco sign the United Nations Charter.

1947 The UN General Assembly adopts a resolution declaring October 24 as UN Day.

1948 The UN approves the Universal Declaration of Human Rights.

1995 The UN celebrates its 50th anniversary on UN Day.

October 24. Some cities also hold international fairs, featuring food, music, performers, and artwork from around the world. In the United states, the president issues an annual proclamation asking citizens to reflect upon the importance of the United Nations to our national interest. Many American and Canadian communities fly the United Nations flag from the town hall, courthouse, or other official building on October 24.

Elementary and high school teachers use the occasion to educate young people about the diversity of the nations that make up the global community and about the role of the United Nations in maintaining peaceful relations among them.

World Fairs

World fairs are huge international expositions that showcase developments in science, technology, industry, and the arts. Held in major cities throughout the world, they typically run for six months, from spring to fall. Exhibitors include governments, corporations, and large private organizations. The Crystal Palace Exhibition held in London in 1851 began the modern era of international expositions. Staged to demonstrate the superiority of British industry, the Crystal Palace housed exhibits of machinery, art, and crafts. Since then, world fairs have become more than demonstrations of industrial progress and have acquired symbolic purposes. The Philadelphia Centennial Exposition of 1876 commemorated the anniversary of the Declaration of Independence. The 1893 World Columbian Exposition in Chicago celebrated the anniversary of Christopher Columbus's arrival in America. In 1915 the San Francisco Panama-Pacific International Exposition honored the opening of the Panama Canal and the city's recovery from the earthquake of 1906.

World fairs held in the United States during the 1930s helped visitors cope with the Great Depression. In 1933–34 Chicago's Century of Progress International Exhibition took shape around the theme of scientific and industrial progress since the city's founding. The 1939–40 New York World's Fair introduced television and promoted suburban living and pollution-free, automated factories. World War II and its aftermath precluded international expositions until the late 1950s. The United States did not host a postwar world fair until the 1962 Century 21 Exposition in Seattle, which featured the 605-foot Space Needle, the monorail, and many exhibitions demonstrating the nation's scientific prowess. The 1964–65 New York World's Fair offered striking pavilion architecture and pioneered audio-visual display techniques. It included 200 buildings and the Unisphere, a 140-foot-high stainless steel globe signifying "Peace Through Understanding." The United States has hosted three fairs dealing with energy conservation and the environment: Spokane (1974), Knoxville (1982), and New Orleans (1984). Since 1928 the Bureau of International Expositions has overseen the planning and administration of world fairs.

Many teachers ask their students to complete readings, compositions, and artwork with United Nations–related themes. Students may also watch special videos about the history of the United Nations, and hold classroom discussions about world peace, human rights, the global economy, and other areas in which the United Nations is active. Students may also learn songs, dances, and games from around the world. At colleges and other educational institutions United Nations Day is observed with serious exhibits, lectures, and debates on issues confronting the United Nations and its member nations.

United Nations Day observances were especially elaborate in 1995, the fifty-year anniversary of the organization's formation. That year, a special commemorative meeting was held at United Nations headquarters, during which U.S. president Bill Clinton, Canadian prime minister Jean Chretien, and the leaders of many other member nations addressed the General Assembly. An additional anniversary celebration was held on June 26 in San Francisco, the date and location of the signing of the United Nations Charter.

The United Nations sponsors numerous other international holidays to draw attention to issues of concern to the global community. One of the most important is International Women's Day (March 8), which honors the struggle of women for equality, justice, peace, and development around the world. Women's Day has been designated a national holiday in many countries. Other important annual United Nations observances include Universal Children's Day (November 20), dedicated to celebrating worldwide fraternity and understanding among children and to promoting the welfare of children; International Day of Disabled Persons (December 3), dedicated to raising awareness and improving the situation of persons with disabilities; World Food Day (October 16), dedicated to heightening public awareness of the lack of adequate food in many parts of the world and to strengthening solidarity in the struggle against hunger, malnutrition, and poverty; and World AIDS Day (December 1), dedicated to raising awareness of the pandemic proportions of the acquired immunodeficiency syndrome (AIDS) and to promoting efforts to combat the disease.

Other United Nations–sponsored international holidays include: International Day for the Elimination of Racial Discrimination (March 21), World Day for Water (March 22), World Meteorological Day (March 23), World Health Day

> *"Let there be no doubt: there are some very basic standards of human behavior, violations of which are simply unacceptable. Fundamental human rights are a product of human nature – indeed human life – itself."*
> Kofi Annan, 1997

(April 7), World Press Freedom Day (May 4), International Day of Families (May 15), World Telecommunication Day (May 17), World No-Tobacco Day (May 31), World Environment Day (June 5), International Day in Support of Victims of Torture (June 26), World Population Day (July 11), International Day of the World's Indigenous People (August 9), International Literacy Day (September 8), International Day of Peace (third Tuesday of September), World Habitat Day (first Monday in October), International Day of Older Persons (October 1), World Food Day (October 16), International Day for Tolerance (November 16), Africa Industrialization Day (November 20), International Day of Solidarity with the Palestinian People (November 29), Human Rights Day (December 10), and International Day for Biological Diversity (December 29). ◆

Valentine's Day

INTERNATIONAL ● FEBRUARY 14

The celebration of Valentine's Day stems from a complex mix of Christian and pagan traditions with roots in the ancient world. Saint Valentine appears to have been a Christian priest in imperial Rome, martyred along with other Christians under the emperor Claudius II in about the year 270 C.E. Traditionally, Saint Valentine was commemorated on the Catholic calendar on February 14.

Some people have tried to connect the historical Saint Valentine with the later practices of Valentine's Day by saying that the saint married couples despite the emperor's prohibition, or that he sent a note signed "from your Valentine" to the daughter of his jailer. However, the early Christian saint Valentine probably had nothing to do with the traditions later celebrated on his feast day; it is simply by his placement in the Christian calendar that his name became associated with it. Later, the word *valentine* may have been confused with the Norman French word *galantin*, meaning lover of women, as the *g* and *v* were often interchangeable in common pronunciation. In any case, February 14 gradually became a traditional date for exchanging love messages, and Saint Valentine became the patron saint of lovers.

The more amorous side of Valentine's Day originates in popular traditions rather than in religion. According to ancient European beliefs, birds began to pair off for the nesting season in mid-February. Because people generally referred to specific days by naming the saint commemorated on that day rather than a specific date, by the Middle Ages Saint Valentine's Day became

The early Christian saint Valentine probably had nothing to do with the traditions later celebrated on his feast day; it is simply by his placement in the Christian calendar that his name became associated with the holiday.

A mother helps her daughter make Valentine cards for her teachers.

associated with the time that birds chose their mates. In his *Parlement of Foules*, the medieval writer Geoffrey Chaucer refers to the date in this way:

> For this was Seynt Valentyne's day.
> When every foul cometh ther to choose his mate.

This folk tradition continued into the beginning of this century in the United States. In the Ozarks, tradition held that birds and rabbits started their mating seasons on February 14.

The practice of exchanging romantic messages and gifts that we follow today most likely originated in the ancient Roman observance of *Lupercalia*, a festival that celebrated early spring and fertility with singing and dancing. Gods associated with Lupercalia included Juno, the Roman goddess of women and marriage, and Lupercus, the god of nature. According to legend, one of the traditions of Lupercalia was name drawing. On the eve of the festival each local boy randomly drew from a jar the name of a girl, who was deemed to be his sweetheart for the year and with whom he exchanged gifts.

The tradition of name drawing and gift giving continued, and by the seventeenth century in France, it was customary for both sexes to draw names from a valentine box. Around the same time in England, some couples also exchanged jewelry or gloves. By the eighteenth century, valentine "writers," or books of verses from which one could choose just the right message, were widely available in England. Some of these European customs soon were brought to the New World.

Today, the most enduring tradition of the holiday is sending notes—valentines—with sentimental verses or love poems. In

A baker prepares heart-shaped cakes for Valentine's Day.

the United States, commercial valentines were introduced in the 1800s, as the holiday gained popularity around the period of the American Civil War. By the early part of the twentieth century, the Chicago post office accepted over a million valentines a year. Today, over a billion valentine cards are delivered every year in the United States, second only to Christmas in the number of greetings sent. The post office in Loveland, Colorado does a booming business on Valentine's Day, using a special red seal to stamp the valentines. Conventional valentine messages are now being sent in unconventional ways, including by E-mail, or classified ads in the newspaper.

Although sweethearts and spouses exchange valentine greeting cards, chocolates, perfume, jewelry, and flowers on Valentine's Day, the holiday remains a favorite of children. As early as kindergarten children are taught to make their own valentines using colored paper, lace doilies, and glitter. For those who choose to buy rather than make their valentines, stores overflow with an ever-increasing variety. In grammar school, kids decorate shoeboxes with brightly colored paper and lace to carry the many valentines offered by their classmates.

In England, traditional belief holds that the first boy a girl sees on Valentine's Day will be her future spouse; some girls have their friends lead them to school in the morning with closed eyes, in order to open them at just the right moment. In Italy, February 14 has become a traditional date for announcing engagements, and in the United States it is a popular date for weddings.

While more elaborate gifts are usually reserved for a sweetheart or spouse, valentine messages can be sent to any friend, relative, or love interest. Valentines use short, sentimental messages such as "Be mine" or "You are loved," though some are comical or even mean-spirited. Many valentines are sent anonymously, with an elusive message such as:

> Roses are red, violets are blue,
> Sugar is sweet, and so are you.
> From: Guess who?

Certain symbols are associated with Valentine's Day in the United States. The heart—once believed to be the organ responsible for human emotion—still stands as a symbol of love and Valentine's Day. The red rose has long been associated with love, and is a traditional gift for a sweetheart. Lace—used to

> **In England, traditional belief holds that the first boy a girl sees on Valentine's Day will be her future spouse.**

decorate chocolate boxes and valentines—connotes romance because of an old tradition in which a woman would drop a lace handkerchief before a particular man, who would pick it up and return it to her, perhaps sparking romance. Lovebirds, brightly colored birds from Africa that sit closely together in pairs, are sometimes associated with Valentine's Day, as are doves, birds that mate for life and stand as symbols of loyalty and love. Cupid is one of the most enduring symbols of the holiday. The son of Venus, the Roman goddess of love, Cupid could cause people to fall in love by piercing them with one of his magic arrows. ◆

Vappu

FINLAND ● MAY 1

Vappu is the Finnish May Day (May 1), an enthusiastic street carnival with an "anything goes" spirit, a joyous release of energies pent up during the long northern winter. With a strong "spring break" gusto among university students and a general zest for drinking and merrymaking, Vappu is a time for all Finns to rejoice in the springtime, even though, at this time of year, snow may still be falling in Helsinki.

May 1 is also Labor Day in Finland, so the age-old impulse to celebrate the return of spring joins with a recognition of the workers and the common cause of international solidarity that is celebrated in May Day festivities in many other countries. With the "party animal" spirit there is also a serious sense of solidarity: the raucous white-capped university students celebrate with the industrial workers, tradesmen celebrate with professors.

The celebration begins on Vapunnatto, or May Day eve, when university students and even white-haired elders wear white student caps and "let loose" in just about any form of revelry that is not indecent or criminal. Vapunnatto is not a night for sleeping—not for more than a few hours, anyway. Anyone trying to get to sleep on Vapunnatto probably regards Vappu as a festival of the obnoxious. Chances are, though, that you won't have to go in for work on May Day, for most businesses are closed. Vappu is second only to Christmas on Finland's calendar; factories that "never close" do shut down for Vappu, or at least scale back their operations, as they do for Christmas.

It is a Vappu tradition in Helsinki, Finland's capital, for students to wade across the moat surrounding a large statue of the mermaid Havis Amanda and climb up to place caps on her head.

368

On May Day, the revelry continues as students lead processions through the streets, and townspeople attend carnivals and concerts. All day long the students and workers wear masks and parade through town with music and streamers, blowing horns and dancing in the streets. Sobriety is not required. It is a tradition in Helsinki, Finland's capital, for students to wade across the moat surrounding a large statue of the mermaid Havis Amanda and climb up to place their caps on her head. In the smaller towns of Finland the celebrations tend to be more solemn and ceremonial, with parades and speeches to honor the workers and welcome the warmer days of spring.

First of May celebrations around Europe have their roots in ancient pagan celebrations marking the beginning of the new year. It is also traditional for the May festivities to include singing, dancing, or chanting a rhyme for money, and often that money is given to the poor. Seen in this way, it is quite consistent with tradition for the young people, the university students, to find common cause with the workers: the tailor and the clerk drinking with the ironsmith. ◆

Veterans Day

On November 11
1918 Germany signs
an armistice end-
ing World War I.

President
Woodrow Wilson
1919 proclaims
November 11 as
Armistice Day.

Arlington
National Ceme-
tery's Tomb of the
1921 Unknown Soldier
is dedicated on
Armistice Day.

The U.S. Con-
gress changes
1954 the holiday's
name to Veterans
Day.

On November 11, 1918, the heads of the Allied and Central armies that were fighting against each other in World War I met in a railroad car in a French forest. That morning they signed an armistice (cease-fire), even though an actual peace treaty was not signed until the following year. On the first anniversary of the cease-fire in 1919, Armistice Day was celebrated in the United States through a presidential proclamation.

In 1921 the Tomb of the Unknown Soldier was dedicated in Virginia's Arlington National Cemetery on Armistice Day. The remains of an unidentified American soldier who had died in France during World War I were placed in the tomb, as a reminder of all who had sacrificed their lives during the war. The tome is carved with the inscription

Here rests in honored glory
An American Soldier
Known but to God.

In later years unidentified soldiers from other wars also were buried in this memorial, which was renamed the Tomb of the Unknowns.

By 1926 more than half the states celebrated Armistice Day as a legal holiday. That year Congress passed a resolution asking that the flag be displayed in public places on Armistice Day and that the day be commemorated "with thanksgiving and prayer and exercises designed to perpetuate peace through good will

Veterans from the
Vietnam War remember
their fallen comrades
on Veterans Day at
the Vietnam Veterans
Memorial in
Washington, D.C.

and mutual understanding between nations." In 1938 Congress
declared Armistice Day a federal legal holiday.

World War I did not lead to continuing peace among nations,
and United States troops fought and died in several further conflicts during the twentieth century, beginning with World War II
(1939–45), followed by the Korean War (1950–53). In 1954
President Eisenhower proclaimed that November 11 would be

renamed Veterans Day, to honor American soldiers from all wars, which later included the Vietnam War (1957–75) and the Persian Gulf War (1991). The Uniform Holiday Bill of 1968 changed the date on which several federal holidays would be celebrated to a Monday, resulting in three-day holiday weekends as of 1971. Under this law, Veterans Day was moved to the fourth Monday in October. But many states continued to cele-

A color guard approaches the Tomb of the Unknown Soldier at Arlington National Cemetery in Washington, D.C., on Veterans Day.

brate the holiday on November 11, and military service organizations were opposed to the change. In 1975 President Ford signed a law that returned Veterans Day to its original date as of 1978.

One of the oldest traditions of Veterans Day is a two-minute period of silence at 11:00 A.M. (the eleventh hour of the eleventh day of the eleventh month), the time when the 1918 armistice was signed. This "Great Silence" has been traced back to 1918 when an Australian journalist, George Honey, suggested a period of respectful silence after the signing; even radio broadcasts in many countries observed the silence.

On Veterans Day, the United States president or vice president honors veterans by laying a wreath at the Tomb of the Unknowns. Other events that traditionally occur on Veterans Day include parades where living veterans of America's wars march in formation, often wearing their old military uniforms. Volunteers also sell artificial poppies to raise money for disabled veterans. Blue and gold stars often are displayed on the windows of veterans' homes, a blue star if the veteran is alive and a gold star if the veteran is dead.

The anniversary of the 1918 armistice is observed as Armistice Day in France. The soldiers of France are honored, along with the many soldiers from other countries who died and were buried there. Canada's Remembrance Day also is on November 11. In Great Britain, Remembrance Day (sometimes called Poppy Day) is celebrated on the second Sunday in November. ◆

One of the oldest Veterans Day traditions is a two-minute period of silence at 11:00 A.M.

Voodoo Festivals

In Haiti, different spirits are associated with each village, city, and region, and people in those areas observe feasts at various times during the year to honor the local spirit.

Voodoo is an African-based, Catholic-influenced religion practiced by 80 to 90 percent of the people of Haiti. Various forms of voodoo are also practiced in parts of Brazil, the United States, Canada, Martinique, and other Caribbean countries. The essential elements of voodoo were brought by slaves from West Africa, where the name originated. Among the Ewes of West Africa, *vodu* means fear of the gods; *Vodun*, in Dahomey, West Africa, is said to be a name for all deities. New Orleans blacks often pronounce voodoo as "hoodoo"; in Haiti, it is frequently called Vodun. Voodoo as a religion or practice probably originated in Santo Domingo (Haiti) as an amalgam of ancient African elements of the Fon (or Dahomey), Yoruba, and Kongo tribes.

Followers of voodoo believe in numerous spirits called lwa (from a Yoruba word for spirit or mystery), sint (saints), miste (mysteries), and zanj (angels). Different spirits are associated with villages, cities, and regions and people in those areas observe feasts at various times during the year in honor of the local spirits. Voodoo also involves a belief in fetishes that manifest the powers of the spirits, who are called upon during ceremonies and feasts to heal, to hold someone's love, bring harm to someone, or to provide protection to one's self or loved ones.

Though primarily of African origin, voodoo reveals the Roman Catholic influence through its use of certain saints and the choice of St. John's Eve as a date for a major feast day in some locations. A Haitian-American follower of voodoo in Brooklyn, for example, keeps a statue of St. Lazarus, represent-

374

ing the Haitian divinity Legba, the gatekeeper (and door opener) between the material world and the spirit world.

There are many different types of voodoo ceremonies, including individual acts of piety, such as lighting of candles for particular spirits, and large feasts, sometimes of several days' duration, which include animal sacrifices as part of a meal offered to the spirits. Energetic drumming, singing, and dancing accompany the more elaborate festivals. In the countryside, feasts often take place outdoors on family land that has been set aside for the spirits. On this land there is often a small cult house, which houses the voodoo altars. In urban areas, voodoo feast and rituals occur in a temple called an ounfo.

During a voodoo festival, participants pound drums, sing, and dance in order to energize the atmosphere sufficiently to bring on possession by the spirits. As a particular spirit is summoned, a devotee enters a trance and becomes the spirit's "chwal" or horse, thus providing the means of direct communication between human beings and the spirits. Using that person's body, the spirit is said to sing, dance, and eat with the people. The spirit may also offer them advice and chastisement. The people, in turn, offer the spirit a wide variety of gifts and acts of obeisance whose goal is to placate the spirit and ensure his or her continuing protection.

For many years, voodoo has been central to the culture of New Orleans. In an unusually clear and impartial article on voodoo in New Orleans, Blake Touchstone explains that in the early days voodoo appealed to blacks, both slave and free, "who were denied most educational and religious opportunities, severely restricted in their overt expressions of violence, and limited in their means of retribution for the many injustices they suffered." Touchstone suggests that voodoo's heyday in the United States was probably in pre–Civil War New Orleans— that is, before slaves were freed by the Emancipation Proclamation (1863).

Voodoo probably first entered the Western Hemisphere in 1724 when West African slaves were brought to the Caribbean. Shipments of slaves from the French colonies of Martinique, Guadeloupe, and Santo Domingo (present-day Haiti), which historian Herbert Asbury says were "veritable hotbeds of Voodooism," appear to have introduced such a menace (and a fear of slave rebellion) that in 1782 the Spanish governor of Louisiana, Bernardo de Gálvez, prohibited further importation of slaves from Martinique, "as they are too much given to

During a voodoo festival, participants pound drums, sing, and dance in order to energize the atmosphere sufficiently to bring on possession by the spirits.

A young man performs an energetic dance during a voodoo ceremony in Gonaïves, Haiti.

voudouism and make the lives of the citizens unsafe." At least two more official prohibitions against slaves from Santo Domingo were issued in the next two decades. Following Haitian independence in 1804, at least five thousand refugees from Haiti, both free and slave, arrived in New Orleans between 1806 and 1810.

Priestesses, known as queens, were the holders of power in voodoo circles; priests were understood to be subservient to the will of the queen. The first powerful voodoo queen in New Orleans was Sanité Dédé, from Santo Domingo. In the 1820s Dédé fixed St. John's Eve as the major celebration of the year. Early eyewitness accounts record a ceremony including about sixty blacks and a few whites assembled at night in an abandoned building. A table served as an altar on which stood a large black doll decorated with snake and alligator bones. A live snake was kept in a box beneath the doll, and stuffed cats, one black and one white, stood at each end of the altar. While drums pounded and gourd rattles kept rhythm, Dédé called forth four priests whom she sprinkled with liquid from a gourd as she spoke an incantation. At her command, a priest removed the snake from the box, coaxed it to rise up straight, and passed the snake over the gathering of celebrants while he chanted the name of the god and the sect. The snake was then thrown into a fire. At that point the drumbeats increased in tempo, singers chanted a ritual song, and a woman stepped into the center of the circle of celebrants and began a ritual dance (later named the Calinda) that imitated the movements of a snake. After a long erotic dance, she tore a white kerchief from her head, at which the whole assembly sprang forward and entered the dance.

Although Dédé was a pioneer, the most famous voodoo queen of all was Marie Laveau, who reigned during the 1850s and '60s. Also known as "Madame L" and the "Widow of Paris," Marie Laveau presided over the public Sunday gatherings in Congo Square as well as the secret rituals. She worked as a hair-dresser to many prominent Creole families, was a practicing Catholic, and spared no effort to comfort and cure victims of the yellow fever epidemics that periodically ravaged the city. She was genuinely a woman of remarkable powers, but Marie Laveau's fame must in part be attributed to what would be called today her "media-savvy" influence with reporters. Her tomb in New Orleans's St. Louis Cemetery No. 1, near the Basin Street entrance, is one of the most frequented sites in the city.

An influx of immigrants from Haiti in recent decades has carried voodoo, and hence voodoo feasts, to several cities in the United States and Canada. In Miami, New York, and Montreal, the cities with the greatest concentrations of Haitian immi-grants, voodoo ceremonies are carried on in storefronts, rented rooms, and high-rise apartment buildings. North American voodoo feasts are usually simplified and shortened versions of their Haitian counterparts. There may be no drums and the only animals sacrificed may be chickens. ◆

Walpurgis Night

EUROPE ● APRIL 30

According to legend, Walpurgis Night is a magical night when witches are said to ride through the air to meet with the devil on Brocken Mountain in Germany.

Walpurgis Night is a festival day with roots in the pagan celebration of spring. It falls on April 30, on the eve of the Feast of Saint Walpurgis. Walpurgis was an English nun of the eighth century and the daughter of King Richard of England. She became a missionary to Germany and the head of an abbey of nuns in Heidenheim. Because Saint Walpurgis was believed to protect against black magic, her feast day may also have become associated with April 30, when the power of witches and demons was said to be at its height. The name for the festival may also be a confused usage of the name of the German fertility goddess Waldborg, who was known in the region where Walpurgis served as a missionary.

According to legend, Walpurgis Night is a magical night when witches are said to ride through the air to meet with the devil on Brocken Mountain, the highest peak in the Harz Mountains of central Germany. There, witches were believed to engage in wild dancing with demons and to perform evil rituals and rites of initiation with the devil. Long ago, the Harz Mountains were the site of pagan sacrifices and spring rituals designed to foster bumper crops and to celebrate fertility and the Earth Mother. As a result of these wild rituals and sacrifices, the area probably became known as a popular gathering place for witches.

The specter of the Brocken and the power they wielded on Walpurgis Night instilled fear in many people of central Europe. To frighten off witches, Germans rang church bells, banged on pots and pans, and burned torches made with pungent herbs. Farmers put crosses and bunches of herbs on stable doors and burned bonfires in the orchards to drive away the witches and the devil. People hid their broomsticks so that the witches would not use them. And in the evening, a cross of stockings was left on children's beds to protect them while they slept. Today, some Germans still observe Walpurgis by building bonfires, dressing up like witches, and celebrating in the streets.

The Swedes are also known to celebrate Walpurgis Night. In Sweden, the festival marks the end of the long, dark winter, and a time for jubilation over the coming days of warmth and light. People celebrate with bonfires and fireworks. Students in university towns also traditionally gather in the midafternoon and at the stroke of three give a cheer and throw their student caps into the air. A speaker welcomes the coming of spring to the land, and the crowd breaks into a robust chorus of old Scandinavian and Latin school songs. Dances go late into the evening. ◆

Wedding Anniversary

VARIOUS DATES

A wedding anniversary is an annual celebration marking the date on which a couple was married. The ways in which wedding anniversaries are celebrated are as unique as the couples themselves, but some traditions prevail.

Most couples exchange gifts on their wedding anniversary. In the United States, traditional gifts include paper for the first anniversary, wood for the fifth, tin or aluminum for the tenth, china for the twentieth, and gold for the fiftieth. In more recent times, these traditional materials have been supplanted by more modern gifts, including clocks for the first, silverware for the fifth, leather for the tenth, and platinum for the twentieth. However, some gift traditions remain; the fiftieth anniversary is referred to as the "golden anniversary" because gold is usually exchanged. Traditional anniversary gifts vary from country to country.

In addition to traditional gifts, a precious gemstone is associated with each anniversary. In fact, jewelry ranks among the most commonly exchanged wedding anniversary gifts. For example, turquoise is the traditional stone for the sixth anniversary, yellow diamond for the twentieth, emerald for the thirty-fifth, and imperial topaz for the fiftieth.

In the United States, couples mark wedding anniversaries with plans such as a romantic dinner at a fancy restaurant or a weekend retreat to a special spot. Some couples take a second honeymoon or renew their wedding vows in a religious ceremony. Traditionally, a couple celebrating their first anniversary eats the top layer of their wedding cake, which has been stored in the freezer since their wedding day.

The tenth, twenty-fifth, fortieth, and fiftieth anniversaries are marked with more special celebrations, often elaborate parties including other members of the couple's extended family and friends. The fiftieth wedding anniversary celebration, in particular, is widely celebrated in the United States with large parties. Family and friends give speeches and toast the couple. In some cases, the couple dresses in a tuxedo and bridal gown, occasionally even the ones they wore at their own wedding ceremony a half-century earlier.

Gifts for Wedding Anniversaries

	Traditional	*Modern*	*Alternative Modern*
1	paper	plastics	clocks
2	cotton	cotton/calico	china
3	leather	leather	crystal/glass
4	flowers	linen/silk/nylon	appliances
5	wood	wood	silverware
6	candy/iron	iron	wood
7	copper/wool	copper/wool/brass	desk sets
8	bronze/pottery	bronze/appliances	linens
9	pottery/willow	pottery	leather
10	tin	aluminum	diamond
11	steel	steel	jewelry
12	silk/linen	silk/linen	pearl
13	lace	lace	textiles/fur
14	ivory	ivory	gold
15	crystal	glass	watches
20	china	china	platinum
25	silver	silver	silver
30	pearl	pearl	pearl
35	coral	coral/jade	jade
40	ruby	ruby/garnet	ruby
45	sapphire	sapphire	sapphire
50	gold	gold	gold
55	emerald	emerald/turquoise	emerald
60	diamond	gold	diamond
75	diamond	diamond/gold	diamond

◆

Appendix A

Lunar and Solar Calendars

A lunar calendar is based on the length of the lunar month (29.5 days, the time from one new moon to the next) and disregards the length of the solar year. The Islamic calendar, which is a lunar calendar, contains the following twelve lunar months (some with 29 days and some with 30 days, supplying an average of 29.5 days):

Muharram (the sacred month)
Safar (the month that is void)
Rabi I (the first spring)
Rabi II (the second spring)
Jumada I (the first month of dryness)
Jumada II (the second month of dryness)
Rajab (the revered month)
Shaban (the month of division)
Ramadan (the month of great heat)
Shawwal (the month of hunting)
Dhu al-Qadah (the month of rest)
Dhu al-Hijja (the month of pilgrimage)

These twelve months, however, provide a lunar year of only 354.367056 days. Because the lunar year is 10.875143 days shorter than the solar year, the months regress (move backward) each solar year, causing the seasons to occur at earlier and earlier dates. In fact, any given month of the Islamic calendar will have regressed through an entire solar year in 33.585 solar years. Another complicating factor is that the decimal value of the length of a lunar year (which amounts to about 11.012 days in 30 lunar years) is unaccounted for in the Islamic calendar. Instead, 11 days are intercalated (inserted) once every thirty years to restore the accuracy with respect to the moon.

A solar calendar ignores the lunar cycle and adheres to the set length of the solar year, with this period divided into twelve set months. There are four critical periods in the solar cycle: two equinoxes and two solstices. The accuracy of a solar calendar can be judged based on the accuracy with which these four events occur on the same days each year. The two most relevant solar calendars are the Julian calendar and the Gregorian calendar. The Julian calendar was the result of an order by Julius Caesar to convert from the Roman lunar calendar to a solar calendar in 46 B.C.E This conversion involved an intercalation of 90 days (23 days after February, and two months of 34 and 33 days added between November and December) to correct for a discrepancy that had been growing between the seasons and the calendar periods in which they had traditionally fallen. The intercalation meant that 46 B.C.E. had a total of 445 days, but thereafter, Caesar ordered that the normal length of the year would be 365 days, with one day added to February every four years to adjust for the true length of the solar year. However, this meant that a solar year would be calculated as 365.25 days, which exceeds the true solar year of 365.242199 days by 11 minutes and 14 seconds. This might seem to be a small discrepancy, but over time the calendar once again began to fall out of synchronization with the seasons. To correct for this discrepancy, Pope Gregory XIII instituted two alterations to the Julian calendar: (1) 10 days were dropped from the calendar of 1582, so the day after October 4 became October 15, a change that restored the vernal equinox date to March 21, and (2) century years were changed to common years (rather than leap years), unless the century year was divisible by 400. These modifications of the Julian calendar to create the Gregorian calendar restored the synchronization between the months and the seasons. Although the Gregorian calendar has become the most widely used of the two solar calendars, the Julian calendar is still used by Orthodox Christian churches.

A lunisolar calendar is generally a compromise between following a lunar calendar and the need to synchronize dates and the seasons. This type of calendar traditionally follows the lunar cycle but intercalates an additional month as necessary to maintain synchronization. Two examples of lunisolar calendars are the Jewish calendar and the Hindu calendar. The Jewish calendar contains the following twelve calendar months, which alternate between 30 and 29 days in length:

Tishri (September–October)
Heshvan (October–November)
Kislev (November–December)
Tevet (December–January)
Shevat (January–February)
Adar (February–March)
Nisan (March–April)
Iyyar (April–May)
Sivan (May–June)
Tammuz (June–July)
Av (July–August)
Elul (August–September)

A thirteenth month is intercalated into the Jewish calendar in the third, sixth, eighth, eleventh, fourteenth, seventeenth, and nineteenth years of a nineteen-year cycle. The standard months of the Hindu lunisolar calendar are as follows:

Asvina (September–October)
Karttika (October–November)
Margasirsa (November–December)
Pausa (December–January)
Magha (January–February)
Phalguna (February–March)
Caitra (March–April)
Vaisakha (April–May)
Jyaistha (May–June)
Asadha (June–July)
Sravana (July–August)
Bhadrapada (August–September)

A thirteenth month is intercalated in the Hindu calendar every sixty months.

Appendix B

National Holidays
Around the World

January 1

Haiti Independence Day: honors Jean-Jacques Dessalines's 1804 proclamation of independence.

Independence Day for Western Samoa: honors the 1962 declaration of independence from New Zealand.

Liberation Day in Cuba: celebrates the end of Spanish rule in 1899.

New Year's Day: marks the first day of the year according to the Gregorian calendar.

Taiwan Foundation Day: commemorates the founding of the Republic of China in 1912.

January 2

Berchtoldstag: observed in Switzerland in honor of the twelfth-century Duke Berchtold V, who founded the city of Bern.

Granada Day in Spain: commemorates the recapture of Granada from the Moors in 1492.

January 4

Burma Independence Day: commemorates the 1948 establishment of Burma as a free nation.

January 11

Albanian Republic Day: commemorates the 1946 establishment of the republic.

Hostos Day: marks the anniversary of the 1839 birth of Eugenio Maria de Hostos, a Puerto Rican philosopher and patriot.

January 22

Ukrainian Day: marks the 1918 proclamation of the free Ukrainian Republic.

January 25

Burns Day: commemorates the 1759 birth of Robert Burns, the national poet of Scotland.

January 26

Duarte Day: a holiday in the Dominican Republic honoring Juan Pablo Duarte, a founder of the republic and a leader in its fight for liberation from Haiti.

India's Republic Day (Basant Panchmi): commemorates the proclamation of the republic in 1950.

January (movable)

Sankranti: Harvest Festival commemorated in several states of southern India.

January (movable; third Monday)

Martin Luther King Jr. Day: celebrates the 1929 birth of the civil rights leader who was assassinated in 1968.

January–February (movable)

Lunar New Year: the celebrations throughout Asia of the Lunar New year vary from country to country, but they all include offerings to household gods, housecleaning and new clothes, large banquets, and ancestor worship. The Chinese festival, known as Chun Chieh (Spring Festival), is characterized by bright colors and loud noises to scare away evil spirits. The Vietnamese celebration, which is the most important festival of the year, is known as Tet (an abbreviation of Tet Nguyen-Den, "first day") and is marked by paying homage to ancestors, wiping out debts, and enjoying family reunions. The Korean New Year, known as Je-sok, is brought in with the lighting of torches and a nightlong vigil to guard against evil spirits.

February 4

Sri Lanka Independence Day: celebrates the 1958 granting of independence of the former British colony, which changed its name from Ceylon to Sri Lanka in 1972.

February 5

Mexican Constitution Day: honors the anniversaries of the constitutions of 1857 and 1917.

Runeberg's Day: commemorates the 1804 birth of Johan Ludvig Runeberg, Finland's leading poet.

February 7

Grenada Independence Day: honors the attainment of complete independence in 1974.

February 11

Japanese National Foundation Day: celebrates the founding of the nation of Japan in 660 B.C.E. by the first emperor.

February 12

Burma Union Day: commemorates the 1947 conference leading to the formation of the Union of Burma.

February 14

Fjortende Februar (Fourteenth of February): traditional day for the exchange of tokens and gifts among schoolchildren in Denmark.

February 21

Shaheel Day: observed in Bangladesh as the national day of mourning.

February 23

Guyana Republic Day: commemorates the 1970 establishment of Guyana as a sovereign democratic state in South America and within the British Commonwealth.

February 24

Estonia National Day: honors the 1920 peace treaty that confirmed Estonian independence.

February 25

Fiesta sa EDSA (People Power Anniversary): commemorates the bloodless People Power Revolution that toppled the Marcos regime in the Philippines in 1986.

February 27

Independence Day in the Dominican Republic: honors the independence obtained with the 1844 withdrawal of the Haitians.

February (movable; third Monday)

Presidents' Day: jointly honors the birthdays of George Washington and Abraham Lincoln but is generally considered to be a day to honor all former presidents of the United States.

February–March (movable)

Prajatantradivasa: celebrated on the seventh day of the month of Phalguna (according to the Hindu calendar) to commemorate the victory of the Nepalese people over the Panchayat and Rana autocratic regimes in Nepal.

March 1

Independence Day in South Korea: celebrates the anniversary of demonstrations in 1919 protesting Japanese occupation, although independence did not occur until the Japanese surrender in 1945 at the end of World War II.

Pinzón Day: marks the return of Martín Pinzón to Spain, bringing the news of the discovery of the New World.

March 3

Bulgaria Liberation Day: marks the anniversary of Bulgaria's release from Ottoman domination by the 1878 Treaty of San Stefano.

March 6

Discovery Day in Guam: commemorates the 1521 discovery of Guam by Ferdinand Magellan.

Ghana Independence Day: commemorates the establishment of the former British Crown colony of the Gold Coast as a sovereign nation in 1957.

March 8

Syrian Revolution Day: marks the anniversary of the 1963 assumption of political power by the National Council of Revolution.

March 9

Amerigo Vespucci Day: honors the fifteenth-century Italian navigator for whom the Americas were named.

Taras Shevchenko Day: marks the anniversary of the 1814 birth of the foremost Ukrainian poet of the nineteenth century.

March 13

National Day in Grenada: commemorates the bloodless revolution of 1979, which was led by the Joint Endeavor for Welfare, Education, and Liberation (JEWEL).

March 20

Lajos Kossuth Day: marks the anniversary of the 1894 death of Lajos Kossuth, the symbol of Hungarian nationalism.

Nawruz: the first day of this thirteen-day celebration of the Iranian New Year begins at the vernal equinox, which coincides with the first day of spring.

March 21

Juárez Day: commemorates the 1806 birth of Benito Pablo Juárez, the first Mexican president of Amerindian descent.

March 23

Pakistan Republic Day: commemorates the establishment of Pakistan in 1956.

March 25

Greek Independence Day: honors the day in 1821 when the Greek flag was first raised against Ottoman domination.

March 26

Bangladesh Independence Day: marks the anniversary of the 1971 proclamation establishing Bangladesh.

March 27

Resistance Day: honors the movement of guerrilla forces in Burma to oppose invaders during World War II.

March 30

Land Day: observed by Palestinians since 1976 to commemorate the confiscation of Palestinian land by Israeli authorities.

March (movable; second Sunday)

Commonwealth Day: honors the British Empire and was formerly known as Empire Day and British Commonwealth Day.

March–April (movable)

Ugadi: marks the Telugu New Year's Day.

April 4

Liberation Day in Hungary: commemorates the defeat of the Germans in 1945 and their departure from Hungary.

April 6

Chakri Day: commemorates the enthronement of Rama I, who founded the Chakri dynasty in Thailand in 1782.

April 14

Pan-American Day: commemorates the 1890 founding of the Organization of American States, which includes Argentina, Bolivia, Brazil, Chile, Colombia, Costa Rica, Cuba, the Dominican Republic, Ecuador, El Salvador, Guatemala, Haiti, Honduras, Mexico, Nicaragua, Panama, Paraguay, Peru, the United States, Uruguay, and Venezuela.

April 16

De Diego Day: marks the anniversary of the 1867 birth of Puerto Rican patriot José de Diego.

April 17

Evacuation Day in Syria: commemorates the withdrawal of French troops from Syria in 1946.

Flag Day in American Samoa: commemorates the 1900 signing of the Instrument of Cession by the seven high chiefs at the invitation of President Theodore Roosevelt and the establishment of the Samoan constitutional government in 1960.

April 21

Tiradentes Day in Brazil: commemorates the execution of the dentist José da Silva Xavier, a conspirator in the 1789 revolt against the Portuguese.

April 24

Armenian Martyrs' Day: memorializes the Armenian victims of the killings in Turkey in 1915–16.

April 25

Italian Liberation Day: celebrated to commemorate the Allied victory in World War II.

Liberation Day in Portugal: marks the anniversary of the 1974 coup that led to the downfall of the Salazar-Caetano dictatorship that had lasted for forty-two years.

April 30

Walpurgis Night: observed since ancient times in Germany, Finland, and the Scandinavian countries to ward off witches, warlocks, and demons.

April (movable)

Festival of the Tombs: observed on the third day of the third moon as a day for the Chinese to honor their dead.

April (movable; first Thursday)

Glarus Festival: Swiss commemoration of the 1388 defeat of the Austrians by the men of Glarus, Switzerland.

April–May (movable)

Naya Varsha: observed on the first day of the month of Vaisakha (according to the Hindu calendar) as the Nepalese New Year.

May 1

International Labor Day: day set aside by many countries to honor workers.

May Day: the traditional day of flower festivals.

May 3

Japanese Constitution Day: celebrates the 1947 establishment of a democratic form of government under parliamentary rule.

Polish Constitution Day: commemorates the Polish constitution of 1791.

May 5

Cinco de Mayo: Mexican holiday celebrating the defeat of the French at the Battle of Puebla in 1862.

Dutch Liberation Day: commemorates the expulsion of German forces from Holland by the Allies in 1945.

May 6

Dukhnovych Day: commemorates the 1803 birth of Aleksander Dukhnovych, the "National Awakener of the Carpatho-Rusyns."

May 8

French Liberation Day: commemorates the expulsion of German forces from France at the end of World War II.

May 9

Carpatho-Rusyn National Day: commemorates the day in 1919 when Rusyns living south of the Carpathians voluntarily united with Czechoslovakia to form their own autonomous province of Subcarpathian Rus.

May 12

Snellman Day: Finnish observation of the anniversary of the birth of J. V. Snellman, journalist, statesman, and leader of the Nationalist movement.

May 17

Constitution Day in Norway: marks the adoption of the constitution in 1814 and the gaining of independence from Sweden by Norway in 1905.

May 18

Haitian Flag Day: honors the flag that bears the country's national arms.

May 19

Flag Day of the Army: honors those who died to preserve Finland's freedom.
Youth and Sports Day: Turkish holiday commemorating the day Mustafa Kemal Atatürk landed in Samsun and began his national movement for independence.

May 20

Botev Day: marks the anniversary of the death of Khristo Botev, Bulgarian poet and hero in the revolutionary movement against the Turks.

May 21

Chilean Navy Day: commemorates the Battle of Iquique in 1879.
The Anasternarides Feast: Macedonian celebration in accordance with classic traditions.

May 22

Haitian National Day: observed as a day to celebrate Haitian culture.
Sri Lanka Republic Day (Heroes' Day): honors the ratification of the constitution in 1972.

May 24

Bulgarian Day of Slavonic Letters (Culture Day): pays tribute to Bulgarian culture, education, and communications.

Independence Battle Day: commemorates the Battle of Pinchincha, which liberated Ecuador from Spanish rule in 1822.

May 25

Argentine National Day: marks the anniversary of the beginning of the 1810 revolution in Argentina.

Jordan Independence Day: honors the 1946 treaty that gave Jordan autonomy and set up a monarchy.

May 26

Guyana Independence Day: commemorates the agreement that gave independence to the former British colony in 1966.

Independence Day in Georgia: marks the declaration of independence of the first Georgian Republic, which lasted from 1918 to 1921.

May 28

Armenian Independence Day: commemorates the founding of the First Republic in 1918.

May 30

Croatian Independence Day: marks the 1991 declaration of independence.

May (movable; Monday preceding May 25)

Victoria Day: Canadian celebration honoring the birth of Queen Victoria.

May (movable; last Monday)

Memorial Day: honors all U.S. citizens who have died in war, although the observance was originally known as Decoration Day and was created to honor Union soldiers who died in the U.S. Civil War.

May–June (movable)

Dragon Boat Festival: celebrated on the fifth day of the fifth moon with the sending out of boats in a reenactment of the search for the body of Qu Yuan (c. 328–298 B.C.E.), a Chinese poet and statesman of the Chu Dynasty who drowned himself in Tungting Lake to protest the corruption and injustice of Prince Huai's court.

June 2

Italian Republic Day: commemorates the proclamation of the republic established by referendum in 1946, in which a majority vote was cast for the republic as opposed to the retention of the monarchy.

Seaman's Day: honors the sailors and fishermen of Iceland, who represent the lifeline of the country's economy.

June 4

Flag Day of the Finnish Armed Forces: commemorates the 1867 birth of Marshall Carl Gustaf Mannerheim, Finland's great military leader.

June 5

Denmark Constitution Day: honors the 1849 constitution and the new constitution signed in 1953.

June 6

Constitution and Flag Day in Sweden: recognizes the adoption of the Swedish constitution in 1809 and the ascension of Gustavus I to the throne in 1523.

June 10

Portugal National Day: commemorates the 1580 death of the Portuguese poet Luíz Vaz de Camoëns.

June 11

King Kamehameha Day: commemorates the victories of Kamehameha I, who unified the Hawaiian islands in the eighteenth century.

June 12

Helsinki Day: commemorates the founding of the city of Helsinki, Finland, in 1550.

Philippine Independence Day: commemorates the 1898 declaration of independence from Spain.

June 15

Flag Day in Denmark: honors the first appearance of the Danish flag in 1219, when, according to legend, a red banner with a white cross floated down from the sky during a battle to conquer the Estonians and convert them to Christianity; a voice from the clouds promised that the Danes would win if they raised the banner before their enemies.

Magna Charta Day: marks the anniversary of King John's signing in 1215 of the "great charter," the foundation of England's constitutional monarchy.

June 17

Iceland Independence Day: commemorates the reestablishment of an independent republic in 1944.

Okinawa Day: marks the anniversary of the 1971 treaty between the United States and Japan that returned Okinawa, which had been seized by the United States during World War II, to Japan.

June 18

> Evacuation Day in Egypt: marks the anniversary of the 1956 departure of the last British troops from the Suez Canal bases.
>
> Waterloo Day: marks Napoleon's 1815 defeat at the Battle of Waterloo.

June 20

> Argentina Flag Day: honors the history of the country's flag, which dates back to 1812.

June 24

> Bannockburn Day in Scotland: commemorates Robert Bruce's winning of independence for Scotland in 1314 by expelling the English.
>
> Battle of Carabobo Day: commemorates the battle fought at Carabobo (west of Caracas) in 1821, a battle that assured Venezuela's independence.
>
> Day of the Indian: celebrated in Peru and other Latin American countries to honor and preserve native customs, music, folklore, and poetry.
>
> San Juan Bautista Day: Puerto Rican holiday commemorating the Battle of San Juan, which ended in victory for the Americans over the Spanish. The island was ceded to the United States at the end of the Spanish-American War.

June 26

> United Nations Charter Day: commemorates the signing of the charter in five official languages—Chinese, English, French, Russian, and Spanish—in 1945.

June 30

> Guatemala Army Day: commemorates the 1871 Guatemalan revolution for agrarian reform.

July 1

> Canada Day (Dominion Day): commemorates the confederation of the provinces of Canada into the Dominion of Canada under the terms of the British North America Act of 1867.
>
> Ghana First Republic Day: commemorates the 1960 change from dominion status to that of a republic in the British Commonwealth.

July 2

> Bahia Independence Day: commemorates the consolidation of Brazilian independence in the state of Bahia with the 1823 defeat of Portuguese troops.

July 4

Caricom Day: celebrates the Caribbean Community and Common Market, which was founded in 1973 to promote cooperation among the Caribbean states.

Garibaldi Day in Italy: commemorates the 1807 birthday of Giuseppi Garibaldi, an important figure in the nineteenth-century unification of Italy.

Independence Day in the United States: celebrates the signing of the Declaration of Independence in 1776.

July 5

Independence Day in Cape Verde: commemorates the country's 1975 independence from Portugal's colonial rule.

Independence Day in Venezuela: commemorates the 1811 declaration of independence from Spanish rule.

July 6

The Fiesta de San Fermin: includes the famous running of the bulls in Pamplona, Spain.

July 9

Independence Day in Argentina: marks the 1816 declaration of independence from Spain.

July 12

Orangeman's Day (Battle of the Boyne Day): dedicated to the anniversary of the 1690 Battle of the Boyne, a statutory public holiday in Northern Ireland.

July 13

Night Watch (La Retraite aux Flambeaux): French holiday celebrating the eve of the fall of the Bastille.

July 14

Bastille Day (Fête Nationale): French holiday commemorating the storming of the Bastille in 1789 and the release of political prisoners.

Iraq 1958 Revolution Day: commemorates the revolution ending Hashemite rule.

July 17

Constitution Day in South Korea: commemorates the adoption of the constitution in 1963.

July Revolution Day in Iraq (Peaceful Revolution Day): commemorates the Iraqi revolts of 1968.

Muñoz Rivera Day: marks the anniversary of the 1859 birth of Luis Muñoz Rivera, Puerto Rican patriot and journalist.

July 18

Constitution Day in Uruguay: commemorates the adoption of the 1951 constitution.

July 19

Sandinista Day: commemorates the revolution ending the rule of the Samoza regime in Nicaragua.

July 20

Independence Day in Colombia: celebrates the 1810 declaration of independence from Spanish rule.

July 21

Belgium Independence Day: commemorates the accession of the first Belgian king, Leopold I, following separation from the Netherlands in 1831.

Liberation Day in Guam: honors the freeing of the island from the Japanese in 1944.

July 22

Manifesto Day: commemorates the anniversary of the issuance of Catherine the Great's 1763 manifesto urging foreign colonists to settle in the Russian Empire, a date considered by many to be the "birthday" of the Germans from Russia.

Polish National Liberation Day: honors the end of World War II in 1944 and the enactment of a constitution in 1952.

July 23

Egyptian Revolution Anniversary Day: commemorates the 1952 revolutionary command terminating the Egyptian royal government and declaring the nation to be a republic.

July 24

Bolívar Day: celebrated in Ecuador and Venezuela to honor Simón Bolívar, known as the "George Washington of South America."

July 25

Constitution Day: honors the 1952 proclamation of Puerto Rico's constitution.

July 26

Bellman Day: honors the memory of Sweden's Carl Michael Bellman, an eighteenth-century troubadour.

Cuban Revolution Day: commemorates Fidel Castro's "26th of July Movement" of 1953 against the Batista military dictatorship.

July 27

Barbosa Day: honors the 1857 birth of José Celso Barbosa, black physician and political hero of nineteenth-century Puerto Rico.

Sovereignty Day in Belarus: marks the anniversary of the declaration of sovereignty in Belarus in 1990.

July 28

Peruvian Independence Day: commemorates the declaration of independence from Spain in 1821, which led to war and complete freedom in 1824.

July 30

Marseillaise Day: commemorates the first signing of the French national anthem, which took place in 1792 at the port city of Marseilles.

August 1

Swiss Confederation Day: celebrates the 1291 founding of the Swiss Confederation.

August 2

Constitution Day in Iceland: marks the anniversary of the granting of a constitution to the country in 1874 by the Danish king and commemorates the 874 settlement, according to legend, of the first Norwegians in Iceland.

Freedom Day in Guyana: commemorates the enactment of the Emancipation Act of 1837, which freed the slaves in the then colony of British Guiana.

August 7

Battle of Boyacá Day: Colombian holiday commemorating the victory of the South American insurgents over Spanish forces in 1819.

August 10

Ecuador Independence Day: commemorates the 1809 proclamation of independence.

August 14

Pakistan Independence Day: commemorates the establishment of Pakistan as a free nation in 1947.

August 15

Independence Day in India: commemorates the day the Indian Independence Act went into effect in 1947.

Republic Day in South Korea: commemorates the 1945 liberation of South Korea from Japanese occupation and the 1948 proclamation of the Republic of South Korea.

August 16

Cyprus Independence Day: marks the anniversary of the 1960 agreement between the British and the Greek and Turkish Cypriots to provide independence for Cyprus.

Dominican Restoration Day: commemorates the restoration of the Dominican Republic's independence in 1963.

August 17

Indonesia Independence Day: honors the proclamation of independence made by the Indonesian revolutionaries in 1945, although full independence for Indonesia did not come until 1949.

San Martín Day: commemorates the 1850 death of José Francisco de San Martín, Argentinean soldier and statesman.

August 20

Constitution Day in Hungary: commemorates the institution of the country's constitution in 1949.

August 23

Romanian Liberation Day: commemorates the 1944 coup that deposed the Fascist Iron Guard dictatorship.

August 25

Independence Day in Belarus: marks the anniversary of the declaration of the independence of Belarus in 1991.

August 30

Victory Day in Turkey: honors the memory of those individuals who died in the 1922 Battle of Dumlupinar, the final battle for Turkish independence.

August 31

Merdeka Day: celebrates Malaysia's achievement of the status of an independent member of the British Commonwealth in 1957; full independence was gained in 1963.

Trinidad and Tobago Independence Day: commemorates the independence achieved in 1962 within the British Commonwealth of Nations.

August (movable)

Pjodhatid: commemorates the granting of Iceland's constitution on July 1, 1874, which permitted the nation, formerly under Danish control, to handle its own domestic affairs.

August (movable; first Monday)

Jamaican Independence Day: commemorates the achievement of independence in 1962.

August–September (movable)

Mid-Autumn Festival: Asian celebration on the fifteenth day of the eighth moon to honor the moon goddess and mark the harvesttime with a day of thanksgiving.

September 3

Cromwell's Day: commemorates the day in 1650 when Oliver Cromwell led the British to victory in the Battle of Dunbar, the day in 1651 when he led the victory at the Battle of Worcester against the Scots, and the day in 1658 on which he died.

Treaty of Paris Day: marks the anniversary of the 1783 signing of the treaty between the United States and England ending the American Revolution.

September 7

Brazilian Independence Day: honors Dom Pedro's 1822 proclamation of independence from Portugal.

September 9

Bulgarian National Day: memorializes the 1944 joining of the Bulgarian partisans and Soviet troops to drive out the Nazis.

September 11

Enkutatash (Ethiopian New Year): marks the first day of the Ethiopian month of Maskarem, which coincides with the end of the rainy season.

Jinnah Day: marks the anniversary of the 1948 death of Quaid-i-Azam Mohammed Ali Jinnah, the founder of a free and independent Pakistan.

September 12

National Day in Ethiopia: commemorates the 1974 termination of the Ethiopian Empire and the deposing of Haile Selassie.

September 14

Battle of San Jacinto Day: commemorates the Nicaraguan defeat of foreign invaders in 1856.

September 15

Central American Independence Day: observed in El Salvador, Guatemala, Honduras, and Nicaragua to commemorate the overthrow of Spanish rule in 1821.

September 16

Mexican Independence Day: commemorates the country's establishment of independence.

September 18

Independence Day in Chile: commemorates the declaration of independence from Spain, although complete independence was not gained until February 12, 1818.

September 19

Chilean Armed Forces Day: celebrated as part of the independence festivities.

September 21

Armenian Independence Day: commemorates the founding of the Second Republic in 1991.

September (movable)

Odwira: celebrates the national identity of the Asante people of Ghana.

September (movable; first Monday)

Labor Day: established as a national holiday in Canada and the United States to honor the worker.

September–October (movable)

Festival of the Kites: observed on the ninth day of the ninth moon as a Chinese family-remembrance day to honor ancestors with visits to their graves and to go to the hills for picnics and kite flying, since kites are believed to carry misfortune into the skies.

Oktoberfest: first celebrated in honor of the 1810 marriage of Crown Prince Ludwig of Bavaria to Princess Therese von Saxe-Hildburghausen, Oktoberfest now serves as a celebration of German ancestry.

October 1

National Day in China: commemorates the establishment of the People's Republic of China in 1949.

October 2

Gandhi Day: commemorates the 1869 birth of Mahatma Gandhi, a dominant political figure in India's struggle for independence.

October 3

Leyden Day: celebration in the Netherlands commemorating the lifting of the Siege of Leyden in 1574 through a storm that carried the Spanish fleet out into the ocean.

Morazán Day: honors Francisco Morazán, an early nineteenth-century Honduran statesman whose dream was a unified Central America.

October 5

Portuguese Republic Day: honors the proclamation of the republic in 1910.

October 6

Armed Forces Day in Egypt: marks the surprise attack on Israel that began the October War of 1973.

October 9

Day of National Dignity: marks the anniversary of the Peruvian government's seizure of the oil fields on behalf of the Peruvian nation; often regarded as a second Independence Day.

Guayaquil Independence Day: marks the 1820 declaration of the Ecuadorian city's independence.

Leif Eriksson Day: celebrated in Iceland and Norway to honor the landing of the Norsemen in Vinland around 100 C.E.

October 10

Aleksis Kivi Day: honors the 1834 birth of the "Father of the Finnish novel and drama."

National Day in Taiwan: commemorates the anniversary of the Proclamation of the Republic in 1911.

October 11

Beginning of Independence Wars Day: honors the guerrilla wars of the 1950s that were led by Fidel Castro to overthrow the Batista regime.

Panama Revolution Day: commemorates the 1968 revolt.

Pulaski Day: honors Count Casimir Pulaski, who, upon being forced to flee Poland because of his efforts to preserve Polish independence, fought in the American Revolution and died in a 1779 battle to free Savannah, Georgia, from British control.

October 12

Dia de la Raza (Day of the Race): celebration in Latin American countries paying tribute to the contributions of Spanish civilization to the American continent.

National Day in Spain: honors the landfall of Christopher Columbus in the New World.

October 14

Yemen National Day: honors the revolts of 1962.

October 17

Dessalines Day: commemorates the 1806 death of Jean Jacques Dessalines, a revolutionist who was proclaimed emperor of Haiti in 1805.

October 20

Guatemala Revolution Day: commemorates the revolution of 1944.

October 21

Honduras Army Day: commemorates the 1956 revolt.

October 23

Chulalongkorn Day: commemorates the 1868 birth of Rama V, a progressive ruler who abolished slavery in Thailand (then called Siam) and introduced numerous reforms.

Revolution Day in Hungary: marks the anniversary of the 1956 revolution.

October 24

United Nations Day: commemorates the 1945 founding of the United Nations in the wake of World War II.

October 26

Austria National Day: commemorates the passing of the neutrality law by the Austrian parliament in 1955.

October 28

Greek National Day: commemorates the anniversary of Greece's successful resistance to Italian aggression in 1940.

October 29

Turkey's Republic Day: commemorates the 1923 proclamation of the republic.

October 31

Halloween (All Hallows Eve): ancient Celtic harvest festival.

October (movable; second Monday)

Canadian Thanksgiving Day: commemorates the arrival of the fall harvest.

November 1

Day of the Awakeners (Den na Buditelite): commemorates the patriots, writers, and revolutionaries who helped foster the spirit of Bulgarian nationalism.

November 2

Balfour Declaration Day: celebration, observed particularly by Jews in Israel, to mark the 1917 establishment of a Jewish national home.

November 3

Cuenca Independence Day: marks the 1820 declaration of the Ecuadorian city's independence.

Independence Day in Panama: commemorates the 1903 declaration establishing Panama's independence from Colombia.

November 4

Panama Flag Day: celebrated in conjunction with the country's independence festivities.

Victory of Vittorio Veneto: honors the Italian Unknown Soldier.

November 5

First Cry for Independence Day: commemorates the first battle for El Salvador's freedom from Spain.

Guy Fawkes Day: marks the anniversary of the 1605 "Gunpowder Plot" to blow up England's parliament and the king.

November 6

Gustavus Adolphus Day: honors the Swedish king who laid the foundations of the modern Swedish state, turned the country into a major European power, and died in battle in 1632.

November 7

Bangladesh Revolution Day: marks the anniversary of the 1975 takeover of the government by the military.

November 9

Crystal Night: marks the anniversary of the street riots of November 9 and 19, 1938, when Nazi storm troopers raided Jewish homes and synagogues; the name comes from the shattering of glass in Jewish homes and stores.

Iqbal Day: marks the anniversary of the 1877 birth of Muhammad Iqbal, Pakistan's philosopher-poet.

November 11

Independence Day in Poland: commemorates the restoration of Polish independence in 1918.

Veterans Day: originally called Armistice Day and observed to commemorate the signing of the 1918 armistice between the Allied and Central Powers that marked the end of World War I, it was later renamed Veterans Day and expanded to honor those who served their countries in other wars as well.

November 15

Republic Day in Brazil: honors the 1889 proclamation that dethroned Dom Pedro II.

November 18

Vertières Day: commemorates the 1803 defeat of the French by the Haitian army in the Battle of Vertières.

November 19

Settlement Day: commemorates the arrival of Garifuna in Belize but is observed in the United States as a day of ethnic celebration of Garifuna for all nationalities.

November 20

Mexico Revolution Day: marks the anniversary of the Mexican Revolution of 1910.

November 22

Lebanese Independence Day: celebrates Lebanon's achievement of independence in 1943.

November 28

Albanian Independence Day: commemorates the 1912 proclamation of independence, issued at the end of the Balkan War, which terminated Turkish rule.

November 29

Albanian Liberation Day: celebrates the 1944 withdrawal of foreign troops.

November 30

Barbados Independence Day: commemorates the island's becoming an independent member of the British Commonwealth of Nations in 1966.

Bonifacio Day (National Heroes' Day): commemorates the birth of Andres Bonifacio, the Philippine patriot who led the 1896 revolt against the Spanish.

November (movable; fourth Thursday)

U.S. Thanksgiving Day: commemorates the Pilgrims' 1621 harvest feast that celebrated the completion of their first year in the Plymouth Colony.

December 1

Iceland National Day: marks the anniversary of the 1918 treaty recognizing Iceland as an independent state under the Danish crown.

December 1

National Day in Romania: commemorates the unification in 1918 of Romania and Transylvania and the formation of the Romanian State.

December 2

Republic Day in Laos: commemorates the founding of the Lao People's Democratic Republic in 1975.

December 6

Finnish Independence Day: commemorates the 1917 declaration of freedom from Russia.

December 10

Thailand Constitution Day: commemorates the 1932 constitution, the first for the Thai.

December 11

Scaling Day (Escalade): honors the night in 1602 when the citizens of Geneva, Switzerland, routed the Savoyards, who were scaling the walls of the city.

December 16

Bangladesh Victory Day: commemorates the end of the 1971 conflict with Pakistan.

Nepal Constitution Day: honors the 1962 adoption of a constitution for the Kingdom of Nepal.

December 25

Taiwan Constitution Day: honors the 1946 adoption of the constitution.

December 26

Boxing Day: customary day for distributing gifts to public servants and employees.

Kwanzaa: marks the first day of a seven-day celebration of oneness in the African-American community that honors the seven principles of unity, self-determination, collective work and responsibility, cooperative economics, purpose, creativity, and faith.

December 30

Rizal Day: commemorates the 1896 death of José Mercado Rizal, Philippine doctor and author whose books denouncing the Spanish administration were an inspiration to the Philippine nationalist movement.

December 31

Evacuation Day: celebrated the withdrawal of French troops from Lebanon in 1946.

Appendix C
Religious Holidays

BAHA'I HOLIDAYS

February 26

Ayyam-i-Ha: marks the first of the four (five in leap years) intercalary days in the Baha'i calendar, a calendar made up of nineteen months of nineteen days each; Ayyam-i-Ha is followed by a nineteen-day fasting period (from March 2 through March 20), which in turn is followed by the Baha'i New Year's Day (Now Ruz) on March 21.

April 21

Feast of Ridvan: marks the first day of the twelve-day celebration commemorating the 1863 declaration by Mirza Husain Ali Nuri (Baha Allah), the founder of the Baha'i religion, that he was God's messenger for the age.

May 23

Declaration of the Bab: celebrates the announcement by Mirza Ali Muhammad Shirazi, that he was the "gate" (the Bab) to the coming of the promised one of all religions, a proclamation considered to be the beginning of the Baha'i religion.

May 29

Ascension of Baha Allah: marks the anniversary of the 1892 death of Mirza Husain Ali Nuri, the founder of the Baha'i religion.

July 9

Martyrdom of the Bab: commemorates the 1850 execution of Mirza Ali Muhammad Shirazi, the first prophet of the Baha'i religion.

October 20

Birth of the Bab: celebrates the 1819 birth of Mirza Ali Muhammad Shirazi, who was the founder of the Babi faith and considered by those in the Baha'i religion to be the herald whose chief task was to announce the advent of the dispensation of Baha Allah (the founder of the Baha'i religion).

November 12

Birth of Baha Allah: marks the anniversary of the 1817 birth of Mirza Husain Ali Nuri, the founder of the Baha'i religion.

November 26

Day of the Covenant: commemorates the covenant that Baha Allah, the founder of the Baha'i religion, made with humanity and his followers, appointing his eldest son, Abd al-Baha, to be the head of the Baha'i religion and interpret Baha'i teachings.

November 28

Ascension of Abd al-Baha: commemorates the 1921 death of Abbas Effendi, the eldest son of the founder of the Baha'i religion, Mirza Husain Ali Nuri.

BUDDHIST HOLIDAYS

Margasirsa (the nineteenth day)

Birthday of the Goddess of Mercy: honors Kuan Yin, the goddess of infinite compassion and mercy.

Magha (full Moon)

Magha Puja: commemorates the occasion when 1,250 followers ordained by the Buddha arrived by coincidence at Veluvan monastery in Rajagriha, India, to hear him lay down monastic regulations and predict his own death.

Phalguna (the sixth day)

Airing the Classics: commemorates the time when the boat carrying the Buddhist scriptures from India to China was upset at a river crossing and all the books had to be spread to dry.

Vaisakha (full moon)

Vesak (Buddha Purnima): commemorates the Buddha's birth, enlightenment, and attainment of Nirvana.

Jyaistha (full moon)

Poson: commemorates the bringing of Buddhism to Sri Lanka in the third century B.C.E.

Asadha (the twenty-fifth day)

Ganden Ngamcho (Festival of Lights): commemorates the birth and death of Tsongkhapa (1357–1419), a saintly scholar and teacher in Tibetan Buddhism, whose successors became the Dalai Lamas.

Asadha to Asvina

Waso (Buddhist Lent): three-month period of abstinence and meditation, the day prior to that which commemorates the Buddha's first sermon to his five disciples, forty-nine days after his enlightenment.

CHRISTIAN HOLIDAYS

January 1

St. Basil's Day: celebrated in Greece to honor the fourth-century bishop of Caesarea.

January 5

Twelfth Night: celebrated the evening before Epiphany as the traditional end to the Christmas season.

January 6

Feast of the Epiphany: commemorates the worshiping of Jesus by the Three Kings (emphasized in Roman Catholic and Protestant churches) and the baptism of Jesus (emphasized in Eastern Orthodox churches), the first two occasions on which Christ was manifested. Epiphany is observed on January 19 by the Eastern Orthodox Churches, which base religious observations on the Julian calendar.

January 8

St. Gudula's Day: honors the patron saint of Brussels.

January 13

St. Knut's Day: observed as the Swedish day for dismantling Christmas trees.
Tyvendedagen: celebrates the official end of the Yuletide in Norway.

January 15

Feast of Christ of Esquipulas (The Black Christ Festival): observed at Esquipulas in Guatemala and named after a figure of Christ that was carved out of dark brown balsam.

January 19

St. Henry of Uppsala's Day: honoring the patron saint of Finland.

January 21

St. Altagracia's Day: celebrated in the Dominican Republic with a pilgrimage to the St. Altagracia shrine.

January 26

St. Nino's Day: honors St. Nino of Cappadocia, who introduced Christianity to Georgia in the fourth century.

January 27

St. Sava's Day: a Serbian children's festival in honor of St. Sava, a king's son who built schools and monasteries all over Serbia.

January 30

St. Charles's Day: observed in commemoration of the 1649 execution of King Charles I for his defense of the Anglican church.

February 1

St. Bridget's Day: honors the patron saint of Ireland who established the first Irish convent, around which the city of Kildare eventually grew.

February 2

Candlemas (Feast of the Purification of the Blessed Virgin Mary): the blessing of candles is a great tradition of the Roman Catholic and Anglican observance that is particularly popular in Mexico and other Latin American countries.

February 2–March 8 (movable)

Shrove Monday: observed the Monday before Ash Wednesday as a preparation day for Lent.

February 3

St. Anskar's Day: honors the patron saint of Denmark, who was a missionary to Denmark, Sweden, Norway, and northern Germany.

February 3–March 9 (movable)

Shrove Tuesday (Mardi Gras): celebrated the day before Ash Wednesday as the last day of preparation for Lent.

February 4–March 10 (movable)

Ash Wednesday: marks the first day of Lent, the forty-day period of abstinence before Palm Sunday, recalling the fasts of Moses, Elijah, and Jesus.

February 14

St. Cyril and St. Methodius's Day: honors the two brothers from Thessalonica who became the "Apostles of the Slavs" and created the Glagolithic alphabet (from which the Cyrillic alphabet was later derived) to aid in their mission. (The feast day is observed on May 24 by Eastern Orthodox churches, which calculate religious dates according to the Julian calendar.)

March 1

St. David's Day: honors the patron saint of Wales, who founded many churches in southern Wales in the sixth century and moved the seat of ecclesiastical government from Caerleon to Mynyw, the present cathedral city of Saint David's.

March 4

St. Casimir's Day: honors the patron saint of Poland and Lithuania.

March 15–April 18 (movable)

Palm Sunday: celebrated on the Sunday preceding Easter to commemorate the arrival of Jesus in Jerusalem, where palm branches, the symbol of victory, were spread before him by the people who viewed him as the leader who would deliver them from the domination of the Roman Empire.

March 17

St. Patrick's Day: honors the patron saint of Ireland who, after becoming a bishop, returned to Ireland about 432 as a missionary to the pagans.

March 18–April 21 (movable)

Spy Wednesday: observed on the Wednesday before Easter to commemorate the betrayal of Jesus by Judas Iscariot in the Garden of Gethsemane.

March 19

St. Joseph's Day: honors the patron saint of Belgium and Colombia.

March 19–April 22 (movable)

Maundy Thursday: celebrated the Thursday before Easter to commemorate Jesus Christ's institution of the Eucharist in the Last Supper.

March 20–April 23 (movable)

Good Friday: observed on the Friday before Easter to commemorate the crucifixion of Jesus.

March 21–April 24 (movable)

Holy Saturday: celebrated on the day before Easter, bringing the season of Lent to a close.

March 22

St. Nicholas von Flüe's Day: honors the patron saint of Switzerland.

March 22–April 25 (movable)

Easter: celebrated the first Sunday after the first full moon on or following the vernal equinox to commemorate the anniversary of Jesus Christ's resurrection from the dead.

March 25

Feast of the Annunciation (Lady Day): celebrates the appearance of the Archangel Gabriel to the Virgin Mary announcing that she was to become the mother of Jesus.

April 2

Martyrdom of Blessed Diego Luis de San Vitores: commemorates the 1672 death of the priest who introduced Catholicism to Guam.

April 23

St. George's Day: honors the patron saint of England, Canada, Portugal, Germany, Genoa, and Venice.

May 10–June 13 (movable)

Pentecost (Whitsunday, Pinkster Day): celebrated on the seventh Sunday (fifty days) after Easter to commemorate the Holy Spirit's visit to the Apostles, giving them the gift of tongues that allowed them to preach about Jesus Christ to people all over the world.

May 15

St. Isidore the Husbandman's Day: honors the patron saint of Madrid.

May 18

St. Eric of Sweden's Day: honors the patron saint of Sweden.

May 30

St. Joan's Day: honors Joan of Arc, who helped save the French city of Orleans from the British in the fifteenth century.

May (movable)

Ascension Day (Holy Thursday): celebrated forty days after Easter to commemorate Jesus Christ's ascension to heaven.

May (third week)

Carabao Festival: honors San Isidro Labrador (St. Isidore the Farmer), the patron saint of the Filipino farmer.

June 5

St. Boniface's Day: honors the patron saint of Germany.
St. Euphrosynia of Polack's Day: honors the patron saint of Belarus.

June 9

St. Columba's Day: honors the patron saint of Ireland who went into self-imposed exile on the island of Iona, where he founded a monastery and school from which he and his disciples preached the Gospel.

June 13

St. Anthony of Padua's Day: honors the patron saint of Portugal.

June 24

Feast of the Nativity of St. John the Baptist: celebration, especially by the French in Canada, of the birth of the cousin of Jesus.

June 28

St. Vitus's Day: commemorates the Serbian defeat by the Turks at Kosovo in 1389.

July 8

St. Elizabeth's Day: honors the saint who was the mother of John the Baptist and a cousin of the Virgin Mary.

July 25

St. James the Great's Day: honors the patron saint of Chile and Spain.

July 26

St. Anne's Day: honors the patron saint of Canada.

July 28

St. Prince Vladimir of Kiev's Day: honors (with celebrations of the Russian culture involving lectures, readings, and concerts) the saint who introduced Christianity to ancient Rus in 988.

July 29

St. Olav's Day: commemorates the death of Olav Haraldsson (the second King Olav), who brought Christianity to Norway and was later killed in the Battle of Stiklestad in 1030.

August 15

Feast of the Assumption: commemorates the belief that when Mary, the mother of Jesus, died, her body did not decay but was assumed into heaven and reunited there with her soul.

August 25

St. Louis's Day: honors the patron saint of France.

August 30

Rose of Lima Day: honors the patron saint of South America and the Philippines.

September 8

Feast of the Nativity of the Blessed Virgin Mary: celebrates the birth of Mary, the mother of Jesus.

September 14

Feast of the Exaltation of the Cross: commemorates the finding of the cross on which Jesus was crucified, the dedication of a basilica built in 335 on the supposed site of Christ's crucifixion on Golgotha, and the recovery in 629 of the relic of the cross that had been stolen by the Persians.

September 28

St. Vaclav's Day: honors the patron saint, widely known as Good King Wenceslas, of the Czech Republic.

September 29

Michaelmas: honors St. Michael, traditionally viewed as the leader of the heavenly host of angels.

October 4

St. Francis of Assisi's Day: honors the patron saint of Italy.

October 9

St. Denis's Day: honors the patron saint of France.

October 15

St. Teresa of Avila's Day: honors the patron saint of Spain.

October 18

El Señor de los Milagros Day: honors the patron saint of Peru with special services and foods, as well as the wearing of purple, the symbolic color of the saint.

October 26

St. Demetrius's Day: honors the patron saint of Greece.

November 1

All Saints' Day: celebration of all Christian saints, particularly those that do not have special feast days of their own.

November 2

All Souls' Day: commemorates the souls of all the faithful departed.

November 8

Saints, Doctors, Missionaries, and Martyrs Day: celebrated in England in memory and commemoration of the "unnamed saints of the nation."

November 11

Beggar's Day in the Netherlands: honors St. Martin with children dressing as beggars and going from door to door.

November 30

St. Andrew's Day: honors the patron saint of Scotland, Russia, and Greece.

November (movable; Sunday closest to November 30)

Advent: marks the beginning of the Christian year and consists of a period varying in length from twenty-two to twenty-eight days, beginning on the Sunday nearest to St. Andrew's Day and encompassing the next three Sundays, ending on Christmas Eve.

December 4

St. Barbara's Day: celebrated in parts of France, Germany, and Syria as the beginning of the Christmas season.

December 6

St. Nicholas's Day: honors the patron saint of Russia and children.

December 12

Festival of Our Lady of Guadalupe: religious ceremony commemorating the appearance of the Blessed Virgin to an Indian boy in Mexico in 1531.

December 13

St. Lucia's Day: Swedish celebration of the festival of lights honoring St. Lucia, the "Queen of Light."

December 16

Posadas: marks the first day of a nine-day celebration in Mexico commemorating the journey Mary and Joseph took from Nazareth to Bethlehem, where Jesus was born.

December 25

Christmas Day: Christian celebration of the birth of Jesus. Christmas is celebrated on January 7 by Eastern Orthodox churches, which base religious observations on the Julian calendar.

December 26

St. Stephen's Day: honors the patron saint of Hungary.

December 28

Holy Innocents' Day: commemorates the massacre of all male children under two years of age ordered by King Herod in an attempt to kill the baby Jesus.

December 31

St. Sylvester's Day: honors the saint who was pope in 325, the year Emperor Constantine declared the pagan religion of Rome abolished in favor of Christianity.

CONFUCIAN HOLIDAY

September 28

Confucius's Birthday: commemorates the birth in the sixth century B.C.E. of the Chinese philosopher and teacher.

HINDU HOLIDAYS

Karttika (fifteenth day of the waning moon)

Divali (Deepavali, Festival of Lights): commemorates Rama's rescue of Sita from Ravana, an important episode in the *Mahabrahata*, and marks the Hindu New Year.

Phalguna (fourteenth day of the waxing moon)

Holi: a Hindu spring festival marking the triumph of Good over Evil with celebrants throwing red and yellow powder over one another and lighting bonfires to remember the burning of the demoness Holika.

Phalguna (full moon)

Dol Purnima: commemorates the birthday of Chaitanya Mahaprabhu (1486–1534), also known as Gauranga, the sixteenth-century Vishnavite saint and poet of Bengal who is regarded as an incarnation of Krishna.

Phalguna (full moon)

Meenakshi Kalyanam: honors the marriage of the goddess Meenakshi, an incarnation of Parvati, and the Lord Shiva.

Phalguna (thirteenth day of the waning moon)

Shivaratri: commemorates the night Lord Shiva, the god of destruction and the restorer, danced the Tandav, his celestial dance of creation, preservation, and destruction.

Caitra

Hanuman Jayanti: honors Hanuman, the Monkey-God and central figure in the Hindu epic *Ramayana*.

Caitra (ninth day of the waxing moon)

Ramanavami (Ram Navami): honors the birth of Rama, the seventh incarnation of Lord Vishnu.

Jyaistha

Ganga Dussehra: honors the healing power of the Ganges River, which originally flowed only in heaven but was brought down to earth in the form of the goddess Ganga by King Bhagiratha to purify the ashes of his ancestors.

Jyaistha (sixth day of the waxing moon)

Sithinakha: honors the birthday of Kumara, the Hindu god of war and the firstborn son of Lord Shiva.

Sravana (waxing moon)

Naag Panchami: honors the sacred serpent Ananta, on whose coils Lord Vishnu rested while he created the universe.

Sravana (fourteenth day of the waning moon)

Ghanta Karna: commemorates the death of Ghanta Karna, who caused death and destruction wherever he went until a god in the form of a frog persuaded him to leap into a well, after which the people beat him to death and dragged his body to the river for cremation.

Bhadrapada (waxing moon)

Ganesh Chathurthi: honors Ganesh, the elephant-headed Hindu god of wisdom and success.

Bhadrapada (waning moon)

Indra Jatra: eight-day celebration to pay homage to the recently deceased and to honor the Hindu god Indra and his mother, Dagini, so they will bless the coming harvest.

Bhadrapada (new moon)

Janmashtami (Krishnastami; Krishna's Birthday): celebrates the birthday of Lord Krishna, the eighth incarnation of Vishnu.

Asvina (waxing moon)

Durga Puja: honors Durga, one aspect of the Mother Goddess and the personification of energy, who rides a lion and destroys demons.

IGBO HOLIDAYS

April

Awuru Odo Festival: celebrated among the Igbo people of Nigeria in honor of the biannual visit of the Odo (the spirits of the dead).

August–September

Agwunsi Festival: honors the god of healing and divination among the Igbo people of Nigeria.

September

Okpesi Festival: ceremony of the Igbo people of Nigeria honoring their ancestors.

ISLAMIC HOLIDAYS

Muharram (first day)

Ashura: commemorates the death of Muhammad's grandson, Hussein, in the year 680 C.E. during a battle between Sunnis and the group of Shiite supporters with whom he was traveling.

Rabi I (the twelfth day)

Mawlid al-Nabi (Prophet's Birthday): honors the birth of the Prophet Muhammad, the founder of Islam, who was born in Mecca in 570 C.E.

Rajab (the twenty-seventh day)

Laylat al Miraj: commemorates the ascent of the Prophet Muhammad into Heaven.

Shaban (night of the fifteenth)

Shab-Barat: a period of intense prayer in preparation for Ramadan during which individuals ask Allah to forgive the people who they know have died.

Ramadan

Ramadan: the holiest period of the Islamic year commemorates the time when the Koran, the Islamic holy book, was revealed to the Prophet Muhammad. Devout Muslims abstain from food, drink, smoking, sex, and gambling from sunrise to sunset during this period.

Ramadan (last ten days)

Laylat al-Qadr: commemorates the night in 610 C.E. when Allah revealed the entire Koran to Muhammad.

Shawwal (first day)

Id al-Fitr (Feast of Fast Breaking): marks the end of the monthlong fasting period of Ramadan.

Dhu al-Hijjah (between the eight and thirteenth days)

Hajj (Pilgrimage to Mecca): a fundamental duty of each Muslim to be completed at least once in a lifetime.

Dhu al-Hijjah

Id al-Adha (Feast of Sacrifice): three-day feast serving as the concluding rite for those performing a pilgrimage to Mecca and, for those not performing a pilgrimage, as a commemoration of Ibrahim's (Abraham') near sacrifice of his son.

JAIN HOLIDAYS

Caitra (thirteenth day of the waxing moon)

Mahavir Jayanti: honors Vardhamana Jnatrputra, who lived during the fifth century B.C.E. and is regarded by the Jains as the twenty-fourth and last in a series of Tirthankaras (Enlightened Teachers).

Bhadrapada

Paryushana: a festival to focus on the ten cardinal virtues (forgiveness, charity, simplicity, contentment, truthfulness, self-restraint, fasting, detachment, humility, and continence) by individuals asking those whom they may have offended for forgiveness and restoring lapsed friendships.

JEWISH HOLIDAYS

Tishri (the first day)

Rosh Ha-Shanah: marks the first day of the two-day observance of the Jewish New Year, which are also the first two days of the ten High Holy Days that conclude with Yom Kippur, the Day of Atonement.

Tishri (the third day)

Tsom Gedaliah (Fast of Gedaliah): fast to commemorate the assassination of Gedaliah ben Ahikam, the Jewish governor left in charge by King Nebuchadnezzar to administer the affairs of Judah after the destruction of Jerusalem and the fall of the First Temple in 586 B.C.E.

Tishri (the tenth day)

Yom Kippur (Day of Atonement): the holiest and most solemn day in the Jewish calendar and the last of the ten High Holy Days (Days of Penitence) that begin with the Jewish New Year (Rosh Ha-Shanah).

Tishri (the fifteenth day)

Sukkot: marks the first day of the eight-day commemoration of the forty years after the Exodus that Jews wandered in the desert under the leadership of Moses.

Tishri (the twenty-first day)

Hoshana Rabbah: considered to be the last possible day on which one can seek forgiveness for the sins of the preceding year.

Tishri (the twenty-second day)

Shemini Atzeret (Eighth Day of Solemn Assembly): marks the eighth day of the festival of Sukkot but is celebrated as a separate holiday dedicated to the love of God.

Tishri (the twenty-third day)

Simhat Torah: celebrates the annual completion of the public reading of the Torah, the first five books of the Bible.

Kislev (the twenty-fifth day)

Hanukkah: marks the first day of an eight-day celebration to commemorate the successful rebellion of the Jews against the Syrians in the Maccabean War of 162 B.C.E. and the associated miracle of a small bottle of consecrated oil for the menorah (perpetual lamp) lasting eight days until more could be obtained.

Tevet (the tenth day)

Asarah be-Tevet (Tenth of Tevet): fast day commemorating the beginning of the siege of Jerusalem by the Babylonians under King Nebuchadnezzar in 586 B.C.E. that was a prelude to the destruction of the First Temple.

Nisan

Hagodol: observed on the Sabbath just prior to Passover to commemorate the Sabbath before the Exodus from Egypt that ended more than four hundred years of slavery.

Nisan (the fifteenth day)

Passover: marks the first day of the eight-day celebration of the deliverance of the Jews from slavery in Egypt.

Nisan (the twenty-seventh day)

Yom Hashoah (Holocaust Day): observed, as a memorial to the six million Jews killed by the Nazis between 1933 and 1945, on the anniversary of the date on which the Allied troops liberated the first Nazi concentration camp, Buchenwald, in Germany, in 1945.

Sivan (the sixth day)

Shavuot: observed fifty days after Passover to mark the end of the barley harvest and the beginning of the wheat harvest and to celebrate the return of Moses from the top of Mt. Sinai with the Ten Commandments, the fundamental laws of the Jewish faith.

Tammuz (the seventeenth day)

Shivah Asar be-Tammuz (Fast of the Seventeenth of Tammuz): commemorates the breaching of the walls of Jerusalem in 586 B.C.E., when the Babylonians conquered Judah, destroyed the First Temple, and carried most of the Jewish population off into slavery.

Av (the ninth day)

Tishah be-Av (Fast of Av): a twenty-four-hour period of fasting, lamentation, and prayer in memory of the destruction of both the First Temple (586 B.C.E.) and the Second Temple (70 C.E.) in Jerusalem.

ZOROASTRIAN HOLIDAYS

January 30

Joshne Sadeh: celebration of the fire-building festival with people saying prayers as they circle large bonfires.

March 16

> Pange Porse Hamagoni: observed on the first of the five days preceding New Year's day as the second of the two days of the year for commemoration of all deaths.

March 27

> Tavalode Zartosht: observed six days after Nawruz (the Iranian New Year) to commemorate Zoroaster's birthday and the day he was named the prophet.

April 3

> Sizda be Dar: observed on the thirteenth day after the New Year with traditional picnics and the throwing out of the greens (from the New Year's table), which helps a young woman find a mate.

June 14

> Ziarat Pir Sabz: a pilgrimage to Pir Sabz, a shrine (the most important of all shrines for most Zoroastrians) near Yazd in Iran.

June 19

> Porse Hamagoni: the first of two celebrations commemorating all deaths together.

July 1

> Tirgan: celebration of the water (or rain) festival.

September 2

> Joshne Mehregan: celebration of the fall festival.

Article Sources

The following articles in **Macmillan Profiles**: *Festivals and Holidays* were newly written for this title:

Article	Author
Abu Simbel Festival	Brigit Dermott
All Saints' Day	Mark LaFlaur
All Souls' Day	Mark LaFlaur
Anzac Day	Geraldine Azzata
Armed Forces Day	Geraldine Azzata
Ash Wednesday	Mary Mary Carvlin
Bastille Day	Mark LaFlaur
Boxing Day	Michael Levine
Butter Sculpture Festival	Patricia Ohlenroth
Canada Day	Mary Mary Carvlin
Cinco de Mayo	Mary Mary Carvlin
Columbus Day	Michael Levine
Confederate Memorial Day	Mark LaFlaur
Confucius Birthday	Patricia Ohlenroth
Corpus Christi	Mary Mary Carvlin
Day of the Dead	Mary Mary Carvlin
Dionysia	Mary Mary Carvlin
Dragon Boat Festival	Patricia Ohlenroth
Earth Day	Mary Carvlin
Emancipation Day	Michael Levine
Fastelavn	Mark LaFlaur
Feast of Our Lady of Gaudalupe	Mary Carvlin
Feast of Saint Francis of Assisi Feast	Mary Carvlin
Flag Day	Geraldine Azzata
Great American Smokeout	Mary Carvlin
Groundhog Day	Geraldine Azzata
Guy Fawkes Day	Mark LaFlaur
Hiroshima Peace Day	Patricia Ohlenroth

The remaining articles in **Macmillan Profiles**: *Festivals and Holidays* were adapted from articles in *The Encyclopedia of Religion*, published by Macmillan Library Reference in 1987; *Encyclopedia of Africa South of the Sahara*, published by Charles Scribner's Sons, 1997; and the *Encyclopedia of Latin American History and Culture*, published by Charles Scribner's Sons, 1996.

Article	Author
April Fools' Day	Leonard Norman Primiano
Anthesteria	Klaus-Peter Koepping
Ashura	Mahmoud M. Ayoub
Buddha's Day	Donald K. Swearer
Carnival	Maria Julia Goldwasser
Chinese New Year	Laurence G. Thompson
Christmas	John F. Baldovin, S.J.
Divali	Maire Louise-Reiniche
Easter	John F. Baldovin, S.J.
Epiphany	John F. Baldovin, S.J.
Fiestas in Latin America	Amalia Cortina Aravena
Halloween	Leonard Norman Primiano
Hanukkah	Louis Jacobs
Holi	Maire Louise-Reiniche
Kumbh Mela	William S. Sax
Masquerades in Africa	Mary Jo Arnoldi
Mawlid	Dale F. Eickelman
Medieval Festivals in Europe	Madeleine Pelner Cosman
May Day	John Forrest
Navaratri	Maire Louise-Reiniche
Nawruz	Ehsan Yarshater
Passover	Louis Jacobs
Potlatch	Stanley Walens
Purim	Louis Jacobs
Rosh Ha-Shanah and Yom Kipper	Louis Jacobs
Shavuoth	Louis Jacobs
Sukkot	Louis Jacobs
Sun Dance	Joseph Epes Brown

Photo Credits

Abu Simbel Festival (page 2): CORBIS/Roger Wood
All Souls' Day (page 8): Victor Englebert
Anzac Day (page 14): CORBIS/Richard Glover
Arbor Day (page 20): CORBIS/Joseph Sohm; ChromoSohm Inc.
Arbor Day (page 21): CORBIS/Dan Lamont
Ash Wednesday (page 26): PhotoEdit/Stephen McBrady
Bastille Day (page 32): CORBIS/Charles & Josette Lenars
Bastille Day (page 33): CORBIS/Owen Franklin
Buddha's Day (page 40): Reuters/Jonathan Drake/Archive Photos
Butter Sculpture Festival (page 43): CORBIS/Tom Nebbia
Canada Day (page 46): CORBIS/Earl Kowall
Canada Day (page 48): CORBIS/Michael S. Yamashita
Carnival (page 51): Aldo Torelli/Tony Stone Images
Carnival (page 54): CORBIS/Stephanie Maze
Chinese New Year (page 61): CORBIS/Douglas Peebles
Christmas (page 66): CORBIS/Mark Theissen
Christmas (page 67): CORBIS/Danny Lehman
Cinco de Mayo (page 70): CORBIS/Richard Cummins
Cinco de Mayo (page 71): CORBIS/Richard Cummins
Columbus Day (page 75): PhotoEdit/Spencer Grant
Confederate Memorial Day (page 79): PhotoEdit/Robert Ginn
Confucius's Birthday (page 82): Reuters/C. Yao/Archive Photos
Corpus Christi (page 85): Victor Englebert
Day of the Dead (page 89): CORBIS/Charles & Josette Lenars
Day of the Dead (page 90): CORBIS/Danny Lehman
Divali (page 96): CORBIS/Lindsay Hebberd
Dragon Boat Festival (page 99): CORBIS/Derek M. Allan; Travel Ink
Earth Day (page 103): CORBIS/D. Robert Franz
Earth Day (page 104): CORBIS/Todd Gipstein
Easter (page 109): PhotoEdit/Paul Conklin
Father's Day (page 122): Superstock
Feast of Our Lady of Guadalupe (page 124): CORBIS/Danny Lehman

Feast of St. Francis of Assisi (page 127): PhotoEdit/Richard Lord
Flag Day (page 135): Jeffrey Markowitz/Sygma
Groundhog Day (page 140): Keith B. Srakocic/AP/Wide World Photos
Halloween (page 147): CORBIS/Joseph Sohm; ChromoSohm Inc.
Halloween (page 149): CORBIS/Annie Griffiths Belt
Hanukkah (page 152): PhotoEdit/Michael Newman
Hiroshima Day (page 155): CORBIS/David Samuel Robbins
Holi (page 161): CORBIS/Lindsay Hebberd
Holy Week (page 165): CORBIS/Craig Lovell
Homecoming (page 170): CORBIS/Richard A. Cooke
Id al-Adha (page 175): CORBIS/AFP
Independence Day (page 178): CORBIS/Kevin R. Morris
Independence Day (page 179): Hiroyuki Matsumoto/Tony Stone Images
Janmashtami (page 183): Reuters/Savita Kirloskar/Archive Photos
Junkanoo (page 188): CORBIS/Philip Gould
Kumbha Mela (page 194): Corbis/Earl Kowall
Kwanzaa (page 201): PhotoEdit/Pat Olear
Labor Day (page 205): CORBIS/Joseph Sohm; ChromoSohm Inc.
Mardi Gras (page 212): Louisiana Office of Tourism
Mardi Gras (page 213): Louisiana Office of Tourism
Mardi Gras (page 214): Louisiana Office of Tourism
Mardi Gras (page 215): Louisiana Office of Tourism
Mardi Gras (page 216): Louisiana Office of Tourism
Martin Luther King Day (page 219): PhotoEdit/A. Ramey
Masquerades in Africa (page 226): CORBIS/Charles & Josette Lenars
May Day (page 233): CORBIS/Robert Maass
May Day (page 234): CORBIS/Dean Conger
Mexican Independence Day (page 248): CORBIS/Morton Beebe, S.F.
New Year's Day (page 270): Steven Weinberg/Tony Stone Images
Oktoberfest (page 273): CORBIS/Peter Turnley
Passover (page 277): Kathy Sloane
Potlatch (page 283): MIRA
Presidents' Day (page 287): CORBIS/Richard T. Nowitz
Quinceañera (page 292): CORBIS/Patrick Ward
Rosh ha-Shanah (page 295): PhotoEdit/A. Ramey
St. Patrick's Day (page 302): PhotoEdit/Robert Brenner
St. Patrick's Day (page 303): CORBIS/Sandy Felsenthal
Sallah (page 306): Victor Englebert
San Fermin Fest (page 309): CORBIS/Nik Wheeler
Songkran (page 322): CORBIS/Kevin R. Morris
Sukkot (page 325): Alain Keler/Sygma
Take Our Daughters to Work® Day (page 336): PhotoEdit/Michael Newman
Tet (page 340): CORBIS/Steve Raymer

Tet (page 341): Kathy Sloane
Thanksgiving (page 345): Bob Krist/Tony Stone Images
Thanksgiving (page 346): CORBIS/Joseph Sohm; ChromoSohm Inc.
Timquat (page 352): Victor Englebert
United Nations Day (page 358): CORBIS/Jack Fields
Valentine's Day (page 364): David J. Sams/Tony Stone Images
Valentine's Day (page 365): CORBIS/Lyn Hughes
Veterans Day (page 371): CORBIS/Bettmann
Veterans Day (page 372): CORBIS/Joseph Sohm; ChromoSohm Inc.
Voodoo Festivals (page 376): CORBIS/Philip Gould

Suggested Reading

Books about Holidays in General

Abbas, Jailan, and Abd el Wahab Bilal. *Festivals of Egypt*. AMIDEAST Publications. 1995.

Angell, Carole S. *Celebrations Around the World: A Multicultural Handbook*. Fulcrum Publishing. 1996.

Bachmann, Ramona. *Simply Kosher: Exotic Food from Around the World*. Gefen Publishing House, Limited. 1994.

Berger, Gilda, and Peter Catalanotto, illus. *Celebrate! Stories of the Jewish Holidays*. Scholastic Trade. 1998.

Brownlie, Alison. *West Africa (Food & Festivals)*. Raintree/Steck Vaughn. 1999.

Clynes, Tom. *Wild Planet! 1,001 Extraordinary Events for the Inspired Traveler*. Visible Ink Press. 1995.

Davies, Horton. *Holy Days and Holidays*. Bucknell University Press. 1982.

Dill, Judith D. *Cooking for the Holidays with Judy*. Judyco. 1995.

Franklin, A., and S. Phillips. *Pagan Feasts: Seasonal Food for the Eight Festivals*. Holmes Publishing. 1997.

Gerson, Ruth. *Traditional Festivals in Thailand (Images of Asia)*. Oxford University Press. 1996.

Heale, Jay, Jan Tin Hock, and Tan Jin, ed. *South Africa (Festivals of the World)*. Gareth Stevens. 1998.

Henderson, Helene, ed. *Holidays, Festivals, and Celebrations of the World Dictionary: Detailing More Than 2,000 Observances from All 50 States and More Than 100 Nations*. Omnigraphics, Inc. 1997.

Howard, Michael. *The Sacred Ring: The Pagan Origins of British Folk Festivals & Customs*. Holmes Publishers. 1995.

Margolis, Isidor, Rabbi Sydney L. Moscowitz, and John Teppich, illus. *Jewish Holidays and Festivals*. Citadel Press. 1989.

Pennick, Nigel. *The Pagan Book of Days: Celebrating Festivals & Sacred Days Through the Millenium*. Inner Traditions International Ltd. 1992.

Toulson, Shirley. *The Celtic Year: A Celebration of Celtic Christian Saints Festivals and Sites*. Element. 1996.

Books Describing Individual Holidays

All Saints' Day

Chambers, Catherine. *All Saints, All Souls, and Halloween (World of Holidays)*. Raintree/Steck Vaughn. 1997.

Lasky, Kathryn. *Days of the Dead*. Hyperion Press. 1996.

All Souls' Day

Morris, Bill. *All Souls' Day*. Avon Books. 1997.

Santino, Jack, ed. *Halloween and Other Festivals of Death and Life*. University of Tennessee Press. 1994.

Anzac Day

Bruce, Jill B. *Anzac Day: Australia's Forces in War and Peace*. Seven Hills Book Distributors. 1998.

April Fools' Day

Kroll, Steven, and Jeni Bassett. *It's April Fools' Day!* Scholastic Inc. 1990.

Arbor Day

Schauffler, Robert Haven. *Arbor Day: Its History, Observance, Spirit and Significance: With Practical Selections on Treeplanting and Conservation, and a Nature Anthology*. Omnigraphics, Inc. 1990.

Skinner, Charles R. *Arbor Day Manual: An Aid in Preparing Programs for Arbor Day Exercises*. Books for Libraries. 1977.

Armed Forces Day

James, D. Clayton. *From Pearl Harbor to V-J Day: The American Armed Forces in World War II (American Ways Series)*. Ivan R Dee, Inc. 1995.

Ash Wednesday

Bloom, James M. and Michael L. Sherer, ed. *Ashes and Tears: Worship Resources for Ash Wednesday*. CSS Publishing Company. 1988.

Ashura

Ayati, Ibrahim. *A Probe into the History of Ashura*. Islamic Seminary. 1985.

Buddha's Day

Demi, Hitz Demi. *Buddha*. Henry Holt & Company, Inc. 1996.

Lippman, Marcia, photographer. *Buddha*. Chronicle Books. 1996.

Rahula. *What the Buddha Taught*. Grove Press. 1986.

Canada Day

Barlas, Robert, Norm Thompsett, and Susan McKay, ed. *Canada (Festivals of the World)*. Gareth Stevens. 1997.

Cohen, David C., and Rick Cohen, ed. *A Day in the Life of Canada (Day in the Life)*. Harper Collins Canada. 1986.

Carnival

Chambers, Catherine. *Carnival (World of Holidays)*. Raintree/Steck Vaughn. 1998.

Chandler, Clare. *Carnival (Festivals)*. Millbrook Press. 1998.

Mason, Peter. *Bacchanal: The Carnival Culture of Trinidad*. Temple University Press. 1999.

Chinese New Year

Brown, Tricia, and Fran Ortiz, photographer. *Chinese New Year (An Owlet Book)*. Henry Holt & Company, Inc. 1997.

Chambers, Catherine. *Chinese New Year (World of Holidays)*. Raintree/Steck Vaughn. 1997.

Hoyt-Goldsmith, Diane. *Celebrating Chinese New Year*. Holiday House. 1998.

MacMillan, Dianne M. *Chinese New Year (Best Holiday Books)*. Millbrook Press. 1998.

Madruga, Jan. *The Chinese New Year Dragon (Globalfriends Adventures Series)*. Globalfriends Collection Inc. 1997.

Vaughan, Marcia K. *The Dancing Dragon*. Mondo Publishing. 1996.

Christmas

Adkins, Jan. *Solstice: A Mystery of the Season*. Walker & Company. 1990.

Baum, L. Frank, and Max Apple, designer. *The Life and Adventures of Santa Claus (Signet Classic)*. Signet. 1994.

Bosco, Anthony J. *The Beginning of Christmas*. Dorrance Publishing Company. 1997.

Dickens, Charles, and James Rice, illus. *A Christmas Carol*. Pelican Publishing Company. 1990.

Metropolitan Museum of Art, Richard Muhlberger, designer. *Christmas Story: Told Through Paintings*. Harcourt Brace. 1990.

Paterson, Katherine. *Angels and Other Strangers: Family Christmas Stories*. HarperTrophy. 1988.

Pratt, J. *Christmas & Easter Ideas Book*. Sheed & Ward, Limited. 1990.

Silverman, Jerry, and Kenneth B. Clark, designer. *Christmas Songs (Traditional Black Music)*. Chelsea House Publishing Paperbacks. 1992.

Zapel, Theodore O., ed. *Christmas on Stage: An Anthology of Royalty-Free Christmas Plays for All Ages*. Meriwether Publishing. 1990.

Cinco de Mayo

Bradley, Mignon L. *Cinco de Mayo: An Historical Play*. LUISA Productions. 1981.

MacMillan, Dianne M. *Mexican Independence Day & Cinco de Mayo*. Enslow Publishers, 1997.

Riehecky, Janet. *Cinco De Mayo (Circle the Year with Holidays)*. Children's Press. 1994.

Vasquez, Sarah. *Cinco De Mayo (World of Holidays)*. Raintree/Steck Vaughn. 1998.

Columbus Day

Ansary, Mir Tamim. *Columbus Day (Holiday Histories)*. Heineman Library. 1998.

Carpenter, Eric. *Young Christopher Columbus: Discoverer of the New Worlds (First-Start Biographies)*. Troll Assoc. 1992.

deRubertis, Barbara. *Columbus Day: Let's Meet Christopher Columbus (Holidays & Heroes)*. Kane Press. 1996.

Durham, Jimmie. *Columbus Day*. University of New Mexico Press. 1983.

Liestman, Vicki. *Columbus Day*. First Avenue Editions. 1992.

Confederate Memorial Day

Brown, Warren, and William Golding. *Robert E. Lee (World Leaders Past & Present)*. Chelsea House Publishing. 1992.

Gurganus, Allan. *Oldest Living Confederate Widow Tells All*. Ballantine Books. 1996.

King, Perry Scott. *Jefferson Davis (World Leaders Past & Present)*. Chelsea House Publishing. 1990.

Potter, Robert R. *Jefferson Davis: Confederate President (American Troublemakers)*. Raintree/Steck Vaughn. 1993.

Confucius's Birthday

Bruya, Brian, trans., and Tsai Chih Chung. *Confucius Speaks: Words to Live By*. Anchor Books. 1996.

Rosemont, Henry, and Roger T. Ames, trans. *The Analects of Confucius: A Philosphical Translation (Classics of Ancient China)*. Ballantine Books. 1998.

Sargent, Claudia Karabaic, ed. *Confucius: The Wisdom*. Bulfinch Press. 1995.

Day of the Dead

Ancona, George. *Pablo Remembers: The Fiesta of the Day of the Dead*. Lothrop Lee & Shepard. 1993.

Carmichael, Elizabeth. *The Skeleton at the Feast: The Day of the Dead in Mexico*. University of Texas Press. 1992.

Greenleigh, John, photographer, and Rosalind Rosoff Beimler. *The Days of the Dead: Mexico's Festival of Communion with the Departed*. Pomegranate. 1998.

Krull, Kathleen. *Maria Molina and the Days of the Dead*. Simon & Schuster. 1994.

Hoyt-Goldsmith, Diane. *Day of the Dead: A Mexican-American Celebration*. Holiday House. 1994.

Johnston, Tony. *Day of the Dead*. Harcourt Brace. 1997.

Divali

Gupta, Shakti M. *Festivals, Fairs and Feasts of India*. Facet Books International. 1990.

Hirst, Mike. *A Flavor of India (Food & Festivals)*. Raintree/Steck Vaughn. 1999.

Kododwala, Dilip. *Divali (World of Holidays)*. Raintree/Steck Vaughan, 1998.

MacMillan, Dianne M. *Diwali: Hindu Festival of Lights (Best Holiday Books)*. Enslow Publishers, Inc. 1997.

Sharma, B. N. *Festivals of India*. South Asia Books. 1978.

Sholapurkar, G. R. *Religious Rites and Festivals of India*. South Asia Books. 1990.

Thomas, R. *Festivals and Holidays of India*. Stosius Inc./Advent Books Division. 1981.

Dragon Boat Festival

Barker, Pat. *Dragon Boats: A Celebration*. Weatherhill. 1996.

Earth Day

Gardner, Robert. *Celebrating Earth Day: A Sourcebook of Activities and Experiments*. Millbrook Press. 1992.

Oelschlaeger, Max, ed. *After Earth Day: Continuing the Conservation Effort (Philosophy and Ecology)*. University of North Texas Press. 1992.

Stefoff, Rebecca. *The American Environmental Movement (Social Reform Movements)*. Facts on File, Inc. 1995.

Easter

Amery, Heather. *Easter Story*. Bible Tales Series. 1999.

Barth, Edna. *Lilies, Rabbits and Painted Eggs: The Story of the Easter Symbols*. Houghton Mifflin Company. 1981.

Evelegh, Tessa. *Easter; A Spring Celebration of Traditional Crafts and Recipes*. Simon & Schuster. 1994.

Pratt, J. *Christmas & Easter Ideas Book*. Sheed & Ward, Limited. 1990.

The Services of Holy Week and Easter Sunday Greek Orthodox Archdiocese of North and South America. Holy Cross Orthodox Press. 1993.

Umnik, Sharon Dunn, ed. *175 Easy-to-Do Easter Crafts (Easy-to-Do Crafts—Easy-to-Find Things)*. Boyds Mills Press. 1994.

Emancipation Day

Trefousse, Hans L. *Lincoln's Decision for Emancipation*. Lippincott. 1975.

Young, Robert. *The Emancipation Proclamation: Why Lincoln Really Freed the Slaves*. Dillon Press. 1994.

Epiphany

O'Neal, Debbie Trafton. *Before and After Christmas: Activities for Advent and Epiphany*. Augsburg Fortress Publications. 1991.

Feast of Our Lady of Gaudalupe

Castillo, Ana, ed. *Goddess of the Americas: Writings on the Virgin of Guadalupe*. Riverhead Books. 1997.

Poole, Stafford. *Our Lady of Guadalupe: The Origins and Sources of a Mexican National Symbol, 1531–1797*. University of Arizona Press. 1996.

Rengers, Christopher. *Mary of the Americas: Our Lady of Guadalupe*. Alba House. 1989.

Rodriguez, Jeanette. *Our Lady of Guadalupe: Faith and Empowerment Among Mexican-American Women*. University of Texas Press. 1994.

Feast Day of Saint Francis of Assisi

Bonsanti, Georgio, and Ghigo Roli, photographer. *The Basilica of St. Francis of Assisi: Glory and Destruction*. Harry N Abrams. 1998.

Di Monte Santa Maria, Ugolino. *The Little Flowers of St. Francis of Assisi (Vintage Spiritual Classics)*. Vintage Books. 1998.

Dunlap, Lauren Glen, and Kathleen Fruge-Brown, illus. *And I, Francis: The Life of Francis of Assisi in Word and Image*. Chiron Publications. 1996.

Frugoni, Chiara. *Francis of Assisi: A Life*. Continuum Publishing Group. 1998.

Hodges, Margaret. *Brother Francis and the Friendly Beasts*. Atheneum. 1991.

Romanini, Angiola Maria. *Assisi: The Frescoes in the Basilica of St. Francis*. Rizzoli Bookstore. 1998.

Fiestas in Latin America

Perl, Lila. *Pinatas and Paper Flowers: Holidays of the Americas in English and Spanish: Pinatas Y Flores De Papel: Fiestas De Las Americas En Ingles Y Espanol*. Houghton Mifflin Company. 1983.

Winningham, Geoff. *In the Eye of the Sun: Mexican Fiestas*. W. W. Norton & Company. 1996.

Flag Day

Furlong, William R., and Byron McCandless. *So Proudly We Hail: The History of the United States Flag*. Smithsonian Institution, 1981.

Schauffler, Haven, ed. *Flag Day: Its History, Origin and Celebration as Related in Song and Story*. Robert Omnigraphics, Inc. 1997.

Sedeen, Margaret. *Star-Spangled Banner: Our Nation and Its Flag*. National Geographic Society. 1993.

Groundhog Day

Magorian, James. *Ground Hog Day*. Black Oak Press. 1987.

Halloween

Bannatyne, Pratt. *Halloween: An American Holiday, an American History*. Lesley Pelican Publishing Company. 1998.

Chambers, Catherine. *All Saints, All Souls, and Halloween (World of Holidays)*. Raintree/Steck Vaughn. 1997.

Suckow, Will. *50 Nifty Super Scary Crafts and Other Things to Do*. Lowell House. 1996.

Umnik, Sharon Dunn, ed. *175 Easy-to-Do Halloween Crafts*. Boyds Mills Press. 1995.

Hanukkah

Berman, Nancy M. *The Art of Hanukkah*. Levin Associates. 1996.

Hall, Melanie W. *On Hanukkah*. Atheneum. 1998.

Hoyt-Goldsmith, Diane. *Celebrating Hanukkah*. Holiday House. 1998.

Kimmel, Eric A., ed. *A Hanukkah Treasury*. Henry Holt & Company, Inc. 1998.

Hiroshima Peace Day (Atomic Bomb Day)

Hersey, John. *Hiroshima*. Vintage Books. 1989.

Hogmanay

Banks, M. M., ed. *British Calendar Customs, Scotland: Fixed Festivals, The Quarters, Hogmanay, January to March*. Periodicals Service Company. 1989.

Holi

Allison, Lynda. *Celebration Banners Dance Holi*. Celebration Ministries. 1995.

Gupta, Shakti M. *Festivals, Fairs and Feasts of India*. Facet Books International. 1990.

Hirst, Mike. *A Flavor of India (Food & Festivals)*. Raintree/Steck Vaughn. 1999.

Kadodwala, Dilip. *Holi (World of Holidays)*. Raintree/Steck Vaughn. 1998.

Sharma, B. N. *Festivals of India*. South Asia Books. 1978.

Sholapurkar, G. R. *Religious Rites and Festivals of India*. South Asia Books. 1990.

Thomas, R. *Festivals and Holidays of India*. Stosius Inc./Advent Books Division. 1981.

Holy Week

Aycock, Don M. *Eight Days That Changed the World: A Devotional Study from Palm Sunday to Easter*. Kregel Publications. 1997.

Kennedy, Pamela. *An Easter Celebration: Traditions and Customs from Around the World*. Ideal Childrens Books. 1991.

Strong, Dina. *Hosanna and Alleluia: Stories of Holy Week and Easter (The Story Teller Series)*. Morehouse Publishing Company. 1997.

Id al-Adha

Mohamed, Mamdouh N. *Hajj & Umrah: From A to Z*. Halalco Books. 1995.

Parker, Ann. *Hajj Paintings: Folk Art of the Great Pilgrimage*. Smithsonian Institution Press. 1995.

Peters, F. E. *The Hajj: The Muslim Pilgrimage to Mecca and the Holy Places*. Princeton University Press. 1994.

Id al-Fitr

Buitelaar, Marjo. *Fasting and Feasting in Morocco: Women's Participation in Ramadan (Mediterranean Series)*. Berg Publishing Ltd. 1994.

Ghazi, Suhaib Hamid. *Ramadan*. Holiday House. 1996.

Jones-Bey, Hassaun Ali. *Better Than a Thousand Months: An American Muslim Family Celebration*. Ibn Musa. 1997.

MacMillan, Dianne M. *Ramadan and Id Al-Fitr (Best Holiday Books)*. Enslow Publishers, Inc. 1994.

Independence Day in the United States

Marrin, Albert. *The War for Independence: The Story of the American Revolution*. Atheneum. 1988.

Nielsen, Shelly. *Celebrating Independence Day (Holiday Celebrations)*. Abdo & Daughters. 1992.

Thomas, Jane Resh. *Celebration!* Disney Press. 1997.

Travers, Len. *Celebrating the Fourth: Independence Day and the Rites of Nationalism in the Early Republic*. University of Massachusetts Press. 1997.

Juneteenth

Abernethy, Francis Edward, ed. *Juneteenth Texas: Essays in African-American Folklore (Publications of the Texas Folklore Society, No. 54)*. University of North Texas Press. 1996.

Barrett, Anna Pearl. *Juneteenth: Celebrating Freedom in Texas*. Eakin Publications. 1999.

Branch, Muriel Miller. *Juneteenth—Freedom Day: Freedom Day*. Cobblehill. 1998.

Ellison, Ralph. *Juneteenth*. Random House. 1999.

Kathin

Erricker, Clive. *Buddhist Festivals*. Heineman Library. 1997.

Snelling, John. *Buddhist Festivals (Holidays and Festivals)*. Element Library, 1996.

Krishnajanmastami

Rosen, Steven J. *Vaisnavi: Women & the Worship of Krishna*. South Asia Books. 1997.

Kumbha Mela

Gupta, Shakti M. *Festivals, Fairs and Feasts of India*. Facet Books International. 1990.

Hirst, Mike. *A Flavor of India (Food & Festivals)*. Raintree/Steck Vaughn. 1999.

Sharma, B. N. *Festivals of India*. South Asia Books. 1978.

Sholapurkar, G. R. *Religious Rites and Festivals of India*. South Asia Books. 1990.

Thomas, R. *Festivals and Holidays of India*. Stosius Inc./Advent Books Division. 1981.

Kupalo Festival

Bassis, Volodymyr. *Ukraine (Festivals of the World)*. Gareth Stevens. 1998.

Whyte, Harlinah. *Russia (Festivals of the World)*. Gareth Stevens. 1997.

Kwanzaa

Gumbs, Ida R. *How to Plan a Kwanzaa Celebration: Ideas for Family, Community and Public Events*. Cultural Expressions Inc. 1998.

Hoyt-Goldsmith, Diane. *Celebrating Kwanzaa*. Holiday House. 1993.

Humphrey, Imani A. *First Fruits: The Family Guide to Celebrating Kwanzaa*. Third World Press. 1993.

Riley, Dorothy Winbush. *The Complete Kwanzaa: Celebrating Our Cultural Harvest*. Harperperennial Library. 1996.

Robertson, Linda. *The Complete Kwanzaa Celebration Book*. Creative Acrylic Concepts. 1994.

Labor Day

Ansary, Mir Tamim. *Labor Day (Holiday Histories)*. Heineman Library. 1998.

Lupercalia

Holleman, A. W. J. *Pope Gelasius I and the Lupercalia*. John Benjamins Publishing Company. 1974.

Mardi Gras/Shrove Tuesday

Hearin, Emily S. *Queens of Mobile Mardi Gras, 1893–1986*. Museum of the City of Mobile. 1986.
Huber, Leonard V. *Mardi Gras: A Pictorial History of Carnival in New Orleans*. Pelican Publishing Company. 1989.
Loccisano, Elio. *A Decade of the Sydney Mardi Gras*. Stampyourself. 1998.
Mitchell, Reid. *All on a Mardi Gras Day: Episodes in the History of New Orleans Carnival*. Harvard University Press. 1995.
Schindler, Henri. *Mardi Gras: New Orleans*. Abbeville Press, Inc. 1997.

Martin Luther King's Birthday

Archer, Jules. *They Had a Dream: The Civil Rights Struggle from Frederick Douglass to Marcus Garvey to Martin Luther King and Malcolm X*. Puffin. 1996.
Clayton, Ed. *Martin Luther King: The Peaceful Warrior*. Archway. 1996.
Kasher, Steven, and Myrlie Evers-Williams, intro. *The Civil Rights Movement: A Photographic History, 1954–68*. Abbeville Press, Inc. 1996.
King, Martin Luther, Jr. *The Autobiography of Martin Luther King, Jr.* Warner Books. 1998.
Rowland, Della. *Martin Luther King, Jr.: The Dream of Peaceful Revolution (History of Civil Right Series)*. Silver Burdett Press. 1990.
Shuker, Nancy. *Martin Luther King; World Leaders*. Chelsea House Publications. 1987.

Masquerades in Africa

Phillips, Ruth B. *Representing Woman: Sande Masquerades of the Mende of Sierra Leone*. UCLA Fowler Museum. 1995.

Mawlid al-Navi

Knight, Khadijah. *Islamic Festivals (Celebrate)*. Heineman Library. 1997.

May Day

Foner, Philip Sheldon. *May Day: A Short History of the International Workers' Holiday, 1886–1986*. International Publishers Company. 1986.

Memorial Day

Ansary, Mir Tamim. *Memorial Day (Holiday Histories)*. Heineman Library. 1998.
Sorensen, Lynda. *Memorial Day (Holidays)* The Rourke Book Company, Inc. 1994.

Mexican Independence Day

MacMillan, Dianne M. *Mexican Independence Day and Cinco De Mayo (Best Holiday Books)*. Enslow Publishers, Inc. 1997.

Mother's Day

Eick, Jean. *Mother's Day Crafts*. Child's World. 1998.
Hautzig, Esther. *A Gift for Mama*. Puffin. 1997.
Minshyll, Evelyn. *Abingdon's Mother's Day Recitations*. Abingdon Press. 1990.
Nielsen, Shelly. *Celebrating Mother's Day (Holiday Celebration)*. Abdo & Daughters. 1996.

Ncwala

Bechky, Allen. *Adventuring in Southern Africa: Botswana, Zimbabwe, Zambia, Namibia, South Africa, Malawi, Lesotho, and Swaziland*. Sierra Club Books. 1997.
Blauer, Ettagale. *Swaziland (Enchantment of the World)*. Children's Press. 1996.

New Year's Day

Cabot, Laurie. *Celebrate the Earth: A Year of Holidays in the Pagan Tradition*. Delta. 1998.
Lyon, Todd. *New Year's Eve Compendium: Toasts, Tips, Trivia, and Tidbits for Bringing in the New Year*. Clarkson Potter. 1998.
Roch, Carrier. *A Happy New Year's Day*. Tundra Books. 1990.

Oktoberfest

Jaros, Patrick. *Oktoberfest: A Fest Feast: A Book of Traditional Recipes (Ever Series)*. TASCHEN America Llc. 1998.

Passover

Avrutick, Frances R. *The Complete Passover Cookbook*. Jonathan David Publishing. 1981.
Cohen, Jeffrey M. *1001 Questions and Answers on Pesach*. Jason Aronson. 1996.
Parnes, Stephan O. *The Art of Passover*. Levin Associates. 1997.
Segal, Eliezer. *Uncle Eli's Special for Kids Most Fun Ever, Under the Table Passover Haggadah*. No Starch Press. 1999.
Wolfson, Ron. *The Art of Jewish Living: The Passover Seder*. Jewish Lights Publishing. 1996.

Pentecost

Cotter, Theresa. *Christ Is Risen: Celebrating Lent, Easter & Pentecost*. St. Anthony Messenger Press. 1994.

Purim

Cohen, Barbara. *Here Come the Purim Players!* Union of American Hebrew Congregations. 1998.
Feder, Harriet K. *It Happened in Shushan: A Purim Story*. Kar-Ben Copies. 1988.
Isaacs, Ronald H. *Every Person's Guide to Purim*. Jason Aronson. 1999.
Rotenberg, Rabbi Shlomo. *And These Days of Purim*. Philipp Feldheim. 1996.
Simon, Norma. *Happy Purim Night*. United Synagogue Book Service. 1959.

Potlatch

Harris, Lorle. *Tlingit Tales, Potlatch and Totem Pole*. Naturegraph Publishing. 1985.
Hoyt-Goldsmith, Diane. *Potlatch: A Tsimshian Celebration*. Holiday House. 1997.
Jonaitis, Aldona, ed. *Chiefly Feasts: The Enduring Kwakiutl Potlatch*. University of Washington Press. 1991.

Presidents' Day

Ansary, Mir Tamim. *Presidents' Day (Holiday Histories)*. Heineman Library. 1998.

Blassingame, Wyatt. *The Look-It-Up Book of Presidents*. Random Library. 1996.

Burns, Roger. *Abraham Lincoln (World Leaders Past and Present)*. Chelsea House Publishing. 1987.

Meltzer, Milton. *George Washington and the Birth of Our Nation*. Franklin Watts, Incorporated. 1986.

Wellman, Sam. *Abraham Lincoln*. Barbour & Company. 1998.

Rosh ha-Shanah and Yom Kipper

Apisdorf, Shimon. *Rosh Hashanah Yom Kipper Survival Kit*. Leviathan Press. 1997.

Groner, Judyth. *All About Yom Kippur*. Kar-Ben Copies. 1997.

Hall, Melanie W. *On Rosh Hashanah and Yom Kippur*. Atheneum. 1997.

Hammer, Reuven. *Entering the High Holy Days: A Guide to the Origins, Themes, and Prayers*. Jewish Publication Society. 1998.

Simon, Norma. *Yom Kippur*. United Synagogue Book Service. 1959.

Quinceañera

Bertrand, Diane Gonzales. *Sweet Fifteen*. Arte Publico Press. 1995.

King, Elizabeth. *Quinceañera: Celebrating Fifteen*. Dutton Books. 1998.

Lankford, Mary D. *Quinceañera; A Latina's Journey to Womanhood*. The Millbrook Press. 1994.

Salcedo, Michele. *Quinceañera!: The Essential Guide to Planning the Perfect Sweet Fifteen Celebration*. Henry Holt & Company, Inc. 1997.

Saint Patrick's Day

Barth, Edna. *Shamrocks, Harps and Shillelaghs*. Houghton Mifflin Company. 1982.

Blazek, Sarah Kirwan. *A Leprechaun's St. Patrick's Day*. Pelican Publishing Company. 1997.

Dauwer, Leo P. *Boston's St. Patrick's Day Irish*. Christopher Publishing House. 1984.

Fallon, Michael James. *The Definitive St. Patrick's Day Festivity Book*. Educare (CA). 1997.

Farrington, Karen. *St. Patrick's Day*. Book Sales. 1998.

Sallah

Nigeria (Fiesta!). Grolier Educational Corp. 1997.

San Fermin Fest

McKay, Susan. *Spain (Festivals of the World)*. Gareth Stevens. 1999.

Ross, Christopher J. *Contemporary Spain: A Handbook*. Edward Arnold. 1997.

Saturnalia

Fleischman, Paul. *Saturnalia*. Harpercollins Juvenile Books. 1992.

Shavuoth

Goodman, Philip (Editor). *Shavuot Anthology*. Jewish Publication Society. 1992.

Isaacs, Ronald H. *Every Person's Guide to Shavuot*. Jason Aronson. 1998.

Sol

Frances, M. Koh. *Korean Holidays and Festivals*. East West Press. 1990.

Korea (Fiesta!). Grolier Educational Corp. 1997.

Siow Yen Ho. *South Korea (Festivals of the World)*. Gareth Stevens. 1998.

Songkran

Gerson, Ruth. *Traditional Festivals in Thailand (Images of Asia)*. Oxford University Press. 1996.

Whyte, Harlinah. *Thailand (Festivals of the World)*. Gareth Stevens. 1998.

Sukkot

Abrams, Judith Z. *Sukkot: A Family Seder*. Kar-Ben Copies. 1993.

Golden, Barbara Diamond. *Night Lights: A Sukkot Story*. Gulliver Books. 1995.

Groner, Judyth Saypol. *All About Sukkot*. Kar-Ben Copies. 1998.

Isaacs, Ronald H. *Every Person's Guide to Sukkot, Shemini Atzeret and Simchat Torah*. Jason Aronson. 1999.

Take Our Daughters to Work® Day

Echevarria, Pegine. *For All Our Daughters: How Mentoring Helps Young Women and Girls Master the Art of Growing Up*. Chandler House Press. 1998.

The Ms. Foundation for Women. *Girls Seen and Heard: 52 Life Lessons for Our Daughters*. Putnam Publishing Group. 1998.

Tet

MacMillan, Dianne M. *Tet: Vietnamese New Year (Best Holiday Books)*. Enslow Publishers, Inc. 1994.

Wonder Kids Publications Group Staff. *Celebrating New Year – Miss Yuan-Shiau/Vietnamese English Version*. Wonder Kids Publications. 1992.

Thanksgiving

Dickson, Paul. *The Book of Thanksgiving*. Perigee. 1995.

Hayward, Linda. *The First Thanksgiving*. Demco Media. 1990.

Lewicki, Krys. *Thanksgiving Day in Canada*. Napoleon Publishing. 1995.

Morley, Fran, ed. *An American Thanksgiving*. Ideals Publishing. 1995.

Rodgers, Rick. *Thanksgiving 101: Celebrate America's Favorite Holiday with America's Thanksgiving Expert*. Broadway Books. 1998.

Timqat

Beckwith, Carol. *African Ark: People and Ancient Cultures of Ethiopia and the Horn of Africa*. Harry N Abrams. 1990.

Fradin, Dennis Brindell. *Ethiopia (Enchantment of the World)*. Children's Press. 1994.

Pankhurst, Richard. *The Ethiopians (Peoples of Africa)*. Blackwell Publishing. 1998.

Twelfth Night

Brokaw, Meredith. *The Penny Whistle Christmas Party Book: Including Hanukkah, New Year's and Twelfth Night Family Parties*. Fireside. 1991.

United Nations Day

Pollard, Michael. *United Nations (Organizations That Help the World)*. Silver Burdett Press. 1994.

Valentine's Day

Arnsteen, Katy Keck. *Make Your Own Valentine Cards*. Troll Assoc. 1992.

Barth, Edna. *Hearts, Cupids and Red Roses*. Demco Media. 1982.

Corwin, Judith Hoffman. *Valentine Crafts (Holiday Crafts)*. Franklin Watts, Incorporated. 1994.

Etter, Roberta B. *Tokens of Love*. Abbeville Press, Inc. 1990.

Vappu

Chung Lee Tan. *Finland (Festivals of the World)*. Gareth Stevens. 1998.

Tan Chung Lee. *Finland (Cultures of the World)*. Benchmark Books. 1996.

Veterans Day

Ansary, Mir Tamim. *Veterans Day (Holiday Histories)*. Heineman Library. 1998.

Bosco, Peter. *World War I (America at War Series)*. Facts on File, Inc. 1991.

Isserman, Maurice. *World War II (America at War Series)*. Facts on File, Inc. 1991.

Sorensen, Lynda. *Veterans Day (Holidays)*. The Rourke Book Company, Inc. 1994.

Walpurgis Night

Confrancesco, Joan. *Walpurgis Night*.

Voodoo Festivals

Davis, Rod. *American Voudou: Journey into a Hidden World*. University of North Texas Press. 1998.

Hurbon, Laennec. *Voodoo: Search for the Spirit (Discoveries)*. Harry N Abrams. 1995.

Hurston, Zora Neale, and Ishmael Reed. *Tell My Horse: Voodoo and Life in Haiti and Jamaica*. HarperCollins. 1990.

Glossary

abatement (əbāt′mənt)   A legal defense or plea to end an action, or law, on the grounds that a factual or technical error prevents the continuation of the action or law.

abbot (ăb′ət)   The title given to the leader, or superior, of a monastery.

abode (ə-bōd′)   A house or other place for living.

abolitionist (ăb′ə-lĭsh′ə-nĭst)   Most commonly used to refer to a person or policy that supported the abolition of slavery in the southern states prior to the Civil War.

abstinence (ăb′stə-nəns)   The deliberate restraint or avoidance of something. The term is most often used to refer to abstention from alcoholic beverages or sexual activity.

acacia (ə-kā′shə)   The overall term for a number of various trees or shrubs with feathery leaves and the heads or spikes of flowers.

acculturation (ə-kŭl′chə-rā′shən)   The changes brought to the culture of a group or individual as the result of contact with a different culture.

Achaemenids (ə-kē′ə mənĭds)   The name given to the dynasty that ruled Persia (now Iran) from about 550 B.C.E. to 330 B.C.E. The name is derived from Achaemenes, a minor 7th-century B.C.E. king of Anshan, but the true founder of the dynasty was his great-great-grandson, Cyrus the Great, who is credited with creating the Persian Empire.

adjudicator (ə-jōō′dĭ-kāt′ or)   A person who hears and settles a case by legal procedures; a judge.

admonish (ăd-mŏn′ĭsh)   To reprove, warn, or caution, often in reminder of an obligation.

Afrocentric (ăf′rōsĕn′trĭk)   One who believes that Africa, African culture, or the people of Africa or of African descent, are most important, or superior.

agrarian (ə-grâr′ē-ən)   A sociological term used to refer to cultures or economies that are based on or derive their primary economic means from uses of the land, such as farming.

allegory (ăl′ĭ-gôr′ē, -gōr′ē)   The use of characters or events as representative of larger ideas or principles in a work of fiction or art.

Allies (ə-lī′s)   This term given to the group of countries, consisting of the United States, Canada, Great Britain, France, and the USSR, that fought against the Axis powers during World War II.

allusion (ə-lōō′zhən)   To refer to by indirect reference.

alms (ämz)   Money or goods given to the poor; charitable contributions.

almsgiving (ämzgĭvĭng)   The practice of giving money or goods to the poor, in some cases considered an obligation or religious duty.

altar (ôl′tər)   An elevated, central place or structure at or upon which religious rituals or ceremonies are performed.

alumni (ə-lŭm′nī′)   The collective term for the graduates of a college or university.

ambivalence (ăm-bĭv′ə-ləns)   To feel two conflicting or opposing opinions at the same time; to waver between conflicting opinions or feelings.

amulet (ăm′yə-lĭt)   An object or talisman, often worn around the neck, as a charm or protection against evil or injury.

anachronism (ə-năk′rə-nĭz′əm)   Something that is noticeably outside its normal chronological or historical place or order.

anarchy (ăn′ər-kē)   The absence of government, central authority, or law. As a political or philosophical belief, anarchism holds that all forms of government are inherently oppressive and unnecessary, and should be abolished.

Anglican (ăng′glĭ-kən)   An adherent of or relating to the Church of England or its associated churches.

anthem (ăn′thəm)   Most often used to refer to a song or hymn of loyalty, often to a country, as in "the National Anthem."

Antioch (ăn′tē-ŏk′) (also **Antiochus**)   An ancient city, founded by Seleucus I, one of the generals and successors of Alexander the Great, in 301 B.C.E. Located at the crossroads of several strategically important caravan routes, it became a center of commercial activity and an architectural marvel. In 64 B.C.E., Antioch became the eastern capital of the Roman Empire, and it later became the center of Christendom outside of Palestine. The city was conquered by the Persians in 260, and over the following centuries repeated war and natural disasters reduced it to relative unimportance. The city, now known as Antakya, is now a part of Turkey.

aphrodisiac (ăf′rə-dĭz′ē-ăk′)   A food or drug that is intended to arouse or intensify sexual desire.

apocryphal (ə-pŏk′rə-fəl)   A statement or event of questionable origin or authenticity. The term is often used to refer to stories or acts attributed to famous or notorious people that probably did not actually occur.

apostolic (ăp′ə-stŏl′ĭk)   A term used to refer to material relating to the teachings of the twelve Apostles of Jesus, or to the Apostles themselves.

apotropaic (ăp′ə-trō-pā′ĭk)   A term used to describe an object meant to avert evil, such as a charm or talisman.

Arapaho (ə-răp′ə-hō′)   A Native American tribe, inhabiting originally what is now Minnesota and later the Great Plains. Although bound in an alliance with the Cheyenne, they were friendly toward white settlers. The Arapaho were noted for their art and religious ceremonies, characteristic of Plains culture. They now live in three settlements, with other Native American tribes, in Wyoming, Oklahoma, and Montana.

arboretum (är′bə-rē′təm)   A place for the study and exhibition of trees.

armistice (är′mĭ-stĭs)   A truce, or temporary stop to fighting, agreed on by both parties involved.

Armistice Day   Currently referred to as Veterans Day, a holiday proclaimed in 1919 to commemorate the termination of World War I. A minute of silence is often recognized across the United States at 11 A.M. on this holiday.

arsenal (är′sə-nəl)   A place for the storage or manufacture of weapons. The term is also used to refer to the weapons themselves.

arsenic disulfide (är′sə-nĭk dī-sŭl′fīd′) (As_2S_2)   Also known as realgar, red orpiment, and ruby arsenic, a mineral used as a pigment in the manufacture of fireworks and paints.

arsuras   From the Sanskrit for "air of life." In Hindu Vedic tradition, one of the two classes of gods (the other being Vedas) that later divided into two groups. The asuras were demonic, the enemies of humans, and the forces of chaos in the cosmic struggle between chaos and order.

Atharvaveda (äthär′vä vēdə) (also ***Atharva-Veda***)   One of the four collections of hymns that are the primary parts of the ancient Hindu sacred texts known as the Veda, or Samhitas.

Atlas (ăt′ləs)   In Greek mythology, one of the twelve Titans who were banished for waging a war against the deities of Mount Olympus. As part of his punishment, Atlas was forced to bear the earth and heavens and the pillar that separates them on his shoulders.

atonement (ə-tōn′mənt)   A penance or reparation made for a wrongdoing, sin, or crime.

attar (ăt′ər)   A type of oil or essence obtained from flowers. It is used in the making of perfumes.

aura (ôr′ə)   From the Greek term for "breath," a term used to refer to a distinctive quality that surrounds a person or thing.

auspicious (ô-spĭsh′əs)   A favorable or good sign.

auxiliaries (ôg-zĭl′yə-rēs)   Smaller, satellite groups that serve to support or supplement a larger central organization.

axiomatic (ăk′sē-ə-măt′ĭk)   A term referring to a universal or self-evident truth.

Axis (ăk′sĭs)   The coalition of countries that opposed the United States and its allies in World War II. It originated as the Rome–Berlin axis, a result of the 1936 accord between Hitler and Mussolini and their military alliance in 1939. It was extended to include Japan with the Berlin Pact in 1940, and ultimately encompassed many eastern European nations.

Aztec (ăz′tĕk′)   A Native American tribe who created one of the world's great civilizations and empires in central and southern Mexico from the 14th to 16th centuries. The Aztecs built great cities and developed complex and advanced social structures, and their capital, Tenochtitlan, located where the modern Mexico City now stands, was possibly the largest city in the world. The Aztec Empire was conquered by the Spanish in 1519.

Bacchus (băk′əs)   A later name for Dionysus, the god of wine and vegetation in Greek mythology. The name was commonly used after the 5th century B.C.E., and was derived from the loud cries with which Dionysus was worshiped.

baptism (băp′tĭz′əm)   A Christian ceremony in which water is used to symbolize a spiritual rebirth and purification. The water is usually sprinkled on the person's forehead, referred to as "aspersion," although some ceremonies require pouring ("affusion") or total immersion. Customarily, a baptism is performed on newborns as a symbol of the Lord's grace and forgiveness, which remains throughout their life.

baptistery (băp′tĭ-strē)   A part of a church set aside to perform baptisms.

barbarous (bär′bər-əs) (also **barbarian** [bär-bâr′ē -ən])   From the Greek word *barbaros*, meaning "foreign," the term refers to primitive cultures lacking refinement and often marked by savage, brutal behavior.

Bastille (bă-stēl′)   A French prison, built around 1370 as part of the fortification of the east wall of Paris. During the 17th and 18th centuries, the Bastille housed political prisoners who were often placed in the prison without accusation or trial. In 1789 the Bastille was attacked and captured by regular citizens who were assisted by armed troops. July 14 is now celebrated in France as Bastille Day, in commemoration of the destruction of the stronghold.

Beltane (bĕl′tān)   In Celtic tradition, a festival held on May Day, to mark the first flowers and the coming of spring.

boon   A term referring to something that is beneficial or a blessing. Boon is also used to describe someone who is jolly, as in "a boon companion."

boycott (boi′kŏt′)   A form of protest in which a person or group refuses to buy products from or support companies, individuals, nations, or other groups with which they disagree.

Brahmin (brä′mən)   In the Hindu hierarchy, or caste system, a member of the elite or highest class.

buckthorn (bŭk′thôrn′)   A common name for about 875 species of plants that customarily grow in dry locations and are known for their medicinal properties. The name most often refers to a shrub with large spines, small, oval leaves, and small white flower clusters.

Buddhism (boo′dĭz′əm)   One of the world's major religions, Buddhism began in northeastern India and is based on the teachings of Siddhartha Gautama, known as the Buddha, or Enlightened One. Originally a monastic movement within the Brahman tradition, it developed in a destinctive direction, as the Buddha rejected significant aspects of the Hindu philosophy and structure. In its present form, it consists of two major branches known as Theraveda, the Way of the Elders, and Mahayana, the Great Vehicle. Buddhism has great force and significance not only in India, but throughout much of southeast Asia.

buffoonery (bə-foo′nə-rē)   Behavior relating to the antics of a clown or jester.

bureaucracy (byoo-rŏk′rə-sē)   A general term for the employees and administrative structure of a company or organization, characterized by a specific hierarchy of authority or responsibility.

burlesque (bər-lĕsk′)   A type of vaudeville entertainment or comic art characterized by ridiculous exaggeration and racy humor.

campaign (kăm-pān′)   A series of military operations enacted to achieve a large-scale objective, or distinct phase, during a war.

cavalcade (kăv′əl-kād′, kăv′əl-kād′)   A procession, often ceremonial, of riders or horse-drawn carriages.

cavalier (kăv′ə-lîr′)   Traditionally, a mounted soldier or knight. The term is also used to describe behavior that is carefree and nonchalant.

celestial (sə-lĕs′chəl)   Used to refer to objects of or relating to the sky or the heavens. It is also commonly used as a superlative.

chanticleer (chăn′tĭ-klîr)   An Old French term for a rooster.

chapel (chăp′əl)   A place of worship that is smaller than a traditional church, often found in hospitals, colleges, and prisons.

charter (chär′tər)   In legal terms, a document issued or granted by a government, creating a business or political entity such as a corporation or colony, and defining its privileges and purposes.

chastity (chăs′tĭ-tē)   The abstention from sexual activity.

Cheyenne (shī-ĕn′)   A Native American tribe originally from the western Great Plains, now living in Montana and Oklahoma.

Chicano (chĭ-kä′nō)   A term used to describe someone who is from Mexican-American descent.

christianization (krĭs′-chə-nĭ-zā′shən)   The movement of introducing and converting people of a different religious faith to Christianity and Jesus' teachings.

chthonic (thŏn′ĭk)   A term used to describe something from, or relating to, the underworld.

circumambulate (sûr′kəm-ăm′byə-lāt′)   The act of circling something on foot.

clan (klăn)   A traditional social unit, originating from the Highlands of Scotland, that consists of a number of families claiming a common ancestor.

clergy (klûr′jē)   A term used to describe someone who is ordained for religious service.

cockerel (kŏk′ər-əl)   A Middle English term used to describe a young rooster.

colonialism (kə-lō′nē-ə-lĭz′əm)   A political philosophy or policy by which a governing nation maintains control over its foreign colonies. The term is also used to refer to an attitude in which a citizen of the ruling country may view citizens of a subject nation with a certain disdain or sense of superiority.

colonist (kŏl′ə-nĭst)   The term used to refer to an inhabitant or one of the original settlers of a colony.

commemorative (kə-měm′ər-ə-tĭv)   An object or token issued to mark a special ceremony or observation, usually in a limited quantity.

commercialism (kə-mûr′shə-lĭz′əm)   A term used to describe an environment or behavior that is based in the spirit, insitution, or method of business and commerce.

commoner (kŏm′ə-nər)   A person who is not of noble rank or status.

commune (kə-myoon′)   A collective living arrangement or community, in which individual members contribute resources and labor to the group as a whole.

communism (kŏm′yə-nĭz′əm)   A political theory and model for a government system in which all resources, businesses, and means of production are jointly owned by all members of the community.

compatriot (kəm-pā′trē-ət, -ŏt′)   A person from the same country as another. The term is also used to refer to people who share a common cause.

concession (kən-sĕsh′ən)   In business, a concession most often refers to the right of an individual or company to sell a particular item in a particular place. Concessions are usually contracts negotiated to allow a subsidiary business, such as a food stand or souvenir shop, to operate in a public place such as a ballpark or restaurant.

concubine (kŏng′kyə-bīn′)   A woman who lives with a man. The term is often used to refer to a woman who has a sexual or conjugal relationship with a man outside of marriage.

Confederate (kən-fĕd′ər-ĭt)   During the American Civil War, a term used to describe someone who was a member of the American Confederacy. The Confederacy was a group of 11 states that seceded from the United States in 1860 and 1861.

Confirmation (kŏn′fər-mā′shən)   A religious rite or sacrament admitting a baptized person to full membership in a church. In Judaism, the term refers to a ceremony that marks the completion of a young person's religious training.

confluence (kŏn′floo-əns)   The term used to describe the point at which two streams meet. The term also refers to a gathering together.

confraternities (kŏn′frə-tûr′nĭ-tēs)   A group or association of people who unite in a common purpose, belief, or profession.

congregation (kŏng′grĭ-gā′shən)   The members of a specific religion who regularly worship together at a church or synagogue.

Congress (kŏng′grĭs) A branch of the United States government, consisting of both the Senate and the House of Representatives, which act as representatives from their state of origin. Congress acts to pass laws and make decisions on behalf of the citizens within the congressperson's district.

connote (kə-nōt′) A term used to describe something that relates to, and suggests, something else in addition to its literal meaning. For example, spring connotes flowers and new life.

consecrate (kŏn′sĭ-krāt′) To declare, or set something apart, as being sacred.

consensus (kən-sĕn′səs) A decision or opinion that is reached by the whole or majority of a group.

conservationist (kŏn′sûr-vā′shə-nĭst) Someone who advocates the preservation and protection of the environment.

consul general (kŏn′səl jĕn′ər-əl) A British official appointed by the government to act as the ruler of a foreign country under British power and reign.

Continental Congress (kŏn′tə-nĕn′tl kŏng′grĭs) The assembly of about 50 representatives from the American colonies that became the revolutionary government that initiated the Declaration of Independence and the American Revolution. The First Continental Congress met in Philadelphia on September 5, 1774.

contrition (kən-trĭsh′ən) In the Catholic and other Christian churches, the deep, sincere sorrow for sin expressed as a form of penance, or voluntary act of self-mortification.

coreligionist (kō′rĭ-lĭj′ə-nĭst) A person who has the same religion or religious faith as another.

corollary (kôr′ə-lĕr-ē) A consequence or effect that stems from an action. In science or mathematics, a proposition that follows from another that has already been proved.

coronation (kôr′ə-nā′shən) The formal ceremony in which a sovereign, such as a king or queen, is formally crowned and invested with office.

Corpus Christi Festival (kôr′pəs krĭs′tē fĕs′tə-vəl) In the Catholic Church, a festival held on the Thursday after Trinity Sunday, celebrating the presence of Christ in the sacrament of the Eucharist. In 1969 some countries, including the United States, transferred the feast of Corpus Christi to the Sunday after Trinity Sunday.

Creole (krē′ōl′) A person of European descent born mostly in the West Indies or Spanish America; also refers to white persons descended from early French or Spanish settlers in the U.S. Gulf states, especially Louisiana.

Crow (krō) (also **Absoraka** [bird people]) A Native American tribe of the Plains culture. Unlike many tribes, they were not originally nomadic, living in permanent settlements along the upper Missouri River, but in the 18th century they moved west to the Yellowstone area and became mounted buffalo hunters. In 1868 they moved to a reservation in Montana.

cult (kŭlt) A religious or other type of spiritualist sect that is considered extremist or radical.

cumbia (kŭm′bē-ə) A Latin American folk dance, usually accompanied by traditional instruments along with African-style drums, shakers, and scrapers.

debauchery (dĭ-bô′chə-rē) An extreme indulgence or obsession with sensual pleasures.

Decalogue (dĕk′ə-lôg′, -lŏg′) Also known as the Ten Commandments, rules or guidelines for conduct believed to have been inscribed by God Himself on two stone tablets, then given to Moses to take back to the Hebrew exodus.

Declaration of Independence (dĕk′lə-rā′shən ŭv ĭn′dĭ-pĕn′dəns) The document, written by Thomas Jefferson and adopted by the Second Continental Congress on July 4,

1776, that outlined the complaints of the American colonies against the King of England, and declared them in revolt from Great Britain, as a free and independent nation to be called the United States of America.

decorum (dĭ-kôr′əm)   Polite behavior or appropriate conduct.

deity (dē′ĭ-tē)   A god or goddess.

delegate (dĕl′ĭ-gāt′, -gĭt)   A representative for another person.

demigod (dĕm′ē-gŏd′)   Meaning literally "partly [a] god," a term used in mythology to refer to a male offspring of a god and a mortal.

deportation (dē′pôr-tā′shən)   The act of expelling a person from a country. Deportation is often used in the cases of criminals or illegal aliens.

despotism (dĕs′pə-tĭz′əm)   A form of government in which a single ruler has absolute power. Also called a tyranny.

Deuteronomy (doo′tə-rŏn′ə-mē)   One of the Old Testament books of the Bible, consisting mostly of homilies and sermons attributed to Moses, along with a recapitulation of events from the journey of the Israelites and a repetition of the Ten Commandments.

devas (dē-văs)   From the Sanskrit for "deity." In Hindu Vedic tradition, one of the two classes of gods (the other being asuras) that would later divide into two groups. The Vedas govern the three regions of heaven, earth, and air, assist humankind, and are the forces of order in the struggle between order and chaos.

Devi (dā′vē)   In the Hindu religion, a goddess of the Goddess, sometimes referred to as the prime force, who orders the male gods to the work of creation and destruction. There are various goddesses who are sometimes considered aspects of Devi, including Durga and Kali.

diaspora (dī-ăs′pər-ə)   The dispersion or separation of culture. The term is often used to refer to the pattern of immigration that spreads an ethnic group beyond its native land.

Dionysus (dī′ə-nī′səs)   In Greek and Roman mythology, the god of wine, drama, and the celebration of the power and fertility of nature.

divination (dĭv′ə-nā′shən)   A supernatural ability to predict future events, or the process of predicting them.

doctrine (dŏk′trĭn)   The collective term for the body of principles, or beliefs, accepted by a religious, political, or philosophic group.

dogmatist (dôg′mə-tĭst)   A person or doctrine characterized by the authoritative, sometimes arrogant assumption of unproved principles.

doubloon (dŭ-bloon′)   A Spanish gold coin, no longer in use.

dreidel (drād′l)   A small, spinning top, traditionally used in games played by children of the Jewish faith during Hanukkah.

druid (droo′ĭd)   A Celtic term for priest in the animistic religions of ancient Gaul and Britain. In myth and legend, druids are often portrayed as prophets or sorcerers.

durbar (dûr′bär′)   A court or formal reception held by an Indian prince or African ruler.

ecclesiastical (ĭ-klē′zē-ăs′tĭ-kəl)   A term describing something that relates to a church, as an institution.

ecology (ĭ-kŏl′ə-jē)   The science or study of the relationships between living things and their environment.

ecosystem (ĕk′ō-sĭs′təm)   The collective term for all living things and the environment of a particular area, most often identified by the interlocking relationships of the various parts.

edifice (ĕd′ə-fĭs)   A building or structure, often of imposing size.

effigy (ĕf′ə-jē)   A derogatory figure used to represent a hated group or culture.

Emancipation Proclamation (ĭ-măn′sə-pā′shən prŏk′lə-mā′shən)   Proclamation issued by U.S. president Abraham Lincoln on January 1, 1863, effectively ending slavery in the United States. Although excluding some slaves in areas of the Confederacy held by Union armies, the Emancipation Proclamation was a radical change in governmental policy, and was instrumental in leading to the enactment of the 13th Amendment to the Constitution in 1865, by which slavery was wholly abolished.

emir (ĭ-mîr′)   A term often used to refer to a Middle Eastern chief or prince.

Endymion (ĕn-dĭm′ē-ən)   In Greek mythology, a male youth of exceptional beauty who was loved by the goddess of the moon, Selene. She visited him nightly as he slept in a cave and bore him 50 daughters, but put him to sleep eternally to keep him to herself.

epicenter (ĕp′ĭ-sĕn′tər)   Literally meaning the point on the earth's surface directly above the center of an earthquake, the term is often used to refer to the central location or person(s) of a movement or event.

Epiphany (ĭ-pĭf′ə-nē)   In the Christian faith, a feast celebrated on the sixth of January to celebrate the visit of the magi to Jesus shortly after his birth. The term is often used to refer to an inspiration or revelatory moment.

episcopal (ĭ-pĭs′kə-pəl)   Of or relating to a Bishop.

etymology (ĕt′ə-mŏl′ə-jē)   The study of the origin and development of a language through its earliest known use, changes in form, and relation to other languages.

Eucharist (yōō′kər-ĭst)   Also called the Lord's Supper or Holy Communion, the institution or sacrament of the Christian religion in which bread and wine are consecrated by an ordained minister, and then shared by the minister and members of the congregation. As commanded by Jesus at the Last Supper, the bread and wine symbolize the body and blood of Christ, and the rite was to be conducted "in rememberance of me [Jesus]."

eulogy (yōō′lə-jē)   A spoken or written tribute, most often given when a person has died.

exegesis (ĕk′sə-jē′sĭs)   The critical explanation or interpretation of a text.

exorcise (ĕk′sôr-sīz′)   In mythology or religion, to expel a demon or malevolent spirit through incantation and prayer.

extinction (ĭk-stĭngk′shən)   The complete death of all members of a race or species, to the point where there are no living examples on earth.

Ezekiel (ĭ-zē′kē-əl)   A book of the Old Testament, for the most part attributed to the prophet Ezekiel and written in the early part of the 6th century, B.C.E.

farce (färs)   In theater, a comedic play characterized by an improbable plot and ludicrous, exaggerated characters.

fast   A form of self-mortification, often used as a religious discipline, that requires abstaining from food.

Fatimids (făt′ə-mĭds′)   A medieval caliphate, or ruling family, of northern Africa. The name derives from Fatima, the daughter and only child of the prophet Muhammad.

fennel (fĕn′əl)   A plant with aromatic seeds used as flavorings, or the seeds or edible stalks of the plant.

festal (fĕs′təl)   Of or related to a feast or festival.

festival (fĕs′tə-vəl)   A feast or celebration.

fete (fāt, fĕt)   From the French, a festival or feast.

feudal (fyōōd′l)   Of or relating to the political and economic system known as feudalism, common in Europe in the Middle Ages, in which a landowner granted land to a vassal in exchange for fealty and military service.

fiesta (fē-ĕs′tə)   From the Spanish word meaning feast, a term commonly used in Spanish-speaking regions for a festival or feast, often religious in nature.

filial (fĭl′ē-əl)   A term describing a relationship or object appropriate for a son or daughter.

filibuster (fĭl′ə-bŭs′tər)   A negotiating or debating tactic, often prolonged speechmaking or other form of delay or obstructionist tactics, intended to delay action.

flagellate (flăj′ə-lāt′)   To whip, flog, or scourge.

frankincense (frăng′kĭn-sĕns′)   An aromatic gum resin, primarily used as incense.

fraternal (frə-tûr′nəl)   Of or relating to brotherhood. The term is often used to refer to the relationship between members of a guild or union, or to members of a college fraternity.

fraternity (frə-tûr′nĭ-tē)   Most often used to refer to one of the organizations of male college students, the term also describes a group associated by similar backgrounds, interests, or occupations, such as a club or guild.

frescoe (frĕs′kō) (also **fresco**)   A style of art in which paint or pigments are applied to a layer of plaster. Frescoes were often used for decoration on walls and churches.

Fulani Jihad (foō′lä′nē jĭ-häd′)   A holy war, known as a jihad, carried out in the 19th century in the Jos Plateau region, in Nigeria, by Islamic leader Usuman dan Fodio.

General Assembly   The main deliberative body of the United Nations, comprising one representative of each member nation.

Genesis (jĕn′ĭ-sĭs)   The first book of the Old Testament. It describes God's creation of the heaven and earth, and contains, among others, the stories of Adam and Eve, Noah and the Flood, the Hebrew patriarchs Abraham, Isaac, and Jacob, and the origins of the Hebrew nation.

genteel (jĕn-tēl′)   A social classification referring to one whose manners are refined and free from rudeness.

gentile (jĕn′tīl′)   A person who is not a Jew. The term is often used to refer specifically to Christians, or to heathens and pagans.

gnostic (nŏs′tĭk)   An adherent of gnosticism, from *gnosis*, intellectual knowledge of spiritual truth. Gnosticism refers to the doctrines of certain pre- or early-Christian sects.

gravity (grăv′ĭ-tē) (also **gravitation**)   The name given to the force of attraction between the masses of two physical bodies, such as a planet and a sun.

Great Depression   The worst and longest economic collapse in modern industrial society, the Great Depression in the United States began in late 1929 and lasted through the early 1940s, spreading to most of the world's other industrial countries.

grotto (grŏt′ō)   A cave or large underground, mostly enclosed, space.

habitat (hăb′ĭ-tăt′)   The environment in which a creature or species makes its home. In a broad sense, a habitat includes not only the physical characteristics of an area, but the entire ecological community.

Haman (hā′mən)   A figure from the Old Testament Book of Esther, an influential minister of the Persian king Ahasuerus.

Hausa (hou′sə)   An African people, living in northwestern Nigeria and southwestern Niger.

Hedonism (hēd′n-ĭz′əm)   The pursuit or devotion to things that provide pleasure, especially to the senses.

henna (hĕn′ə)   A tree or shrub with fragrant white or reddish flowers. The term also refers to a type of dye, often used as hair coloring, prepared from the leaves of the plant.

hierarchy (hī′ə-rär′kē)   Most often used to refer to the structure of authority in a group or organization, ranked by authority or ability.

Hillelites   Name given to the followers and descendents of Hillel (c. 70 B.C.E.–10 C.E.), a Jewish rabbi and teacher. He was an authority on the Law, head of a religious council in Jerusalem, and his ethical philosophy and moral teachings anticipated those of Jesus.

Hinduism (hĭn′do͞o-ĭz′əm)   One of the world's most followed and enduring religions, which organized in India and is still practiced by most of its inhabitants. The basic principles of Hinduism are defined more by the way people behave than what they think or believe; there are very few common practices and beliefs shared by all. Some practices observed by mostly all Hindis include reverence for Brahmans, the highest caste or class, and for cows; the abstention from eating meat; and worship of the gods Shiva, who personifies both the destructive and creative forces in the universe, and Vishnu, considered the preserver of the universe.

Holy Trinity (hō′lē trĭn′ĭtē) (also **Trinity** [trĭn′ĭtē])   In Christian theology, the belief that God exists in three parts: the Father (God), the Son (Jesus), and the Holy Spirit. The term is also used to refer to the members collectively.

Holy Week   In the Christian religion, the week preceding Easter, beginning with Palm Sunday and including Maundy Thursday and Good Friday.

homiletical (hŏm′ə-lĕt′ĭ-kəl)   Of or relating to a homily or sermon, or preaching.

hominy (hŏm′ənē)   Hulled and dried kernels of corn. They are prepared as food by boiling.

homophonous (hō-mŏf′ə-nəs)   Two or more words that are pronounced the same way, but spelled differently, and with different meanings.

hotbed (hŏt′bĕd′)   A colloquial term for an area of environment that fosters growth or activity, as in "a hotbed of intrigue."

House of Lords   The name given to a legislative branch of the British government, comprised of the bishops of the Church of England and the hereditary and life peers, or nobility, all of whom are appointed by the crown. Its powers, once equal to that of the Commons, has become limited for the most part to the ability to delay bills, providing additional time for study and reflection.

hybrid (hī′brĭd)   Something that is made up of several parts. In sociology, the term refers to the mixing of different cultures to form a new culture.

hymn (hĭm)   A religious song of praise or worship.

iconography (ī′kə-nŏg′rə-fē)   A term used in art history to refer to the study of subject matter in artistic works, as a means of determining the artist's intended meaning through the objects that are portrayed.

ideology (ī′dē -ŏl′ə-jē , ĭd′ē -)   The collective term for the body of ideas and principles reflecting the social needs and aspirations of an individual, group, or culture.

imam (ĭ-mäm′)   From the Muslim word meaning "leader" or "exemplar," the title indicating the political leader of a Muslim community or the person who leads the prayer services. In Shiite Islam, the term refers to the person who is both the political and religious leader, and who is a descendent of Ali and Fatima, the daughter of the Prophet Muhammad.

incarnation (ĭn′kär-nā′shən)   In theology, the term used to describe a god who has taken earthly form. In Christian doctrine, the Incarnation refers to God the Son become man in the person of Jesus.

incense (ĭn-sĕns′)   An aromatic substance, often a spice, oil, or essence, burned to produce a pleasant smell.

indigenous (ĭn-dĭj′ə-nəs)   A person or object originating and living in an area or environment.

inner sanctum (ĭn′ər săngk′təm)   A place within the structure of a building, often a temple or other place of worship, reserved for private contemplation by the highest-ranking members of the organization or priesthood.

inversion (ĭn-vûr′zhən)   A reversal of the normal order or place of things.

Isis (ī′sĭs)   In Egyptian mythology, the goddess of fertility and motherhood. She is often represented in human form, but was frequently described as wearing the horns of a cow.

itinerant (ī-tĭn′ər-ənt)   A term referring to one who travels from place to place, especially as a means of finding work.

jai alai (hī′lī′)   A type of court game in which players use an extended, hand-shaped basket to hurl a ball against a wall.

Jayanta   One of the gods featured in the myth or folklore that forms the basis of the Hindu fair or festival of Kumbha Mela.

jongleur (zhôN-gl÷r′)   An itinerant medieval entertainer, a precursor of the troubadour, proficient in juggling, acrobatics, music, and recitation.

juggernaut (jŭg′ər-nôt)   An overwhelming advancing force, against which nothing can stand. The term is often used to refer to popular or cultural movements that cannot be stopped by the existing establishment.

jurisdiction (jŏŏr′ĭs-dĭk′shən)   The term used to refer to the territory or area in which a specific authority has control over the laws and residents.

jurist (jŏŏr′ĭst)   A judge or other person skilled in the law.

Kama (kä′mə)   A river in eastern Russia, a tributary of the Volga and an important inland waterway for travel and transportation of goods.

Kislev (kĭs′ləv)   A month of the Jewish calendar.

Koran (kə-răn′) (also **Qur'an** or **Alcoran**)   From the Arabic word *qaraa*, meaning "to read," the sacred scripture of the Islamic religion. It is comprised of 114 suras, or chapters, containing all the divine revelations given to the Prophet Muhammad by God, or Allah. It is the earliest known work of Arabic prose, contains the Islamic religious, social, civil, commercial, military, and legal codes, and is considered above doubt or criticism.

laurel (lôr′əl)   A type of evergreen tree, also called a bay, having aromatic leaves. The term is often used to refer to a wreath made up of laurel, conferred as a mark of honor.

lay (also **laymen** [lā′mən])   A term most often used to refer collectively to all people not members of a professional group, or clergy.

leaven (lĕv′ən)   In cooking, to add an agent, such as yeast, to dough or batter, that causes it to rise.

Lent (lĕnt)   In the Christian religion, a period of fasting, reflection, and pentinence observed in preparation for Easter. It begins on Ash Wednesday and lasts for 40 days, ending the day before Easter.

leprosy (lĕp′rə-sē)   (also **leper**)   Also called Hansen's disease, a degenerative, chronic, infectious disease that affects primarily the skin, mucous membranes, and nerves. In biblical references, the term is used to refer to a variety of diseases, many not related to actual leprosy, that were considered a mark of defilement, or punishment from God for sin.

libidinous (lĭ-bĭd′n-əs)   A person or type of behavior that strongly reflects the influnce of the libido, or emotional energy associated with biological drives, often sexual desire.

licentious (lī-sĕn′shəs)   A term referring to characteristics that lack moral or sexual restraint.

lignum vitae (lĭg′nəm vī′tē)   From the Latin meaning "wood of life," a type of tree or shrub native to the tropical Americas. The term also refers to the wood of the sandarac, a cypress pine found in Africa and Australia.

lineage (lĭn′ē-ĭj)   A line of descent, usually traced from a specific ancestor.

liturgy (lĭt′ər-jē)   A set of public forms followed in Christian ceremony or ritual.

lunar (lōō′nər)   Of or relating to earth's moon.

lustration (lŭs′trāshən)   A ceremonial purification.

Maccabees (măk′ə-bēz′)   Four books of religious scripture, two of which (1 Maccabees and 2 Maccabees) are contained in the Old Testament used by Roman Catholics and Orthodox Christians, and in the Apocrypha in Protestant faiths. The third and fourth books are considered variously by different Christian traditions.

Magi (mā′jī′)   Originally the name given to a priestly caste of ancient Persia, thought to have been followers of Zoroaster, by the 1st century C.E. the term was used generically for wise men and soothsayers. It is often used to refer to the Three Wise Men from the East, who, in Christian tradition, were led to the birthplace of Jesus by a star.

mainstream (mān′strēm′)   A social term referring to the prevailing thoughts, influences, or activities of a specific area or period.

manifesto (măn′ə-fĕs′tō)   A public declaration of principles, often political in nature.

Maori (mou′rē)   The native inhabitants of New Zealand. Polynesian in origin, the Maori originally came to New Zealand by canoe from other Pacific islands.

maraca (mə-rä′kə)   A percussive instrument made from a hollow gourd containing pebbles or beans.

mariachi (mä′rē-ä′chē) (also **mariachi band**)   A Mexican street band. The term also refers to the type of music commonly performed by such groups.

martyr (mär′tər)   Generally used to refer to a person who dies rather than renounce his or her religious principles, or one who makes great sacrifices for a cause.

marzipan (mär′zə-păn)   A type of sweet or candy made from ground almonds, egg whites, and sugar.

masthead (măst′hĕd′)   Most often used to refer to the portion of a newspaper or other periodical that lists information about the staff, operation, and circulation.

matador (măt′ə-dôr′)   From the Spanish word *matar,* meaning "kill," the man in the sport of bullfighting who performs the final passes and kills the bull.

maypole (mā′pōl′)   A pole, used in the celebration of May Day, that is decorated with streamers that are wrapped around the pole as people dance around it.

Mecca (mĕk′ə)   A place that is considered to be the center of activity or interest. The term derives from the Islamic holy city of Mecca, in Saudi Arabia, the birthplace of the Prophet Muhammad.

medieval (mē′dē-ē′vəl)   A term used to describe someone or something as belonging to, or a part of, the Middle Ages.

meditation (mĕd′ĭ-tā′shən)   A period or practice of contemplation and reflection.

menorah (mə-nôr′ə)   A nine-branch candelabra, used in the Jewish faith during the celebration of Hanukkah.

mercantile (mûr′kən-tēl, -tīl′, -tĭl)   A social classification characterized by the selling of goods and trade.

merengue (mə-răng′)   A ballroom dance of Dominican and Haitian folk origin, characterized by a sliding step.

mestizo (mĕs-tē′zō)   A term commonly used to refer to a person of mixed racial ancestry, often such as Native American and European.

metaphysical (mĕt′ə-fĭz′ĭ-kəl)   Referring to a branch of philosophy concerned with the ultimate nature of reality and the relationship between mind and matter.

Mihragan (mîr′əgən)   A festival of ancient Persia that marked the end of summer.

militant (mĭl′ĭ-tənt)   A person, political party, or course of action that is combative or aggressive, usually for a cause or to achieve a specific objective.

minaret (mĭn′ə-rĕt′)   A tall, slender tower, most often found on and characteristic of a mosque.

Mishnah (mĭsh′nə)   The first part of the Talmud, the primary scripture of the Jewish faith, codifying the oral law of the Old Testament and the political and civil laws of the Jewish people.

missionary (mĭsh′ə-nĕr′ē)   A member of a particular religious organization whose tradition is to "witness" by word and deed to the beliefs of his or her religion, so that others may come to know and understand it.

Mithra (mĭth′rə)   The ancient Persian god of light and wisdom. Mithraism was one of the major religions of the Roman Empire, and its many similarities to Christianity made the eventual conversion of its followers possible.

mnemonic (nĭ-mŏn′ĭk)   Most commonly used to refer to a device or scheme, such as a formula or a rhyme, used to aid the memory or memorization.

moat (mōt)   An artificial lake or ditch surrounding a castle or town. It was used as a form of defense in medieval times.

monastery (mŏn′ə-stĕr′ē)   The residence of monks.

monsoon (mŏn-sōōn′)   A wind or wind system, prevailing mainly in the Indian Ocean, that reverses direction seasonally and brings dramatic climactic changes to regions such as India and southern Asia. The term is sometimes used to refer to the torrential rains that often accompany the monsoon winds.

mosque (mŏsk)   A house of worship in the Muslim faith.

motif (mō-tēf′)   An artistic or literary term referring to a dominant theme or central idea.

Muhammad (mŏŏ-hăm′ĭd, -hä′mĭd)   (c. 570–632) Founder of the Islamic religion, which is based upon his prophetic teachings. Born in Mecca, he experienced a visitation from the archangel Gabriel, who declared him a prophet of God. The verses of his revelations came to be known as the Koran, which serves as the foundation of virtually all aspects of Islamic life and law.

munitions (myŏŏ-nĭsh′ən)   War materiel, such as weapons and ammunition.

Muslim (mŭz′ləm)   A follower or believer of the Islamic faith.

myrrh (mûr)   An aromatic gum resin, obtained from any of several African or Asian trees or shrubs, used in the making of perfume and incense.

nationalism (năsh′ə-nə-lĭz′əm)   The devotion to the beliefs and interests of a specific nation.

naturalist (năch′ər-ə-lĭst)   A scientist in one of the fields of natural history, especially zoology or botany. The term also refers to a believer in naturalism.

neopaganism (nē′ō-pā′gənĭz′əm)   A contemporary revival of the practice of witchcraft.

Nubian (nŏŏ′bē-ən)   A member of the kingdom of Nubia, which occupied both sides of the Nile River from Aswan, Egypt, to Khartoum, Sudan. Called Kush in ancient times and ruled by Egypt for almost 2,000 years, Nubians achieved independence in the 8th century B.C.E. and conquered Egypt. Nubia itself was conquered by Arabs in the 14th century, and by Egypt in 1820.

oba (ō′bə)   A king or war leader of the Kingdom of Benin, a state of West Africa that flourished from the 15th to 17th centuries in what is now present-day Nigeria.

obeisance (ō-bā′səns)   Often used to refer to a gesture or body movement, such as a bow or salute, expressing deference.

octave (ŏk′tāv)   A term used to represent a series of eight parts, or an eighth.

Oijik (ō-ĭjĭk)   The formal or ancestral word for a groundhog, in the language of the Native American Delaware tribe.

oppression (ə-prĕsh′ən)   To be kept down or denied rights through an unjust use of force or authority. The term is often used to refer to social and legal discrimination against certain ethnic groups.

orthodoxy (ŏr′thə-dŏk′sē)   An accepted or established doctrine or creed, and the adherence to it. The term "orthodox" is also often used to refer to the most conservative or traditional element, especially of a religion.

pagan (pā′gən)   A follower of a religion or sect not Christian, Muslim, or Jewish.

pagoda (pə-gō′də)   A type of tower common in Buddhist temples, comprised of one to thirteen stories, each with a separate projecting roof, traditionally housing a memorial, shrine, or tomb.

pandemic (păn-dĕm′ĭk)   An epidemic or other mass reaction which takes place over a wide geographic area.

panegyrical (păn′ə-jĭr′ĭ-kəl)   Commending, or in praise of.

Pantheon (păn′thē-ŏn′)   The most completely preserved structure dating to ancient Roman times, considered one of the most significant and influential buildings in architectural history. Originally built as a temple dedicated to the Roman gods, who are collectively referred to as the Pantheon, it was erected by the emperor Hadrian between 118 and 128 C.E.

papal (pā′pəl)   Of or relating to the Pope or papacy.

papier mâché (pā′pər-mə-shā′)   A type of building or sculpting material made from the pulp or scraps of paper that when wet can be easily molded.

paschal cycle (păs′kəl sī′kəl)   A liturgical cycle of the Orthodox church, which begins with Lent and includes the 50 days separating Easter and Pentecost and is continued on Sundays throughout the year.

Passover (păs′ō′vər)   A festival of the Jewish faith, celebrating the exodus of the Hebrews from Egypt and their safe passage across the Red Sea. The name derives from the Hebrew word *pesach*, meaning "passing over" or protection.

pastoral (păs′tər-əl)   Most often used to refer to a lifestyle or setting that is simple, serene, or idyllic, usually possessing elements of rural life.

penance (pĕn′əns)   In the Christian faith, a voluntary act of contrition, a sacrament performed for the forgiveness of sins.

Petronius Arbiter (pĭ-trō′nē-əs är′bĭ-tər)   A Roman writer of the 1st century C.E. believed to have written *Satyricon*, generally considered the earliest example in European literature of the picaresque novel. Petronius was noted for his sense of elegance and style, and planned entertainments for the emperor Nero. A rival, jealous of his influence with the emperor, brought false accusations against him, arousing Nero's anger, and Petronius committed suicide in 66 C.E.

phalanx (fā′lăngks′)   In military history, a type of infantry formation in which soldiers carried overlapping shields and long spears. It was first developed in Greece in the 4th century B.C.

pharaoh (făr′ō)   In ancient Egypt, the name originally used to refer to the palace of the king, it was later used to refer to the kings themselves.

piety (pī′ĭ-tē)   The demonstration of devotion and reverence to God or family.

pilgrim (pĭl′grəm) A person who travels to or visits a place of spiritual or political importance to seek refuge or insight.

pilgrimage (pĭl′grə-mĭj) The voyage taken by a pilgrim to a site of spiritual or political importance. Most often used to refer to a religious journey.

pious (pī′əs) Adamantly observant of religion and religious practices.

pope (pōp) From the Latin word *papa*, meaning father, since the 8th century the title given to the bishop of Rome, the head of the Roman Catholic church.

posset (pŏs′ĭt) A hot drink, made of sweetened and spiced milk, curdled with wine or ale.

proselyte (prŏs′ə-līt′) A new religious convert.

Protestant (prŏt′ĭ-stənt) In religious terms, an individual or church organization that follows a religious belief denying the universal authority of the Pope, and ascribes to the beliefs of the Reformation. In the United States, Lutherans, Methodists, and Baptists are among the most widely followed Protestant faiths.

punchinello (pŭn′chə-nĕl′ō) The short, fat buffoon or clown in an Italian puppet show.

purgatory (pŭr′gətôr′ē) In Christian theology, a state of the afterlife, considered to be between heaven and hell, in which a soul is either cleansed of sins or endures a period of waiting that remains after the guilt of mortal sin has been remitted.

pyre (pīr) A funeral rite in which the body is placed on fire atop a pile of combustible material.

Qur'an An alternate spelling of "Koran," the primary sacred text of the Islamic faith.

rabbi (răb′ī) The highest ranking position within a Jewish congregation, similar to a minister in Christian religions.

rabbinate (răb′ə-nāt′, -nĭt) A term used to describe the office and functions of a rabbi.

raconteur (răk′ŏn-tûr′) A person who tells stories with wit and skill.

realgar (rē-ăl′gär′) Another name for arsenic disulfide, a mineral used as a pigment in the manufacture of fireworks and paints.

reformist (rĭ-fôr′mĭst) A person with the political intent of bringing about change, or reform.

rehabilitation (rē′hə-bĭl′ĭ-tāt-shən) The process of restoring something to usefulness, or to its former condition.

relic (rĕl′ĭk) In religion, a physical object of veneration that has some connection to a holy person or sacred site.

reliquary (rĕl′ĭ-kwĕr′ē) A container, often a shrine or coffer, used for displaying or storing sacred relics.

Remus (rē′məs) With Romulus, one of the two brothers who according to legend established the city of Rome. Romulus and Remus were said to be the twin sons of Rhea Silvia, a vestal virgin and the daughter of Numitor, the king of Alba Longa.

requiem (rĕk′wē-əm, rēk′wē-) A mass for a deceased person, or the music written for the mass.

resurrection (rĕz′ə-rĕk′shən) From the Latin *resurrectus*, meaning to rise again, in Christian theology the belief that on the third day after his death, Jesus rose from the dead. The term is also used to refer to the rising of the dead at the Last Judgment.

rogation (rō-gā′shən) (also **Rogation Day**) The days of prayer observed on the three days before Ascension Day. Rogation Day is also observed by Roman Catholics on the 25th of April.

Romulus (rŏm′yə-ləs) With Remus, one of the brothers who according to legend established the city of Rome. Romulus and Remus were said to be the twin sons of Rhea Silvia, a vestal virgin and the daughter of Numitor, the king of Alba Longa.

rosary (rō′zə-rē)   A term used to describe both a series of prayers dedicated to the Virgin Mary, and to the string of beads on which the prayers are counted.

rosemary (rōz′mâr′ē)   The leaves of an aromatic evergreen shrub, used in cooking and making perfumes.

Sabbath (săb′əth)   The first day of the week, Sunday, observed as the day of rest and worship by most Christians.

sackcloth (săk′klôth′)   Clothing made from a rough, coarse cloth. In Christian tradition, often worn as a sign of mourning or penitence.

sacrament (săk′rəmənt)   Any of several rites or liturgical actions in the tradition of the Christian church that are believed to be instituted by Jesus. They include marriage, the Eucharist, or communion, baptism, and Holy Orders, and are thought to communicate the grace or power of good through material objects and ritual.

sacred (sā′krĭd)   A term used to classify an object that is dedicated for the worship of a god.

saint (sānt)   In the Roman Catholic church, a person who is considered holy, and worthy of public veneration.

samba (săm′bə)   A Brazilian ballroom dance, of African origins.

Samhain (sămhān)   The Celtic festival of the dead. Samhain was later adapted by the Roman Catholic church as All Saints Day, which falls on November 1.

sanctify (săngk′tə-fī′)   To reserve something for sacred use, or to grant something religious sanction with an oath or vow, such as marriage.

sanctions (săngk′shəns)   In political terms, restrictions or prohibitions, usually economic, against dealings or interactions with other countries.

Sanhedrin (săn-hĕd′rĭn, hē ′drĭn, săn-)   The supreme national tribunal of the Jewish people, established at the time of the Maccabees.

Sanskrit (săn′skrĭt′)   The classical sacred and literary language of the Hindus of India.

Sarasvati (săr′ə-svə-tē)   One of the manifestations of the Goddess in the Hindu religion. Sarasvati, associated with the Sarasvati River, is the wife of Brahma.

Sassanid (să-să′nĭd)   The ruling dynasty of Persia from 224 until the Islamic conquest in 641. Under the first Sassanid king and founder of the dynasty, Ardashir I, Zoroastrianism became the official religion of Persia.

Saturnalia (săt′ər-nā′lē-ə)   A type of festival or celebration based on the Roman festival of Saturn, which began on December 17.

sect (sĕkt)   A smaller, distinct unit, sometimes separated from a larger group or denomination by variations in common beliefs.

secular (sĕk′yə-lər)   A term referring to an approach that does not relate to religious or spiritual views.

Seder (sā′dər)   The feast, celebrated on the first two nights of Passover, commemorating the exodus of the Jewish people from Egypt.

segregation (sĕg′rĭ-gā′shən)   To be separated, usually through force, from the mainstream for reasons of race or creed. The term is most often used to refer to the forced separation of blacks and whites, most notable in the southern United States.

sermon (sûr′mən)   A homily or lesson, delivered as part of a religious service or liturgy.

shaman (shä′mən)   A member of certain tribal societies who communes and meditates between the physical and spiritual world for the purposes of healing, divination, and control over natural events.

Shammaites   Followers of the Jewish leader Shammai, also called Shammai the Elder, considered to have been the leader of the Sanhedrin.

Shoshoni (shō-shō′nē) A member of or relating to the Native American tribe Shoshoni, part of the Plains culture area. The Shoshoni originally lived in a number of states, from Wyoming to Nevada, and many currently live on reservations in Wyoming, Idaho, and Nevada.

Sioux (soō) (also **Lakota, Dakota**) The collective name for one of the largest confederacies of Native American peoples occupying the heartland of the northern Great Plains. It was comprised of seven tribes, in three major divisions: the Senatee, the Nakota, and the Teton.

St. Peter's Basilica (sānt pē ′tərz bə-sĭl′ĭkə) One of the most important buildings of the Vatican, St. Peter's was built between the 15th and 17th centuries, and features designs and works of art by Michelangelo and Bernini, among many others. It is considered the center of Roman Catholic worship.

strata (strā′tə) Various layers or divisions.

strike (strīk) An organized work stoppage carried out by a group of employees, usually as a tactic to enforce demands or protest unfair labor conditions.

Sukkot (soō-kôt′) **(also Sukkoth)** Also called the Feast of Tabernacles and the Feast of Ingathering, a festival held to mark the end of the harvest in Palestine.

sultanate (sŭl′tənāt′) The country or area ruled by a sultan, a Muslim title commonly used in the Ottoman Empire.

summer solstice (sŭm′ər sŏl′stĭs) The time of year in the northern hemisphere when the noon sun appears to be farthest north. It occurs on or around June 21, and mark s the beginning of summer.

supplication (sŭp′lĭ-kā-shən) A humble, earnest petition.

Swahili (swä-hē′lē) Most often used to refer to a member of the Muslim people or culture of the coast and islands of eastern Africa. The term is also used for the Bantu language, which is widely used in eastern and east-central Africa.

synagogue (sĭn′ə-gŏg′) A place of worship and religious instruction for those of the Jewish faith.

Tabernacle (tăb′ər-năk′əl) According to the Old Testament, he tent in which the Ark of the Covenant, containing the Ten Commandments, was conveyed.

Talmud (täl′mo͞od, tăl′məd) The primary body of Jewish religious and civil law, consisting of the Mishnah, the codification of laws, commentary on the Mishnah, along with commentaries on the Torah, the Halakah, and the Haggada.

Taoist (tou′ĭst) A follower of the Chinese philosophical and religious system Taoism. Taoists seek harmony with the underlying pattern of the universe, called the Tao, meaning "way," which cannot be described in words or conceived by the human mind.

temple (tĕm′pəl) A place of religious worship.

theology (thē-ŏl′əjē) A discipline that attempts to express the content of a religious expression in words that are contained in faith.

theophany (thē-ŏf′ə-nē) The visible manifestation of a deity.

Theravadists (thĕr′ə-vä′dĭsts) Followers of Theraveda Buddhism, with Mahayana Buddhism one of the two principle branches of the Buddhist faith.

transubstantiation (trăn′səb-stăn′shē-ā′shən) The literal or symbolic changing of one substance into another. In Christian theology, the sacrament of the Eucharist changes bread and wine into the body and blood of Christ.

trope (trōp) A figure of speech, using words in nonliteral ways.

troupe (tro͞op) An acting company. The term is often used to refer to a traveling or touring group of performers.

underworld (ŭn′dər-wûrld′)   The world of the dead, in Greek and Roman mythology.

Veda (vā′də)   From the Sanskrit, meaning "knowledge," the oldest sacred literature of the Hindu religion. The term is also used to refer to the individual collections of hymns: the *Rig-Veda*, the *Sama-Veda*, the *Yajur-Veda*, and the *Atharva-Veda*.

vernal equinox (vûr′nəl ē′kwə-nŏks′)   One of the two points during the year when day and night are of equal length, occurring on or about March 21 and marking the beginning of spring.

viceroy (vīs′roi′)   The political leader of a vassal or colonial country or province, who rules as a representative of the sovereign.

Visnu (also **Vishnu** [vĭsh′nōō])   A major god of Hindu and Indian mythology. Vishnu is considered an all-pervasive spirit, and the preserver of the world.

voodoo (vōō′dōō)   The primary religion of Haiti, voodoo combines elements of Roman Catholicism with tribal religions of Africa. The religious beliefs include cult worship of a high god (Bon Dieu), the dead, twins, and spirits called Ioa. As in Roman Catholicism the use of candles, prayer, crosses, and the sign of the cross are common elements. African elements include dancing, drumming, and the worship of ancestors and twins.

wassailing (wŏs′əlĭng)   Toasting or drinking to someone's health, or drinking and merriment.

winter solstice (wĭn′tər sŏl′stĭs)   In the northern hemisphere, the time of year, on or about December 21, when the noon sun appears farthest south, marking the beginning of winter.

witchcraft (wĭch′krăft′)   The practice of ritualistic, and/or herbal magic by people outside the religious mainstream. The term is used differently in different societies, and has historical roots in many different traditions.

Wojak   One of the names for the ancestral groundhog in the language of the Native American Delaware tribe. This is the origin of the English word "woodchuck."

Yamuna   A river in northern India, which joins with the Ganges at Allahabad. The confluence of the two rivers is a destination of pilgrimages for those of the Hindu faith.

yogi (yō′gē)   A person who practices yoga. The term is often used to refer to those of the Buddhist faith who use yoga as a form of divine communication or meditation.

Zarathustra   The ancient Persian name for Zoroaster, the religious prophet who founded Zoroastrianism.

Zionism (zī′ə-nĭz′əm)   A movement aimed at uniting the Jewish people of the exile and settling them in Palestine. Founded in the late 19th century by journalist Theodor Herzl, the organization eventually grew to settle the State of Israel in 1948. Their main goal of statehood was to defend and consolidate Israel and to justify its existence. In the 1970s and 1980s, Zionist aid was turned to Soviet Jews and today guarantees a Jewish nationality to any Jew in need of it.

Zoroastrianism (also **Zoroaster**)   A religion founded in ancient Persia by the prophet Zoroaster, also known as Zarathustra. Among its tenets are the belief in a single god, known as Ahura Mazda, and in the principle of ethical dualism represented by the emanations of Ahura Mazda called Spenta Mainyu (the Holy or Incremental Spirit), representing good, and Angra Mainyu (the "Fiendish Spirit") representing evil. Over the course of the centuries, Zoroastrianism was replaced in Persia by Islam, but adherents, today called Parsis, meaning "Persians," still live in parts of Iran and in India.

Zulu (zōō′lōō)   The sociological term for a member of a people from southeast Africa. A dominant tribe in the 19th century, the Zulu defeated numerous tribes in an effort to settle in an area rich in land and food.

Index